Chartered Institute of
Management Accountants

This book comes with free EN-gage online resources so that you can study anytime, anywhere. This free online resource is not sold separately and is included in the price of the book.

How to access your on-line resources

You can access additional online resources associated with this CIMA Official book via the EN-gage website at: **www.EN-gage.co.uk**.

Existing users

If you are an **existing EN-gage user**, simply log-in to your account, click on the 'add a book' link at the top of your homepage and enter the ISBN of this book and the unique pass key number contained above.

New users

If you are a new EN-gage user then you first need to register at: **www.EN-gage.co.uk**. Once registered, Kaplan Publishing will send you an email containing a link to activate your account - please check your junk mail if you do not receive this or contact us using the phone number or email address printed on the back cover of this book. Click on the link to activate your account. To unlock your additional resources, click on the 'add a book' link at the top of your home page. You will then need to enter the ISBN of this book (found on page ii) and the unique pass key number contained in the scratch panel below:

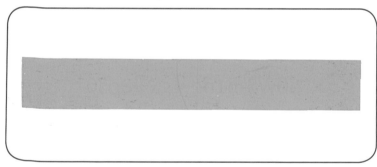

D0683354

Then click 'finished' or 'add another book'.
Please allow 24 hours from the time you submit your book details for the content to appear in the My Learning and Testing area of your account.

Your code and information

This code can only be used once for the registration of one book online. This registration will expire when this edition of the book is no longer current - please see the back cover of this book for the expiry date.

Existing users

If you are an **existing EN-gage user**, simply log-in to your account, click on the 'add a book' link at the top of your homepage and enter the ISBN of this book and the unique pass key number contained above.

CIMA

Paper E2

Project and Relationship Management

Study Text

Published by: Kaplan Publishing UK

Unit 2 The Business Centre, Molly Millars Lane, Wokingham, Berkshire RG41 2QZ

Acknowledgements

We are grateful to the CIMA for permission to reproduce past examination questions. The answers to CIMA Exams have been prepared by Kaplan Publishing, except in the case of the CIMA November 2010 and subsequent CIMA Exam answers where the official CIMA answers have been reproduced.

Notice

British Library Cataloguing in Publication Data

A catalogue record for this book is available from the British Library.

ISBN: 978-1-78415-297-0

Printed and bound in Great Britain.

Contents

Introduction

How to use the materials

These official CIMA learning materials have been carefully designed to make your learning experience as easy as possible and to give you the best chances of success in your Objective Test Examination.

The product range contains a number of features to help you in the study process. They include:

- a detailed explanation of all syllabus areas;
- extensive 'practical' materials;
- generous question practice, together with full solutions.

This Study Text has been designed with the needs of home study and distance learning candidates in mind. Such students require very full coverage of the syllabus topics, and also the facility to undertake extensive question practice. However, the Study Text is also ideal for fully taught courses.

The main body of the text is divided into a number of chapters, each of which is organised on the following pattern:

- **Detailed learning outcomes.** These describe the knowledge expected after your studies of the chapter are complete. You should assimilate these before beginning detailed work on the chapter, so that you can appreciate where your studies are leading.

- **Step-by-step topic coverage.** This is the heart of each chapter, containing detailed explanatory text supported where appropriate by worked examples and exercises. You should work carefully through this section, ensuring that you understand the material being explained and can tackle the examples and exercises successfully. Remember that in many cases knowledge is cumulative: if you fail to digest earlier material thoroughly, you may struggle to understand later chapters.

- **Activities.** Some chapters are illustrated by more practical elements, such as comments and questions designed to stimulate discussion.

- **Question practice**. The text contains three styles of question:
    - Exam-style objective test questions (OTQs)
    - 'Integration' questions – these test your ability to understand topics within a wider context. This is particularly important with calculations where OTQs may focus on just one element but an integration question tackles the full calculation, just as you would be expected to do in the workplace.
    - 'Case' style questions – these test your ability to analyse and discuss issues in greater depth, particularly focusing on scenarios that are less clear cut than in the Objective Test Examination, and thus provide excellent practice for developing the skills needed for success in the Management Level Case Study Examination.

- **Solutions.** Avoid the temptation merely to 'audit' the solutions provided. It is an illusion to think that this provides the same benefits as you would gain from a serious attempt of your own. However, if you are struggling to get started on a question you should read the introductory guidance provided at the beginning of the solution, where provided, and then make your own attempt before referring back to the full solution.

If you work conscientiously through this Official CIMA Study Text according to the guidelines above you will be giving yourself an excellent chance of success in your Objective Test Examination. Good luck with your studies!

Quality and accuracy are of the utmost importance to us so if you spot an error in any of our products, please send an email to mykaplanreporting@kaplan.com with full details, or follow the link to the feedback form in MyKaplan.

Our Quality Co-ordinator will work with our technical team to verify the error and take action to ensure it is corrected in future editions.

Icon Explanations

Definition – These sections explain important areas of knowledge which must be understood and reproduced in an assessment environment.

Key point – Identifies topics which are key to success and are often examined.

Supplementary reading – These sections will help to provide a deeper understanding of core areas. The supplementary reading is **NOT** optional reading. It is vital to provide you with the breadth of knowledge you will need to address the wide range of topics within your syllabus that could feature in an assessment question. **Reference to this text is vital when self studying**.

Test your understanding – Following key points and definitions are exercises which give the opportunity to assess the understanding of these core areas.

Illustration – To help develop an understanding of particular topics. The illustrative examples are useful in preparing for the Test your understanding exercises.

Exclamation mark – This symbol signifies a topic which can be more difficult to understand. When reviewing these areas, care should be taken.

Study technique

Passing exams is partly a matter of intellectual ability, but however accomplished you are in that respect you can improve your chances significantly by the use of appropriate study and revision techniques. In this section we briefly outline some tips for effective study during the earlier stages of your approach to the Objective Test Examination. We also mention some techniques that you will find useful at the revision stage.

Planning

To begin with, formal planning is essential to get the best return from the time you spend studying. Estimate how much time in total you are going to need for each subject you are studying. Remember that you need to allow time for revision as well as for initial study of the material.

With your study material before you, decide which chapters you are going to study in each week, and which weeks you will devote to revision and final question practice.

Prepare a written schedule summarising the above and stick to it!

It is essential to know your syllabus. As your studies progress you will become more familiar with how long it takes to cover topics in sufficient depth. Your timetable may need to be adapted to allocate enough time for the whole syllabus.

Students are advised to refer to the notice of examinable legislation published regularly in CIMA's magazine (Financial Management), the students e-newsletter (Velocity) and on the CIMA website, to ensure they are up-to-date.

The amount of space allocated to a topic in the Study Text is not a very good guide as to how long it will take you. The syllabus weighting is the better guide as to how long you should spend on a syllabus topic.

Tips for effective studying

(1) Aim to find a quiet and undisturbed location for your study, and plan as far as possible to use the same period of time each day. Getting into a routine helps to avoid wasting time. Make sure that you have all the materials you need before you begin so as to minimise interruptions.

(2) Store all your materials in one place, so that you do not waste time searching for items every time you want to begin studying. If you have to pack everything away after each study period, keep your study materials in a box, or even a suitcase, which will not be disturbed until the next time.

(3) Limit distractions. To make the most effective use of your study periods you should be able to apply total concentration, so turn off all entertainment equipment, set your phones to message mode, and put up your 'do not disturb' sign.

(4) Your timetable will tell you which topic to study. However, before diving in and becoming engrossed in the finer points, make sure you have an overall picture of all the areas that need to be covered by the end of that session. After an hour, allow yourself a short break and move away from your Study Text. With experience, you will learn to assess the pace you need to work at. Each study session should focus on component learning outcomes – the basis for all questions.

(5) Work carefully through a chapter, making notes as you go. When you have covered a suitable amount of material, vary the pattern by attempting a practice question. When you have finished your attempt, make notes of any mistakes you made, or any areas that you failed to cover or covered more briefly. Be aware that all component learning outcomes will be tested in each examination.

(6) Make notes as you study, and discover the techniques that work best for you. Your notes may be in the form of lists, bullet points, diagrams, summaries, 'mind maps', or the written word, but remember that you will need to refer back to them at a later date, so they must be intelligible. If you are on a taught course, make sure you highlight any issues you would like to follow up with your lecturer.

(7) Organise your notes. Make sure that all your notes, calculations etc. can be effectively filed and easily retrieved later.

Objective Test

Objective Test questions require you to choose or provide a response to a question whose correct answer is predetermined.

The most common types of Objective Test question you will see are:

- Multiple choice, where you have to choose the correct answer(s) from a list of possible answers. This could either be numbers or text.

- Multiple choice with more choices and answers, for example, choosing two correct answers from a list of eight possible answers. This could either be numbers or text.

- Single numeric entry, where you give your numeric answer, for example, profit is $10,000.

- Multiple entry, where you give several numeric answers.

- True/false questions, where you state whether a statement is true or false.

- Matching pairs of text, for example, matching a technical term with the correct definition.

- Other types could be matching text with graphs and labelling graphs/diagrams.

In every chapter of this Study Text we have introduced these types of questions, but obviously we have had to label answers A, B, C etc rather than using click boxes. For convenience we have retained quite a few questions where an initial scenario leads to a number of sub-questions. There will be questions of this type in the Objective Test Examination but they will rarely have more than three sub-questions.

Guidance re CIMA on-screen calculator

As part of the CIMA Objective Test software, candidates are now provided with a calculator. This calculator is on-screen and is available for the duration of the assessment. The calculator is available in each of the Objective Test Examinations and is accessed by clicking the calculator button in the top left hand corner of the screen at any time during the assessment.

All candidates must complete a 15-minute tutorial before the assessment begins and will have the opportunity to familiarise themselves with the calculator and practise using it.

Candidates may practise using the calculator by downloading and installing the practice exam at http://www.vue.com/athena/. The calculator can be accessed from the fourth sample question (of 12).

Please note that the practice exam and tutorial provided by Pearson VUE at http://www.vue.com/athena/ is not specific to CIMA and includes the full range of question types the Pearson VUE software supports, some of which CIMA does not currently use.

Fundamentals of Objective Tests

The Objective Tests are 90-minute assessments comprising 60 compulsory questions, with one or more parts. There will be no choice and all questions should be attempted.

Structure of subjects and learning outcomes

Each subject within the syllabus is divided into a number of broad syllabus topics. The topics contain one or more lead learning outcomes, related component learning outcomes and indicative knowledge content.

A learning outcome has two main purposes:

(a) To define the skill or ability that a well prepared candidate should be able to exhibit in the examination.

(b) To demonstrate the approach likely to be taken in examination questions.

The learning outcomes are part of a hierarchy of learning objectives. The verbs used at the beginning of each learning outcome relate to a specific learning objective, e.g.

Calculate the break-even point, profit target, margin of safety and profit/volume ratio for a single product or service.

The verb '**calculate**' indicates a level three learning objective. The following tables list the verbs that appear in the syllabus learning outcomes and examination questions.

CIMA VERB HIERARCHY

CIMA place great importance on the definition of verbs in structuring Objective Test Examinations. It is therefore crucial that you understand the verbs in order to appreciate the depth and breadth of a topic and the level of skill required. The Objective Tests will focus on levels one, two and three of the CIMA hierarchy of verbs. However they will also test levels four and five, especially at the management and strategic levels. You can therefore expect to be tested on knowledge, comprehension, application, analysis and evaluation in these examinations.

Level 1: KNOWLEDGE

What you are expected to know.

VERBS USED	DEFINITION
List	Make a list of.
State	Express, fully or clearly, the details of/facts of.
Define	Give the exact meaning of.

For example you could be asked to make a list of the advantages of a particular information system by selecting all options that apply from a given set of possibilities. Or you could be required to define relationship marketing by selecting the most appropriate option from a list.

Level 2: COMPREHENSION

What you are expected to understand.

VERBS USED	DEFINITION
Describe	Communicate the key features of.
Distinguish	Highlight the differences between.
Explain	Make clear or intelligible/state the meaning or purpose of.
Identify	Recognise, establish or select after consideration.
Illustrate	Use an example to describe or explain something.

For example you may be asked to distinguish between different aspects of the global business environment by dragging external factors and dropping into a PEST analysis.

Level 3: APPLICATION

How you are expected to apply your knowledge.

VERBS USED	DEFINITION
Apply	Put to practical use.
Calculate	Ascertain or reckon mathematically.
Demonstrate	Prove with certainty or exhibit by practical means.
Prepare	Make or get ready for use.
Reconcile	Make or prove consistent/compatible.
Solve	Find an answer to.
Tabulate	Arrange in a table.

For example you may need to calculate the projected revenue or costs for a given set of circumstances.

Level 4: ANALYSIS

How you are expected to analyse the detail of what you have learned.

VERBS USED	DEFINITION
Analyse	Examine in detail the structure of.
Categorise	Place into a defined class or division.
Compare/ contrast	Show the similarities and/or differences between.
Construct	Build up or compile.
Discuss	Examine in detail by argument.
Interpret	Translate into intelligible or familiar terms.
Prioritise	Place in order of priority or sequence for action.
Produce	Create or bring into existence.

For example you may be required to interpret an inventory ratio by selecting the most appropriate statement for a given set of circumstances and data.

Level 5: EVALUATION

How you are expected to use your learning to evaluate, make decisions or recommendations.

VERBS USED	DEFINITION
Advise	Counsel, inform or notify.
Evaluate	Appraise or assess the value of.
Recommend	Propose a course of action.

For example you may be asked to recommend and select an appropriate course of action based on a short scenario.

E2
PROJECT AND RELATIONSHIP MANAGEMENT

Syllabus overview

E2 emphasises a holistic, integrated approach to managing organisations, from external and internal perspectives. It builds on the understanding of organisational structuring gained from E1 and is centred on the concept of strategy and how organisational strategy can be implemented through people, projects, processes and relationships. It provides the basis for developing further insights into how to formulate and implement organisational strategy, which is covered in E3.

Summary of syllabus

Weight	Syllabus topic
30%	**A.** Introduction to strategic management and assessing the global environment
20%	**B.** The human aspects of the organisation
20%	**C.** Managing relationships
30%	**D.** Managing change through projects

E2 – A. INTRODUCTION TO STRATEGIC MANAGEMENT ASSESSING THE GLOBAL ENVIRONMENT (30%)

Learning outcomes
On completion of their studies, students should be able to:

Lead	Component	Indicative syllabus content
1 discuss developments in strategic management.	(a) discuss the concept of strategy and the rational/formal approach to strategy development	<ul><li>Defining strategy and strategic management.</li><li>Core areas of strategic management.</li><li>Levels of strategy within organisations.</li><li>Stages in the rational approach to strategy developments.</li></ul>
	(b) compare and contrast alternative approaches to strategy development	<ul><li>Intended, emergent, logical incrementalism, and political approaches.</li><li>Resource-based view – resources and competencies, internal value and dynamic capabilities.</li><li>Strategy development in different contexts, e.g. SMEs, public sector, not-for-profit.</li><li>Strategy and structure.</li></ul>
	(c) explain the approaches to achieving sustainable competitive advantage.	<ul><li>The concept of competitive advantage.</li><li>Generic competitive strategies.</li><li>Value, rarity, inimitability, non-substitutability as bases of competitive advantage.</li><li>Achieving sustainable competitive advantage.</li></ul>
2 analyse the relationship between different aspects of the global business environment.	(a) distinguish between different aspects of the global business environment, including the competitive environment	<ul><li>The macro and micro environments.</li><li>LoNGPEST analysis and its derivatives.</li><li>Globalisation.</li><li>Country and political risk factors.</li><li>Emerging markets.</li><li>Porter's Diamond and its use for assessing the competitive advantage of nations.</li><li>Porter's Five Forces model and its use for analysing the external environment.</li></ul>

Learning outcomes

On completion of their studies, students should be able to:

Lead	Component	Indicative syllabus content
	(b) discuss the approaches to competitor analysis including the collection and interpretation of trend data.	<ul><li>Key concepts in competitor analysis.</li><li>The role of competitor analysis.</li><li>Approaches to collecting competitor information.</li><li>Sources, types and quality of competitor data.</li><li>Analysing and interpreting competitor data.</li><li>The application of Big Data to competitor analysis.</li></ul>

E2 – B. THE HUMAN ASPECTS OF THE ORGANISATION (20%)

Learning outcomes
On completion of their studies, students should be able to:

Lead	Component	Indicative syllabus content
1 discuss the concepts associated with managing through people.	(a) discuss the concepts of leadership and management	• Fundamental and contemporary concepts in management. • The concepts of power, authority, delegation and empowerment. • Different approaches to leadership, including personality/traits, style, contingency/situation, transactional/transformational, distributive. • Leadership in different contexts.
	(b) discuss HRM approaches for managing and controlling individuals' performance.	• HR policies and procedures. • Different approaches to employee performance appraisals. • The contribution of coaching and mentoring in enhancing individual and organisational performance. • Equality and diversity practices. • Disciplinary and grievance procedures in resolving poor performance. • Dismissal and redundancy. • Employer and employee responsibilities in managing the work environment (e.g. health and safety).

2 discuss the hard and soft aspects of people and organisational performance.	(a) discuss behavioural aspects of management control	• Theories of behavioural aspects of control.
		• Performance management and measurement frameworks, e.g.
		  – target setting
		  – management by objectives
		  – the Balanced Scorecard (BSC).
		• Trust and control.

Learning outcomes

On completion of their studies, students should be able to:

Lead	Component	Indicative syllabus content
	(b) explain the importance of organisational culture.	• Explaining the concept and importance of culture. • Levels of culture. • Influences on culture. • Analysing organisational culture – the cultural web framework. • Models for categorising culture. • National cultures and managing in different cultures.

E2 – C. MANAGING RELATIONSHIPS (20%)

Learning outcomes
On completion of their studies, students should be able to:

Lead	Component	Indicative syllabus content
1 discuss the effectiveness of organisational relationships.	(a) evaluate the issues associated with building, leading and managing effective teams	• Building effective and high-performing teams. • Leading and managing teams. • Factors associated with effective team work. • Motivating team members. • Resolving problems and conflict in teams.
	(b) discuss the effectiveness of handling relationships between the finance function and other parts of the organisation and the supply chain	• Management of relationships between the finance function and other parts of the organisation (internal). • The concept of the Chartered Management Accountant as a business partner in creating value. • Transaction cost theory in the context of shared service centres and outsourcing, including contractual relationship, SLAs (service level agreements), bounded rationality and co-creation with customers.
	(c) discuss the effectiveness of handling relationships between the finance function and external experts and stakeholders	• Management of relationships with professional advisors (external) e.g. accounting, tax and legal, auditors and financial stakeholders such as shareholders and other investors to meet organisational objectives and governance responsibilities.
2 discuss management tools and techniques in managing organisational relationships.	(a) discuss the roles of communication, negotiation, influence and persuasion in the management process	• The communication process, types of communication tools and their use, ways of managing communication problems. • The importance of effective communication skills for the Chartered Management Accountant. • The importance of non-verbal communication and feedback. • Developing effective strategies for influence/persuasion/negotiation. • The process of negotiation. • Negotiation skills.

Learning outcomes

On completion of their studies, students should be able to:

Lead		Indicative syllabus content
	Component	
	(b) discuss approaches to managing conflict.	<ul><li>The sources and causes of conflict in organisations.</li><li>The different forms and types of conflict.</li><li>Strategies for managing conflict to ensure working relationships are productive and effective.</li></ul>

E2 – D. MANAGING CHANGE THROUGH PROJECTS (30%)

Learning outcomes

On completion of their studies, students should be able to:

Lead	Component	Indicative syllabus content
1 advise on important elements in the change process.	(a) discuss the concept of organisational change	• Types of change. • External and internal triggers for change. • Stage model of change management. • Principles of change management.
	(b) recommend techniques to manage resistance to change.	• Problem identification as a precursor to change. • Reasons for resistance to change. • Approaches to managing resistance to change.
2 discuss the concepts involved in managing projects.	(a) discuss the characteristics of the different phases of a project	• Definition of project attributes. • Time, cost and quality project objectives. • The purpose and activities associated with the key stages in the project lifecycle. • Examples of the role of project management methodologies in project control (e.g. PRINCE2, PMI).
	(b) apply tools and techniques for project managers	• Key tools for project management, including work breakdown schedule (WBS), Gantt Charts, and Network analysis. • Managing project risk. • PERT charts. • Scenario planning and buffering. • The contribution of project management software.
	(c) discuss management and leadership issues associated with projects, including the roles of key players in projects.	• Project structures, including matrix structure and their impact on project achievement. • The role and attributes of an effective project manager. • The role of the Chartered Management Accountant in projects. • The role of other key players in a project. • Managing key project stakeholders. • The lifecycle of project teams. • Leading and motivating project teams.

The concept of strategy and the rational/formal approach to strategy development

Chapter learning objectives

Discuss the concept of strategy and the rational/formal approach to strategy development.

More detail on the levels of strategy

Corporate strategy

The corporate centre is at the apex of the organisation and will contain the corporate board. Corporate strategy is typically concerned with determining the overall purpose and scope of the organisation, in other words what type of business or businesses should the organisation be in. Common issues at this level include:

- decisions on acquisitions, mergers and sell-offs or closure of business units

- relations with key external stakeholders such as investors, the government and regulatory bodies

- decisions to enter new markets or embrace new technologies (sometimes termed diversification strategies)

- development of corporate policies on issues such as public image, employment practices or information systems.

Decisions at this level tend to be complex and non routine in nature because they often involve a high degree of uncertainty based on what might happen in the future.

Business strategy

This level of strategy is concerned with how an operating or strategic business unit approaches a particular market. Management of the SBU will be responsible for winning customers and beating rivals in its particular market. Consequently, it is at this level that competitive strategy is usually formulated. The considerations at this level will include:

- marketing issues such as product development, pricing, promotion and distribution.

- how should it segment the market and which segments should it operate in.

- how can it gain competitive advantage?

Business strategy should be formulated within the broad framework of the overall objectives laid down by the corporate centre to ensure that each SBU plays its part. The extent to which the management of the SBU is free to make competitive strategy decisions varies from organisation to organisation and reflects the degree of centralisation versus decentralisation in the management structure of the firm.

Functional strategies

The functional (sometimes called operational) level of the organisation refers to main business functions such as sales, production, purchasing, human resources and finance. Functional strategies are the long-term management policies of these functional areas. They are intended to ensure that the functional area plays its part in helping the SBU achieve the goals of its corporate strategy.

Case study style question 1

V operates in the leisure and entertainment industry. It has a range of different ventures worldwide including fitness centres, casinos, cinemas and sports bars, each of which operates as a separate business. PC, the new CEO of V is concerned about how to manage an integrated strategy within the organisation, while allowing the managers of each business unit to act autonomously. PC has invited you to do a presentation to the managers of V at their next management meeting covering the levels of strategy.

Required:

Produce notes for your presentation, distinguishing between the different levels at which strategy should exist in V, briefly explain what would be involved at each level.

(15 minutes)

4 The rational/formal approach to strategy development

The rational approach is also referred to as the formal, traditional or top-down approach.

The rational strategic planning process model is based on rational behaviour, whereby planners, management and organisations are expected to behave logically. First defining the mission and objectives of the organisation and then selecting the means to achieve this. Cause and effect are viewed as naturally linked and a strong element of predictability is expected.

The model below shows a framework of the rational/formal approach and clearly shows the various stages which management may take to develop a strategy for their organisation.

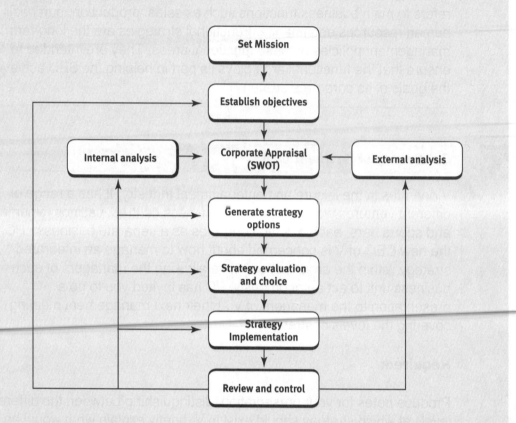

The rational/formal approach follows a logical step-by-step approach:

- Determine the mission of the organisation.

- Set corporate objectives.

- Carry out corporate appraisal (SWOT) – involving analysis of internal and external environments.

- Identify and evaluate strategy options – select strategies to achieve competitive advantage by exploiting strengths and opportunities or minimising threats and weaknesses.

- Evaluate each option in detail for its fit with the mission and circumstances of the business and choose the most appropriate option.

- Implement the chosen strategy.

- Review and control – reviewing the performance of the organisation to determine whether objectives have been achieved. This is a continuous process and involves taking corrective action if changes occur internally or externally.

Each of the different stages in the model will be looked at in more detail in this, and the following chapters.

Ensure you are comfortable with this model as you will refer back to it throughout this syllabus area.

A formal top-down strategy process within a large organisation

Large organisations will often formalise the process of strategy development. The following are typical features of the process:

(1) *A designated team responsible for strategy development.* There are several groups involved in this process:

    (a) A permanent strategic planning unit reporting to top management and consisting of expert staff collecting business intelligence, advising divisions on formulating strategy and monitoring results.

    (b) Groups of managers, often the management teams of the SBUs, meeting periodically to monitor the success of the present strategies and to develop new ones. These are sometimes referred to as strategy away days because they often take place away from the office to avoid interruptions.

    (c) Business consultants acting as advisers and facilitators to the process by suggesting models and techniques to assist managers in understanding their business environments and the strategic possibilities open to them. You will be reading about many of these models and techniques later.

(2) *Formal collection of information for strategy purposes.* The management team will gather information from within and outside the firm to understand the challenges they face and the resources at their disposal. This information can include:

    (a) Environmental scanning reports compiled by the business intelligence functions within the firm, including such matters as competitor behaviour, market trends and potential changes to laws.

    (b) Specially commissioned reports on particular markets, products or competitors.

    (c) Management accounting information on operating costs and performance, together with financial forecasts.

    (d) Research reports from external consultancies on market opportunities and threats.

(3) *Collective decision-taking by the senior management team*. This involves the senior management team working together to develop and agree business strategies. Techniques such as brainstorming ideas on flip charts and using visual graphical models to summarise complex ideas will assist this process. Also, arriving at a decision will involve considerable conflict as particular managers are reluctant to see their favoured proposal rejected and a different strategy adopted.

(4) *A process of communicating and implementing the business strategy*. This can be accomplished using a combination of the following methods:

    (a) Writing a formal document summarising the main elements of the plan. This will be distributed on a confidential basis to other managers and key investors, and also perhaps to other key stakeholders such as labour representatives, regulatory bodies, major customers and key suppliers.

    (b) Briefing meetings and presentations to the stakeholders mentioned above. Frequently, reporters from the business press will be invited to ensure that the information reaches a broader public. Naturally, the fine detail will remain confidential.

    (c) The development of detailed policies, programmes and budgets based on achieving the goals laid out in the business strategy.

    (d) The development of performance targets for managers and staff. These ensure that everyone plays their part in the strategy (and perhaps receive financial rewards for doing so).

(5) *Regular review and control of the strategy*. Management will monitor the success of the strategy by receiving regular reports on performance and on environmental changes. Today, the sophisticated competitive strategies of many firms have necessitated the development of more complex performance measurement systems to supplement traditional budgetary control information, such as enterprise resource management systems and balanced scorecards. There has also been an increased emphasis on competitor and other environmental information to assist managers in steering their businesses.

5 Mission, goals and objectives

From the diagram of the rational/formal model, the first step of the model is setting the mission for the organisation.

Mission

A mission is a broad statement of the overall purpose of the business and should reflect the core values of the business. It will set out the **overriding purpose of the business** in line with the values and expectations of stakeholders. (*Johnson and Scholes*)

Examples of reasons for existence

Companies within the same industry may have different reasons for existing.

Manufacturing

- Rolls Royce exists to make a small number of high quality luxury cars with a distinctive image.
- Ford exists to sell a large volume of different types of car to a global market.

Travel

- Ryanair and EasyJet exist to provide low-cost, no frills flights from the UK to destinations in Europe.
- British Airways exists to provide a quality service to economy, business and first class passengers to destinations around the world.

Financial services

- Coutts and Co exists to provide an individualised banking service to a particular group of customers.
- First Direct exists to provide low-cost telephone-based financial services to a wide range of customers.

Mission statement

The mission statement is a statement in writing that describes the basic purpose of an organisation, that is, what it is trying to accomplish. It is possible to have a strong sense of purpose or mission without a formal mission statement.

There is no one best mission statement for an organisation as the contents of mission statements will vary in terms of length, format and level of detail from one organisation to another.

Mission statements are normally brief and address **three main questions**:

- Why do we exist?
- What are we providing?
- For whom do we exist?

For example:

Starbucks mission is to '*inspire and nurture the human spirit   one person, one cup and one neighbourhood at a time.*'

Purposes of mission statements (Hooley et al.):

- To provide a basis for consistent planning decisions.
- To assist in translating purposes and direction into objectives suitable for assessment and control.
- To provide a consistent purpose between different interest groups connected to the organisation.
- To establish organisational goals and ethics.
- To improve understanding and support from key groups outside the organisation.

Role and content of a mission statement

Roles of mission statements

Mission statements help at four places in the rational model of strategy:

(1) Mission and objectives. The mission sets the long-term framework and direction for the business. It is the job of the strategy to progress the firm towards this mission over the coming few years covered by the strategy.

(2) Corporate appraisal. Assessing the firm's opportunities and threats, strengths and weaknesses must be related to its ability to compete in its chosen business domain. Factors are relevant only insofar as they affect its ability to follow its mission.

(3) Strategic evaluation. When deciding between alternative strategic options, management can use the mission as a benchmark against which to judge their suitability. The crucial question will be, 'Does the strategy help us along the road to being the kind of business we want to be?'

(4) Review and control. The key targets of the divisions and functions should be related to the mission, otherwise the mission will not be accomplished.

David provides a useful list of what areas should be included in a mission statement:

- **Customers.** A statement making reference to who the organisation's customers are.

- **Markets.** A statement of where the firm competes.

- **Products or services.** A description of the firm's major products or services.

- **Concern for survival, growth and profitability.** The broad economic objectives of the firm.

- **Philosophy.** A statement of the organisation's basic values and standards of behaviour.

- **Concern for employees.** A statement of the firm's attitude to its employees.

- **Concern for public image.** A statement as to how much concern the organisation has of its public image and all its stakeholders.

- **Self-concept.** A statement of the organisation's strength and distinction relative to competitors.

Vision

While a mission statement gives the overall purpose of the organisation, a vision statement describes a picture of the "preferred future."

A vision statement describes how the future will look if the organisation achieves its mission.

For example BBC's mission is to "*to enrich people's lives with programmes and services that inform, educate and entertain.*"

And their vision is "*to be the most creative organisation in the world.*"

The link between mission, goals and objectives

Once the mission has been established, the rational model moves on to establishing objectives. Often organisations set high level goals first, which feed into more measurable objectives.

Goals

Mintzberg defines goals as the intention behind an organisation's decisions or actions. He argues that goals will frequently never be achieved and may be incapable of being measured. Thus for example 'the highest possible standard of living to our employees' is a goal that will be difficult to measure and realise. Although goals are more specific than mission statements and have a shorter number of years in their timescale, they are not precise measures of performance.

Objectives

Mintzberg goes on to define objectives as goals expressed in a form in which they can be measured. Thus an objective of 'profit before interest and tax to be not less than 20% of capital employed' is capable of being measured.

Objectives generally possess four characteristics which set it apart from a mission statement:

(1) a precise formulation of the attribute sought

(2) an index or measure for progress towards the attribute

(3) a target to be achieved

(4) a time-frame in which it is to be achieved.

The mission is normally an open-ended statement of the organisation's purpose and strategies, goals and objectives translate the mission into strategic milestones for the organisation's strategy to reach.

Objectives

The acronym often used when setting objectives is **SMART:**

- **S**pecific means 'clearly expressed', e.g. 'improve performance' is too vague; 'improve operating profit' is better.

- **M**easurable means quantifiable, e.g. 'improve image' is not measurable, but 'increase operating profit to 20% of turnover' is.

- **A**chievable means perceived as achievable by those being held responsible for achieving them, e.g. 'improve operating profit to 80% of turnover' probably will be impossible to achieve. Unachievable objectives demotivate those held responsible for them.

- **R**elevant means explicitly linked to the overall goals of the business, e.g. 'increase customer retention by 5%' is relevant to the overall goal of 'delight our customers'.

- **T**imely means that timescales have to be set if the objective is ever to be achieved, e.g. 'by 31 December 20X2'.

Objectives perform a number of functions:

- **Planning.** Objectives provide the framework for planning. They are the targets which the plan is supposed to reach.

- **Responsibility.** Objectives are given to the managers of divisions, departments and operations. This communicates to them:
  - the activities, projects or areas they are responsible for
  - the types of output required
  - the level of outputs required.

- **Integration.** Objectives are how senior management coordinate the firm. Provided that the objectives handed down are internally consistent, this should ensure goal congruence between managers of the various divisions of the business.

- **Motivation.** Management will be motivated to reach their objectives in order to impress their superiors, and perhaps receive bonuses. This means that the objectives set must cover all areas of the mission. For example, if the objectives emphasise purely financial outcomes, then managers will not pay much attention to issues such as social responsibility or innovation.

- **Evaluation.** Senior management control the business by evaluating the performance of the managers responsible for each of its divisions.

You may be familiar with these five functions (often recalled using the acronym **PRIME**).

The goal structure:

Once the mission, goals and objectives have been set, these can be broken down into **Critical Success Factors** (CSFs). A CSF is defined as '*something which must go right if the objectives and goals are to be achieved*'

CSFs may be financial or non-financial, but they must be high level.

Each CSF must have a **Key Performance Indicator** (KPI) attached to it to allow it to be measured. KPIs are low level and detailed. They are used to measure performance which indicates whether the CSFs have been achieved or not.

KPIs can be further broken down into **individual performance targets**.

It is important to note that target setting motivates staff and enables the entity to control its performance and that the objectives set will apply to the entity as a whole, to each business unit, and also to each individual manager or employee.

If the goals of the individual are derived from the goals of the business unit, and these are in turn derived from the goals of the entity, **'goal congruence'** is said to exist. Attainment by individuals or units of their objectives will directly contribute towards the fulfilment of corporate objectives.

You can see from this that the company's mission is translated into goals and then objectives:

Strategic objectives reached by following strategies communicated to management as numerous......

Tactical objectives which in turn are implemented and reviewed through setting a large number of......

Operational objectives which may be communicated to managers and staff responsible through their......

Critical Success Factors, Key Performance Indicators and individual performance targets. Whilst the mission is normally an open-ended statement of the firm's purposes and strategies, strategic objectives and goals translate the mission into strategic milestones for the business strategy to reach. In other words the outcomes that the organisation wants to achieve.

6 Corporate Appraisal (SWOT)

Look back to the diagram of the rational/formal model, you can see that once the mission and objectives have been set, the next stage is analysis. Analysis is made up of internal and external analysis which feed into corporate appraisal.

Corporate appraisal (SWOT) provides the framework to summarise the key outputs from the external and internal analysis.

The strengths and weaknesses normally result from the organisation's internal factors, and the opportunities and threats relate to the external environment.

The strengths and weaknesses can be ascertained from internal position analysis, using tools such as resources audits and Porter's value chain, and the opportunities and threats come from external position analysis using tools such as PESTLE and Porter's five forces model. The analysis tools used in corporate appraisal can be summarised as shown:

Elements of SWOT	Environment	Analytical tools
Strengths and Weaknesses	Internal	• Resource audit • Porter's value chain
Opportunities and Threats	External	• PESTLE • Porter's five forces

Each of these tools will be examined in more depth in the following chapters.

How to carry out a good SWOT analysis

- Identify key strengths, weaknesses, opportunities and threats. It can be useful to show them as follows:

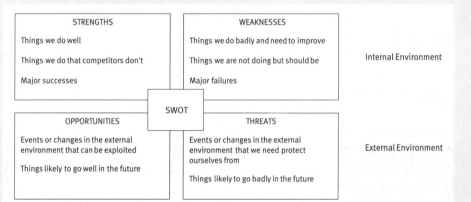

- Try to suggest how to convert weaknesses to strengths, threats to opportunities

- Advise on how to remove weaknesses that leave the organisation exposed to threats

- Match strengths to opportunities

- Remember, if something is a threat to us, it is likely to be a threat to our rivals. Can we exploit this?

Corporate appraisals are useful for organisations in a number of ways:

- they provide a critical appraisal of the strengths, weaknesses, opportunities and threats affecting the organisation.

- they can be used to view the internal and external situation facing an organisation at a particular point in time to assist in the determination of the current situation.

- they can assist in long-term strategic planning of the organisation.

- they help to provide a review of an organisation as a whole or a project.

- they can be used to identify sources of competitive advantage.

Case study style question 2

E operates a chain of retail clothing stores specialising in ladies' designer fashion and accessories. J, the original founder, has been pleasantly surprised by the continuing growth in the fashion industry during the last decade.

The company was established 12 years ago, originally with one store in the capital city. J's design skills and entrepreneurial skills have been the driving force behind the expansion. Due to unique designs and good quality control, the business now has ten stores in various cities.

Each store has a shop manger that is completely responsible for managing the staff and stock levels within each store. They produce monthly reports on sales. Some stores are continually late in supplying their monthly figures.

E runs several analysis programmes to enable management information to be collated. The information typically provides statistical data on sales trends between categories of items and stores. The analysis and preparation of these reports are conducted in the marketing department. In some cases the information is out of date in terms of trends and variations.

As the business has developed J has used the service of a local IT company to implement and develop their systems. She now wants to invest in website development with the view of reaching global markets.

Required:

(a) Construct a SWOT analysis with reference to the proposal of website development.

(15 minutes)

(b) Write an email to J explaining how the use of SWOT analysis may be of assistance to E.

(10 minutes)

7 Options, choice and implementation

Look back at the diagram of the rational/formal model, you can see that once the mission and objectives have been set and the corporate appraisal (SWOT) has been carried out, the next steps are to generate strategic options and make strategic choices.

Generate strategic options, evaluation and choice

Strategic choice is the process of choosing the alternative strategic options generated by the SWOT analysis. Management need to seek to identify and evaluate alternative courses of action to ensure that the business reaches the objectives they have set. This will be largely a creative process of generating alternatives, building on the strengths of the business and allowing it to tackle new products or markets to improve its competitive position.

The strategic choice process involves making decisions regarding:

- On what basis should the organisation compete?

- What are the alternative directions available and which products or markets should the organisation enter or leave?

- What alternative methods are available to achieve the chosen direction?

Strategic direction

The organisation also has to decide how it might develop in the future to exploit strengths and opportunities or minimise threats and weaknesses. There are various options that could be followed. **Ansoff Matrix** can be used to show the alternatives:

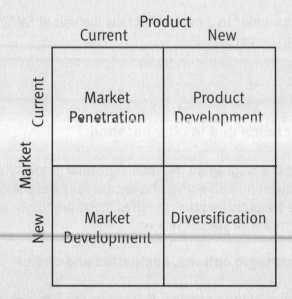

- **Market penetration**. This is where the organisation seeks to maintain or increase its share of existing markets with existing products.
- **Product development**. Strategies are based on launching new products or making product enhancement which are offered to its existing markets.
- **Market development**. Strategies are based on finding new markets for existing products. This could involve identifying new markets geographically or new market segments.
- **Diversification**. Strategies are based on launching new products into new markets and is the most risky strategic option.

Strategic methods

Not only must the organisation consider on what basis to compete and the direction of strategic development, it must also decide what methods it could use. The options are:

- **Internal development**. This is where the organisation uses its own internal resources to pursue its chosen strategy. It may involve the building up a business from scratch.

- **Takeovers/acquisitions or mergers**. An alternative would be to acquire resources by taking over or merging with another organisation, in order to acquire knowledge of a particular product/market area. This might be to obtain a new product range or market presence or as a means of eliminating competition.

- **Strategic alliances**. This route often has the aim of increasing exposure to potential customers or gaining access to technology. There are a variety of arrangements for strategic alliances, some of which are very formalised and some which are much looser arrangements.

Evaluation of strategic options

The evaluation stage considers each strategic option in detail for its feasibility and fit with the mission and circumstances of the business. By the end of this process, management will have decided on a shortlist of options that will be carried forward to the strategy implementation stage. The various options must be evaluated against each other with respect to their ability to achieve the overall goals. Management will have a number of ideas to improve the competitive position of the business.

Strategy implementation

The strategy sets the broad direction and methods for the business to reach its objectives. However, none of it will happen without more detailed implementation. The strategy implementation stage involves drawing up the detailed plans, policies and programmes necessary to make the strategy happen. It will also involve obtaining the necessary resources and committing them to the strategy. These are commonly called tactical and operational decisions:

- Tactical programmes and decisions are medium-term policies designed to implement some of the key elements of the strategy such as developing new products, recruitment or downsizing of staff or investing in new production capacity. Project appraisal and project management techniques are valuable at this level.

- Operational programmes and decisions cover routine day-to-day matters such as meeting particular production, cost and revenue targets. Conventional budgetary control is an important factor in controlling these matters.

Johnson, Scholes and Whittington

The Johnson, Scholes and Whittington (JSW) model of strategic planning is a modern development of the rational planning model. It consists of three elements (analysis, choice, implementation) but instead of presenting these linearly, it recognises interdependencies. For example, it might only be at the strategy into action (implementation) stage that an organisation discovers something that sheds light on its strategic position. The other key difference is that Johnson, Scholes and Whittington argue that strategic planning can begin at any point. For example, firms might decide that they will launch an internet sales division without first carrying out any strategic analysis or choosing how the new strategy might compete.

> ### Strategic analysis
> - External analysis to identify opportunities and threats
> - Internal analysis to identify strengths and weaknesses
> - Stakeholder analysis to identify key objectives and to assess power and interest of different groups
> - Gap analysis to identify the difference between desired and expected performance.

> ### Strategic choice
> - Strategies are required to 'close the gap'
> - Competitive strategy – for each business unit
> - Directions for growth – which markets/products should be invested in
> - Whether expansion should be achieved by organic growth, acquisition or some form of joint arrangement.

> ### Strategic implementation
> - Formulation of detailed plans and budgets
> - Target setting for KPIs
> - Monitoring and control.

8 Review and control

The last step in the rational/formal model is review and control. From the model you can clearly see the review and control process. Where issues are discovered, parts of the model will have to be re-visited.

This is a continuous process of reviewing both the implementation and the overall continuing suitability of the strategy. It will consider two aspects:

(1) Does performance of the strategy still put the business on course for reaching its strategic objectives?

(2) Are the forecasts of the environment on which the strategy was based still accurate, or have unforeseen threats or opportunities arisen subsequently that might necessitate a reconsideration of the strategy?

9 Stakeholder analysis

There are a number of different individuals and interest groups both inside and outside the organisation who will have views of the strategic development of the organisation and who can affect or be affected by the performance of the organisation, These groups or individuals are referred to as stakeholders.

Strategic decision-making requires managers to consider stakeholders when setting the mission and objectives of the firm. This is for two broad reasons:

- **Stakeholder power**. Management must recognise that stakeholders can affect the success of a strategy, depending on whether they support or oppose it. For example, customers refusing to buy products, shareholders selling their shares or staff striking would disrupt any strategy. The view concludes that management should consider stakeholders before setting strategic objectives.

- **Organisational legitimacy**. This more radical view suggests that firms are required to be good citizens because they are only permitted to exist by society on sufferance of not abusing their power. Consequently, although working primarily for the shareholders, management must ensure that its decisions do not ignore the interests of other stakeholders.

Stakeholders may include any or all of the following groups:

- Shareholders
- Directors
- Employees
- Trade unions
- Customers
- Suppliers
- Government
- Pressure groups
- General public and local people

There are different classifications of stakeholders:

- **internal** stakeholders (employees and management)
- **connected** stakeholders (shareholders, customer and suppliers)
- **external** stakeholders (governments, community, pressure groups)
- **primary** stakeholders have a formal contractual relationship in a strategy or a project
- **secondary** stakeholders have no formal relationship.

Managing stakeholders – the Mendelow matrix

It is important that companies recognise the objectives of each group of stakeholders. These vary and can conflict with each other making the task of managing stakeholders more difficult.

A process for managing stakeholders is:

- Identify stakeholders and determine each group's objectives
- Analyse the level of interest and power each group possesses
- Place each stakeholder group in the appropriate quadrant of the Mendelow matrix
- Use the matrix to assess how to manage each stakeholder group.

Level of Interest

	Low	High
Low	Lack of interest and power means they are likely to accept what they are told. **MINIMAL EFFORT**	Present strategy as rational which may stop them joining forces with powerful dissenters. **KEEP INFORMED**
High	Keep them satisfied. Assure them of the likely outcomes of the strategy well in advance. **KEEP SATISFIED**	Can be a major drivers or major opponents of change. Need to assure them that the change is necessary. **KEY PLAYERS**

Level of Power (row axis label)

Assessing the power and interest of stakeholders

Some stakeholder groups wield greater power than others. For example, the government's legislative power is comprehensive, and rulings of the Competition and Markets Authority have a direct effect upon the objectives and strategies of companies affected. Examples are:

- in 2004, UK based supermarket chain, Morrisons bought over rival chain Safeway for £3bn ($5.2bn), making them the fourth largest supermarket chain in the UK. The takeover was only cleared on condition that both groups sold one of its existing stores in towns where both were present;

- in newspaper publishing, Rupert Murdoch was blocked from taking over other newspapers on the grounds of safeguarding freedom of opinion across a range of views.

Assessing power of stakeholders

Factors that may be associated with a particular group having high power are:

- Status of the stakeholders, for example:
    - their place in the organisational hierarchy
    - their relative pay

- their reputation in the firm

- their social standing (e.g. ministers of religion may carry considerable power due to their social status).

- Claim on resources, for example:
  - size of their budget

  - number and level of staff employed

  - volume of business transacted with them (e.g. suppliers and customers)

  - percentage of workers they speak for (e.g. a trade union).

- Formal representation in decision making processes:
  - level of management where they are represented

  - committees they have representation on

  - legal rights (e.g. shareholders, planning authorities).

Assessing interest of stakeholders

This will be more complex because it involves two factors:

- Where their interests rest. We assume that powerful stakeholders will pursue their self-interest. It is important to consider what they wish to achieve. It is possible to make some generalisations, for example:
  - managers – want to further the interests of their departments and functions as well as their own pay and careers;

  - employees – require higher pay, job security, good working conditions and some consultation;

  - customers – want fair prices, reliable supply and reassurance about their purchases;

  - suppliers – want fair prices, reliable orders, prompt payment and advance notification of changes;

  - local government – wants jobs, contribution to local community life, consultation on expansions and so on.

  In practice, we would need to interview the powerful stakeholders to find out precisely what they wanted.

- How interested they are. Not all stakeholders have the time or inclination to follow management's decisions closely. Again, some generalisations are possible about what will lead to interest, for example:
  - high personal financial or career investment in what the business does;
  - absence of alternative (e.g. alternative job, customer, supplier or employer);
  - potential to be called to account for failing to monitor (e.g. local councils or government bodies, such as regulators);
  - high social impact of firm (e.g. well-known, visible product, association with particular issues).

Strategies to deal with stakeholders – Johnson and Scholes

Using a similar approach to Mendelow, **Scholes** suggests the following strategies to deal with stakeholders depending on their level of power and interest.

Low Interest – Low power: Direction

Their lack of interest and power makes them open to influence. They are more likely than others to accept what they are told and follow instructions.

High Interest – Low power: Education/communication

These stakeholders are interested in the strategy but lack the power to do anything. Management need to convince opponents to the strategy that the plans are justified; otherwise they will try to gain power by joining with other, more powerful parties.

Low Interest – High power: Intervention

The key here is to keep these stakeholders satisfied to avoid them gaining interest. This could involve reassuring them of the outcomes of the strategy well in advance.

High Interest – High power: Participation

These stakeholders are the major drivers of change and could stop management plans if not satisfied. Management therefore need to communicate plans to them and then discuss implementation issues.

Stakeholder analysis table

The following table looks at the main stakeholder groupings and assesses the general concerns and objectives of each group.

Stakeholder group	General concerns/objectives	Example
Shareholders	• A steady flow of income (dividends) • Possible capital growth • Continuation of business	If a strategy involves a large capital injection, the shareholders will be unhappy if the injection has an adverse effect on their income stream.
Directors/Managers	• Pay and status • Job security • Individual performance measures	If a strategy results in a particular department being reduced in size or abolished, the manager of that department is likely to be hostile to the plans.
Employees	• Job security • Pay and conditions • Job satisfaction	If a strategy results in workers being given more responsibility for monitoring quality, the employees may be unhappy unless this increased role is supported by an increase in wages.
Trade unions	• The problems of the employees • Taking an active part in the decision-making process	If a strategy results in a manufacturing plant being closed, the union will be unhappy if it has not been consulted and if there is no scheme for helping the employees find alternative employment.

Customers	• Receiving goods and services of a reasonable quality • Paying a reasonable price for those goods and services	If a strategy increases the quality of a product at the same time as increasing the price, *existing* customers may not be willing to pay more for the product, while *new* customers are not attracted to a product that they will view as being of low quality.
Suppliers	• Being paid promptly for goods and services delivered • Receiving regular repayments of any capital provided (e.g. banks)	If a strategy improves the working capital management by paying suppliers late, existing suppliers may decide to stop supplying the organisation, leading to the increased cost of finding new suppliers.
Government/pressure groups/the general public and local people	• The organisation is meeting relevant legal requirements • The organisation does not harm the outside environment	If a strategy relies on increased use of shops based in out-of-town retail centres, this will be affected by government attitudes towards increased road building and society's attitude towards this method of shopping.

Case study style question 3

C Theatre is a charitable trust with the objective of making multicultural films and stage productions available to a regional audience. The organisation is not for profit. The aim to bring diversity of films, plays and dance that would otherwise be inaccessible to a regional audience.

The theatre needs to have strict budget focus, since a charity can become bankrupt. In order to achieve the required income, relationships must be built with a range of stakeholders.

Required:

Write a report to the board of the trust identifying the main stakeholder groups and providing suggestions as to how the trust should build relationships with these stakeholder groups.

(20 minutes)

Managing stakeholders in different organisations

Consider three different types of organisation that are investigating the same strategy of bringing down costs by reducing wages and making employees work more flexible shifts.

The first step is to identify the main stakeholders affected by the decision, and assess their level of power and interest. From this analysis, the Mendelow matrix can be used to guide management on how to manage the stakeholders.

Organisation 1 – Contract cleaning company

- The main employees affected will be the cleaners themselves.

- Since unskilled workers are easy to replace, they have high interest in the decision but low power.

- From the Mendelow matrix, the strategy here should be **'keep informed'**.

- The organisation will therefore keep the cleaners informed of the decision but will probably impose the decision on the workforce.

- This imposition is likely to be enacted quickly, i.e. the strategy will take place almost immediately.

Organisation 2 – Accountancy training company

- The main employees affected will be the lecturers.

- Since these lecturers are very difficult to replace, they have high interest in the decision and high power.

- From the Mendelow matrix, the strategy here should be **'key players'**.

- The organisation may not be able to enforce their strategy without the cooperation of the lecturers. It may decide that this strategy will not succeed.

Organisation 3 – Local public library service

- The main employees affected will be the library staff.

- They will have high interest in the decision.

- Although these employees may be easy to replace, they are likely to be highly unionised. The power of the union will affect the decision-making process.

- From the Mendelow matrix, the strategy here will be **'keep informed'** if the union power is deemed to be low and **'key players'** if the union power is deemed to be high.

- The organisation may decide to consult with the union before any final decisions are made.

- Owing to the lengthy procedures that often exist within the public sector, it is likely that any change in working conditions will be subject to a number of reviews, and implementation will not be rapid.

10 Managing stakeholder conflict

The objectives of the stakeholder groups will inevitably be different and may be in direct conflict. For example, the staff's desire for better pay and work conditions may conflict with the shareholders' desire for higher profits and the customers' desire for lower prices. The job of management is to develop and implement strategy with these differences in mind. This can be further complicated in organisations where the employees are also shareholders.

Cyert and March suggest the following rational techniques for resolving stakeholder conflict:

- **Satisficing** usually by negotiation to keep most and not necessarily all powerful stakeholders happy. It usually emerges as a result of negotiation between the competing stakeholders.

- **Sequential attention** by giving stakeholders turns to realise their objectives. Therefore, staff may get a large pay rise every 3 years but, in between, pay remains static while dividends are paid.

- **Side payments** where compensation is given to make up for not addressing particular stakeholders' objectives. For example, a local community may have a new leisure centre built by a company whose new superstore will inevitably increase noise and traffic congestion in the area.

- **Exercise of power** where deadlock is overcome by powerful figures forcing through their preferred strategic option.

Other techniques used to resolve stakeholder conflict

- **Prioritisation**. Management can specify that any strategy considered must at a minimum satisfy one or more specific objectives before they are prepared to consider it.

- **Weighting and scoring** objectives in terms of importance. Each objective is weighted according to its relative importance to the organisation. Each strategic option is scored according to how well it satisfies the objective. A ranking is calculated for each option by multiplying its weighting by its score, and the strategic option with the highest overall ranking is accepted.

- Creation of a wider **balanced scorecard** set of performance measures.

11 Chapter summary

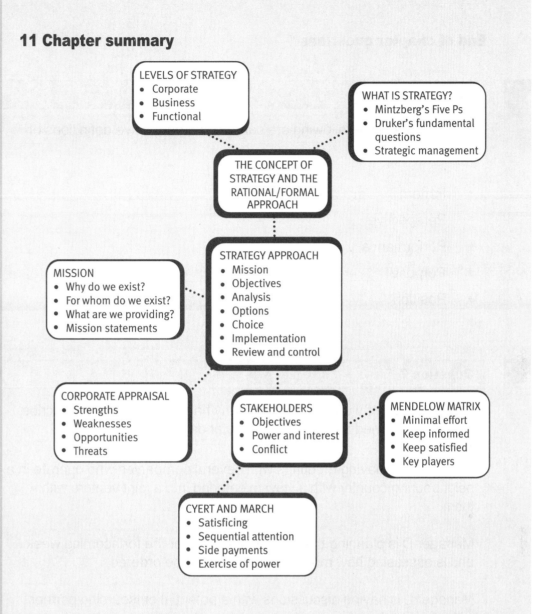

LEVELS OF STRATEGY
- Corporate
- Business
- Functional

WHAT IS STRATEGY?
- Mintzberg's Five Ps
- Druker's fundamental questions
- Strategic management

THE CONCEPT OF STRATEGY AND THE RATIONAL/FORMAL APPROACH

STRATEGY APPROACH
- Mission
- Objectives
- Analysis
- Options
- Choice
- Implementation
- Review and control

MISSION
- Why do we exist?
- For whom do we exist?
- What are we providing?
- Mission statements

CORPORATE APPRAISAL
- Strengths
- Weaknesses
- Opportunities
- Threats

STAKEHOLDERS
- Objectives
- Power and interest
- Conflict

MENDELOW MATRIX
- Minimal effort
- Keep informed
- Keep satisfied
- Key players

CYERT AND MARCH
- Satisficing
- Sequential attention
- Side payments
- Exercise of power

End of chapter questions

Question 1

Which **three** of the following are part of Mintzberg's five definitions of strategy?

- Pattern
- Perspective
- Performance
- Purpose
- Position

Question 2

Three managers working for a company have been asked to describe their main planned activity for a particular day:

Manager H is having meetings with several companies who operate in a neighbouring country with a view to entering into a joint venture with them.

Manager D is planning the staff requirement for the forthcoming week and is assessing how much inventory should be ordered.

Manager L is having discussions with a potential outsourcing partner with a view to transferring elements of production to them in order to reduce the product cost.

Match each manager to the correct level of strategic planning that they are involved with.

Level of strategic planning:

- Corporate
- Business
- Functional

Question 3

Which of the following statements regarding mission, goals and objectives are true? Select all that apply.

- A mission statement addresses the preferred future of the organisation.
- Setting the mission is the first step in the rational/formal model of strategy development.
- A mission statement would consider questions such as, who are competitors, and, how should we compete in our chosen market?
- A mission statement describes the basic purpose of the organisation and what it is trying to accomplish.
- Once the mission for an organisation has been established, the goals and objectives can be set.

Question 4

Which three of the following are functions performed by objectives?

- Responsibility
- Authorisation
- Co-ordination
- Integration
- Communication
- Motivation

Question 5

A Call Centre manager has been set an objective to increase the percentage of call answered within 5 rings to 95%. The current level of calls answered within 5 rings is 89%.

Which of the components for objective setting has not been achieved?

- Specific
- Measurable
- Achievable
- Relevant
- Timely

Question 6

Stakeholders can be classified in a number of different ways.

H is a manufacturing company, considering opening a large, new factory. It is currently at the consultation stage of the project and as part of this has drawn up a list of the main stakeholder groups who would be interested in the development of the new factory.

Place each of the following stakeholder groups under the correct classification.

Employees	Internal	Connected	Secondary
Shareholders			
Pressure Groups			
Customers			

Question 7

K is a retail organisation with three main shareholders; P and his son F, and daughter N.

P is due to retire and has passed the day to day running of the company over to F and N. he spends most of his time abroad and has not had anything to do with any company decision for the last two years.

According to Mendelow, what would be the best method for managing P?

A   Keep informed

B   Minimal effort

C   Keep satisfied

D   Key players

Question 8

The strategy suggested by Cyert and March for managing stakeholder conflict which suggests giving stakeholders turns to realise their objectives is known as:

A   Exercise of power

B   Side payments

C   Satisficing

D   Sequential attention

Question 9

A company has been undertaking a corporate appraisal and has listed the following findings:

- Lack of IT expertise
- Increasing overseas demand for their products
- A popular and charismatic CEO
- A shortage of raw materials

Match these findings to the areas they relate to in the corporate appraisal:

Strengths
Weaknesses
Opportunities
Threats

Question 10

Complete the diagram for the Ansoff Matrix by inserting the correct word in the correct place on the diagram.

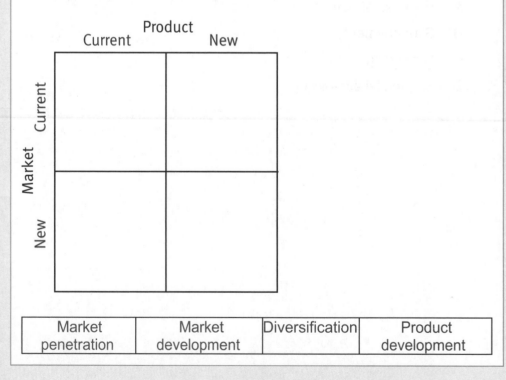

Market penetration	Market development	Diversification	Product development

Test your understanding answers

Case study style question 1

Slide 1: Welcome and introduction

Slide 2: Introduce the three levels of strategy

- Corporate

- Business

- Functional/Operational

Slide 3: Corporate level

At the corporate level, strategy will cover **the purpose and scope of V**.

This will encompass V's mission statement leading to its goals and objectives that feed down to lower levels of strategy. Decisions will be made about the longer term direction of V.

The corporate strategy involves the scope of V's activities and the matching of these to its environment, its resource capabilities and values and the expectations of different stakeholders, e.g. Should V expand into operating theme parks?

Slide 4: Business level

At the business level, strategy will cover **how each of V's strategic business units (SBU) attempts to achieve its mission**.

Within V the fitness centres, casinos, cinemas and sports bars operate as a separate business units. The business level strategy of each SBU will relate to the strategic decisions such as being customer focused, the choice of products, exploring new opportunities and gaining competitive advantage, etc, e.g. Should fitness centres compete on the basis of low cost, value for money or high quality? Which new fitness products/services will be developed and how they will be released to the markets.

Slide 5: Functional level

At the functional level, strategy will cover **how the various functions within the organisation contribute to the achievement of V's overall objectives**.

This strategy focuses on the issues such as resources, processes and people. The activities of the functions within V such as finance, marketing and human resources need to focus on assisting in the achievement of V's overall strategies, e.g. How should V seek to recruit, train and retain croupiers for its casinos?

Slide 6: conclusion/questions and answers

Case study style question 2

(a) A SWOT analysis for E is shown below

Strengths:
Successful company
Steady increase in market share
Experience in the market
Founder's entrepreneurial skills
Good designs
Good quality control
Keen to exploit to technology
Strong IT

Weakness:
Management of information is often out of date
No in-house IT expertise
No web experience
Not sure if the new system will generate new sales
Lack of control over store managers
Out of date reporting from some stores
Over reliance on IT provider

Opportunities:
E-trading can provide a new sales channel and revenue stream
Identification and recording of customer details to enhance customer relationships
Extension of customer base
Global market potential
Cut costs in many areas
Create a vision of a modern company
Develop product range further
Look at employing an IT specialist

Threats:
Customer resistance to on-line shopping
Loss of unique identity; may become just another website trader
Resistance within the company
Effects on existing personnel and working conditions
Costs of developing the website may outweigh the benefits
Security issues
Loss of competitive edge

The above are suggested answers.

(b) Email to J

To: J

From: Management accountant

Date: today

Subject: The use of SWOT analysis

SWOT analysis, or corporate appraisal, is a key tool for organisations. It provides a framework to summarise the key outputs from the external and internal analysis carried out by the organisation. The undertaking of a corporate appraisal is an important step in strategy formulation and would benefit E at this time as you are considering an investment in website development with a view to reaching global markets.

This type of development marks a change for the company and it important that a full analysis is carried out before this strategy is embarked upon. Analysis should be carried out both internally and externally. The SWOT analysis will pull all of the analysis together and will allow you make better, more informed decisions.

The use of SWOT analysis will focus your management's attention on current strengths and weaknesses. It will also enable management to monitor trends and developments in the changing business environment. Each trend or development may be classified as an opportunity or a threat that will provide a stimulus for an appropriate management response.

You will then be able to make an assessment of the feasibility of required actions in order that the company may capitalise upon opportunities whilst considering how best to negate or minimise the effect of any threats.

I hope you have found the above helpful. Please do not hesitate to get in touch if you require any further information.

Case study style question 3

Report to the board of C Theatre charitable trust

In this report, the main stakeholders will be identified and suggestions as to how relationships with these stakeholders can be developed will be put forward.

Loyal customers

One of the main stakeholder groups will be the customers of the theatre. Without the continued support of the loyal customers, the theatre would be unable to survive therefore the building of relationships with the customer is essential for the theatre.

The theatre could use a database to profile the interests and wants of customers. Tailored communication could then be sent. Given the need to contain costs, this might be achieved by getting customers to sign up to electronic communications. Up-to-date news and information on future performances can be easily made available to customers.

The theatre could set up a website with booking facilities which would allow customer to book on line and receive confirmation by email rather than post. This would reduce costs and would provide efficiency for the booking process.

In addition, a friend of the theatre group could be established, providing loyal customers with offers and discounts to encourage their continued support.

First time customers

While loyal customers will always be important to the theatre, it is equally important to attract new customers. The website could be linked to other relevant websites, such as local attractions and tourist boards to attract new customers.

In addition, the theatre could produce an information pack to attract new mailing list subscribers. These could be made available in local churches and shops.

Local arts groups and performers

Another stakeholder group which the theatre will have to develop relationships with are the local arts groups and performers. A partnership agreement could be established with arts groups, to co-sponsor events of special interests to given groups of customers.

The theatre could allow the local groups use of the theatre to encourage locals to come along to performances.

Local organisations

Another stakeholder group would be local organisations and businesses. The theatre could build relations with these groups in order to try to obtain commercial sponsorship. Acknowledgement could be given in the monthly programme mailings and preferential facilities offered for corporate hospitality.

The above is just a selection of potential relationships with stakeholders.

Question 1

- Pattern
- Perspective
- Position

Mintzberg suggested five essential characteristics of strategic planning. As well as pattern, perspective and position, he also suggested:

- Plan
- Ploy

Question 2

Level of strategic planning:

- Corporate – Manager H
- Business – Manager L
- Functional – Manager D

Corporate strategy is concerned with decisions such as which industry to operate in, or whether to enter new markets.

Business strategy is concerned with decisions regarding product development, marketing and how to gain competitive advantage.

Functional strategy is concerned with day to day decisions such as staffing levels and inventory control.

Question 3

The correct statements are:

- Setting the mission is the first step in the rational/formal model of strategy development.
- A mission statement describes the basic purpose of the organisation and what it is trying to accomplish.
- Once the mission for an organisation has been established, the goals and objectives can be set.

A mission statement addresses the preferred future of the organisation. This is incorrect. The preferred future of the organisation is known as the vision.

A mission statement would consider questions such as, who are competitors, and, how should we compete in our chosen market? This is incorrect. Mission statements can address many questions, but tend to be more high level and would not normally address specific questions about who are our competitors.

Question 4

- Responsibility
- Integration
- Motivation

The functions performed by objectives can be remembered by PRIME:

Planning

Responsibility

Integration

Motivation

Evaluation

Question 5

The component for objective setting which has not been achieved is Timely.

Objectives should be SMART:

The call centre manager's target is specific – 95% of calls must be answered within 5 rings.

The technology within the call centre should be capable of measuring this.

Given that the current operating level is 89%, 95% should be seen as achievable.

This is clearly a relevant measurement for a call centre manager.

The component of SMART which is not achieved is Timely as the objective does not specify over what period this improvement should be achieved.

Question 6

Internal	Connected	Secondary
Employees	Shareholders Customers	Pressure Groups

Internal stakeholders are those stakeholders who are within the organisations and would include employees and management.

Connected stakeholders either invest or have dealings with the organisation. This group would include shareholders, customers, suppliers and finance providers.

Secondary stakeholders may have an interest in the organisation but have no contractual link. The public and pressure groups would fall into this category.

Question 7

Answer C

The best method for managing P would be to keep him satisfied. He is a main shareholder therefore would have high power, but he has low interest in the running of the company.

Question 8

D   Sequential attention

Cyert and March suggested four techniques for resolving stakeholder conflict. The sequential attention technique gives stakeholders turns in realising their objectives. An example of this would be paying larger dividends for two years and paying smaller dividends in the third year while staff bonuses are paid.

Question 9

A corporate appraisal analyses internal strengths and weaknesses and external opportunities and threats. The items can be matched to the corporate appraisal as follows:

Strengths	A popular and charismatic CEO
Weaknesses	Lack of IT expertise
Opportunities	Increasing overseas demand for their products
Threats	A shortage of raw materials

Question 10

The completed Ansoff matrix is shown below:

	Product Current	Product New
Market Current	Market Penetration	Product Development
Market New	Market Development	Diversification

chapter

2

Alternative approaches to strategy

Chapter learning objectives

Compare and contrast alternative approaches to strategy
development

1 Session content diagram

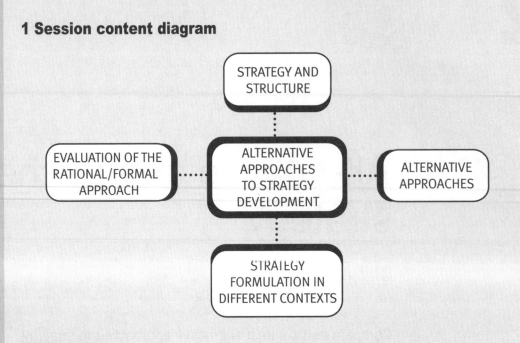

2 Introduction

While the rational model of strategy (covered in the previous chapter) is a well recognised approach with many benefits, not all organisations will adopt this approach. Many organisations find the rational approach inflexible, too bureaucratic and too costly. The rational approach is not suitable for all types of organisations and all circumstances. There are alternative approaches to strategy development which many organisations favour and these will be covered in this chapter.

3 Advantages and disadvantages of the rational/formal approach

The rational/formal approach can take a significant amount of time and requires a lot of organisational resources. It is important that organisations can see the benefits from the effort required with this approach:

The benefits of the rational/formal approach to strategy formulation

- Long term view – it avoids organisations focusing on short term results.

- Identifies key strategic issues – it makes management more proactive.

- Goal congruence – it ensures that the whole of the organisation is working towards the same goals.

- Communicates responsibility – everyone within the organisation can be made aware of what is required from them.

- Co-ordinates SBU's – it helps business units to work together.

- Security for stakeholders – it demonstrates to stakeholders that the organisation has a clear idea of where it is going.

- Basis for strategic control – clear targets and reports enabling success of the strategy to be reviewed.

However, some writers are critical of the rational approach. In addition to the time required to undertake the rational approach and the cost of the process, there are other areas of criticism.

The problems with the rational/formal approach to strategy formulation

- Inappropriate in dynamic environments – a new strategy may only be established say every five years, which may quickly become inappropriate if the environment changes.

- Bureaucratic and inflexible – radical ideas are often rejected and new opportunities which present themselves may not be able to be taken.

- Difficulty getting the necessary participation to implement the strategy – successful implementation requires the support of middle and junior management and the nature of the rational approach may alienate these levels of management.

- Impossible in uncertain environments – it is impossible to carry out the required analysis in uncertain business environments.

- Stifles innovation and creativity – the rational approach encourages conformity among managers.

- Complex and costly for small businesses with informal structures and systems.

Further detail on the benefits and drawbacks of the rational/formal

Benefits of the rational/formal top-down approach to strategy

Business strategy formulation obviously uses a lot of organisational resource. What are the benefits?

- Avoids short-termist behaviour. It ensures that management considers the long-term development of the business rather than focusing solely on short-term results and operational results.

- Helps identify strategic issues. By encouraging management to consider the business environment in their plans and decisions, it will help them keep ahead of change and to be more proactive.

- Goal congruence. There are many aspects to this:
  - It will help coordinate the different business units, divisions and departments and ensure that they work together to realise the full potential of the organisation.
  - Asset investment decisions will be taken with the long-term needs of the business in mind. This could include design or acquisition of buildings and capital equipment, information systems or acquisitions of other businesses.
  - Business and operational level decisions will be congruent with the overall strategy. This might affect the types of staff recruited and developed, the location of production and distribution facilities or the sorts of products and brands created.

- Improves stakeholder perceptions. If the organisation demonstrates that it has a clear idea of where it is going, it enables others to make plans based on its future. This may lead to:
  - higher share price because investors are confident of higher future return;

    attraction and retention of staff and higher morale because employees can see that their career aspirations may be met within the firm;
  - improved relations with suppliers who feel they can rely on orders in the future.

- Provides a basis for strategic control. By having a formal process of formulation and implementation, this ensures that:
  - There is someone looking after the development of strategy.
  - There are clear programmes and policies being developed to implement the chosen strategy.
  - There are targets and reports enabling review of the success of the strategy.

- Develops future management potential and ensures continuity. This relates to the fact that formal strategy formulation is a collective process. This means that:
  - Different functional managers (e.g. finance or marketing) gain an appreciation of the other disciplines of business and so develop into stronger general managers.
  - Providers of information to the strategy process become more deeply involved in the business and develop as a pool of expertise from which the next generation of managers may be recruited.
  - Avoids succession problems when members of senior management retire or move on. The strategy of the firm is understood by all and will outlast the loss of key members of the management team.

Drawbacks of the formal top-down approach to strategy

Some writers are critical of the formal process discussed above, because:

- It is too infrequent to allow the business to be dynamic. This view emphasises the infrequency of the 'strategy round', say every five years, and the time it takes to achieve any change to the strategy. If the environment changes unexpectedly, the firm's performance may deteriorate as it continues to follow a business strategy which has now become inappropriate to its business environment, for example by continuing to make a product no one wants.

- It discourages the development of radical or innovative strategies. The need to retain consensus among the management team means that radical ideas are too often rejected.

- There is loss of entrepreneurial spirit. Entrepreneurs are persons who break rules and make changes to conventional ways of doing business. On the other hand, a middle manager in a strategically managed firm will be rewarded for carrying out their allotted part in the strategy and for not breaking the rules. The effect will be to encourage conformity among managers. This will lose the firm potentially successful ventures and perhaps also the services of gifted entrepreneurial managers who may leave in frustration.

- It suffers from difficulties of implementation. The formal process is management-led and seeks to pursue the goals of the business. Successful implementation requires the participation of middle and junior management, together with operative staff. There is a danger that the formal process will not build the support of these people and hence will be misunderstood or resisted. The result will be that the goals of the strategy are not realised.

- It is impossible in uncertain business environments. Formal business strategy requires that the strategists are able to make reliable assumptions about the future and particularly about the opportunities and threats facing them. The business environment is now more uncertain than ever before. Some writers argue that management efforts should be diverted from trying to plan strategies and instead should focus on improving the ability of their businesses to respond and adapt to change. (Managing change will be dealt with in a later chapter).

- It is too expensive and complicated for small businesses. The manager of a small business is unlikely to be skilled in the techniques needed for developing the kinds of business strategy described above. Moreover, the opportunity cost in terms of the time away from direct management of the operational parts of the business are likely to be too great.

> ### Case study style question 1
>
> Your manager has been asked to do a presentation to the next board meeting about the typical features of the rational approach to strategy and the disadvantages of such an approach. He is unfamiliar with this approach and has asked you to provide him with some information which he could use in his presentation.
>
> **Required:**
>
> Produce a memo for your manager detailing the typical features of the rational/formal approach to strategy and the disadvantages of such an approach.
>
> **(20 minutes)**

4 Environmental uncertainty

Earlier in the chapter we mentioned that the rational/formal model is not appropriate in dynamic or uncertain environments.

> CIMA defines **uncertainty** as: *'The inability to predict the outcome from an activity due to a lack of information about the required input/output relationships or about the environment within which the activity takes place.'*

Managers' perception of uncertainty will be increased by two factors – complexity and dynamism.

- **Complexity.** This is the number of variables which can impact on the organisation and how difficult they are to predict or understand. Also if the relationships between the variables is complex, this will also increase uncertainty.

- **Dynamism.** This is the rate of change of the business environment. Increased dynamism means that management's models of 'how things work' will become out of date much quicker. It also suggests that competitors will be able to respond more quickly to a firm's initiatives.

  Examples of the factors which have increased dynamism include:

  - Faster information flows. These mean that something happening on one side of the world will have global impacts very quickly.

  - Shorter product life cycles. Modern competitive strategy leads most firms to invest heavily in research and development to render rivals' products obsolete.

Impact of uncertainty

High uncertainty affects business strategy in several ways:

- Reduces the planning horizon. If a firm operates in an uncertain environment its management are unlikely to develop plans for more than a few years ahead because they accept that they will be subject to large margins of error.

- May lead to conservative strategies. Managers will tend to stay closer to the 'strategic recipes' that have worked in the past because they fear trying anything new due to not being able to forecast its effects. This approach is flawed because under conditions of high uncertainty there is no reason to believe that old 'recipes' will still work.

- Increases information needs of the organisation. Where the environment is no longer predictable, management will require more regular information and on a greater range of factors to make it more certain.

These factors have led organisations to abandon the rational/formal approach to strategy in favour of alternative approaches which take more account of the changing nature of the environment in which the organisation is operating. Approaches such as the emergent approach have become more popular. This and other approaches will now be considered in more detail.

Has uncertainty really increased?

The modern assumption is that the business environment has become more uncertain and that more information is needed by management in order to restore certainty. **Hatch** (1997) observes that 'Environments do not feel uncertain, people do', and the only thing which has demonstrably increased is the amount of environmental information available to management. She ventures that perhaps the world has always been dynamic and complex but that we never fully appreciated it before.

Hatch's suggestion is deliberately far-fetched to make a point. The more environmental data we provide to managers, the more uncertain and stressed-out they may become. This gives weight to the argument that in strategy formulation management should focus on only a few key success variables and ignore the rest.

5 Other approaches to strategy formulation

You can see from the above that the rational/formal approach has a number of drawbacks and is not suitable in all situations. There are other recognised approaches to strategic planning, including:

- Emergent approach
- Incremental approaches
- Freewheeling opportunism
- Political approaches

Emergent approach

Mintzberg argues that successful strategies can emerge in an organisation without formal, deliberate prior planning. The 'pattern' is often made up of the intended (planned) strategies that are actually realised and any emergent (unplanned) strategies.

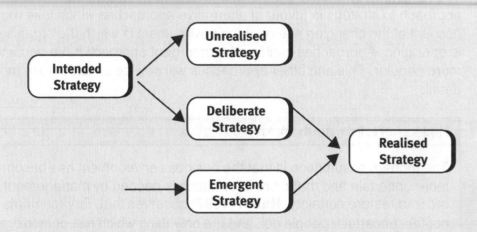

Under the emergent approach a strategy may be tried and developed as it is implemented. If it fails a different approach will be taken. This is likely to result in a more short-term emphasis than with the rational model. To successfully use the emergent approach, the organisation needs to have a culture of innovation.

Mintzberg was not surprised at the failure of intended strategies to be fully realised as deliberate strategies. He regarded it as unlikely that a firm's environment could be as totally predictable as it would need to be for all intended strategies to work out. The emergent strategy is often a response to unexpected contingencies and the resulting realised strategy may, in the circumstances, be superior to the intended strategy.

Emergent strategies

Some strategies may be deliberately emergent, in that managers may create the conditions for new ideas to flourish and strategies to emerge. This has the effect of focusing attention on the role of the manager as at the heart of the strategy and reduces the importance of the rational process. To do this, Mintzberg suggested that a manager must exhibit the following skills:

- **Manage stability**. Managers should be able to master the details of running their business and not feel compelled to constantly rethink the business's strategic future.

- **Detect discontinuity**. This is the ability to detect the subtle environmental changes that may affect the business and be able to assess their potential impact on its future performance. The key to this is that managers must 'know the business'. Formal strategy systems can distance managers from their business and they can subsequently lack the knowledge they need to run it.

- **Manage patterns**. Management should encourage strategic initiatives to grow throughout the business and watch to see how they develop and intervene once this is clear.

- **Reconcile change and continuity**. Managers must realise that radical changes and new patterns of strategy will create resistance and instability in the firm. They must keep radical departures in check, while preparing the ground for their introduction.

Illustration 1 – Honda's emergent strategy

When Honda executives arrived in Los Angeles, they did so with the intention of setting up a subsidiary to sell 250cc and 350cc machines to existing motorcycle enthusiasts. They had no intention of trying to sell smaller bikes such as the 50cc machines that were so popular in Japan because they could not envisage a market for these in a country where everything was bigger and better than back home.

As things turned out, the sales of the 250cc and 350cc bikes were disappointing. One of the reasons was to do with the mechanical failure of some of their machines. The intended strategy looked to be failing. In the course of their work, however, the Honda executives were using the 50cc machines to run errands around Los Angeles and their presence attracted a lot of attention.

One day the Honda team received a call from a Sears' buyer who proposed selling the 50cc machines through the department chain outlets. For their part the Honda team was reluctant to sell the small bikes because they feared it would alienate serious bikers who might associate the Honda company with 'wimp' machines. Eventually, however, their failure to sell the expected quota of larger machines pushed them into selling the small 50cc machines and to sell them not through specialist motor cycle distributors but through general retailers. Sales took off and a new strategy was born.

Incremental approaches

Lindblom – 'Muddling through'

Lindblom described how government administrators 'muddle through' from year to year rather than carry out bold strategic initiatives. He criticised the rational model as follows:

- In practice, managers confuse the goals and the strategy of the company.

- It is unrealistic to imagine a strategic planner carefully sifting through every possible option to achieve predetermined goals.

- At best, formulation of strategy is a process of evaluating a few slight extensions to existing policies.

Lindblom argued that strategic choice takes place by comparing possible options against each other and considering which would give the best outcome. This approach does not try to identify and review all the potential strategies available to the organisation. Rather it provides a way of monitoring the progress and the direction the organisation is moving in, and allows a change in 'course' if required.

Lindblom did not advocate this approach, he simply recorded its existence. He agreed with critics that in an environment of turbulence and rapid change, minor adjustments to current policies will not allow organisations to adapt sufficiently. The same could be said in circumstances where organisations face threats to their survival, a more radical approach may be required.

Quinn – Logical incrementalism

Quinn takes a more positive view of incrementalism than Lindblom. For Quinn, a manager must map where he or she wants the organisation to go and then proceed towards it in **small steps**, being prepared to adapt if the environment changes or if support is not forthcoming. Quinn's logical incrementalism falls somewhere between the rational approach and the 'muddling through' approach.

He identified that:

- **Managers generally know where they want their organisations to go**. Effective strategists initially work out only a few integrating concepts, principles, or philosophies that can help rationalise and guide the company's overall actions.

- **Strategy is an incremental, step-by-step, learning process**. They proceed step-by-step from early generalities toward later specifics, clarifying the strategy as events both permit and dictate.

- **Managers consciously keep their decisions small and flexible**. In early stages, they consciously avoid over-precise statements that might impair the flexibility or imagination needed to exploit new information or opportunities.

The outcome of this approach is a deliberate policy of small strategic changes within the framework provided by a general sense of strategic direction.

Managerial functions in incrementalism

In the incremental approach, the manager's skill is crucial. The main managerial functions are:

- The manager sits at the centre of a network of **formal and informal communications** with staff, customers and others. They will be attuned to the problems and issues confronting the organisation. They may use formal strategy models and techniques to understand these.

- Once they sense that a **need for change** has arisen and that events are pushing the firm in a particular direction, they will start to develop a general strategic vision for the organisation.

- Rather than present the full-blown strategy, and risk opposition, the manager will **build political support** for the ideas from key committees or individual managers.

- Commitment will be gained to an **initial trial of the strategy**. This will build further commitment among those charged with making the project a success and erode the consensus in favour of the old way of doing business.

- This consensus will build and **press the strategic change forward incrementally**.

> The use of formal strategic frameworks is valuable in developing and communicating the changed strategy. This is the logical element in Quinn's methodology because it ensures that the process leads somewhere. The incrementalism comes from the need to subordinate rapid change to the process of gaining consensus and avoiding resistance.

As we can see, Mintzberg and Quinn are essentially making the same point: that strategies are not always planned or revealed in advance and that management skill is crucial. Unlike Lindblom, they do not see this as unacceptably conservative, but see it as realistic.

Freewheeling opportunism

The alternative to having a long-term strategic plan is having little or no plan.

Freewheeling opportunism is a term used to describe the essentially reactive process of management as an alternative to strategic planning. This would often be used by entrepreneurs and innovators who enjoy taking risks.

This suggests:

- a flexible and dynamic approach
- opportunities are taken as they arise
- fast reaction to changes in the environment

Consider market traders who quickly change the goods they are selling depending on short-term trends.

Some criticisms of this approach are that it:

- may encourage managers to pursue their own agenda, which may conflict with the company's aims
- may restrict the ability of the whole organisation to respond to major environmental changes
- may result in pursuit of short-term profit rather than long-term strategy.

6 Strategy Safari

It can be seen that there are numerous approaches to strategy development.

In their 1998 (updated 2008) book Strategy Safari, Mintzberg et al. attempted to define strategic management, and they identified ten approaches to strategy (schools of thought). Their work analyses each of the ten schools of thought and identifies the advantages and disadvantages of each. The schools of thought are shown below. Elements of these approaches should be recognised from the material already covered in this chapter.

The schools are split into two main categories; prescriptive and descriptive. The prescriptive schools attempt to explain how strategy **should** be formulated, while the descriptive schools attempt to describe how strategies actually **are** formed.

Prescriptive schools

Design school (conception) – Strategy development is a rational process which seeks to establish a fit between internal capabilities and external possibilities.

Planning school (formal) – Strategy is developed by specialists in the science of developing strategy using rigorous strategy planning methodologies.

Positioning school (analytical) – Strategy is a combination of defensive and offensive moves, based on the premise that industry structure drives strategy position which drives organisational structure.

The Design and Planning schools are closely linked to the rational/formal model. The main tool used in the Design school is SWOT. Within the Planning school, strategy is seen as a formal process and relies on rigorous strategy planning methodologies. Elements of the Positioning school which uses tools such as the Boston Consulting Group, Porter's generic strategies and Porter's value chain will be covered in the next chapters.

The descriptive schools

Environmental school (reactive) – Strategy develops as a response to forces in the environment within which it operates.

Cognitive school (mental) – Strategy development is an act of understanding how the mind works and processing information is the key to understanding strategy development.

Entrepreneurial school (visionary) – Strategy development is dependent on the vision and direction of one entrepreneurial individual.

Power school (negotiation) – Strategy results from power struggles within the organisation and in the market place.

Cultural school (collective) – Strategy development is a process of social interaction that takes place within the context of beliefs and shared values of the members of the organisation.

Learning school (emergent) – Strategy emerges as a result of trial and error and learning within the organisation.

Configuration school (transformation) – Strategy is a conscious act of transforming an organisation from one state to another.

From this group of approaches, the Learning school can be seen to have elements of the emergent and incremental approaches.

It can be seen that there are many different approaches to strategy, each offering different views and concepts. Mintzberg et al. were not advocating any particular viewpoint. No one approach is seen as right, or better that the others. In fact the book goes on to argue that strategy planning is not always a good thing in all cases.

Strategy as a political process

With the Power school the exercise of power is seen as the key influence in strategy development and uses bargaining and negotiation as its key tools. This approach views strategy formulation as a political process, where political and stakeholder analysis must be carried out in order to identify the main sources of power. This power may be found internally, or may be external to the organisation. Once the key players have been identified, a power struggle may then take place which, through negotiation, results in the formulation of strategy.

It was felt that this approach is more appropriate in larger, more mature organisations where the power structures were more established.

There are many influences in strategy with some being influenced by the environment or market influences, while others rely more on the analysis of internal capabilities. The important aspect for each approach is to identify what, or who, influences the strategy.

7 Strategy and structure

When organisations are developing their strategy, thought must be given to their structure.

There has always been some debate as to whether strategy follows structure, or vice versa. This was looked at by Mintzberg. When discussing the Positioning approach, it is considered that the industry structure drives the strategic position, which in turn drives the organisational structure. In the Design school, however it is viewed that strategy precedes structure. The more widely held belief is that strategy dictates structure and that structure must support strategy.

A structure is necessary in order to facilitate the implementation of strategy and the achievement of objectives. It has been described as the 'shape' of the business but can be defined as the established pattern of relationships between individuals, groups and departments within the organisation.

According to Drucker, '*Structure is a means for attaining the objectives and goals of an organisation'* and according to Johnson, Scholes and Whittington, a key aspect of strategy implementation is considering whether the firm needs to change its organisational structure.

Whether it is believed that strategy follows structure or structure follows strategy will largely depend on the view on strategic management adopted. Regardless of which view is taken, it is accepted that strategy and structure are linked and are both key determinants of an organisation's success.

The influences that have a bearing on organisational structure and design include:

- The organisation's strategic objectives – if coordination between specific parts of the organisation is of key importance then the structure should facilitate relationships between them.

- The nature of the environment in which the organisation is operating, now and in the future. Generally, product based structures are more flexible and are more suitable in a dynamic or complex environment where organisations have to be adaptable.

- The diversity of the organisation – the needs of a multinational are different from those of a small company.

- The future strategy – for example, if a company may be making acquisitions in the future, then adopting a divisional structure now will make the acquired companies easier to assimilate.

- The technology available – IT has a significant impact on the structure, management and functioning of the organisation because of the effect it has on patterns of work, the formation and structure of groups, the nature of supervision and managerial roles. New technology has resulted in fewer management levels because it allows employees at clerical/operator level to take on a wider range of functions.

- The people within the organisation and their managerial skills.

Case study style question 2

Your 18 year old neighbour, J, has recently left school and has decided that he wants to pursue an entrepreneurial career. He has inherited a sum of money from his grandmother that he aims to invest in his first business venture. In order to be better prepared for the business world he enrolled in a Business Studies course at a local college. After only 6 weeks of the course, J decided that he had gained enough knowledge and decided not to continue with the course. He was impatient to launch his career and wanted to focus his energy on his first business venture.

The key element that J picked up on the college course was that the key to business success was planning. The lecturer explained that there are different levels of planning (from strategic down to operational) and different types of planning. J didn't pay attention to all the detail, but he came away with a clear understanding that planning was important.

For his first business venture J intends to set up a computer games development company. He has always had a keen interest in computer games and is skilled in computer technology. He believes he knows the types of games which would sell. He has developed a plan for his business:

(1) Buy a top level gaming computer

(2) Set aside one month to create the game

(3) Approach local games stores directly and convince them to sell the game

(4) Also use word of mouth and the internet to promote the game

J has a lot of belief in himself and his ability but asks you for a second opinion to ensure he's not missed anything vital.

Required:

Write an email to J explaining three different approaches to strategic planning and recommending which might be most appropriate for him.

(15 minutes)

8 Strategy development in different contexts

Strategy is required in all organisations. While much of what is covered about strategy relates to large, commercial, profit-seeking organisations, we have to consider the additional considerations when developing strategy in smaller organisations, in public organisations and in organisations which are not-for-profit.

SMEs (small and medium sized enterprises)

SMEs often lack the management skills required for formal planning approaches and often rely more on informal planning using their intuition and understanding of their businesses. In small organisations, formal structures and controls may be lacking.

According to **Birley** (1982), the formal top-down process may be unsuitable for small businesses for four reasons:

Differences in goals. In a small firm, the goals of the business are often inseparable from the goals of the owner-manager and immediate family group. Small businesses often do not exhibit the economic rationality and single-minded pursuit of dividends and growth often associated with businesses governed by external shareholders. In many small, family run businesses, goals may be a satisfactory income and lifestyle, or passing the business to family members when they retire. Growth may not be a primary consideration

Limited scope of product/market choices. Small-business managers typically consider a much narrower range of strategic options than do their large-business counterparts. The business will often have a narrow scope, based on the skills and knowledge of the proprietor. Management may be reluctant to move too far away from their core business.

Limited resources. Smaller firms lack the resources to invest in new strategic ventures and rapid growth. Therefore, they do not exhibit the sudden strategic leaps envisaged by the rational model. Given their smaller income streams, an unsuccessful strategic investment could destroy the firm.

Organisational structure. Strategic implementation demands the setting up of an appropriate structure and selection of an appropriate team to carry it out. Small firms may not have the personnel available, or the owner may be unwilling to lose their absolute control.

Public sector and not-for-profit organisations

Public sector organisations such as schools and hospitals, charities and not-for-profit organisations often have difficulty in developing strategy due to their difficulty in using traditional private sector based approaches to objective setting since profit is not their main objective.

With such organisations a discussion of objectives is likely to be problematic for the following reasons:

- It is more likely to have multiple objectives. A large teaching hospital may want to give the best quality care and treat as many patients as possible and train new doctors and research new techniques. Conflict is inevitable.

- It will be more difficult to measure objectives. How can one measure whether a school is educating pupils well? Performance in exams? Percentage going on to university? Percentage getting jobs? Percentage staying out of prison once they leave?

- There may be a more equal balance of power between stakeholders. In a company, the shareholders hold ultimate power. If they do not use it, the directors generally get their way. In a school, the balance of power may be more even (or even undefined) between parents, governors, the headmaster and the local education authority.

- The people receiving the service are not necessarily those paying for it. The government and local NHS trusts determine a hospital's funding, not the patients. Consequently, there may be pressure to perform well in national league tables at the expense of other objectives.

The 'three Es approach'

One way to address this problem is to use the 'three Es approach' of the Audit Commission:

- **Effectiveness** looks at the outputs (the goal approach); the 'goal approach' looks at the ultimate objectives of the organisation, i.e. it looks at output measures. For example, for an NHS hospital, have the waiting lists been reduced? Have mortality rates gone down? How many patients have been treated?

- **Efficiency** looks at the link between outputs and inputs (the internal processes approach); The 'internal processes approach' looks at how well inputs have been used to achieve outputs – it is a measure of efficiency. For example, what was the average cost per patient treated? What was the average spend per bed over the period, and what was the bed occupancy rate that this achieved?

- **Economy** looks solely at the level of inputs, e.g. did the hospital spend more or less on drugs this year, or on nurses' wages?

The best picture of the success of an organisation is obtained by using all of the above approaches and by examining both financial and non-financial issues. Think about effectiveness meaning 'doing the right things' and efficiency 'about doing things right'.

This problem with objective setting has important implications in the following areas:

- *Development of consistent strategies*. If the organisation does not have clear objectives, or if its objectives are in conflict with one another, then it will not be able to follow consistent courses of action. For example, a firm that seeks to satisfy objectives for short-term dividends while also pursuing long-term growth will eventually be forced to sacrifice one or the other due to lack of funds.

- *Deciding between strategic options*. Options are evaluated against the objectives of the business before management agree to devote resources. However, if one option provides a good financial return while another provides jobs in an area of high unemployment, a firm with both financial and social responsibility objectives will find it difficult to choose.

- *Development of appropriate performance measures.* The more objectives an organisation has, the more control measures it will need to monitor performance towards them. If the objectives are competing, there is a danger of conflicting signals or, worse, excessive focus on one at the expense of the rest. For example, a school will have many objectives such as producing good citizens, ensuring emotional development, catering for special needs, and so on. However, parents and government prefer to have a single measure to decide whether a school is performing well or badly and tend to focus on examination results. This immediately distorts behaviour in the school towards exam results at the expense of other equally worthy objectives.

9 Chapter summary

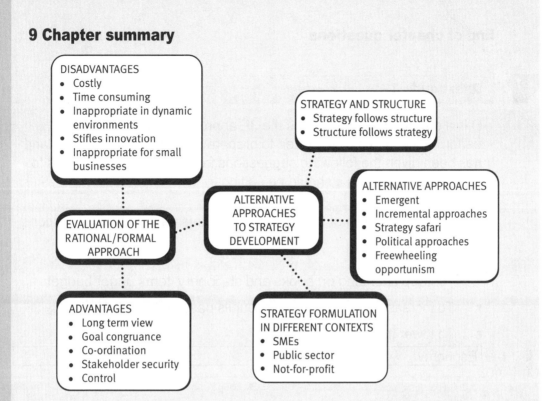

DISADVANTAGES
- Costly
- Time consuming
- Inappropriate in dynamic environments
- Stifles innovation
- Inappropriate for small businesses

EVALUATION OF THE RATIONAL/FORMAL APPROACH

ADVANTAGES
- Long term view
- Goal congruance
- Co-ordination
- Stakeholder security
- Control

ALTERNATIVE APPROACHES TO STRATEGY DEVELOPMENT

STRATEGY AND STRUCTURE
- Strategy follows structure
- Structure follows strategy

ALTERNATIVE APPROACHES
- Emergent
- Incremental approaches
- Strategy safari
- Political approaches
- Freewheeling opportunism

STRATEGY FORMULATION IN DIFFERENT CONTEXTS
- SMEs
- Public sector
- Not-for-profit

End of chapter questions

Question 1

D is a state-run school. It uses the 3E approach to measuring performance. It has been asked to prepare objectives for next year and has been given the following suggestions from the local authority as to the type of objectives it should be setting.

Under which heading of the 3E approach does each of the suggestions belong?

- To keep spending on books and stationery items under budget

- To increase the percentage of pupils passing their final exams

- To lower the pupil to staff ratio

Economy	Efficiency	Effectiveness

Question 2

Which **three** of the following are advantages of the rational/formal approach to strategy formulation?

- Prevents focus on short-term results

- Suitable in dynamic environments

- Encourages innovation and creativity

- Appropriate for small businesses

- Ensures goal congruence

- Provides security for stakeholders

Question 3

Under which of the following environmental conditions would the rational/formal approach to strategy formulation be **LEAST** suitable?

A   Stable and unchanging

B   Gradually changing in a predictable fashion

C   Rapidly changing in an unpredictable fashion

D   Stable with minor fluctuations

Question 4

In which of the following ways would high uncertainty impact business strategy? Select ALL that apply.

Encourages the use of the rational approach

Reduces the planning horizon ·

Encourages emergent strategies ,

Encourages long-term planning

Encourages risk taking behaviour ¨

Increases the information needs of the organisation

Question 5

Consider the following two organisations:

H has a culture of innovation and is willing to develop its strategy over time in relation to changes in the market place.

X has mapped where it wants the organisation to go but is moving towards this in small steps.

Which of the following approaches to strategic development is each organisation adopting?

- Emergent approach
- Logical incrementalism
- Freewheeling opportunism
- Muddling through

Question 6

Which **three** of the following are seen as advantages of the freewheeling opportunism approach to strategy formulation?

- Provides the ability to react quickly to changes in the environment
- Provides more security for stakeholders
- Opportunities can be taken as they arise
- Encourages managers to pursue short-term profit

- It is a flexible and dynamic approach
- Ensures goal congruence

Question 7

Which of the following statements regarding environmental uncertainty are correct? Select ALL that apply.

- High uncertainty would tend to increase the likelihood of risky strategies being pursued.

- Dynamism within the business environment has increased due to shorter product lifecycles.

- Where a business is experiencing high uncertainty, they are likely to increase their planning horizon and develop more long-term plans.

- Complexity refers to the number of variables which can impact on the organisation and how difficult they are to understand or predict.

- Increased uncertainty will increase the information needs of an organisation.

Question 8

Complete the diagram for the emergent approach to strategy formulation using the words given below:

Deliberate strategy	Intended strategy	Realised strategy	Emergent strategy	Unrealised strategy

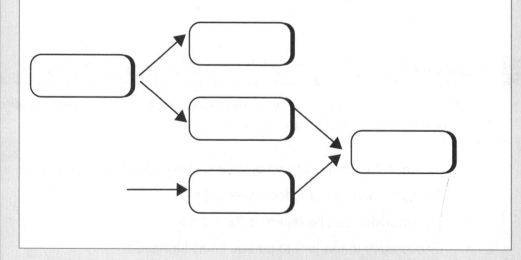

Question 9

The rational/formal approach to strategy formulation may **not** be as suitable for small and medium sized enterprises (SMEs) for which of the following reasons? Select all that apply.

- SMEs typically have a more limited range of strategic options
- Strategy is not required in small and medium sized enterprises
- There may be insufficient personnel available to carry it out
- In small businesses, the goals of the business may not be growth but may come from the goals of the owners

Question 10

Match the descriptions with the schools of thought identified by Mintzberg:

Configuration	Cultural	Design	Learning

- Strategy develops as a rational process which seeks to establish a fit between internal and external capabilities
- Strategy emerges as a result of trial and error
- Strategy is a conscious act of transforming an organisation from one state to another
- Strategy development is a process of social interaction within the context of the belief and shared values of the organisation

Test your understanding answers

Case study style question 1

MEMORANDUM

To: Manager

From: Management Accountant

Date: Today

Subject: Rational/formal planning process

The following are typical features of the process:

The strategy team is developed:

The team will be selected and report to top management. They will consist of expert staff collecting business intelligence. Groups of managers of SBU's will meet periodically and discuss business operations and progress.

Business consultants may be involved as advisors and facilitators recommending models and techniques in understanding their business environments.

Formal collection of information from both inside and outside the organisation:

Environmental scanning reports will be produced detailing competitor behaviour and market trends. Specially commissioned reports may be produced upon request on particular markets. Management reports on operating costs and performance will be regularly produced. Research reports on market opportunities and threats will be issued also.

Collective decisions are made:

The senior management team will work together to develop and agree strategies. The use of brainstorming may be used, which may involve conflict but will lead ultimately to a decision about strategy.

Communication and Implementation of decisions:

A formal document will be issued summarising the elements of the plan. Briefing meetings will be held with the stakeholders. There will be regular development of detailed policies, programmes and budgets. Performance targets for managers and staff will be set.

Regular reviews will be undertaken:

Regular reviews will take place and reports will be produced for management on performance and environmental changes.

The problems of the rational/formal approach to strategy formulation:

The rational approach can be Inappropriate in dynamic environments – a new strategy may only be established say every five years, which may quickly become inappropriate if the environment changes. In addition, it is often bureaucratic and inflexible – radical ideas are often rejected and new opportunities which present themselves may not be able to be taken. It is often said that it stifles innovation and creativity.

There can be difficulty getting the necessary participation to implement the strategy – successful implementation requires the support of middle and junior management and the nature of the rational approach may alienate these levels of management.

The rational approach is also not suitable in all situations. It is impossible in uncertain environments as it is impossible to carry out the required analysis in uncertain business environments. It is also inappropriate for small businesses as it is viewed as too complex and too costly.

I hope you have found the above helpful, please do not hesitate to get in touch if you need any more information.

Case study style question 2

EMAIL

To: J

From: Neighbour

Date: Today

Subject: Approaches to strategic planning

There are a number of ways in which a business might choose to carry out its strategic planning process. Three main ones are detailed below.

The rational/formal approach

This breaks the process into three distinct steps: strategic analysis (examining the businesses external and internal environment), strategic choice (choosing how best to succeed within this environment) and strategic implementation (putting strategic choices into action). It is a very logical process with clearly defined steps and aims to make a business proactive towards its environment.

Johnson, Scholes and Whittington suggested that each step was interdependent and that each step should be reviewed and possible re-performed after each other step. They also suggested that any step could be the starting step in the process.

The emergent approach

This suggests that strategies emerge over time rather than being developed from an in-depth analysis of the business environment. It aims to recognise the difficulties that some businesses have with strategic analysis. Businesses often start with a planned strategy, but some of this will not be able to be realised due to changes in the market or due to internal factors. Businesses also take advantage of new opportunities which have presented themselves even if these were not in the original plan. The result can be a different outcome than was originally planned.

Logical Incrementalism

Quinn suggested that businesses will have a view as to where they want to be in the future but they will proceed in small steps. With this approach strategy is a step by step learning process. This allows decisions to be small and flexible and allows new opportunities to be exploited.

Given your situation at this point, it is unlikely that the rational approach would suit you as you are not really at the stage of long term planning. Logical Incrementalism may work for you as you would be able to take your plans step by step and let the longer term plan develop from this. You have knowledge of the market and good technical skills. You can use these key skills to create the new game and see where it takes you. The best approach would be to get the business up and running, create a viable product and survive for the first six months or a year. After that time you can be more rational and focused and expand your plans over the longer term.

Please get in touch if you need any additional information.

Regards

Neighbour

Question 1

- To keep spending on books and stationery items under budget is a measure of **Economy**

- To increase the percentage of pupils passing their final exams is a measure of **Effectiveness**

- To lower the pupil to staff ratio is a measure of **Efficiency**

With not-for-profit organisations it can be difficult to measure objectives; also they are likely to have multiple objectives. A method for addressing these issues, used by many not-for-profit organisations, is the 3E approach. This approach measures:

- Effectiveness (outputs)

- Economy (inputs)

- Efficiency (the link between inputs and outputs)

Question 2

- Prevents focus on short-term results
- Ensures goal congruence
- Provides security for stakeholders

The rational/formal approach to strategy formulation has a number of advantages. It is however criticised for being unsuitable in dynamic environments and for stifling innovation and creativity. It is also seen as being less suitable for small businesses.

Question 3

C   Rapidly changing in an unpredictable fashion

One of the main criticisms of the rational/formal approach is that it is inappropriate in dynamic environments. The more the environment is changing, the less appropriate the rational approach will be.

Question 4

Encourages the use of the rational approach	
Reduces the planning horizon	X
Encourages emergent strategies	X
Encourages long-term planning	
Encourages risk taking behaviour	
Increases the information needs of the organisation	X

With uncertainty, the rational approach is less appropriate and organisations tend to move away from long-term planning towards a shorter planning horizon. During periods of uncertainty managers will tend towards more conservative strategies and take fewer risks. In order to try to reduce the impact of uncertainty, managers will require more information.

Question 5

H is adopting an **emergent** approach

X is adopting a **logical incrementalism** approach

With logical incrementalism, the company knows where it wants to go but takes a step-by-step approach keeping decisions small and flexible.

With the emergent approach the company has an intended strategy. Over time elements of this may be disregarded and new strategies will develop in relation to changes in the environment. The company can end up with a realised strategy very different from the original intended strategy.

Question 6

- Provides the ability to react quickly to changes in the environment
- Opportunities can be taken as they arise
- It is a flexible and dynamic approach

Freewheeling opportunism is a reactive process of management as an alternative to long-term strategic planning. This approach can increase flexibility, can give more scope for innovation and creativity and is generally perceived as dynamic and exciting.

The rational/formal approach is seen as providing more security for stakeholders and encourages goal congruence.

Encouraging managers to pursue short term profits is a disadvantage of the freewheeling opportunism approach.

Question 7

- Dynamism within the business environment has increased due to shorter product lifecycles.

- Complexity refers to the number of variables which can impact on the organisation and how difficult they are to understand or predict.

- Increased uncertainty will increase the information needs of an organisation.

High uncertainty would tend to reduce the likelihood of risky strategies being pursued. In times of uncertainty, managers tend to become more conservative and stick to what has worked for them in the past.

In addition where businesses are experiencing high uncertainty, they are likely to shorten their planning horizons.

Question 8

The completed diagram for the emergent approach is shown below:

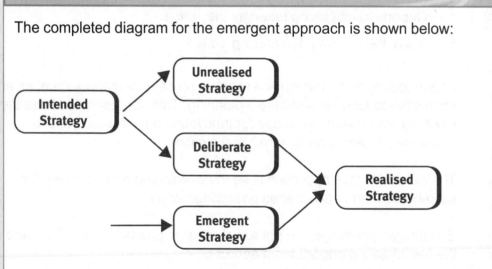

Question 9

- SMEs typically have a more limited range of strategic options

- There may be insufficient personnel available to carry it out

- In small businesses, the goals of the business may not be growth but may come from the goals of the owners

Strategy is required in all organisations, regardless of size.

Question 10

- Strategy develops as a rational process which seeks to establish a fit between internal and external capabilities – **Design**

- Strategy emerges as a result of trial and error – **Learning**

- Strategy is a conscious act of transforming an organisation from one state to another – **Configuration**

- Strategy development is a process of social interaction within the context of the belief and shared values of the organisation – **Cultural**

chapter

3

Competitive advantage

Chapter learning objectives

Explain the approaches to achieving sustainable competitive advantage

Compare and contrast alternative approaches to strategy development

1 Session content diagram

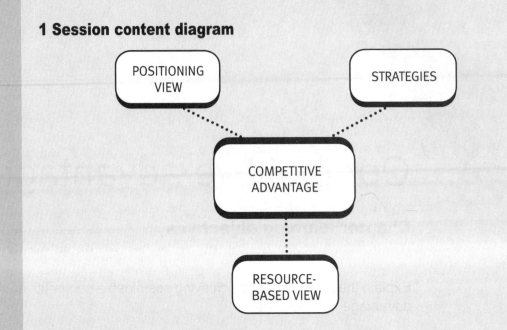

2 Competitiveness and competitive advantage

When developing a corporate strategy, the organisation must decide on which basis it is going to compete in its marketplace. This involves decisions on whether to compete across the whole marketplace or only in certain segments.

Competitiveness is essentially the ability of a firm, sector or economy to compete against other firms, sectors or economies.

The number of competing firms in an industry, their strength and the ease of entry for new firms have an impact on:

- the level of choice for consumers
- the degree of competition in terms of price, promotion, new product developments
- the profitability of firms in the industry
- the likelihood of illegal collusive agreements.

Organisations must consider how they can gain **competitive advantage**, that is anything that gives on organisation an edge over its rivals and which can be sustained over time. To be sustainable, organisations must seek to identify the activities that competitors cannot easily copy and imitate.

> CIMA defines **competitive advantage** as *situations where an organisation exerts more competitive force on its competitors than they exert on it.*

Sustainable competitive advantage

The important aspect of competitive advantage is that is must be **sustainable**. Sustainable means over the long-term, not just for the immediate future. Organisations may enjoy short-term competitive advantage, for example by being the first to get a new product to market, or by using cost leadership techniques, but these benefits may not be sustainable in the longer-term. Competitors will catch up and overtake.

The challenge for organisations is therefore how to build sustainable competitive advantage which will see them staying ahead of their competitors for the longer-term. The competitive advantage which an organisation enjoys must be difficult for competitors to copy, at least in the short-term. If the competitors are able to copy straight away, then the advantage is not sustainable.

Certain sources of competitive advantage are more sustainable than others. For example, patents and licences may by difficult or impossible for competitors to gain. Likewise competitive advantage stemming from reputation, branding and customer loyalty may also be very difficult for competitors to copy.

It is therefore not only important for organisation to understand what it is that gives them competitive advantage, but they must continually monitor and develop in order to ensure that they maintain their advantage in the long-term.

Porter's three generic strategies

According to Porter, there are three generic strategies' through which an organisation can generate superior competitive performance (known as generic because they are widely applicable to firms of all sizes and in all industries):

(1) Cost leadership – offering products and services of the same quality as competitors but at lower prices

(2) Differentiation – changing higher prices by offering more innovative products, or products with a higher perceived quality

(3) Focus – concentrating only on a small part of the market

The adoption of one or other of these strategies by a business unit is made on the basis of:

- an analysis of the threats and opportunities posed by forces operating in the specific industry of which the business is a part
- the general environment in which the business operates
- an assessment of the organisation's strengths and weaknesses relative to competitors.

The general idea is that the strategy to be adopted by the organisation is one which best positions the company relative to its rivals and other threats from suppliers, buyers, new entrants, substitutes and the macro-environment, and to take opportunities offered by the market and general environment.

Decisions on the above questions will determine the generic strategy options for achieving competitive advantage.

Bowman's Strategy Clock

Bowman and Faulkner expanded on the work of Porter and developed the Bowman's Strategy Clock which shows eight strategic positions depending on the combination of price and perceived value to the customer. The eight positions are shown on the following diagram.

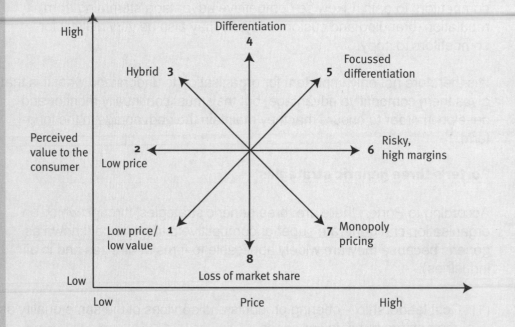

Bowman's Strategy Clock is a very useful model which helps to understand how companies select where to compete in their chosen marketplace.

Position 1: Low Price/Low Value

Not many companies choose to compete in this position as it is difficult to achieve sustained competitive advantage. Known as the bargain basement approach, survival in this position relies on high sales volume and continually attracting new customers. Good have a low perceived value to customers and are seen as inferior quality.

Position 2: Low Price

Similar to position 1, this position relies on high volumes to counteract the low margins. Some large companies have managed to sustain this approach, acting as cost leaders, e.g. Lidl and Aldi. This differs from position 1in that it is not focused on inferior products, just on lower prices than competitors for equivalent products.

Position 3: Hybrid

This is an interesting combination of low cost, but higher perceived value. Companies competing here can build up reputation and customer loyalty for offering reasonable goods at fair prices. This can often be seen in small, local businesses.

Position 4: Differentiation

This approach is the same as Porter's differentiation. Companies in this position can increase their price which customers will accept as they value the features of the product, or they may operate with lower margins and gain higher market share. A good example here is Apple.

Position 5: Focused Differentiation

These companies operate on high margins and highly targeted markets. Consumers will be willing to pay high prices in this category as they value the uniqueness and exclusivity of the product. This can be seen with luxury, designer goods such as Gucci and Channel.)

Position 6: Risky, high margin

Sometimes companies take a gamble and simply increase their prices without any increase to the perceived value. Higher profitability can be enjoyed, but only in the short-term.

Position 7: Monopoly pricing

This high price, low value position can only be achieved where there is only one company in the market or very limited choice for the customer. Catering services at events could use this approach.

Position 8: Loss of market share

This is not really a sustainable position. This involves attempting to sell an inferior product at a price associated with a superior product. Any company that pursues this type of strategy will lose market share. If you have a low value product, the only way you will sell it is on price.

Positions 6, 7, and 8 are not viable competitive strategies in truly competitive marketplaces. Whenever price is greater than perceived value there will always be competitors offering better quality products at lower prices. For a sustainable long-term strategy you have to align your value and price correctly.

3 The positioning and resource-based views

The positioning view and the resource-based view, look at strategy formulation from the point of view of how the organisation attempts to gain competitive advantage.

The positioning view

The **positioning view** sees competitive advantage stemming from the firm's position in relation to its competitors, customers and stakeholders. It is sometimes called an **'outside-in'** view because it is concerned with adapting the organisation to fit its environment.

The positioning approach to strategy takes the view that supernormal profits result from:

- high market share relative to rivals
- differentiated product
- low costs.

Criticisms of the positioning view:

- The competitive advantages gained in this way are not sustainable. These advantages are too easily copied in the long run by rivals. Environments are too dynamic to enable positioning to be effective. Markets are continually changing due to faster product life cycles, the impact of IT, global competition and rapidly changing technologies.

- It is easier to change the environment than it is to change the firm. Supporters of the positioning view seem to suggest that organisations can have its size and shape changed at will to fit the environment.

The resource-based view of strategy

The **resource-based view** sees competitive advantage stemming from some unique resource or competence possessed by the firm. This is called an **'inside-out'** view because the firm must go in search of environments that enable it to harness its internal competencies.

Until the 1990s, most writers took a positioning view; however, more recently, the resource-based perspective has become popular.

Principles of the resource-based view (RBV)

Supporters of the resource-based view believe that, sustainable profitability depends on the firm's possession of **unique resources** or abilities that cannot easily be duplicated by rivals.

Barney (1991) identified four criteria for unique resources:

- **Valuable**. They must be able to exploit opportunities or neutralise threats in the firm's environment.
- **Rare**. Competitors must not have them too, otherwise they cannot be a source of relative advantage.
- **Imperfectly imitable**. Competitors must not be able to duplicate them.
- **Non-substitutability**. It must not be possible for a rival to find a substitute for this resource.

Resources are combined together to achieve a competence. There are two types of competence.

Threshold competencies are those actions and processes that you must be good at just to be considered as a potential supplier to a customer. If these are not satisfied, you will not even get a chance to be considered by the customer.

A core competence is something that you are able to do that is very difficult for your competitors to emulate.

According to the resource-based view core competencies are the key to competitive advantage.

Prahalad and Hamel coined the term core competence, which has three characteristics:

- it provides potential access to a wide variety of markets (extendability)
- it increases perceived customer benefits; and
- it is hard for competitors to imitate.

Prahalad and Hamel's work on core competencies focuses on the strategic intent of an organisation to leverage its internal capabilities and core competencies to confront competition. This is sometimes referred to as **strategic stretch**.

Organisations need to ensure that they are continually monitoring their marketplace to ensure that their core competencies are still valid and that all thresholds are duly satisfied.

It is argued that core competences can be destroyed by failure to invest in them. Prahalad and Hamel's formulation carries profound implications for the management accounting function. Management accounting is traditionally built on a responsibility centre model, whereas the view of several of the resource-based view writers is that the object of control should be competences and processes rather than business units and divisions.

The implications of the resource-based view

The resource-based view challenges the rational model of strategy. It argues that strategy should not be a process of deciding a product/market mission and competing in markets by establishing what the customer wants and exploiting the weaknesses of rivals. Instead, it suggests that strategy involves deciding what makes the firm unique and building strategy on that, extending into any products or markets where it will work. The impacts of this are:

- The RBV of strategy starts with the corporate appraisal, not with the mission of the business. Indeed, the mission must adapt to fit the most recent extension of core competence.

- There is a much higher emphasis on finding an environment to match the firm rather than vice versa (management seems to be saying 'all we have is a hammer so our markets are anything that involves hitting things'). This reasoning could lead to very diverse strategies or perhaps a complete drying-up of strategic avenues (as they run out of things to hit).

- Investors cannot be clear what industry they are investing in. This may increase perceived risk and hence destroy shareholder value by reducing the share price.

The resource-based view can lead to different conclusions. The basis of the resource-based view is the suggestion that the firm should retain any unique strategic resources it has, outsource the remainder, and focus on building up relationships with internal and external stakeholders to develop its internal knowledge so as to improve performance and innovation. Consequently, it fits well with modern concepts in network organisation management such as:

- teamworking
- collaboration with suppliers and customers
- flexible working practices
- creation of participative culture.

However, an alternative conclusion might be that unique knowledge is too valuable to risk losing in networks that could easily be 'burgled' by rivals, through enticing contract staff and suppliers/customers to defect. This might encourage management to deliberately keep knowledge under close control by bringing production in-house, putting staff on restrictive long-term contracts and segmenting trade secrets on a 'need-to-know' basis.

Even where a firm is involved in a range of industries and has a unique core competence across them all, it is no guarantee of competitive advantage against more focused players in each market (e.g. in the 1980s, IBM had a unique global architecture, reputation and ownership of proprietary technology. This did not stop it from being beaten into second or third place by focused rivals in each of its sub-industries of software development, consulting, PCs and mainframe systems).

Companies which have adopted the resource-based view

Amazon

Amazon.com turned the stable, mature industry of book retailing upside-down. Using its skills by developing a user-friendly IT interface, it grasped the opportunity of meeting the customers' needs for convenience whilst paying a low price. Customers enjoy an on-line buying experience that allows them to browse book covers, search from over two million titles, view expert and general reader reviews, choose a basket of books and pay for them including delivery within 24 hours for most titles. They can subsequently track their order.

Amazon.com has achieved success in the way it has focused on its skills (developing one of the best IT interfaces for e-commerce) whilst networking to resource the rest of the business – a network of publishers and book warehouses (for the product), couriers (for handling delivery), credit card operators (for handling payment). To ensure satisfaction to its main customers and keep the well-established book retailers at bay, it does maintain some warehouses which stock the best selling titles. Its prices, including delivery costs, are quite competitive.

Marks & Spencer, recognising their core skills, have asked Amazon.com to manage their on-line shopping infrastructure. Meanwhile Amazon.com have extended the on-line shopping experience to other products including music, household items, clothing and many more.

Saga

Saga established a strong leadership in supplying financial services (e.g. insurance) and holidays to the 'wrinklies and crinklies' or WOOFs (well-off older folks). The core competencies that enable Saga to enter apparently different markets:

- Clear distinctive brand proposition that focuses solely on a closely-defined customer group.

- Leading direct marketing skills – database management; direct-mailing campaigns; call centre sales conversion.

- Skills in customer relationship management.

Apple

It could be argued that when Apple developed the ipad, they were using a resource-based view. the tablet market did not exist but Apple made the product because they had the technology to do so.

Resource-based view versus positioning view

The positioning view focuses on an analysis of competitors and markets before objectives are set and strategies developed. It is an outside-in view.

The essence of this view is ensuring that the organisation has a good "fit" with its environment. The idea is to look ahead at the market and predict changes to enable the organisation to control change rather than having to react to it.

The main problem with the positioning view is that it relies on predicting the future of the market. Some markets are volatile and make estimating future changes impossible in the longer term.

The resource-based view focuses on looking at what the organisation is good at. It is an inside-out view.

The essence of this view is for the organisation to identify its core competencies and build strategies around what they do best, and what competitors find hard to copy.

In practice, more organisations are tending towards the resource-based view for the following reasons:

- Strategic management should focus on developing core competencies.

- Greater likelihood of implementation. Basing a strategy on present resources will reduce the disruption and expenditure involved in implementation.

- It will avoid the firm losing sight of what it is good at.

Case study style question 1

F consists of automobile engine, marine engine and aerospace engine businesses. It has built its global reputation for engine design and quality on its engineering capability. Though the marine engine business has not been performing well for some time, F has dominated the supply of engines for the luxury end of the automobile market for years. Unfortunately for F, however, the market in luxury automobiles is changing. Exchange rate movements and increased production costs have made F less competitive and its rivals are rapidly catching up in terms of engine quality and design. As a result, the latest annual report shows turnover down, margins reduced and the company barely breaking even.

You have just attended a strategy meeting at F in which:

- Manager C said that more attention should be paid to the threats and opportunities of the external environment so that F could position itself more realistically.

- Manager D claimed that the company should really be seeking to develop further its core engineering competence if it were going to regain its competitiveness in the market place.

After the meeting, a junior manager who had been in attendance asks you to explain what his senior colleagues had been talking about.

Required:

Write an email to the junior manager explaining the perspectives on strategy development adopted by Manager C and Manager D.

(20 minutes)

4 Resources and competencies

It is clear that within the resource-based view, an organisation must be able to identify its internal resources and capabilities. It must be able to identify those things that the organisation is particularly good at in comparison to that of its competitors. To do this it must carry out **internal analysis**.

Internal analysis was mentioned as part of the rational/formal approach to strategy development. The findings from the internal analysis highlight the strengths and weaknesses of the organisation and feed in to the corporate appraisal (SWOT).

Two key techniques that can be used are:

- Resource audit
- Porter's value chain model.

Resource audit

The resource audit seeks to establish the **strategic capability** of the organisation. This is the ability of the organisation to perform at the level required to survive and prosper. The resource audit firstly identifies the resources that are available to the organisation and then starts the process to identify the competencies.

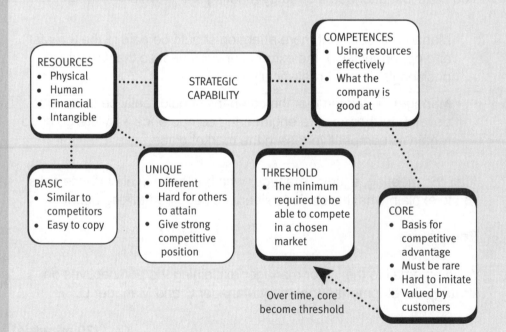

Resources are usually grouped under four headings:

- Physical or operational resources (e.g. land, machinery, IT systems).
- Human resources (e.g. labour, organisational knowledge).
- Financial resources (e.g. cash, positive cash flows, access to finance).
- Intangibles (e.g. patents, goodwill).

Resources can be identified as either basic or unique:

- **Basic resources** are similar to those of competitors and will be easy to obtain or copy.
- **Unique resources** will be different from competitors and difficult to attain. The more unique resources an organisation has, the stronger its competitive position will be.

The key is to know what you have available to you and how this will help you in any strategic initiative. At the same time the organisation needs to know what it is lacking and how things may change in the future.

Competences can also be classified into two types:

- **Threshold competences** – attainment avoids competitive disadvantage. It represents those processes, procedures and product characteristics that are necessary to enter a particular market.
- **Core competences** – these are the activities which the organisation can do better that competitors. These core competencies form the basis of **distinctive capabilities** which can provide the organisation with competitive advantage over others within that market, or allow the organisation to change the competitive forces in that market to their advantage.

Over time core competences can become threshold as customer expectations develop and organisations battle for competitive advantage.

A resource audit analyses how resources are being deployed to create competences and the processes through which these competences may be linked. The key to success is usually found at this level.

Source of distinctive capabilities

Kay (1997) writes of distinctive capabilities arising from four sources:

(1) **Competitive architecture**. These are the relationships that make up the organisation. These can be divided into:

- internal architecture: relations with employees

- external architecture: relations with suppliers and customers

- network architecture: relations between a group of collaborating firms.

These deliver distinctive capabilities that are greater than the sum of the parts.

(2) **Reputation**. This is the high esteem that the public have for the firm. Among customers, it is a reason to buy the product and to remain loyal, while for investors, suppliers and potential employees, it is a reason to become involved and give exceptional levels of support to the firm. Kay argues that reputation must be built and maintained over time and requires detailed attention to all aspects of the firm's products, procedures and processes.

(3) **Innovative ability**. This is the ability to develop new products, services or solutions. These discourage competitors and enable the firm to enjoy the high margins of early lifecycle markets. Innovation frequently demands collaboration among staff and with suppliers and customers. Consequently, it builds on the architectures of the firm.

(4) **Ownership of strategic assets**. The firm may have a unique source of materials or possess exclusive legal rights to a market or invention.

Stalk et al. (1992) suggest four principles of capabilities-based competition:

(1) The building blocks of corporate strategy are business processes, not products and markets.

(2) Competitive success depends on the ability to transform these processes into strategic capabilities able to provide superior value to the customer.

(3) Creating these capabilities requires group-wide investments that transcend traditional functional or business unit boundaries.

(4) Therefore, the champion of capabilities-based strategy is the chief executive officer (CEO).

Superior competitive performance will result from the firm using these competences to outperform rivals on five dimensions:

- **Speed**. More able to quickly incorporate new ideas and technologies into its products.

- **Consistency**. All its innovations satisfy the customer.

- **Acuity**. Ability to see its environment clearly and forecast changing needs.

- **Agility**. Ability to adapt on many fronts simultaneously.

- **Innovativeness**. Ability to generate and combine business ideas in novel ways.

Case study style question 2

The managers of ABC have been discussing adopting the resource-based view of strategy. A few of the managers are unfamiliar with some of the concepts involved and have asked you to arrange a presentation for the next managers' meeting. You have organised for a few of your colleagues to do some of the presentation. You have decided to present a section explaining the importance of continually developing core competencies. Your section is headed "over time core competencies become threshold".

Required:

Produce a briefing note to use during your presentation. Use examples from the mobile phone industry to highlight the points in your presentation.

(15 minutes)

Porter's Value Chain

The second model used for internal analysis is Porter's value chain. Michael Porter suggested that the internal position of an organisation can be analysed by looking at how the various activities performed by the organisation added or did not add value, in the view of the customer. This can be established by using **'the value chain model'**.

This is a model of value activities, those activities that procure inputs, process the inputs, and add value to them in some way to generate outputs for customers, and the relationships between those activities.

Value activity

This is a physically and technologically distinct activity that a firm performs. They are value activities because they should add value to a product or service.

How is it used?

The value chain can be used to design a competitive strategy, by utilising the activities in a strategic manner, it helps identify areas to reduce costs and increase margins. By exploiting linkages in the value chain and improving activities an organisation can obtain a competitive advantage.

Porter views the individual firm as a sequence of value creating activities instead of as an organisation chart detailing business functions. He suggests the business unit of the organisation can be visualised as a business system:

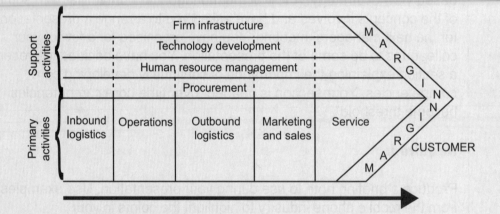

Value chain detail for a manufacturing company

Primary activities

Those activities involved in the physical creation of the product or delivery of the service and its sale and distribution to the buyer as well as after sales service. They add value to the product or service.

- Inbound logistics – receiving, storing and handling raw material inputs; e.g. a just in time system could give a cost advantage.

- Operations – transformation of raw materials into finished goods services; e.g. using skilled craftsmen could give a quality advantage.

- Outbound logistics – storing and distributing finished goods to customers; e.g. outsourcing delivery could give a cost advantage.

- Sales and marketing – making the customer aware of the product or service and providing them with opportunities to buy; e.g. sponsorship a sports celebrity could enhance the image of the product.

- Service – activities that occur after the point of sale, such as installation, training and repair; e.g. Marks and Spencer's approach to returns gives it a perceived quality advantage.

Support activities

Those activities that help the primary activities go more smoothly.

- Infrastructure – how the firm is organised; e.g. centralised purchasing could result in cost savings arising from bulk purchase discounts.

- Technology development – how the firm uses technology; e.g. computer controlled machinery gives greater flexibility to customise products to specific customer requirements.

- Human resources management – all matters relating to staff, including recruitment, appraisal, training and dismissal; e.g. employing expert buyers could enable a supermarket to purchase better quality fruit than competitors.

- Procurement – purchasing including negotiation of contracts and not restricted to raw materials; e.g. buying a building out of a town centre could give a cost advantage over high street competitors.

Linkages

Value activities are interdependent and connected by linkages.

Linkages exist when the way in which one activity is performed affects the cost and effectiveness of other activities – for example, IS/IT can identify where better information and systems are needed to improve or integrate the linkages; better quality production reduces the need for after sales service, which is the link between improving the operations to provide lower costs in the service area of the value chain.

Linkages require co-ordination, which can often be provided by information technology.

Competitors can often imitate the separate activities of a successful organisation, but it is more difficult to copy the linkages with and between the value chain activities.

An example of the value chain applied to the NHS

Primary activities

- Patients, who would either be transported by their own methods or by ambulances in order to receive the treatment.

- Drugs, dressings and other pharmaceutical supplies.

- Staff who may travel to and from hospitals, to and from other medical establishments and from either of the former to a patients home/destination and so on.

- Medical equipment, such as surgical instruments and monitors.

- Non medical equipment such as beds, linen, catering requirements, cleaning equipment and stationery.

- Warehousing of goods.

A wide range of **logistical activities** take place which are managed by different departments and others which are outsourced such as catering and cleaning. Where control of activities is outsourced there is a chance of a weak link. Think of the importance of cleanliness and nutrition to patient's health.

The **operations** transform the various inputs into the level of service. It is therefore a key link in the chain to ensure the correct level of service delivery.

The **marketing and sales** activities are responsible for raising awareness of the services provided by the NHS and the perception of the quality of service it supplies to the public. The NHS is split into multiple trusts with different specialisms. Inter trust relationships are key to the treatment of certain patients, which creates more linkages in the chain and thus more marketing relationships are required.

Support activities

Procurement is 'the processes for acquiring the various resource inputs to the primary activities occurs in many parts of the organisation' (Johnson and Scholes). Within a complex organisation, such as the NHS, there are many ways to procure goods and services from both the physical approach to the electronic methods.

Technology development ranges from the hospital Consultant's know-how, to computer systems used for medical records, to pharmacy systems linked to drugs. All of these will be managed by human resources some directly employed by the trust, some contracted to the trust and some working for contract companies contracted to the trust.

This is all held together by the **infrastructure**, 'the systems of planning, finance, quality control, information management' (Johnson and Scholes).

5 Chapter summary

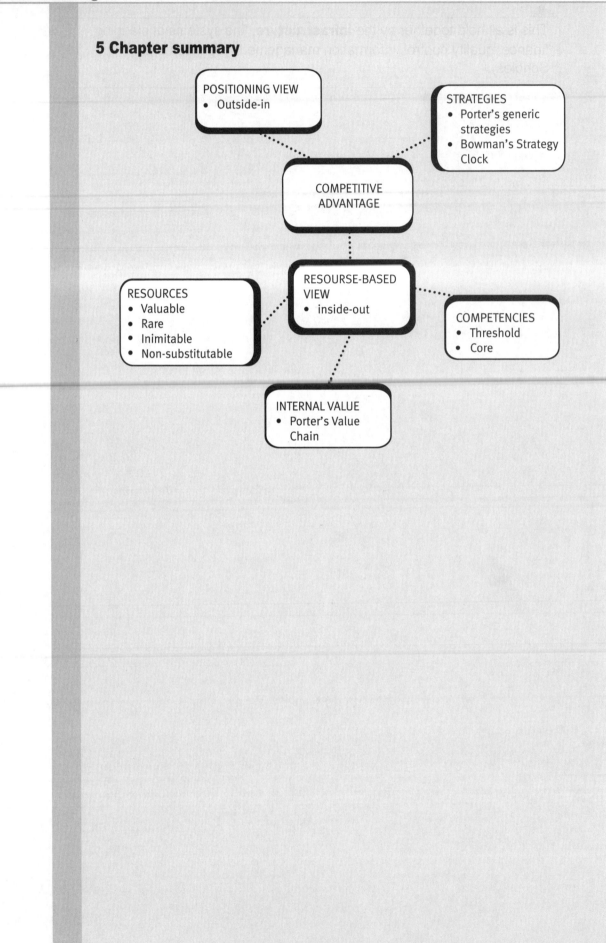

POSITIONING VIEW
- Outside-in

STRATEGIES
- Porter's generic strategies
- Bowman's Strategy Clock

COMPETITIVE ADVANTAGE

RESOURSE-BASED VIEW
- inside-out

RESOURCES
- Valuable
- Rare
- Inimitable
- Non-substitutable

COMPETENCIES
- Threshold
- Core

INTERNAL VALUE
- Porter's Value Chain

End of chapter questions

Question 1

RG manufactures a range of frozen desserts. Their products are marketed as 'high end' products and are sold through the more expensive supermarket chains, and small independent food stores. Its brand is well recognised and it is seen as one of the leading brands within the industry. Much of the success of RG can be attributed to its dedication to fresh, organic ingredients, unusual flavour combinations and tasteful, stylish packaging.

Which of Porter's generic strategies would be most suitable for RG?

A   Differentiation

B   Market leader

C   Focus

D   Cost leadership

Question 2

In the Value chain model, Porter identified nine activities and categorised these as either primary or support activities. Which of the following would be categorised as a support activity. Select all that apply.

Firm infrastructure	☐
Finance	☐
Marketing and sales	☐
Human resource management	☐
Operations	☐
Procurement	☐

Question 3

When carrying out a corporate appraisal, the information used to populate the strengths and weaknesses section would come from which of the following tools or techniques. Select all that apply.

- Porter's value chain
- Bowman's strategy clock
- Porter's generic strategies
- Resource audit
- Ansoff Matrix

Question 4

Match the comments to either the positioning view or the resource-based view.

Positioning view	Resource-based view

- Focuses on analysis of competitors and markets
- Strategies are built around what the organisation does best
- It ensures that the organisation has a good fit with its environment
- It relies on predicting the future of the market

Question 5

Match the five primary activities in Porter's value chain to their description.

- Marketing and sales
- Service
- Outbound logistics
- Inbound logistics
- Operations

Storing, distributing and delivering finished goods
Making customers aware of the product and providing them with opportunities to buy
Transformation of raw materials into finished goods
Activities after the point of sale such as installation and repair
Receiving, storing and handling raw materials

Question 6

Which of the following statements about competencies is true?

A   Over time, threshold competencies become core as customer expectations develop

B   Threshold competencies give the basis for competitive advantage

C   Attainment of core competencies give a company the basis to change competitive forces in the market to their advantage

D   Core competencies must be valuable, rare and difficult to imitate or substitute

Question 7

Prahalad and Hamel's work on core competencies focused on the strategic intent of an organisation to leverage its internal capabilities and core competencies to confront competition. This is referred to as:

- Strategic choice
- Resource-based view
- Strategic stretch
- Gap analysis

Question 8

Which three of the following statements regarding Porter's generic strategies are true?

- Focus involves offering general goods to a small segment of the market at a low price

- Cost leadership involves manufacturing goods more efficiently than rivals

- Businesses may become cost leaders by making their goods a lower quality than their rivals

- A focus strategy tends to allow businesses to charge a premium price

- Differentiation involves charging a premium for a product due to its actual or perceived benefits to the customer

Question 9

One of the principal insights of the resource-based view of the firm is that not all resources are of equal importance or possess the potential to be a source of sustainable competitive advantage.

What are the **four** conditions that must be met by resources in order for them to be advantage-creating resources?

- Valuable

- Core

- Rare

- Intangible

- Sustainable

- Imperfectly imitable

- Non-substitutable

Question 10

AAH buys large rolls of cable from a number of manufacturers, cuts it into shorter lengths and sells it to various retailers.

Department 3 is solely responsible for the cutting of the cable, department 4 deals with delivering the cable to the customers and department 1's role is negotiating with suppliers to buy the rolls of cable.

Which of Porter's value chain activities is each department responsible for?

- Sales and marketing

- Operations

- Inbound logistics

- Procurement

- Outbound logistics

Test your understanding answers

Case study style question 1

EMAIL

To: Junior manager

From: Management accountant

Date: Today

Subject: Approaches to strategy development

Manager C is arguing that the most important consideration for F in setting its strategy is consideration of the external environment.

This entails looking at the immediate environment in which F operates, for example looking at:

- rivals to see what products they are offering (this appears to be a serious problem to F).

- suppliers of raw material to see if any reduction in price might be obtained (to increase margins).

- customer needs to see if any new products might have a market (for example, what kind of engines will be required in the next generation of passenger aircraft).

F should also look at the general environment that affects the entire industry. The company should look at:

- political pressures (in case of any relevant legislation, particularly over engine emissions).

- technology that might alter the way engines are made.

- economic issues such as future exchange rates since these obviously affect F.

- the overall economic situation that will affect the demand for sea and air travel which will have a knock-on effect for F.

- social issues, such as the demand for cleaner car engines (or engines capable of running on alternative fuel sources).

All of the above can be combined to identify the major threats to F as well as any opportunities that can be exploited to expand sales and/or margins.

Manager D, on the other hand, is arguing that the most important consideration for setting strategy is to look inside the company. In other words this entails looking at what sets the company apart from its rivals by making sure that this advantage is not lost due to the functional strategy being adopted. This means that if F has a reputation for manufacturing high-quality products this must be maintained. This may cause difficulties given the current situation since the temptation may be to cut costs in response to external pressures.

I hope you have found the above useful. Please do not hesitate to get in touch if you need any further information.

Regards

Management Accountant

Case study style question 2

Managers' meeting – presentation on the resource-based view

"over time core competencies become threshold".

Core competencies are those elements which make a company or a product stand out from its competitors. It gives the company competitive advantage.

Over time competitors catch up and develop these competencies for themselves which reduces the original advantage. What was originally an innovative or superior feature becomes the norm. To maintain competitive advantage companies must continually strive to develop their core competencies.

In the mobile phone industry we can see many examples of this.

In the early days of mobile phones, phones were large and clumsy and only enabled telephone calls. Over time phones became smaller and manufacturers competed to produce smaller and smaller units.

Then in 1993, Nokia developed the technology to incorporate the sending of text messages. This was innovative and generated huge interest from customers. Over time, all phones incorporated this technology and the advantage Nokia enjoyed disappeared. Now all mobiles have this technology as a minimum requirement.

Another development was the inclusion of a camera on a mobile. This was first developed by Sharp in 2000. Again over time this has become a basic function on a phone.

There have been many recent developments such as music players, smart phones, Internet access and GPS technology. Almost as soon as a new development is unveiled, the competitors quickly incorporate these features and they become threshold.

Mobile manufacturers need to constantly update their technology to keep ahead of the competitors.

The Idea that core competencies eventually become threshold can be applied to all industries. The important point is that companies continually monitor what it is that gives them advantage over their competitors. As competitors catch up, companies must find a new way of gaining that advantage so that they can stay ahead of their competitors.

Thanks for listening. Any questions?

Question 1

A   Differentiation

Porter suggested three generic strategies:

Cost leadership – where the company offers products and services of the same quality as competitors, but at a lower price

Differentiation – where the company charges a higher price than competitors by offering quality products and service with a high perceived value

Focus – where the company concentrates on only a small segment of the market

RG is offering 'high-end' products through more expensive supermarket chains. Differentiation is the best strategy to use for this type of company as RG's products are of a high perceived quality and can therefore be charged at a higher price.

Question 2

Firm infrastructure   X

Finance

Marketing and sales

Human resource management   X

Operations

Procurement   X

Porter's value chain model is shown below:

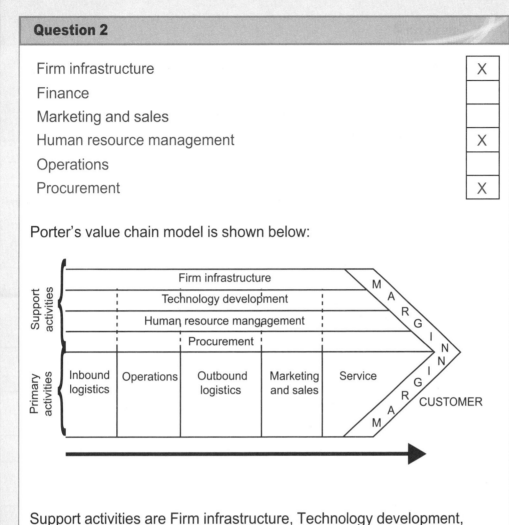

Support activities are Firm infrastructure, Technology development, Human resource management and Procurement. The primary activities are Inbound logistics, Operations, Outbound logistics, Marketing and sales and Service.

Question 3

- Porter's value chain
- Resource audit

Porter's value chain and Resource audits are used to carry out the internal analysis section of the corporate appraisal. This part of the corporate appraisal looks at identifying the strengths and weaknesses within the organisation.

Question 4

- Focuses on analysis of competitors and markets – **positioning view**

- Strategies are built around what the organisation does best – **resource-based view**

- It ensures that the organisation has a good fit with its environment – **positioning view**

- It relies on predicting the future of the market – **positioning view**

Question 5

The correct descriptions of the primary activities are:

Outbound logistics is the storing, distributing and delivering finished goods
Marketing and sales is making customers aware of the product and providing them with opportunities to buy
Operations is the transformation of raw materials into finished goods
Service is the activities after the point of sale such as installation and repair
Inbound logistics is the receiving, storing and handling raw materials

Question 6

C   Attainment of core competencies give a company the basis to change competitive forces in the market to their advantage.

A is incorrect as over time core competencies become threshold as customer expectations develop.

B is incorrect as it is core competencies that give the basis for competitive advantage.

D is incorrect as it is unique resources which must be valuable, rare, and difficult to imitate or substitute.

Question 7

According to Prahalad and Hamel, the strategic intent of an organisation to leverage its internal capabilities and core competencies in order to confront competition is known as **strategic stretch**.

Question 8

- Cost leadership involves manufacturing goods more efficiently than rivals

- A focus strategy tends to allow businesses to charge a premium price

- Differentiation involves charging a premium for a product due to its actual or perceived benefits to the customer

Focus involves offering general goods to a small segment of the market at a low price is incorrect as focus does not necessarily involve competing on the grounds of price.

Businesses may become cost leaders by making their goods a lower quality than their rivals is incorrect as cost leadership does not imply goods of a lesser quality.

Question 9

According to Barney unique, or advantage-creating, resources have four criteria:

- Valuable – they must be able to exploit opportunities or neutralise threats

- Rare – competitors must not have them too

- Imperfectly imitable – competitors must not be able to easily duplicate them

- Non-substitutable – it must not be possible for competitors to find a substitute for this resource

Question 10

Department 1: Procurement

Department 3: Operations

Department 4: Outbound logistics

The negotiation and purchase of the cable would be procurement (department1).

The receipt of the cable from the manufacturers would be inbound logistics.

Cutting the cable down into lengths would be operations. (department 3).

Outbound logistics (department 4) would cover the storing and delivering of the finished product to customers.

The sales and marketing role would be to make the customer aware of the product and providing them to opportunity to buy it.

chapter

4

The nature of the global business environment

Chapter learning objectives

Distinguish between different aspects of the global business environment, including the competitive environment

1 Session content diagram

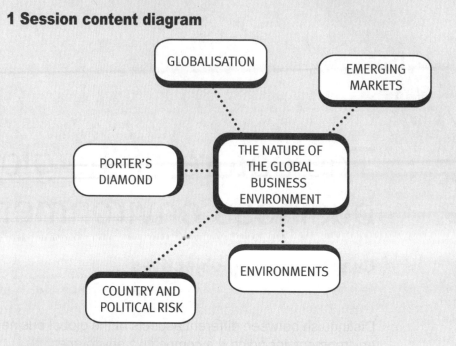

2 Different environments

The environment within which an organisation operates exerts three basic forms of influence upon the organisation:

- It offers **threats** (to the well-being of the organisation, such as government legislation, or, say, national action by trade unions) and **opportunities** (for exploitation, such as growth in market demand, or new technological possibilities).

- It is the source of organisational **resources** (human resources come from outside the organisation, as do funds and supplies generally).

- It contains interest or '**pressure groups**' that have some kind of direct interest in organisational activities (these range from the general public and government bodies to 'action' groups such as Amnesty International, Greenpeace and Animal Rights groups).

Strategy is concerned with the ability of the organisation to fit with, or cope with, its environment. Since an organisation does not operate in a vacuum it is important that it continually scans its external environment in order that it can develop appropriate responses to take advantage of opportunities, or to minimise threats. An understanding of the external environment is, therefore, a critical element in the development of strategy and can help in determining how to achieve a sustainable competitive advantage.

An organisation can react to its environmental situation in several ways. It may:

- **do nothing** if it is convinced that the problem is insignificant or short-term
- decide to **monitor the environment** carefully but not to respond just yet
- **increase its flexibility** through contingency planning and product-market development
- decide that the situation is important and urgent and want to **plan major strategic change**

Strategic implication of different environments

Environments can exhibit different characteristics, which will affect the strategy of organisations operating within that environment:

- **Stable and unchanging** – In this case the organisation can focus its attention on its past decisions and results, and on attempting to correct its past mistakes. Tactical planning is more important than strategic planning.

- **Stable with minor fluctuations** – This describes an environment characterised by cyclical and/or seasonal fluctuations within a fairly stable structure. Here, policies and procedures a can be implemented which only need to be updated to take account of changes in activity levels.

- **Gradually changing in a predictable fashion** – This is where an organisation recognises that its environment is slowly being changed into something new and predictable. With this recognition it can begin to make the necessary adjustments to its goals, strategic direction, organisation structure, and systems so that it can proceed in a meaningful way for the future.

- **Rapidly changing in an unpredictable fashion** – Within this environment an organisation operates in highly turbulent and unpredictable businesses. Strategic planning is much more important than tactical planning, and effectiveness (doing the right things) is just as essential as achieving efficiency (doing things the best way). Organisations must find creative ways of adapting to their environments in order to survive.

e.g

Illustration 1 – Strategies adopted in response to environmental

Consider the airline industry

The industry has changed dramatically in the last ten years, with increased competition. Different airlines have chosen different strategies to deal with their changing environment.

- Integration: for example, Air France and KLM, and Lufthansa and Swissair.

- New routes and new services: 'flat beds', showers and massage facilities in first class.

- Cost cutting: for example, BA has outsourced its ticketing administration to India.

- Better branding: focusing on the service differences with the low-cost carriers.

Consider the retail outlet industry

In the competitive multiple retail outlet industry, Marks & Spencer and Tesco are constantly struggling to make the right decisions. They regularly change their direction to grasp the opportunities presented by changing patterns of consumer behaviour (new fashion trends, new health issues relating to food) and increasing pressure from competitors (Waitrose, Aldi, Lidl, Next, Gap). Marks & Spencer have changed their top management, marketing and design structure to bring in new skills whenever they have found themselves underperforming.

3 Environmental analysis

When establishing its strategy, it is important for an organisation to look at the various factors within its environment that may represent threats or opportunities and the competition it faces.

Corporate appraisal (SWOT) was looked at as part of the rational/formal approach to strategy development. The internal analysis techniques which considered the organisation's internal capabilities (resource audit and Porter's value chain) were looked at in the competitive advantage chapter.

The second element to feed into the corporate appraisal is external analysis, which looks at the environment within which the organisation operates.

The analysis requires an external appraisal to be undertaken by scanning the business external environment for factors relevant to the organisations current and future activities.

External analysis can be carried out at different levels, as seen below. There are a number of strategic management tools that can assist in this process. These included the PESTLE framework which helps in the analysis of the macro or general environment and Porter's five forces model which can be used to analyse the industry or micro environment.

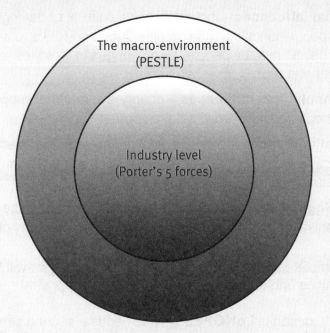

External analysis of the macro environment

An important aspect of strategy is the way the organisation adapts to its environment. The macro environment consists of factors that cannot be directly influenced by the organisation itself and the firm must try to respond to these factors rather than control them.

PESTLE analysis is an approach used in analysing an organisation's environment.

PESTLE is an acronym used to help organise the analysis of the business environment into broad categories. PESTLE analysis divides the business environment into political, economic, social (and cultural), technical, legal and ecological/environmental factors. Analysing these factors can help organisations understand the opportunities and threats within their environment and this understanding is crucial in shaping the organisation's current and future strategic decisions, for example:

- **political influences and events** – legislation, government policies, changes to competition policy or import duties, etc.

- **economic influences** – a multinational company will be concerned about the international situation, while an organisation trading exclusively in one country might be more concerned with the level and timing of domestic development. Items of information relevant to marketing plans might include: changes in the gross domestic product, changes in consumers' income and expenditure, and population growth.

- **social influences** – includes social, cultural or demographic factors (i.e. population shifts, age profiles, etc.) and refers to attitudes, value and beliefs held by people; also changes in lifestyles, education and health and so on.

- **technological influences** – changes in material supply, processing methods and new product development.

- **legal influences** – changes in laws and regulations affecting, for example, competition, patents, sale of goods, pollution, working regulations and industrial standards.

- **ecological/environmental influences** – includes the impact the organisation has on its external environment in terms of pollution etc.

Once completed, the output from the PESTLE analysis will help to form the opportunities and threats part of the corporate appraisal.

Another variation is **LoNGPEST**, which adds a second dimension to the external environment which is the levels at which influences occur. For example local, national and global:

- Lo refers to the local level in which the organisation operates, for example the immediate city or region.

- N is concerned with the home country in which an organisation has its headquarters.

- G represents the global level, which becomes anything outside the local and national environments.

It is irrelevant which acronym is used as long as the analysis is carried out within the company and that they remain aware of the business environment and the changes that are occurring within it.

Illustration 2 – Applying the PESTLE model

In the United Kingdom, railways are facing major challenges. Customers are complaining about poor services. The government is reluctant to spend vast amounts of public money on developing the decaying infrastructure. The inflated costs of commuting by car, such as fuel and congestion charges, are increasing the number of people wanting to use the railways.

Required:

Construct an outline PESTLE analysis for the UK railway industry.

Solution:

Political

The balance of public – private involvement in the running costs and capital investments for rail development is a major issue.

Economic

The growth of commuter travel on the rail system means it is working at close to full capacity. This trend is likely to continue with the high costs of fuel, making car travel expensive.

There is a need for investment in infrastructure in areas such as longer platforms and new signal systems.

Financing this investment may be difficult.

Social/cultural

Increasing concerns about reliability, particularly in rural areas.

Concerns about the effect that railway construction and travel has on the environment.

Safety issues on trains and at railway stations.

Technological

The development of new train technologies such as the tilting train.

Also following the trends set by air travel by introducing ways to improve the customer experience. For example, offering internet access and on-train entertainment.

Legal

The legal framework for the regulation and power of the railways is a major issue for operators.

Environmental

Environmental impact of major infrastructure developments is a key issue.

Overall, the switch to rail travel is seen to have a positive environmental impact, reducing the congestion and pollution associated with car based travel.

Note: it does not matter under which category an influence has been listed. Some influences may be listed under several categories, for example, government regulation has both legal and political dimensions. All that matters is that regulation has been considered in the analysis.

Case study style question 1

DM is the world's largest and best-known food service retailing group with more than 30,000 'fast-food' outlets in over 120 countries. Currently half of its restaurants are in S country, where it first began 50 years ago, but up to 1,000 new restaurants are opened every year worldwide. Restaurants are wholly owned by the group (it has previously considered, but rejected, the idea of a franchising of operations and collaborative partnerships).

As market leader in a fiercely competitive industry, DM has strategic strengths of instant global brand recognition, experienced management, site development expertise and advanced technological systems. DM's basic approach works well in all countries and although the products sold in each restaurant are broadly similar, menus are modified to reflect local tastes. Analysts agree that it continues to be profitable because it is both efficient and innovative.

DM's future plans are to maximise global opportunities and continue to expand markets. DM has long recognised that the external environment can be very uncertain and consequently does not move into new locations or countries without first undertaking a full investigation.

You are part of a strategy steering team responsible for investigating the key factors concerning DM's entry for the first time into the restaurant industry in R country.

Required:

Prepare briefing notes for the next strategy steering team meeting:

(a) Justifying the use of a PESTLE framework to assist your team's environmental analysis for the R country expansion.

(5 minutes)

(b) Discussing some of the main issues arising from each aspect of the framework.

(15 minutes)

External analysis of the industry/competitive environment

As well as the macro environmental factors, part of external analysis also requires an understanding of the industry level, or competitive environment and what are likely to be the major competitive forces in the future.

Porter's five forces

A well-established framework for analysing and understanding the nature of the competitive environment is Porter's five forces model. Porter emphasises that some industries and some positions within an industry are more attractive than others. Therefore central to business strategy is an analysis of industry attractiveness. Porter's five forces model identifies five competitive forces that help determine the level of profitability for an industry or for a firm within an industry.

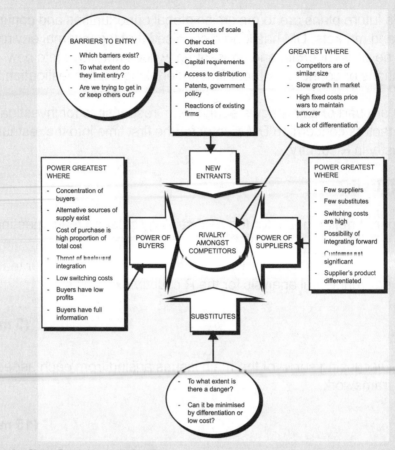

Porter's five forces analysis

Just because a market is growing, it does not follow that it is possible to make money in it. Porter's five forces approach looks in detail at the firm's competitive environment by analysing five forces. Firms must identify these forces and assess the strength of each force. The relative strength of each of these forces (high, moderate or low) will determine the **profit potential of the industry**.

(1) New entrants – new entrants into a market will bring extra capacity and intensify competition.

(2) Rivalry amongst competitors – existing competition & its intensity.

(3) Substitutes – This threat is across industries (e.g. rail travel or bus travel or private car).

(4) Power of buyers – powerful buyers can force price cuts and/or quality improvements.

(5) Power of suppliers – powerful suppliers can charge higher prices, forcing down profit margins.

The model can be used in several ways:

• To help management decide whether to enter a particular industry. Presumably, they would only wish to enter the ones where the forces are weak and potential returns high.

- To influence whether to invest more in an industry. For a firm already in an industry and thinking of expanding capacity, it is important to know whether the investment costs will be recouped.

- To identify what competitive strategy is needed. The model provides a way of establishing the factors driving profitability in the industry. For an individual firm to improve its profitability above that of its competitors, it will need to deal with these forces better than the competitors.

Further detail on Porter's five forces

New entrants

How easy it is for companies to enter a market depends on the **barriers to entry:**

- **Economies of scale**, where the industry is one where unit costs decline significantly as volume increases, such that a new entrant will be unable to start on a comparable cost basis.

- **Product differentiation**, where established firms have good brand image and customer loyalty. The costs of overcoming this can be prohibitive.

- **Capital requirements**, where the industry requires a heavy initial investment (e.g. steel industry, rail transport).

- **Switching costs**, i.e. one-off costs in moving from one supplier to another (e.g. a garage chain switching car dealership).

- **Restricted access to distribution channels** (e.g. for some major toiletry brands 90% of sales go through 12 buying points, i.e. chemist multiples and major retailers). Therefore it is difficult for a new toiletry product to gain shelf space.

- **Cost advantages of existing producers**, independent of economies of scale, e.g. patents, special knowledge, favourable access to suppliers, government subsidies.

- **Government policy**; the government can limit or even foreclose entry to industries with such controls as licence requirements and limits on access to raw materials.

Rivalry amongst competitors

The intensity of the rivalry amongst the existing competition will depend on the following factors:

- Number and relative strength of competitors – where an industry is dominated by a few large companies rivalry is less intense (e.g. petrol industry).

- Rate of growth – where the market is expanding, competition is low key.

- Where high fixed costs are involved, companies will cut prices to marginal cost levels to protect volume, and drive weaker competitors out of the market.

- If buyers can switch easily between suppliers the competitive rivalry will be stronger.

- If the exit barriers (i.e. the cost incurred in leaving the market) are high, companies will hang on until forced out, thereby increasing competition and depressing profit.

- An organisation will be highly competitive if its presence in the market is the result of a strategic need.

Substitutes

Porter explains that, 'substitutes limit the potential returns … by placing a ceiling on the price which firms in the industry can profitably charge'. The better the price-performance alternative offered by substitutes, the more readily customers will switch.

Power of buyers

The bargaining power of buyers is affected by factors such as:

- The proportion of the supplier's business the individual buyer's purchases make up.

- The importance of quality or delivery timing. Where these are less important, the prices will be forced down.

- The level of differentiation. Products with good brand image will be demanded by customers and retailers will be forced to stock these products.

Power of suppliers

The bargaining power of suppliers is affected by factors such as:

- The degree to which switching costs apply and substitutes are available.

- The presence of one or two dominant suppliers controlling prices.

- The extent to which products offered have a uniqueness of brand, technical performance or design not available elsewhere.

e.g Illustration 3 – Applying Porter's five forces model

Following on from illustration 2 on the UK railway system:

Required:

Briefly apply Porter's five forces to the railway industry in the UK.

Solution:

Rivalry amongst competitors

This is largely down to the way the industry operates. Passenger rail services in the UK are divided into regional franchises and run by various operating companies. These companies bid for seven to eight year contracts to run individual franchises. Some firms, including Abellio, National Express Group and Stagecoach Group, run multiple franchises.

Some routes will allow more than one operating company, this is particularly the case on longer distance routes, for example journeys from Scotland to London. On these routes, rail operators may be directly competing with other operators and there can be strong rivalry. For other routes, generally the shorter, local rotes, the franchise will only be granted to a single operator who will face no competition from other rail operators.

The strength of rivalry with therefore vary depending on the route. On routes with direct competition, the rivalry will be high, while on single operator routes, the rivalry will be low.

Substitutes

There are other forms of transport available such as travel by road (e.g. cars and buses) and travel by air. The threat of substitutes will therefore be moderate or high.

Power of buyers

Severe competition over price with low-cost airlines on longer city routes.

Online price comparisons make it easy for customers to select lowest cost option.

The power of buyers is therefore moderate to high.

New entrants

New companies may enter the market when rail franchises become available for re-tender, although the high capital cost is a barrier to new entrants, as is the need to successfully tender for an available franchise. The threat of new entrants is low.

Virgin entered the market in the mid 1990, and initially won two rail franchises, although one of these was lost in 2007.

In 1997 Virgin placed the largest rolling-stock order (£1bn) in British history, for new electric tilting trains. By December 2004 Virgin Trains had replaced all the rolling stock it had inherited from British Rail.

Power of suppliers

With an increasing number of discrete rail and train operators, the allocation of capacity becomes an issue. This is similar to landing slots at airports.

The power of suppliers is therefore high.

Case study style question 2

The directors of JPC, a well-established manufacturer of cardboard boxes, are considering entering the cardboard tube market. Cardboard tubes are required in various sizes ranging from large tubes used for carpets, to small tubes used for films and paper products. The cardboard tubes are usually purchased in very large quantities by customers. On average, the cardboard tubes comprise between 1% and 2% of the total cost of the customers' finished product.

The directors have gathered the following information:

- The lowest cost machine which could be used to manufacture the tubes is priced at $30,000 and requires only one operative for its operation. A one-day training course would be required for the operator.

- The cardboard tubes are made from specially formulated paper which, at times during recent years, has been in short supply.

- At present, four major manufacturers of cardboard tubes have an aggregate market share of 80%. The current market leader has a 26% market share. The market shares of the other three manufacturers are equal in size. The product ranges offered by the four major manufacturers are similar in terms of size and quality. The market has grown by 2% per annum during recent years.

- A recent report on the activities of a foreign-based multinational company revealed that consideration was being given to expanding operations in their packaging division overseas. The division possesses large-scale automated machinery for the manufacture of cardboard tubes of any size.

- Another company, PTC produces a narrow, but increasing, range of plastic tubes which are capable of housing small products such as film and paper-based products. At present, these tubes are on average 30% more expensive than the equivalent sized cardboard tubes sold in the marketplace.

Required:

Write a report to the board of JPC assessing the attractiveness of the option to enter the market for cardboard tubes as an improved strategy for JPC. The report should make reference to Porter's five forces model.

(20 minutes)

Evaluation of environmental models

The benefits from using recognised models, such as PESTLE and Porter's five forces, for external analysis:

- They ensure that management consider a wide range of potential impacts when devising strategy

- They allow the division of the work in environmental analysis – one team deal with buyers another team with suppliers

- They provide a common language between managers – Porter's five forces and PESTLE

- They provide insight into key strategic issues.

However, there are limitations in their use:

- They can distort reality – real business environments do not fit into neat segments

- They present the environment as external – distribution channels as separate and external

- They may cause management to overlook networks – joint ventures & strategic alliances

- They can overload management with analysis.

4 Globalisation

Most commentaries on developments in strategic management start with observations about the changes in the business environment. Today's global business environment is changing at a fast pace.

Companies are able to compete more easily anywhere in the world, with the effect that competition has become even fiercer. Companies have been forced to change the way they manage and operate their businesses.

Today's global managers are expected to possess entrepreneurial qualities beyond those of judgement, perseverance and knowledge of business. Above all, global managers must have an understanding of the complexities of the modern world and how to deal with people from a wide range of backgrounds and cultures.

e.g

Illustration 4 – Globalisation

Most people are affected by globalisation in a number of ways and are aware of global brands either through personal experience or via the media. Thinking about what you are doing at the moment, it is quite possible that:

- You are reading a book written in the UK
- Using software developed in North America
- Which was typeset in India
- Printed locally wherever you live
- Bought using a credit card issued by an international bank
- You are drinking a coffee made from Columbian beans
- Wearing trainers made in Vietnam
- Clothes made in China
- Or possibly from Egyptian cotton
- You may be listening to music recorded locally
- But playing on equipment made in Japan
- You may even be studying in a foreign country where you have gone to work

The impact of globalisation on strategy

As global competition becomes increasingly evident, organisations must choose the geographical boundaries in which they are going to operate, for example do they retain a strong domestic force, or at the other extreme, become a global player. In most industries organisations can no longer afford to formulate and implement strategies in response to just local conditions; they must be willing to adapt to the conditions of a 'borderless world'.

A number of factors will influence an organisation's ability to operate effectively as a global player, for example in terms of organisational structure, cultural issues and the need for a set of specific leadership skills. All these factors have implications for global effectiveness and development and implementation of strategies.

Although on the one hand, markets are becoming global, there is also a trend towards customisation – with the product/service adapted to some extent for local conditions, hence the need to '**think global, act local**'.

Porter states that any organisation structure competing in a global market has to balance two dimensions:

- global dimension for world-wide coordination to achieve economies of scale

- local dimension that enables country managers to respond to local customer needs.

Developments in the business environment

Globalisation and the changes observed in the business environment are seen as the result of a number of developments including:

- The drive by multinational companies to seek new markets as domestic markets become saturated.

- The deregulation and privatisation of industries.

- Consolidation and development of trading blocks.

- Liberalisation of trade.

- Free trade opening up new opportunities in emerging markets.

- Potential cost & market share advantages.

- Lower production costs in developed countries.

- Development in communications network.

- Development in transportation technologies and networks.
- Global financing.
- Developments in the technology of communication and transportation.

The impact of globalisation on firms

Firms are affected by globalisation in many ways, including:

Industrial relocation

Many firms have relocated their manufacturing base to countries with lower labour costs (offshoring).

However, this can give the impression that the only form of expansion is from "First World" to "Third World". This is not always the case as illustrated by Nissan (a Japanese company) building a car factory in Sunderland in the United Kingdom to avoid EU import quotas and tariffs.

Some non-Western countries are developing regional areas of excellence. For example, Bangalore in India is recognised globally for its expertise in telecommunications.

Managing (often complex) global supply chains has only been made possible by the advances in information technology.

Emergence of growth markets

As mentioned above, many previously closed markets, such as China, are opening up to Western firms.

In addition, if tastes are becoming more homogeneous, then this presents new opportunities for firms to sell their products in countries previously discounted.

Access to markets and enhanced competition

The combination of firms' global expansion plans and the relaxation of trade barriers have resulted in increased competition in many markets. This can be seen in:

- greater pressure on firms' cost bases with factories being relocated to even cheaper areas
- greater calls for protectionism.

Developments in information technology have also facilitated greater access to markets, for example by selling via the Internet.

Cross-national business alliances and mergers

To exploit the opportunities global markets offer many firms have sought to obtain expertise and greater economies of scale through cross-national mergers and acquisitions. For example:

- The takeover of UK based Cadbury by US food giant Kraft in 2010. One of Kraft's aims in this was to give them access to European markets.

- American cable company Liberty Global's purchase of UK's Virgin Media in 2013 aimed to strengthen Virgin Media's ability to compete with BskyB in the UK.

Widening economic divisions between countries

Many opponents of globalisation argue that it is creating new gaps between the rich and the poor. For example:

Rich countries have much greater access to the Internet and communications services. In the current information age wealth is created by the development of information goods and services, ranging from media, to education and software. Not all poor countries are taking part in this information revolution and are falling further behind the "digital divide".

The relentless drive to liberalise trade, i.e. to remove trade barriers, promote privatisation, and reduce regulation (including legal protection for workers), has had a negative impact on the lives of millions of people around the world.

Many poor countries have been pressured to orientate their economies towards exporting and to reduce already inadequate spending on public services such as health and education so that they can repay their foreign debt. This has forced even more people into a life of poverty and uncertainty.

5 National competitive advantage – Porter's Diamond

The internationalisation and globalisation of markets raises issues concerning the national sources of competitive advantages that can be substantial and difficult to imitate. **Porter** (1992) explored why some nations tend to produces firms with sustained competitive advantage in some industry more than others.

He tried to answer the following questions:

- Why does a nation become the home base for successful international competitors in an industry? Germany is renowned for car manufacture; Japan is prominent in consumer electronics.

- Why are firms based in a particular nation able to create and sustain competitive advantage against the world's best competitors in a particular field?

- Why is one country often the home of so many of an industry's world leaders?

Porter called the answers to these questions the determinants of national competitive advantage. He suggested that there are four main factors which determine national competitive advantage and expressed them in the form of a diamond.

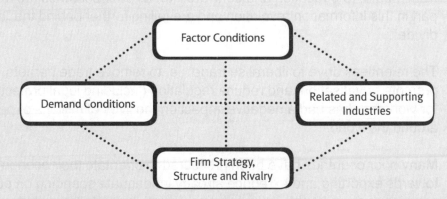

- **Factor conditions.** Factor conditions include the availability of raw materials and suitable infrastructure.

- **Demand conditions.** The goods or services have to be demanded at home: this starts international success.

- **Related and supporting industries.** These allow easy access to components and knowledge sharing.

- **Firm strategy, structure and rivalry.** If the home market is very competitive, a company is more likely to become world class.

Porter concludes that entire nations do not have particular competitive advantages. Rather, he argues, it is specific industries or firms within them that seem able to use their national backgrounds to lever world-class competitive advantages.

Further detail on Porter's Diamond

Demand conditions

The demand conditions in the home market are important for three reasons:

(1) If the demand is substantial it enables the firm to obtain the economies of scale and experience effects it will need to compete globally.

(2) The experience the firm gets from supplying domestic consumers will give it an information advantage in global markets, provided that:

- its customers are varied enough to permit segmentation into groups similar to those found in the global market as a whole

- its customers are critical and demanding enough to force the firm to produce at world-class levels of quality in its chosen products

- its customers are innovative in their purchasing behaviour and hence encourage the firm to develop new and sophisticated products.

(3) If the maturity stage of the product lifecycle is reached quickly (say, due to rapid adoption), this will give the firm the incentive to enter export markets before others do.

Related and supporting industries

The internationally competitive firm must have, initially at least, enjoyed the support of world-class producers of components and related products. Moreover success in a related industry may be due to expertise accumulated elsewhere (e.g. the development of the Swiss precision engineering tools industry owes much to the requirements and growth of the country's watch industry).

Factor conditions

These are the basic factor endowments referred to in economic theory as the source of so-called comparative advantage. Factors may be of two sorts:

(1) Basic factors such as raw materials, semi-skilled or unskilled labour and initial capital availability. These are largely 'natural' and not created as a matter of policy or strategy.

(2) Advanced factors such as infrastructure (particularly digital telecommunications), levels of training and skill, R&D experience, etc.

Porter argues that only the advanced factors are the roots of sustainable competitive advantage. Developing these becomes a matter for government policy.

Firm structure, strategy and rivalry

National cultures and competitive conditions do create distinctive business focuses. These can be influenced by:

- ownership structure

- the attitudes and investment horizons of capital markets

- the extent of competitive rivalry

- the openness of the market to outside competition.

Other events

Porter points out that countries can produce world-class firms due to two further factors:

(1) The role of government. Subsidies, legislation and education can impact on the other four elements of the diamond to the benefit of the industrial base of the country.

(2) The role of chance events. Wars, civil unrest, chance factor discoveries, etc. can also change the four elements of the diamond unpredictably.

---

e.g

Illustration 5 – Porter's diamond illustration

Porter's diamond applied to the Scotch whisky industry

Factor conditions:

Natural factor conditions: Scotland has ready availability of the raw materials required for whisky production. This includes a plentiful water supply and a climate suited to growing the crops required in the production process.

Advanced factor conditions: Over the years, knowledge and a skilled workforce has developed in Scotland. In addition the name 'Scotch' can only be applied to whisky which has been produced in Scotland and 'Scotch' is known throughout the world and recognised for its quality.

Demand conditions:

A strong home demand is the starting point for international competitive advantage. The domestic consumers become more sophisticated and demanding, which drives up the quality of all products. This is true in the case of Scotch whisky, there is a strong home demand (around 15% of all Scotch is sold in Scotland).

Related and supporting industries:

The numerous distilleries in Scotland all require the support of other industries. As a result there are strong bottling, cooperage and distribution industries which support the whisky producers.

Firm strategy, industry structure and rivalry:

There are over 100 working distilleries throughout Scotland, many of these are small and only produce one or two specialist malt whiskies. This has generated competition between the distillers to produce the best quality whisky and this in turn increases the quality of all products in the industry.

Case study style question 3

Kayland is known across the world as the producer of the finest coffee, with the majority of the successful coffee producing companies coming from Kayland. Neighbouring Jayland also produces coffee, but the Jayland coffee companies have not managed the same success, or enjoyed the same reputation as the Kayland companies.

A colleague has just returned from a conference in Kayland where Porter's diamond was discussed. He is keen to find out more about this model and how it could be applied.

Required:

With reference to Porter's Diamond model, write an email to your colleague explaining the different sources of national competitive advantage that the companies from Kayland may enjoy and which could give them a competitive edge over the Jayland companies.

(20 minutes)

Difficulties with Porter's Diamond

Although not as popular as his five forces model, value chain and generic strategies, this model has still achieved a lot of recognition for Porter. It is not, however, without its difficulties:

- **Companies not countries.** The industries that must succeed globally have their own management and strategies. By focusing on their country of origin Porter does not explain why a given country produces both stars and duds in the same industry. For example, Toyota and Honda are both Japanese car makers which are a success. Nissan and Mazda are less successful and have been rescued by Renault and Ford, respectively.

- **Ignore multinational or global corporations.** The idea that Microsoft is an American company seems outdated when we consider that their staff, shareholders and customers are from all over the world. Porter's model seems to apply better to firms that are exporting and less well to ones who are actually setting up outside of their home country.

- **Ignores the target country.** Commercial success or failure will depend more on the environment in the target country than it will on the environment in the home country. Therefore it is necessary to analyse the target country too.

- **Less applicable to services.** Porter's examples are restricted to manufacturing and closely allied industries such as banks and management consultancies. It is hard to see how his model would apply to say Starbucks where so much of the product and staffing depends on the local economy.

6 Emerging markets – the BRIC(S) economies

A recent trend has been a rise in multinational companies from the emerging "BRIC" or "BRICS" economies.

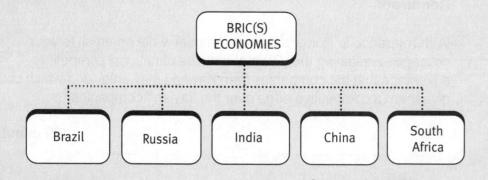

138

BRIC(S) are the world's largest emerging economies.

(Note: until fairly recently South Africa was not included in this group so it was known as the "BRIC" economies)

Two key factors have resulted in the growth of these economies:

- **globalisation**
- **internal developments** – these include:
  - large and rapid growth rates
  - a move towards a free market economy
  - relative political stability
  - availability of labour
  - low wage rates
  - improvements in education
  - availability of natural resources.

Some analysts predict that by 2050, the combined BRIC(S) economies will outstrip the G6 economies (Germany, France, Italy, Japan, UK and the USA).

Some predict that China will become the world's largest economy, as early as 2025. It is currently the second largest behind the USA.

Organisations in BRIC(S) economies are moving from being recipients of foreign direct investment to actually investing in and even becoming owners of major Western businesses. For example, there is a strong move in China to export capital and to make foreign acquisitions.

The future of the BRIC(S) economies

The global financial meltdown in 2008 has resulted in a slowdown in the rate of growth of the BRIC(S) economies. However, BRIC(S) countries have a number of strengths which should allow them to continue to grow including:

- **Strong consumer demand** – high levels of consumer expenditure in the BRIC(S) countries should help drive growth.
- **High levels of foreign exchange reserves** – these reserves will allow the government to boost public spending in the economy, e.g. on transport and infrastructure. This will enhance the environment and lead to further economic growth.

The BRIC(S) economies seem to have withstood the shakings of the world's economic foundations, and emerged more robust than ever.

Other emerging major economies

Other emerging major economies include Argentina, Mexico, Taiwan, South Korea and Singapore.

Threats for the BRIC(S) economies

The global slowdown since 2008 has resulted in a number of threats for the BRIC(S) economies. For example:

- Foreign investment in BRIC(S) economies from developed countries has slowed.

- Consumer demand in the developed world has slowed. This will impact the BRIC(S) economies, e.g. two thirds of China's exports are to the developed world, with exports accounting for over one third of their wealth.

- India's economy depends on developed countries outsourcing services to them. A recession in the developed world will reduce the level of outsourcing.

A second tier of emerging economies, which demonstrates some similar characteristics to those of the BRIC(S) nations, is Indonesia, Vietnam, Colombia and Ukraine. Economic growth in these countries is beginning to drive consumer spending on domestic goods. The size of their populations means there is unlikely to be any reversal of this trend.

7 Country and Political Risk

Globalisation can be a huge opportunity for a company to engage in business with many countries around the world. However, investing abroad may be accompanied by risk. This section will review two such risks:

- Political risk
- Country risk

Political risk

Political risk is the possibility of an unexpected politically motivated event in a country affecting the outcome of an investment.

- Political risk is greater in countries with developing economies.
- A change in government can sometimes result in dramatic changes for a business.

- Political risk could have a **direct** effect on a business. For example:
  - The risk of nationalisation of foreign owned assets.
  - The risk of a government decision to raise taxation.
  - The risk of a government decision to restrict payments to foreign shareholders.
  - The risk that politically motivated terrorists cause damage to property and/or employees.
  - The risk of changes in the law, such as employment law.
  - The risk that contracts are cancelled or revised.
  - The risk that lobby groups within a country put pressure on the government to support home based business rather than foreign business.

- Political risk can also be **indirect**, because of the effect of government policies on the economy, e.g. changes in interest rates and exchange rates.

e.g

Illustration 6

In 2001, British Prime Minister Tony Blair had to personally intervene to protect the investment in the Ukraine by the British oil company JKX Oil and Gas plc. The Ukraine's State Property Fund had attempted to expropriate JKX's investment but after intervention by the British Prime Minister the Ukrainian court ruled that the action was illegal.

Groups that can generate political risk

- Current government
- Opposition groups
- Organised interest groups or protest groups
- Terrorist or anarchist groups
- International organisations such as the UN
- Foreign governments that have entered into international alliances with the country or are supporting the opposition within the country.

Managing political risk

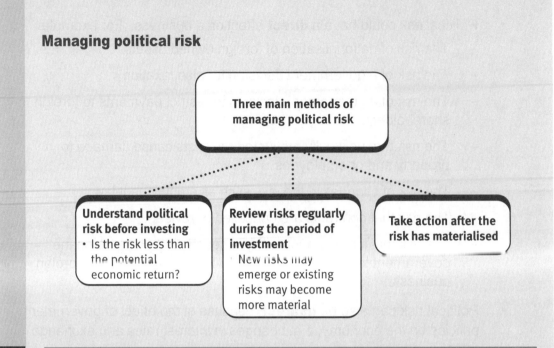

Three main methods of managing political risk

Understand political risk before investing
- Is the risk less than the potential economic return?

Review risks regularly during the period of investment
New risks may emerge or existing risks may become more material

Take action after the risk has materialised

Case study style question 4

You have been brought in as an adviser by the CEO of X. X are considering making a substantial investment in the country of Yland. This would be their first investment outside of their native country.

The CEO is aware of political risk but is unsure of the best way to manage it. He feels that it is something he needs to look into as X operates in a very stable country but he feels that Yland may be less stable.

Required:

Draft a brief report to the CEO of X explaining what steps may be taken to manage political risk. Your report should cover three time periods:

- before the investment takes place.

- during the period of investment.

- after the risk has been realised.

(20 minutes)

Country risk

Country risk is the risk arising from operating or investing in a particular country, with risks relating to matters such as:

- political interference, e.g. currency controls
- political stability
- the social and economic infrastructure
- the culture of the country
- and its attitude to foreign business.

Country risk is a much more general term than political risk and relates to all of the risks of operating or investing in a particular country.

Country risk analysis

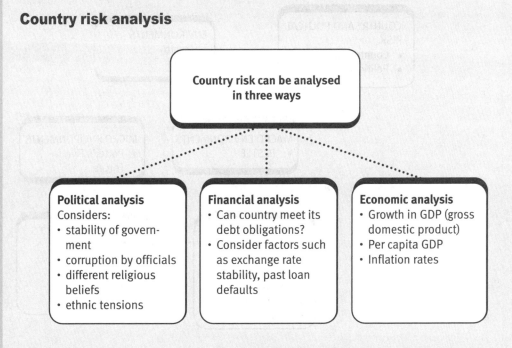

Country risk can be analysed in three ways

Political analysis
Considers:
- stability of government
- corruption by officials
- different religious beliefs
- ethnic tensions

Financial analysis
- Can country meet its debt obligations?
- Consider factors such as exchange rate stability, past loan defaults

Economic analysis
- Growth in GDP (gross domestic product)
- Per capita GDP
- Inflation rates

When all of these risks are taken together, an overall assessment of country risk can be made.

8 Chapter summary

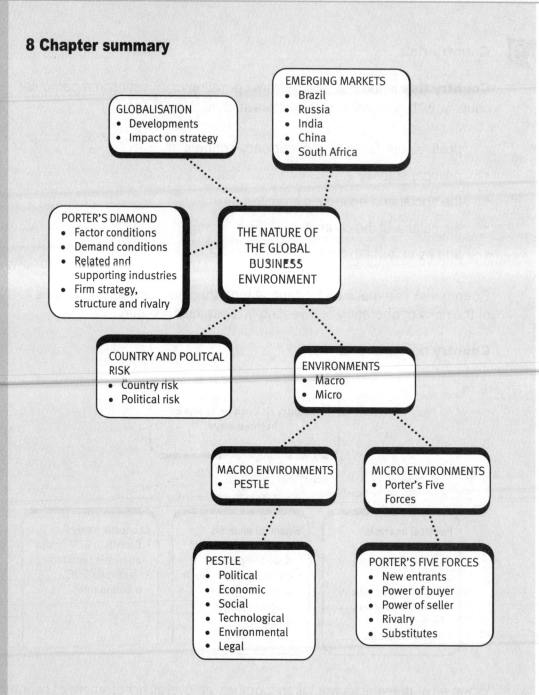

GLOBALISATION
- Developments
- Impact on strategy

EMERGING MARKETS
- Brazil
- Russia
- India
- China
- South Africa

PORTER'S DIAMOND
- Factor conditions
- Demand conditions
- Related and supporting industries
- Firm strategy, structure and rivalry

THE NATURE OF THE GLOBAL BUSINESS ENVIRONMENT

COUNTRY AND POLITCAL RISK
- Country risk
- Political risk

ENVIRONMENTS
- Macro
- Micro

MACRO ENVIRONMENTS
- PESTLE

MICRO ENVIRONMENTS
- Porter's Five Forces

PESTLE
- Political
- Economic
- Social
- Technological
- Environmental
- Legal

PORTER'S FIVE FORCES
- New entrants
- Power of buyer
- Power of seller
- Rivalry
- Substitutes

End of chapter questions

Question 1

X offers accountancy training courses. The market is growing quickly and X's courses are significantly different to those offered by its rivals. Any new company wishing to teach accountancy courses must obtain accreditation by the various accountancy organisations – a process which can take several years.

Based on the above information, which of the following statements can be made about X's competitive environment?

A   Competitive rivalry is likely to be low

B   The threat of substitutes is likely to be high

C   Barriers to entry are likely to be low

D   The threat of new entrants is likely to be low

Question 2

Which of the following relates to the PESTLE analysis model? Select all that apply.

A   The output from it can be used to form the opportunities and threats part of the corporate appraisal

B   It helps to analysis the macro-environment in which an organisation operates

C   It can be used to identify the resources available to an organisation and how these can be used to create competitive advantage

D   One of the factors considered in the model is the level of power held by buyers and suppliers

E   It would include considering the demographics factors of a country

F   It helps organisations to understand the competitive environment in which they operate.

Question 3

Factors such as training and skills or research and development experience would come under which heading in the Porter's diamond model?

A   Related and supporting industries

B   Factor conditions

C   Firm strategy, structure and rivalry

D   Demand conditions

Question 4

The imposition of which one of the following would NOT act as a barrier to international trade?

A   quotas

B   tariffs

C   value added tax

D   embargoes

Question 5

Which of the following statements are true in relation to Porter's five forces model? Select all that apply.

A   Rivalry amongst competitors is high where there is high growth in the market

B   The power of suppliers is high where there are few suppliers

C   The power of buyers is low where there are high switching costs

D   The threat of new entrants is high where capital requirements are low

E   Rivalry amongst competitors is low where fixed costs are high

F   The power of suppliers is low where the supplier's product is differentiated

Question 6

Complete the following statements regarding globalisation using the words provided.

Factors which have contributed towards globalisation include the _____ of industries and the _____ of trade. There have been more opportunities within _____ markets.

Globalisation has also resulted in a requirement for more _____ of products. It is often said that in the current environment, companies must think_____ but act _____.

| local | liberalisation | customisation | deregulation | global | emerging |

Question 7

Which three of the following statements regarding the BRIC(S) economies are correct?

A   South Korea was a later edition to the original BRIC economies.

B   The BRIC(S) economies are India, China, Russia, South Africa and Brazil.

C   China is now the second largest economy in the world and is predicted to be the largest by 2025.

D   It is anticipated that the BRIC(S) economies will outstrip the G6 economies within the next 40 years.

E   India's growth has mainly been the result of an increase in the home demand for domestic products.

Question 8

PC manufactures greeting cards. It is considering moving into the wrapping paper market. It has established that there are four main wrapping paper manufacturers, who have an aggregate market share of 82%. The current market leader has a share of 26%. There four companies produce products of similar size and quality. The market for wrapping paper has grown by 2% per annum in recent years.

Identify which aspect of Porter's five forces would consider this information and identify if the scenario suggests that the force would be high or low.

New entrant	
Power of buyer	
Power of supplier	
Substitutes	
Rivalry	

Low
High

Question 9

Match the statements to whether it relates to country or political risk.

This risk relates to matters such as political stability of a country or the social and economic infrastructure of the country.	Political
This risk can have a direct effect on an organisation such as changes to employment law.	Country
This risk can be analysed by undertaking political analysis, financial analysis and economic analysis.	
The culture of a country could affect this type of risk.	
The risk that interest groups put pressure on the government of a country to support home based rather than foreign business would be this type of risk.	

Question 10

Which of the following could act as a barrier to entry? Select all that apply.

A   Patents and licences

B   Many suppliers

C   Economies of scale

D   Differentiated products

E   Government policy

F   Low initial investment

Test your understanding answers

Case study style question 1

BRIEFING NOTES FOR STRATEGY STEERING TEAM MEETING

Justify the use of PESTLE

(a) PESTLE analysis examines the broad environment in which the organisation is operating. PESTLE is a mnemonic which stands for Political, Economic, Social, Technological, Legal and Environmental factors. These are simply key areas in which to consider how current and future changes affect the business. Strategies can then be developed which address any potential opportunities and threats identified.

In entering a new overseas market, an environmental analysis is important to help the organisation understand the factors specific to that market so that the specific opportunities and threats posed can be assessed and appropriate action taken.

It is a useful tool for the following reasons:

- It ensures completeness. The majority of issues relevant to an organisation will be covered under one of the areas of PESTLE analysis. By reviewing all areas, DM can be sure that it has done a full and complete analysis of the broad environment.

- All elements are relevant to examining new markets:
  - *Political*: Each new country entered will have different political systems. DM will need to understand these differences. They will also want to ensure that there is political stability within the country which will ensure long-term viability of the new operations.

  - *Economic:* Economies are different in different parts of the world. Understanding the local economy in R country and how it is expected to develop enables DM to assess the potential within that market as well as any economic issues which they need to consider.

  - *Social*: Each country will have its own cultural differences, and DM can change how they operate depending on R country's culture. DM has already shown its willingness to change for each country's different tastes and will want to do so in R country too.

- *Technological*: Each country has a different level of technological expertise and experience. DM might need to change processes to accommodate local systems, or implement training programmes for staff unfamiliar with their technology.

- Environmental: Each country will have different laws and concerns about the environment. The importance the public place on conserving the environment could have an impact on the DM's operations.

- *Legal:* Each new country entered will have different laws. DM will need to understand these differences to ensure that they operate within the law in R country.

- It is a well-known tool which is easy to understand and use. PESTLE analysis is a very simple tool that does not require detailed understanding. This means that it is easy to use by the team and simple for Directors to analyse and understand.

The main issues from the PESTLE analysis

(b) **Political factors:**

- Political stability: Given DM's worldwide penetration (over 120 countries) it is likely that R country is in a developing region which may be more politically unstable than many countries in which they currently operate. This may affect the long-term potential in the market.

- Tariffs and other barriers to trade. Tariffs may be imposed on imports into R country. This may put DM at a significant disadvantage compared with local competitors if they aim to import a significant number of items (unlikely on food items, more likely on clothing, fittings etc).

Economic factors

- Economic prosperity: The more prosperous the nation the more money people will have to invest in 'fast-food'. Examining the current and likely future prosperity enables the organisation to understand the potential of this market and the likely future investment required.

- Position in economic cycle: Different countries are often at different positions in the economic cycle of growth and recession. The current position of R country will affect the current prosperity of the nation and the potential for business development for DM.

- Inflation rates: High inflation rates create instability in the economy which can affect future growth prospects. They also mean that prices for supplies and prices charged will regularly change and this difficulty would need to be considered and processes implemented to account for this.

Social factors

- Brand reputation: As a global brand, the reputation of DM might be expected to have reached R country. If not, more marketing will be required. If it has, the reputation will need to be understood and the marketing campaign set up accordingly.

- Cultural differences: Each country has its own values, beliefs, attitudes and norms of behaviours which means that people of that country may like different foods, architecture, music and so on, in comparison with S country restaurants. By adapting to local needs DM can ensure it wins local custom and improve its reputation. Different cultures also need to be considered when employing people, especially given the importance to DM of employee relations. People might have different religious needs to be met or may dislike being given autonomy so the management style needs changing.

Technological factors

- DM may need to train people in the use of their technologies if the local population are unfamiliar with them e.g. accounting systems or tills. In addition, technology might have to be adapted to work in local environments, such as different electrical systems.

- Availability of infrastructure within R country would have to be considered to ensure that it is suitable to allow DM to run its operation.

Legal factors

– Regulation on overseas companies: There may be regulation on how overseas companies can operate in the market. In China, for instance, it is common for joint ventures with local companies to be a prerequisite for western companies entering the market.

– Employment legislation: Each country will have different employment legislation e.g. health and safety, minimum wages, employment rights. DM may have to change internal processes from the S country model to stay within this legislation within R country. Being a good employer is also one of DM's specific strategies.

Environmental factors

– Laws and regulations on emissions and pollution. DM would have to ensure that it could carry out its operations within these guidelines.

– Sustainability of raw materials could be an issue which DM should consider as it could affect how they source their raw materials which could affect the cost.

Case study style question 2

REPORT

To: Board of JPC

From: Management accountant

Date: today

Report on the attractiveness of the cardboard tube market

Introduction

In order to assess the attractiveness of the option to enter the market for spirally-wound paper tubes, the directors of JPC could make use of Michael Porter's five forces model. This model assesses the attractiveness of an industry using five factors. Each factor is discussed in turn in this report.

New Entrants

In applying this model to the given scenario one might conclude that the relatively low cost of the machine together with the fact that an unskilled person would only require one day's training in order to be able to operate a machine, constitute relatively low costs of entry to the market. Therefore one might reasonably conclude that the threat of new entrants might be high. This is especially the case where the market is highly fragmented.

The fact that a foreign-based multinational company is considering entering this market represents a significant threat from a potential new entrant as it would appear that the multinational company might well be able to derive economies of scale from large scale automated machinery and has manufacturing flexibility.

Buyer Power

The fact that products are usually purchased in very large quantities by customers together with the fact that there is little real difference between the products of alternative suppliers suggests that customer (buyer) power might well be very high. The fact that the paper tubes on average only comprise between 1% and 2% of the total cost of the purchaser's finished product also suggests that buyer power may well be very high.

Supplier Power

The threat from suppliers could be high due to the fact that the specially formulated paper from which the tubes are made is sometimes in short supply. Hence suppliers might increase their prices with consequential diminution in gross margin of the firms in the marketplace.

Rivalry

The threat from competitive rivals will be strong as the four major players in the market are of similar size and that the market is a slow growing market. The market leader currently has 26% of the market and the three nearest competitors hold approximately 18% of the market.

Substitutes

The fact that PTC produces a narrow range of plastic tubes constitutes a threat from a substitute product. This threat will increase if the product range of PTC is extended and the price of plastic tubes is reduced.

Conclusion

Low capital barriers to entry might appeal to JPC but they would also appeal to other potential entrants. The low growth market, the ease of entry, the existence of established competitors, a credible threat of backward vertical integration by suppliers, the imminent entry by a multi-national, a struggling established competitor and the difficulty of differentiating an industrial commodity should call into question the potential of JPC to achieve any sort of competitive advantage. If JPC can achieve the position of lowest cost producer within the industry then entry into the market might be a good move. In order to assess whether this is possible JPC must consider any potential synergies that would exist between its cardboard business and that of the tubes operation.

From the information available, the option to enter the market for cardboard tubes appears to be unattractive. The directors of JPC should seek alternative performance improvement strategies.

Case study style question 3

EMAIL

To: Colleague

From: Accountant

Date: today

Subject: Porter's Diamond model

Porter's Diamond looks at why organisations may achieve competitive advantage over their rivals by virtue of being based in a particular country. The theory helps to explain why some nations tend to produce firms with sustained competitive advantage in particular industries using specific sources of advantage that can be substantial and hard to imitate.

In this case, it would appear that the coffee producing companies from Kayland have national competitive advantage over the companies from Jayland.

The model considers four interacting determinants, these are factor conditions; demand conditions; related and supporting industries; firm strategy, structure and rivalry.

- **Factor conditions** refer to the factors of production that go into making a product or service. Different nations have different stocks of factors which can be categorised as human resources; physical resources; knowledge; capital; infrastructure. In this case we can assume that Kayland has the necessary climate to grow coffee beans and they have over the years improved their knowledge of growing and cultivating the coffee beans.

- **Demand conditions** refer to the nature of the domestic customer becoming a source of competitive advantage. Dealing with sophisticated and demanding customers with high expectations in an organisation's home market will help drive innovation and quality, which in turn will help an organisation to be effective in other countries. From the question, it may be the case that Kayland residents are keen coffee drinkers who have demanded the highest quality products over the years. If the customer needs are understood in the home market earlier than in the world market, the firms benefit from the experience.

- **Related and Supporting Industries**. Porter proposes that a nation's competitive industries are clustered, where a cluster is a linking of industries through relationships which are either vertical (buyer-supplier) or horizontal (common customers, technology, skills).

  In other words, competitive success in one industry is linked to the success in related industries. In the coffee producing industry, supporting industries may be jar manufacturers and distribution networks.

- **Firm strategy, industry structure and rivalry** is related to the fact that fierce domestic rivalry and competition will drive innovation, force down costs and develop new methods of competing. This can enhance global competitive advantage. In the scenario it states that there a number of top coffee producing companies in Kayland. These companies are likely to compete against each other in order to improve their products, thus driving up the quality overall.

Hopefully this is helpful to you. Please let me know is you need any more information on this.

Regards.

Case study style question 4

REPORT

To: CEO of X

From: Consultant

Date: today

Report on the management of political risk

Introduction

X are considering a substantial investment in Yland, the first non-domestic investment to be considered by X.

In any international investment, consideration must be given to political risk in the country, in this case, Yland. Management of political risk can be crucial in the success of the investment.

Risk can be managed at three stages; before the investment, during the investment and after the risk has been realised. This report will look at how risks should be managed at each of these stages.

Before the investment takes place

The company should take steps to understand the level and types of political risk. A decision to invest should only be taken if the potential economic return is sufficient to compensate for the political risk. The company should take out appropriate insurance prior to investment.

During the period of investment

During the investment it is important to establish business relations – partnerships with local businesses and suppliers can help the company to learn local business customs and their advice should help to reduce the risks from nationalism and anti-foreign sentiment in the country.

Set up a local operation – this should be headed by a local manager and should help to reduce risks from nationalist attitudes.

Borrow in the local currency – the profit from the business can be used to repay loans. This reduces risks from currency conversion or from restrictions on payments out of a country.

Develop government contacts – winning the support of government should help to reduce the risk of unhelpful political measures such as the refusal of planning permission.

Split operations between countries – this will reduce the incentive for the government to nationalise the business.

Set up a joint venture – risk is shared with another partner

After the risk has been realised

If a risk is realised, litigation or retaliation may be possible, as maybe an insurance claim. Implementation of a contingency plan should come into force at this stage. A contingency plan should have been established at the outset.

Depending on the severity of the realised risk, exit from the market may have to be considered.

Conclusion

Management of political risk is an important process in any non-domestic investment and X must careful consider this before making any investment in Yland.

Question 1

D   The threat of new entrants is likely to be low

The need for accreditation will make it harder for competitors to enter the market, therefore the threat of new entrants will be low. The accreditation will raise the barriers to entry.

The fact that the market is growing would suggest that rivalry within the market would be high as all companies attempt to gain a bigger share of the growing market.

The courses offered by X are significantly different to those offered by rivals, therefore the threat of substitutes is low.

Question 2

A, B and E are correct.

PESTLE analysis involves analysing the external environment under a number of headings:

- Political

- Economic

- Social

- Technological

- Legal

- Environmental

PESTLE analysis analyses the macro-environment in which an organisation operates. This, together with the industry level analysis using Porter's five forces, can be used to form the opportunities and threats part of the corporate appraisal.

The demographic factors of a country would be considered under the social element of PESTLE.

Option C relates to internal analysis which would be carried out using Porter's value chain and resources audits. Options D and F refer to Porter's five forces model.

Question 3

B   Factor conditions

Training and skills or research and development would come under the factor condition section of Porter's diamond. Factor conditions refer to the basic factors endowments which that country has. These can be analysed as either basic factors such as raw materials or labour availability or advanced factors such as infrastructure, training or research and development experience. Advanced factors are created as a matter of strategy or policy and Porter argues that only these advanced factors can bring sustainable competitive advantage.

Question 4

C   value added tax

Quotas, tariffs and embargoes can be put in place by governments to restrict trade from other countries. The existence of these would act as barriers to international trade. Value added tax, or sales tax would have to be applied to the products sold in the country, depending on the tax laws, but this would not act as a barrier to trade.

Question 5

B   The power of suppliers is high where there are few suppliers

C   The power of buyers is low where there are high switching costs

D   The threat of new entrants is high where capital requirements are low

The power of suppliers is high when there are few suppliers is true. If companies are restricted in terms of selecting suppliers, the few suppliers will be able to largely dictate prices and will reduce the margins the company can achieve.

The power of buyers is low when there are high switching costs is true. Where buyers find it costly to move to another supplier then they are likely to continue to buy from the existing company and will have low power to influence the prices imposed by the company.

The threat of new entrants is high where capital requirements are low is true. High capital requirements can make it difficult for new companies to enter the market. Low initial capital requirements can make it easier for new companies to enter the market.

Rivalry amongst competitors is high where there is high growth in the market is incorrect. Where there is high growth in the market competition and rivalry will be low. Rivalry will increase where the market growth is low as all companies will be fighting to maintain their market share. Rivalry amongst competitors is low where fixed costs are high is incorrect. The higher the fixed costs within an industry, the higher the rivalry as all companies are trying to ensure they gain enough revenue to cover their fixed costs.

The power of suppliers is low where the supplier's product is differentiated is incorrect. The power of supplier is low where their product has many substitutes but high if the product is differentiated.

Question 6

Factors which have contributed towards globalisation include the **deregulation** of industries and the **liberalisation** of trade. There have been more opportunities within **emerging** markets.

Globalisation has also resulted in a requirement for more **customisation** of products. It is often said that in the current environment, companies must think **global** but act **local**.

Question 7

B   The BRIC(S) economies are India, China, Russia, South Africa and Brazil.

C   China is now the second largest economy in the world and is predicted to be the largest by 2025.

D   It is anticipated that the BRIC(S) economies will outstrip the G6 economies within the next 40 years.

South Korea was a later edition to the original BRIC economies. This is incorrect – the later edition to the BRIC economies was South Africa.

India's growth has mainly been the result of an increase in the home demand for domestic products. This is incorrect – India's growth has largely been the result of the outsourcing services they supply to the developed countries.

Question 8

Rivalry	High

The aspect of Porter's five forces would be rivalry. There are four main competitors already in the market and between them they hold 82% of the market. Also, the market growth is low at only 2% per annum. These factors would suggest that the rivalry within this market would be high.

Question 9

This risk relates to matters such as political stability of a country or the social and economic infrastructure of the country.	Country
This risk can have a direct effect on an organisation such as changes to employment law.	Political
This risk can be analysed by undertaking political analysis, financial analysis and economic analysis.	Country
The culture of a country could affect this type of risk.	Country
The risk that interest groups put pressure on the government of a country to support home based rather than foreign business would be this type of risk.	Political

Question 10

A   Patents and licences

C   Economies of scale

D   Differentiated products

E   Government policy

Patents and licences can make it difficult, if not impossible, to operate within a particular marketplace.

Economies of scale can also act as a barrier to entry as new entrants to the market will be unable to compete on a comparable cost basis to those already operating within the market as existing companies can enjoy reduced unit costs as a result of their volume of production.

Differentiated products can also act as a barrier to entry. Where established firms have good brand image and customer loyalty, the costs of overcoming this can be prohibitive.

Government policy such as licences to operate or limits on access to raw materials could create a barrier to entry.

Many suppliers will not create a barrier to entry, but could actually make it easier for new entrants to obtain the raw materials they require.

High initial investment would be a barrier to entry, but low initial investment can make it easy for new entrants to set up within the market.

163

Competitor analysis

Chapter learning objectives

Discuss the approaches to competitor analysis including the collection and interpretation of trend data

1 Session content diagram

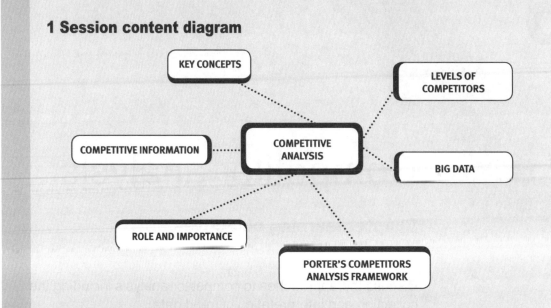

2 Competitor analysis

CIMA defines competitor analysis as: 'Identification and quantification of the relative strengths and weaknesses (compared with competitors or potential competitors), which could be of significance in the development of a successful competitive strategy.'

The role of competitor analysis

According to **Wilson and Gilligan** (1997) competitor analysis has three roles:

- to help management understand their competitive advantages and disadvantages relative to competitors

- to generate insights into competitors' past, present and potential strategies

- to give an informed basis for developing future strategies to sustain or establish advantages over competitors.

To these we may add a fourth:

- to assist with the forecasting of the returns on strategic investments for deciding between alternative strategies.

Key concepts in competitor analysis

There are some key concepts which are helpful when undertaking competitor analysis.

- A useful starting point to competitor is to gain an understanding of **market size**. This is usually based on the annual sales of competitors. A challenge in doing this is in actually defining the 'market' (e.g. if undertaking an analysis of Easyjet, is the market the airline market, or the budget airline market – which is most helpful?)

- A second step involves estimating the **market growth.** The importance of growth is relevant to strategy development, since if an organisation has a strategy which involves quick growth, then it would be more attracted to a market which is growing rapidly.

- A third step involves gaining an understanding of **market share**. This relates to the specific share an organisation has of a particular market. A larger share is usually regarded as being strategically beneficial since it may make it possible to influence prices and reduce costs through economies of scale. The outcome is increased profitability.

The Boston Consulting Group (BCG) model

A model which can be used in competitor analysis when considering market share and market growth is the Boston Consulting Group Model (BCG). This model can look at the position of individual product lines in relation to the market sector they compete in. Each product is assessed in terms of its market share, relative to that of the market leader in their sector. This is mapped against the growth rate of the sector.

By plotting each of its product lines on the BCG grid, the organisation is able to assess whether it has a balanced portfolio in terms of products and market sectors. It can also help in the development of strategic options for each product, depending on the potential growth in the market sector and the relative strength of the product compared to its competitors in that sector.

Four main steps:

(1) Identify the company's products or product lines.

(2) Allocate each product into the matrix depending on the analysis of relative market share and market growth:

Relative market share – the ratio of the product market share to that of largest rival in the market sector. BCG suggests that market share gives a company cost advantages from economies of scale and learning effects.

Market growth rate – represents the growth rate of the market sector concerned. High growth industries offer a more favourable competitive environment and better long-term prospects than slow-growth industries.

(3) Assess the prospects of each product and compare against others in the matrix

(4) Develop strategic objectives for each product.

Boston Consulting Group Growth / Share Matrix

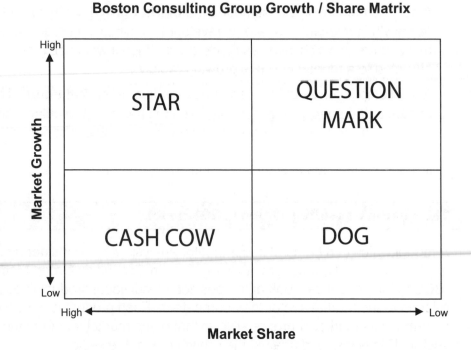

The model suggests that appropriate strategies would be:

Cash cows

Cash cows have a relatively high market share in a low-growth market. These are generally cash generators and profitable.

Recommended strategy: hold, build or harvest

Low market growth implies a lack of opportunity and therefore the capital requirements are low. Profits from this area can be used to support stars and develop question marks.

A defensive strategy is often adopted to protect the position.

Star

Stars have a relatively high market share in a high growth market. They are often the market leader. Stars offer attractive long-term prospects – may one day become a cash cow.

They can require large investment in non-current assets and they need to defend against competitor attacks.

Recommended strategy: hold, divest or build

Question marks

Question marks have a relatively low market share in a high growth market. Opportunity exists for these products, they could become a star, but there is uncertainty. With question marks it may be necessary to invest heavily to secure market share. They may also require substantial management time and may not develop successfully.

Recommended strategy: build, harvest or divest

Dogs

Dogs have a relatively low market share in a low growth market. To cultivate these products would require substantial investment and would be risky. They may be turned into 'niche' products or could be carried as a loss leader.

Recommended strategy: harvest, divest or niche

Limitations of the BCG model:

- Simplistic – only considers two variables.

- Connection between market share and cost savings is not strong – low market share companies use low-share technology and can have lower production costs

- Cash cows do not always generate cash – cash cows can require substantial cash investment just to remain competitive and defend its position.

- Fail to consider value creation – the management of a diverse portfolio can create value by sharing competencies across SBUs, sharing resources to reap economies of scale or by achieving superior governance. BCG would divert investment away from the cash cows and dogs and fails to consider the benefit of offering the full range and the concept of 'loss leaders'.

Why is competitor analysis important?

The actions of competitors will impact on the profits of a business. This may include:

- price cuts
- launching of new products

- aggressive expansion of production and sales which reduces the firm's market share

- upgrading of their product's features which customers then expect

This will have implications for management's choice of strategy. A suitable strategy is one which yields satisfactory financial returns after taking into account the potential responses of competitors.

Porter's competitor analysis framework

Porter suggested four key aspects:

Identifying competitor's strategy. This can be identified from what a company says and does. More often than not what they do will be more important than what they say.

(2) **Identifying competitor's objectives.** Knowledge of competitors' objectives is an essential component of any analysis. Whether they are driven by short-term cash or profit goals or whether they have the reserves to focus on long-term objectives will result in them exhibiting significantly differing behaviours.

(3) **Identifying a competitors' assumptions about the industry.** A competitors' decisions are governed by their perceptions and assumptions about industry structure and the players with whom they compete. These perceptions will often be driven by the value systems of the senior management.

(4) **Identifying the competitors' resources and capabilities.** Without a rigorous analysis of the resources that a competitor possesses there can be no realistic prediction of the seriousness of a possible challenge. It is easy to determine what they are doing but the emphasis here should be on what they are capable of doing. Ideally a company should know as much about its competitors as it knows about itself, this is, of course, unlikely to be achieved but is something for which a company should strive.

All competitor information must be gathered and analysed and presented in the most accessible format to those who will make the decisions on a timely basis. Competitors should be **continuously** monitored for signs of activity and the industry scanned for the emergence of potential rivals.

Levels of competitors

Kotler (2008) identifies four levels of competitors:

- **Brand competitors**. Firms who offer similar products to the same customers we serve and who have a similar size and structure of organisation as ourselves, for example Pepsi and Coca-Cola.

- **Industry competitors**. Suppliers who produce similar goods but who are not necessarily the same size or structure as ourselves, or who compete in a more limited area or product range, for example British Airways and Singapore Airlines.

- **Form competitors**. Suppliers whose products satisfy the same needs as ours, although they are technically quite different, for example speedboats and sports cars.

- **Generic competitors**. Competitors who compete for the same income as the company, for example home improvements and golf clubs.

Understanding the level of competitors will help organisations to understand the basis on which they must try to compete their market place. It will assist them in defining their competitive strategy.

Level of threat posed by competitors

The extent to which competitors pose a threat to the firm depends on factors such as:

- **Number of rivals and the extent of differentiation in the market**. Greater numbers of rivals increases the complexity of the industry, but because they are smaller it reduces the danger of one competitor breaking from the rest in an attempt to deliver a knockout blow. Instead each will try to carve a niche and hence increase differentiation. This makes it less likely that one can invade the market of another.

- **Entry and mobility barriers**. These are costs that the firm must pay to get admission to the industry or to the firm's particular segment of it. For example, the Levi brand has a strong presence in the market for casual clothing. It proved an impediment when the firm tried to make tailored suits.

- **Cost structure**. If the rival has a high-cost structure this effectively denies entry to a market that contains a cost leader. For example, the high-cost structure of an exclusive department store would effectively deny it access to lower market segments.

- **Degree of vertical integration**. Highly vertically integrated firms have considerable strength in a market. However, they are also inflexible because they are committed to buying from their own upstream supply divisions. International oil firms have repeatedly lost out to discounting petroleum retailers able to buy supplies on the world's spot markets.

As a rule of thumb it is likely that the most significant present or potential competitors are the ones who conform most strongly to one or more of the following descriptions:

- they presently serve the same or similar customers to ourselves

- they have a similar or cheaper distribution network

- they are at the same stage of production as ourselves

- they utilise a similar technology in providing their goods and services

- they utilise similar types of management and staff skills

- they have a similar geographical spread.

Case study style question 1

At the first board meeting with the new CEO of WB, the Marketing Director was asked to provide details of the market growth in their industry and the company's market share. The new CEO was shocked to learn that these were not measures which WB had ever considered before.

He immediately instructed the directors to undertake detailed competitor analysis and to provide him with a report at the next board meeting which detailed: the main competitors and their current strategies; the rate of growth in the market and WB's market share.

Required:

The finance director has asked you to draft part of the report. Your draft report should:

(a) Explain why WB should undertake competitor analysis.

(8 minutes)

(b) Discuss why it is important for WB to understand the concepts of high/low market growth and market share when undertaking competitor analysis.

(10 minutes)

3 Competitor information

You need to understand what competitors are offering so you can offer at least as much to customers.

In collecting competitor information, organisations must firstly identify who their main competitors are. There may be a number of organisations operating in the market sector, it is important to identify those which pose the largest threat. This may be the market leader, or other organisations of around the same scale, offering similar products or services. It is however also important to continue to monitor the market for new entrants.

Types of information to collect:

- **Competitor's strategy**. Once the main competitors have been identified, information should be collected on their current strategies. Some of this may be established from looking at the products offered, the markets in which they operate and how they are operating within those markets.

- **Competitor's goals and objectives**. This may be established by looking at activities being undertaken by the competitor, for example moving into new markets, or developing new products.

- **Competitor's products and services**. It is important to know how competitor's products and services compare with those offered by the organisation. From this, information can be gathered on the segment of the market the competitor operates in, their pricing and quality strategy, their branding and image.

- **Competitor's resources and capabilities**. It is important to gauge the strength of the competitor in terms of financial, human, intellectual, technological and physical resources. This will help the organisation judge the threat posed by that competitor.

Types of information to gather about competitors

Fleisher and Bensoussan (2002) give a full listing of the information that an organisation should gather about their competitors. The broad headings are as follows:

- Products and services
- Marketing
- Human resources
- Operations
- Management profiles
- Sociopolitical

- Technology

- Organisational structure

- Competitive intelligence capacity

- Strategy

- Customer value analysis

- Financial.

Sources of information

There are a range of different sources available to organisations undertaking competitor analysis, for example:

- Website of competitor. This may contain information about strategy and objectives, as well as details of past performance. It should also provide information about where they operate, in what sectors and what types of products they offer.

- Annual report and accounts of competitors. This is publically available for larger companies and contains information about financial performance as well as details on governance issues and other general information about the company,

- Newspaper articles and on-line data sources on company. An internet search can highlight any articles relating to the company.

- Magazines and journals including trade media, business management and technical journals.

- On-line data services such as FAME to collect financial and statistical information.

- Directories and yearbooks covering particular industries.

- Becoming a customer of the competitor. This can be a good way to obtain information about the products and services offered by the competitor and the level of service offered by them.

- Market research reports and reviews produced by specialist firms such as Mintel, Economist Intelligence Unit, which might provide information on market share and marketing activity.

- Customer market research could be independently commissioned to establish consumer attitudes. This is the most costly of the data sources, but it will be the most specific in meeting the needs of the competitor analysis.

Competitor analysis must focus on two main issues: acquiring as much relevant information about competitors and subsequently predicting their behaviour.

Information sources

Tudor (1992) provides the following categorisation of information sources (some of it is a little dated now, but it is still a very useful listing):

(1) **Primary sources:**
- Annual reports and statements of competitors or firms in the target market or industry and those of their suppliers.
- Transcript services from newspapers, analysts and on-line data sources such as proprietary company information services.
- Statistical sources such as government censuses and surveys of household expenditure, production and demographics.
- Newspapers and newsletters such as the business press or industry bulletins.
- Magazines and journals including the trade media, business and management journals, technical journals.
- Analysis services such as FAME.
- Patents registered with the national patents office.

(2) **Secondary sources:**
- Directories and yearbooks covering particular industries (who's who) and ownership patterns (who owns what).
- Market research reviews and reports produced by specialist research firms including Mintel, Economist Intelligence Unit, etc.
- Abstracts, index journals and current awareness services. These are specialist databases which index technical articles under codes and keywords. The firm can set up a profile of keywords relevant to its industry and source the material written on it.
- Government publications such as special reports of select committees on particular industries, economic forecasts and reports.
- Grey literature. A generic phrase covering theses, conference reports, special research papers, maps and photographs.

(3) **Computer-based information services:**
- CD-Rom-based abstracts and journals.
- On-line databases of professional and academic journals, newspapers and business information.
- Internet resources.

The internet as a source of competitor information

Some competitor intelligence is freely available from the Internet. This information can provide a valuable starting point for developing detailed competitor profiles. Be cautious about acting on competitor intelligence until you have as much complete, accurate, up-to-date information as possible. Published sources can provide only a partial picture, and more strategic information is likely to be confidential.

The Internet has become part of everyday business and personal life and traffic increases worldwide every day. It provides an unsurpassed opportunity for businesses to access new markets and grow their existing markets locally, nationally and globally There are many challenges to be addressed in ensuring a website is visible and effective. Key amongst these is ensuring that your organisation can measure the effectiveness of its site both in comparison to how it performed last month and last year and how it is performing against its competitors.

An organisations Internet presence is more than just a website and needs to react and evolve to meet competitive and market changes. An organisation needs as much market intelligence and possible to plan and adapt its campaigns and respond to the actions of its competitors.

Case study style question 2

V, the new CEO of D was surprised to find out that the company do not undertake competitor analysis. He was told by J, the Marketing director that D operates in a very dynamic market and that things change too quickly to make analysis worthwhile.

Required:

V has asked you to draft an email to J, explaining why competitor analysis is so important and highlighting the main sources D could use to gather information on competitors.

(15 minutes)

4 Market research

Market research is one of the most useful sources of competitor information as it can be carried out to the exact specification of the organisation. Although more costly than most other sources, it can gather very specific information which would be of more use than the cheaper, but more general information which is more readily available.

Research of this nature largely falls into two distinctive areas that are both useful in their own ways: qualitative and quantitative research.

Quantitative research

Quantitative research tries to answer the **what**, **where** and **when** questions. Undertaking quantitative research will be carried out using questionnaires and surveys. Specific product based research can be carried out face-to-face at the point of purchase, but is more commonly carried out online after purchase. More general surveys may be carried out through the post or on the telephone. Questions asked often have a sliding scale for answers, e.g. 0 = unsatisfied and 5 = very satisfied and participants are able to select the number from 0 to 5 which matches their opinion. Some questions will be more factual or yes/no style questions such as, "would you recommend this product to a friend?", or "how many times in the last month have you purchased this product?"

Statistical methods such as ratios or trend analysis can then be used to analyse this data. Analysis can produce information such as:

- 80% of our customers would recommend our product to a friend

- 90% of purchasers were very satisfied with the service given

When carrying out quantitative analysis, select and discuss those ratios that have an impact on important company issues. These ratios can then be compared with industry averages to discover if the company is out of line with others in the industry.

A typical financial analysis of a firm would include a study of the operating statements for three or five years, including a trend analysis of sales, profit margins, earnings per share, return on investment, liquidity ratios plus a comparison of the firm under study with industry standards.

Non-financial quantitative analysis

Another important aspect of quantitative analysis is the gathering of non-financial data, such as number of customers, customer complaints etc.

The financial indexes are useful, but they cannot show some competitive advantages characteristics such as the product differentiation or the quick responsiveness to customer questions.

This non-financial data is often more useful in terms of competitor analysis. For example a company may want to assess their customer service against the service given by a competitor. They may gather information on the time between order and delivery. This would allow them to ensure that they provide the same, or better service to customers.

Rankings and ratings

Once the quantitative data has been gathered, it can be useful to rank and rate competitors. Competitors can be assigned a score for each product/service area measured. Companies may weight some of these areas if they are viewed as more important. This approach results in an aggregate measure for each competitor which can be compared to the company's own measures for comparison purposes.

Qualitative research

Qualitative research involves the collection of non-numerical data. It investigates more the **why** decisions rather than the what, where and when decisions which are more associated with quantitative analysis. It is used to gain insight into people's attitudes and behaviours.

In terms of competitor analysis, qualitative research would attempt to discover why customers prefer one product or brand over another. It is largely subjective and can be difficult to undertake, but can provide valuable information for decision making.

One aspect of competitor analysis which could be addressed by qualitative research is brand perception. This is an attempt to find out what customers feel about certain brands. A company may attempt to get customers to assess one of their products compared to a competitor's product. Customers' views may not be in line with the company's view about the product, but the customers' views should be listened to as they know what they like and they are the ones buying the product.

This type of research can provide in depth understanding about customer preferences which can aid product development and marketing strategy. However this can be expensive as it often involves employing a specialist agency to undertake the research.

It is worth noting that much of the information required for successful competitor analysis will be qualitative.

How to undertake qualitative research

While quantitative research can be carried out remotely via online or postal surveys, qualitative research requires more direct interaction.

The aim of this type of research is to understand the reasons why, for example, a customer selected a particular product. This cannot be achieved using a simple questionnaire as discussion is required.

There are a number of ways in which this type of research is undertaken:

- **Observation**. Customers or competitors can be observed in how they buy/sell or use the product. The observation can be with or without the knowledge of the customer or competitor and may involve discussion with the customer or competitor.

- **In-depth interviews**. Directly interviewing customers can give a more detailed insight into their views and specific questions about products can be posed. It may even be possible to interview ex-employees of competitors, although care must be taken that no confidentiality rules are breached. These interviews can be carried out in person, or via the telephone. They would take the form of open questioning to encourage discussion.

- **Focus groups**. These involve selecting a group of individuals who are representative of a target market and questioning them on their preferences. This type of research can also be useful in testing out new product ideas.

- **Analysis**. As with quantitative analysis, once the data from the research has been gathered it must be analysed in order to provide meaningful information which the company can use in developing products and setting strategy.

Benchmarking:

Once you have assembled detailed information about your competitors, you can **benchmark** your performance against theirs.

Strategic benchmarks

- market share
- return on assets
- gross profit margin on sales.

Functional benchmarks

- % deliveries on time
- order costs per order
- order turnaround time
- average stockholding per order.

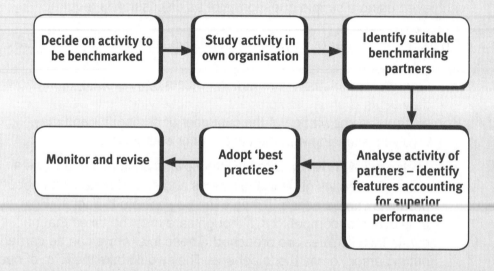

Case study style question 3

RG manufactures a range of sauces and preserves. Their products are marketed as 'high end' products and are sold through the more expensive supermarket chains, and small independent food stores. Its brand is well recognised and it is seen as one of the leading brands within the industry.

Much of the success of RG can be attributed to its dedication to fresh, organic ingredients, unusual flavour combinations and tasteful, stylish packaging.

Although RG has continued to be the market leader and innovator in the last two years, new competitors have entered the market attempting to imitate the company, but offering cheaper products. In response, the Marketing Department at RG is setting up a market analysis team. Its remit will be to undertake competitor analysis to enable the company to keep in touch with the developments of its competitors. This will involve the regular collection of competitor intelligence using qualitative and quantitative research techniques.

Required:

Prepare a briefing note for the market analysis team discussing the techniques of undertaking qualitative and quantitative research and the types of data RG could collect to inform its competitor analysis.

(15 minutes)

5 Big Data

What is Big Data?

There are several definitions of Big Data, the most commonly used referring to **large volumes of data** beyond the normal processing, storage and analysis capacity of typical database application tools. Although Big Data does not refer to any specific quantity, the term is often used when speaking about petabytes and exabytes of data.

The definition can be extended to incorporate the variety of **types of data involved**. Big Data will often include much more than simply financial information and can involve other organisational data which is operational in nature along with other internal and external data which is often unstructured in form.

Big Data management is the storage, administration and control of these vast quantities of both structured and unstructured data. The main aim of Big Data management is to ensure the data stored is high quality and accessible. One of the key challenges of managing Big Data is to identify repeatable business patterns in this unstructured data, significant quantities of which is in text format. Managing such data can lead to significant business benefits such as greater competitive advantage, improved productivity and increasing levels of innovation.

The three V's – the defining characteristics of Big Data

Velocity – Data is now streaming from sources such as social media sites at a virtually constant rate and current processing servers are unable to cope with this flow and generate meaningful real-time analysis.

Volume – More sources of data and an increase in data generation in the digital age combine to increase the volume of data to a potentially unmanageable level.

Variety – Traditionally data was structured and in similar and consistent formats such as Excel spreadsheets and standard databases. Data can now be generated and collected in a huge range of formats including rich text, audio and GPS data amongst others.

Another V which is sometimes added by organisations to the above list is **Veracity.**

Veracity (truthfulness) – it is vital that the organisation gathers data that is accurate. Failure to do so will make analysis meaningless. Match.com has found that when gathering customer data, customers may lie to present themselves in the most positive light possible to prospective partners. This will lead to inaccurate matches. Using nonbiased sources of information (such as purchasing or web browser histories) rather than relying on customer feedback is therefore important.

Why is Big Data so important?

Several major business benefits arise from the ability to manage Big Data successfully, including:

- Innovation and improved product development
- More informed decision making
- Better market segmentation

These benefits can all lead to the gaining of competitive advantage

How is Big Data used in competitor analysis?

Some examples of how Big Data is used:

- Consumer facing organisations monitor social media activity to gain insight into customer behaviour and preferences. This source can also be used to identify and engage brand advocates and detractors and assess responsiveness to advertising campaigns and promotions.

- Sports teams can use data of past fixtures to tracking tactics, player formations, injuries and results to inform future team strategies.

- Manufacturing companies can monitor data from their equipment to determine usage and wear. This allows them to predict the optimal replacement cycle.

- Financial Services organisations can use data on customer activity to carefully segment their customer base and therefore accurately target individuals with relevant offers.

- Health organisations can monitor patient records and admissions to identify risk of recurring problems and intervene to avoid further hospital involvement.

Examples of data which may input into Big Data systems:

- social network traffic
- web server logs
- traffic flow monitoring
- satellite imagery
- streamed audio content
- banking transactions
- audio downloads
- web pages content
- government documentation
- GPS tracking

Big Data analytics

Big Data analytics is the process of scrutinising Big Data to identify patterns, correlations, relationships and other insights. This information can have a wide reaching effect on the organisation's competitive strategy and marketing campaigns and can therefore have a direct impact on future profitability.

Big Data sources may not fit into currently available data warehouses and Big Data analytics may require more advanced software tools than those commonly used in traditional data mining. Open source technologies such as Hadoop are increasingly utilised to manage the constantly evolving data processing requirements of Big Data.

Hadoop is an open source programming framework which enables the processing of large data sets by utilising multiple servers simultaneously.

Big Data examples

Netflix has 44 million users worldwide who watch 2 billion hours of programmes a month. The company uses information gathered from the analysis of viewing habits to inform decisions on which shows to invest in. Analysing past viewing figures and understanding viewer populations and the shows they are likely to watch allows the analysts to predict likely viewing figures before a show has even aired. This can help determine if the show is viable.

Delivery company UPS equips its delivery vehicles with sensors which monitor data on speed, direction, braking performance and other mechanical aspects of the vehicle. Using this data to optimise performance and routes has led to significant improvements, including:

- Over 15 million minutes of idling time were eliminated in one year, saving 103,000 gallons of fuel.

- 1.7 million miles of driving were also eliminated in the same year, saving a further 183,000 gallons of fuel.

Risks associated with Big Data

- Availability of skills to use Big Data systems which is compounded by the fact that many of the systems are rapidly developing and support is not always easily and readily available. There is also an increasing need to combine data analysis skills with deep understanding of industry being analysed and this need is not always recognised.

- Security of data is a major concern in the majority of organisations and if the organisation lacks the resource to manage data then there is likely to be a greater risk of leaks and losses.

- Data Protection issues as organisations collect a greater range of data from increasingly personal sources (e.g. Facebook).

- It is important to recognise that just because something CAN be measured, this does not necessarily mean it should be. There is a risk that valuable time is spent measuring relationships that have no organisational value.

- If organisations are to effectively utilise Big Data, this will require a change in perspective to ensure sense can be made of the information.

- There may be technical difficulties associated with integrating existing data warehousing and Hadoop systems.

Case study style question 4

FM is a multi-channel retailer selling clothes, homewares, furniture and electrical goods through stores, online and via mobile applications. The company operates in a highly competitive environment and seeks to differentiate its products on the basis of good quality and a high level of customer service. In the last twelve months the company has recruited a team of social media experts to develop and manage a Facebook page and Twitter feed. These networks have seen significant increases in traffic since launch and are seen by the company as a key route to understanding customer preferences.

Required:

Write an email to the Managing Director of FM explaining how application of Big Data principles can help FM with competitor analysis.

(15 minutes)

6 Chapter summary

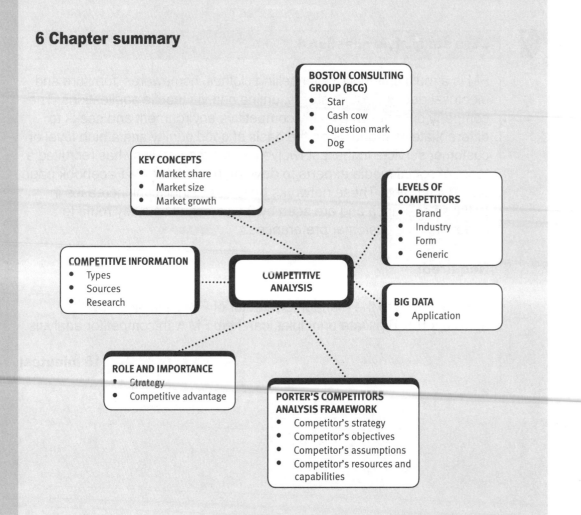

BOSTON CONSULTING GROUP (BCG)
- Star
- Cash cow
- Question mark
- Dog

KEY CONCEPTS
- Market share
- Market size
- Market growth

LEVELS OF COMPETITORS
- Brand
- Industry
- Form
- Generic

COMPETITIVE INFORMATION
- Types
- Sources
- Research

COMPETITIVE ANALYSIS

BIG DATA
- Application

ROLE AND IMPORTANCE
- Strategy
- Competitive advantage

PORTER'S COMPETITORS ANALYSIS FRAMEWORK
- Competitor's strategy
- Competitor's objectives
- Competitor's assumptions
- Competitor's resources and capabilities

End of chapter questions

Question 1

Porter suggested four key aspects of competitor analysis which companies should attempt to identify. Three of the key aspects are included below.

- Identify competitor's strategy
- Identify competitor's key products
- Identify competitor's pricing policy
- Identify competitor's objectives
- Identify competitor's strengths and weaknesses
- Identify competitor's assumptions about the industry

The key aspects which is missing is:

Identify competitor's _____.

Question 2

Match the following statements to the correct category from the Boston Consulting Group model.

This type of product is generally a cash generator and is profitable.	Star
This type of product would have a relatively low market share in a high growth market.	Dog
This product generally requires a large investment in non-current assets and needs to be defended against competitor attacks.	Question mark
The best strategy for this product would be to harvest, divest or niche.	Cash cow

Question 3

DS is a manufacturer, operating in two distinct markets:

Work-wear – this includes industrial overalls, hard hats and protective footwear. These products are sold through MJW's 40 retail outlets across the country and via their website. It is a stable market and MJW have been the recognised market leader for the past five years.

School-wear – this division manufactures generic school-wear in a range of colours which is sold to supermarkets and other large high street retailers. A recent Government directive has encouraged the wearing of school uniforms at all schools in the country. MJW's market share in this market is just behind the market leader. Between them the two companies account for 90% of the market.

Using the BCG model, suggest the category each of the divisions would fall into.

Cash cow	Star	Question mark	Dog

The Work-wear division would be a _____.

The School-wear division would be a _____.

Question 4

According to Kotler's model of levels of competitors, generic competitors can be defined as:

A   Competitors who offer similar products to the same customers

B   Competitors who operate in the same country

C   Competitors whose products satisfy the same needs

D   Competitors who produce similar products but are different in size or structure

E   Competitors who compete for the same income

Question 5

Which of the following techniques would be most likely to be used when undertaking qualitative research? Tick all that apply.

Interviewing customers about their views on the product	
Analysing sales data for the last period	
Testing new products or ideas using focus groups	
Observing customers in how they use the product	
Undertaking ratio analysis	

Question 6

Match the competitor descriptions to the level of competitor defined by Kotler.

Brand	Industry	Form	Generic

- Restaurant X is a family run vegetarian restaurant based in town K. It operates next to restaurant Y which is a franchise of a large worldwide fast food outlet.

- Travel agent W specialises in city breaks and family package holidays while furniture store Z sell reasonably priced, quality furniture.

- Theatre P puts on live music, drama and dance shows throughout the year while Cinema Q shows the latest box office movies.

- Bank A and Bank B are both based in the same country, have similar customer bases and offer very similar banking and insurance products.

Question 7

Qualitative and quantitative research aim to answer different questions. Match the question with the type of research.

What		Qualitative
When		Quantitative
Why		
Where		

Question 8

Which of the following are characteristics of Big Data? Select all that apply.

A   Value

B   Velocity

C   Vision

D   Volume

E   Validation

Question 9

Insert the correct words to complete the sentence about research.

• Qualitative

• Trend

• Why

• Ratios

• Quantitative

• What

_____ research involves the collection of non-numerical data. It investigates the _____ decisions that consumers make.
_____ research involves gathering factual and numerical data which can then be analysed using _____ analysis or _____.

Question 10

Which of the following are seen as advantages for organisations which successfully manage Big Data? Tick all that apply.

More informed decision making	
Improved leadership skills	
Gaining competitive advantage	
Lower IT costs	
Better market segmentation	

Test your understanding answers

Case study style question 1

DRAFT REPORT

To: Finance Director

From: Management Accountant

Date: today

Report on competitive analysis

Why WB should undertake competitive analysis

(a) For any company it is important to know about the market they compete in and this includes an understanding of competitor analysis. In order to maintain growth, companies must be aware of changes in their marketplace. If new competitors have entered the market, this will change the dynamics of the market and the potential profit for all companies competing.

Companies must not view undertaking competitor analysis as a one off exercise, but should continually update it to ensure that they are always aware of new developments in their market and to ensure they are not left behind. This is an important step in strategic planning.

If competitor analysis is not undertaken, or is allowed to get out of date, a new competitor could have entered the market and could reduce the sales of WB. In additional, competitors may be offering new products which are proving popular with customers and WB may need to consider updating its product range. Alternatively others may have tried new products which did not prove successful and this would help WB in deciding what new products to try to develop in the future.

The importance of understanding market growth and market share

(b) Market growth looks at the overall market in which a company competes and how much that market is growing. WB needs to consider the whole market and ascertain if it is growing, and if so if it is experiencing a high or a low level of growth. Market growth is usually measured in sales volume or value.

This information lets WB know the potential for them to expand their business in the future. If the market is experiencing high growth then WB has scope to increase their business by trying to gain the new customers who are entering the market. If the market is experiencing low growth then the opportunities are more limited as all companies in the market will be competing for the same customers.

Market share looks at how much of the overall market one company has. Companies aim to have as large a market share as possible and would like this to be growing. A growing market share suggests that a company is gaining a larger % share of the market.

All companies in the market will be competing for as large a share of the overall market as possible. By undertaking this analysis WB will be able to ascertain how strong their position in the market is and if that position is growing stronger or weaker. The analysis will also tell WB how much scope there is to improve their position in the future.

Case study style question 2

EMAIL

To: J, Marketing director

From: Accountant

Date: today

Subject: The importance of competitor analysis

For any company it is important to know about the markets they compete in so that they can gain an understanding of which other companies are competing in the same market and how they are going to compete against them. Competitor analysis will help the company recognise their own strengths and weaknesses relative to those of their competitors. This will allow them to assess their competitive advantage and how they can use this to drive their business forward. Competitor analysis is therefore an important stage in the formulation of strategy.

In order to maintain growth, companies must be aware of changes in their marketplace. If new competitors have entered the market this will change the dynamics of the market and could affect the company's profitability. Companies must not only undertake competitor analysis but should continually update it to ensure that they are not left behind in terms of market development. If D Company does not undertake adequate competitor analysis, a new company may have entered the market and this could adversely affect their sales, or competitors may be offering a new range of products, or better services than D Company and this could reduce D Company's customer base.

Competitor analysis will:

* Avoid company's sales lagging behind competitors

* Help a company to maintain profitability

* Assist company to increase profitability

* Aid strategic planning

* Allow companies to analyse the goods and services offered by competitors and help them develop their products and services to compete in the way customers want

Competitor information can be gathered from a variety of sources. Some information which is more readily accessible may be less useful, however very specific information which would be most useful may be difficult or costly to obtain.

There are a range of different sources available to D Company which could be accessed to gain information about its potential competitors, for example:

* **Websites of competitors** – this is readily available information, but will only include the information which the competitor wants to share with the public and will be designed to show the company in the most positive way.

* **Annual report and accounts of the competitor**. Again this is information which is available in the public domain for listed companies.

* **Newspaper articles and on-line data sources** on company information.

* **Industry publications, trade media, business management and technical journals**

* **Government reports and statistics** on industrial sectors may be available.

- **Becoming a customer** of the competitor is a good way of sampling the products and service provided by them.

- **Market research reports** and reviews produced by specialist firms might provide information on market share and marketing activity within the chosen industry.

- **Customer market research** could be independently commissioned to establish consumer attitudes and awareness towards D Company's potential competitors in the various regions. This would potentially be the most useful information as the questions could be specific, but this is a costly way to gather information.

Hopefully this is helpful to you. Please let me know is you need any more information on this.

Regards.

Accountant

Case study style question 3

BRIEFING NOTE

To: Market analysis team

Subject: Qualitative and quantitative research

The overriding purpose of research is to gain competitor intelligence in order to understand competitor actions. This would help RG in understanding the strengths and weaknesses of both its known competitors and also its potential competitors and help predict likely competitor behaviour.

Qualitative and quantitative research techniques can be used to collect information. This should be viewed as a continual process, hence the setting up of the market analysis team will enable RG to continuously monitor its competitor rivals for signs of activity and scan the industry for the emergence of potential new rivals.

Qualitative research data would involve RG collecting non-numerical data from in-depth interviews or focus groups. This type of data could be used by the market analysis team to help gain an insight into customers (and customers of its competitors) on attitudes and behaviours.

For instance, information could be collected to help in understanding the decision making process in purchasing sauces and preserves and why consumers prefer one brand over another. It could also be used to test new product ideas, and to gain feedback on consumers' attitudes towards RG's competitors' products.

Quantitative research is often undertaken by conducting surveys with customers and the customers of competitors. Surveys can be undertaken in a number of ways, for example by questionnaires sent electronically via email, face-to-face, or by telephone. The results will generate numerical data and statistical methods can be used to analyse the data. This type of survey research could be used to quantify levels of consumer satisfaction or establish brand awareness of RG. This type of data could also be used to help understand the customer profiles for its own products and for those of its competitors. This, in turn, could help in developing segmentation strategies. Quantitative research could also assist RG understand and track its market share, providing trend data on its competitors' share of the market. This will help RG understand the level of competition it faces and the nature of the market. The results could input into future strategy development decisions, for instance on how RG should respond to its competitors' strategies.

Quantitative data can also be used to collect data which would enable RG to benchmark its performance against its competitors.

Case study style question 4

EMAIL

To: Managing Director, FM

From: Accountant

Date: today

Subject: The application of Big Data principles

Big Data management involves using sophisticated systems to gather, store and analyse large volumes of data in a variety of structured and unstructured formats.

A company like FM is likely to generate large quantities of data about their customers through the various different channels and the use of Customer Relationship Management software in conjunction with Big Data systems will help them to gain significant insight into customer preferences. Traditionally these insights would have been limited to customers already transacting with FM however the emergence of social networks and the data generated within these networks allows companies to also obtain useful insights into their competitors' activities.

Data insight experts will be able to monitor the social media feeds of competitors and gather information regarding the type of customers, their preferences, their complaints and positive comments about the competitor offering. Similar information can be obtained from FM's social networks and compared to competitive information to identify areas of strength and weakness.

As this data is likely to be largely unstructured, Big Data principles will be important in collating it into useful formats in order to gain a sufficient understanding.

There are certain issues involved in using competitor information in this way as the information is limited to those customers currently engaging in social interaction with FM and its competitors. However this is a growing sample and the company will still be making relevant comparisons as the sample for FM is likely to have similar characteristics to the competitor samples.

FM will also have to take into account the fact that they will largely see the extreme views of those customers who are extremely positive or very unhappy with the products but these are the two groups of customers who usually need the most management so this can give useful insights.

FM will have to take care that the target users and objectives of the Facebook page and Twitter feed are similar for each company as some companies use social media as a tool to send out information regarding products and offers, some use it to monitor customer feedback and some offer a more informative and interactive social network to encourage customer engagement. If the competitor networks are set up for different reasons then the information produced may not be as useful to FM.

Hopefully this is helpful to you. Please let me know is you need any more information on this.

Question 1

The missing aspect is:

Identify competitor's **resources and capabilities**.

Porter suggested the following four aspects of competitor analysis:

- Identify competitor's strategy
- Identify competitor's objectives
- Identify competitor's assumptions about the industry
- Identify competitor's resources and capabilities

Question 2

The complete BGC model is shown below:

Boston Consulting Group Growth / Share Matrix

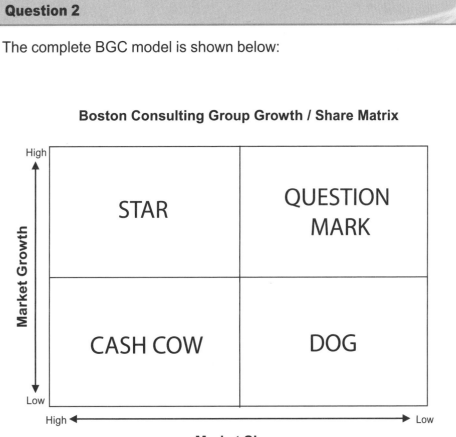

The type of product which is generally a cash generator and is profitable is a **cash cow**.

The type of product which would have a relatively low market share in a high growth market is a **question mark**.

The product which generally requires a large investment in non-current assets and needs to be defended against competitor attacks is a **star**.

The best strategy for a **dog** would be to harvest, divest or niche.

Question 3

Work-wear division is a **cash cow**.

School-wear division is a **star**.

The BCG matrix breaks a business into its component units or products and then considers the performance of each unit/product in terms of the market growth and the relative market share.

- High market growth/high market share – Star
- High market growth/low market share – Question mark/Problem child
- Low market growth/high market share – Cash cow
- Low market growth/high market share – Dog

For DS, the future strategies for the products should be to continue with its work-wear business, and if possible try to extend it and should try to build the school-wear division.

Question 4

E   Competitors who compete for the same income

Kotler identified four levels of competitors:

Brand competitors. Firms who offer similar products to the same customers

Industry competitors. Suppliers who produce similar goods but who are not necessarily the same size or structure

Form competitors. Suppliers whose products satisfy the same needs

Generic competitors. Competitors who compete for the same income

Question 5

Interviewing customers about their views on the product	√
Analysing sales data for the last period	
Testing new products or ideas using focus groups	√
Observing customers in how they use the product	√
Undertaking ratio analysis	

Qualitative research involves the collection of non-numerical data. It investigates more the **why** decisions rather than the what, where and when decisions which are more associated with quantitative analysis. It is used to gain insight into people's attitudes and behaviours.

Qualitative research can be carried out using a number of methods. The main ways are using Interviews, focus groups, observations and analysis.

Question 6

X and Y would be **industry competitors**. (Suppliers who produce similar goods but who are not necessarily the same size or structure)

W and Z would be **generic competitors**. (Competitors who compete for the same income)

P and Q would be **form competitors**. (Suppliers whose products satisfy the same needs)

A and B would be b**rand competitors**. (Firms who offer similar products to the same customers)

Question 7

What	Quantitative
When	Quantitative
Why	Qualitative
Where	Quantitative

Quantitative research will tend to be factual and numerical, while qualitative research aims to understand people's attitudes and behaviours.

Question 8

B   Velocity

D   Volume

The three characteristic of big data are:

Velocity (speed) – Data is now streaming from sources such as social media sites at a virtually constant rate and current processing servers are unable to cope with this flow and generate meaningful real-time analysis.

Volume – More sources of data and an increase in data generation in the digital age combine to increase the volume of data to a potentially unmanageable level.

Variety – Traditionally data was structured and in similar and consistent formats such as Excel spreadsheets and standard databases. Data can now be generated and collected in a huge range of formats including rich text, audio and GPS data amongst others.

Another V which is sometimes added by organisations to the above list is Veracity (truthfulness).

Question 9

Qualitative research involves the collection of non-numerical data. It investigates the **why** decisions that consumers make. **Quantitative** research involves gathering factual and numerical data which can then be analysed using **trend** analysis or **ratios**.

Question 10

More informed decision making	√
Improved leadership skills	
Gaining competitive advantage	√
Lower IT costs	
Better market segmentation	√

Big data offers many advantages to organisations such as:

- Innovation and improved product development
- More informed decision making
- Better market segmentation

Good use of big data can lead to the gaining of competitive advantage.

6

Leadership and management

Chapter learning objectives

Discuss the concepts of leadership and management

1 Session content diagram

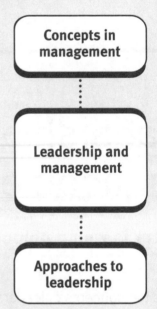

2 What is leadership and management?

Sometimes management and leadership are seen as synonymous. There is, however, a difference between the two and it does not follow that every leader is a manager, or that every manager is a leader.

Management

Management is the process of getting things done through the efforts of other people. It focuses on procedures and results. Managers tend to react to specific situations and be more concerned with solving short-term problems. Management suggests more formality and the term 'manager' refers to a position within a structured organisation and with prescribed roles.

A century ago, in 1916, Fayol identified the common features of management. These are still relevant to management today.

He identified the common features as:

- Planning.
- Organising resources to achieve organisational objectives.
- Co-ordinating company and individual objectives.
- Commanding – giving orders and instructions.
- Controlling – comparing actual performance with expected or budgeted performance.

Leadership

Leadership, on the other hand, can be viewed as providing direction, creating a vision, and then influencing others to share that vision and work towards the achievement of organisational goals. Leadership can be seen as 'getting other people to do things willingly' and can occur at all different levels within the organisation.

3 Important concepts in management

Individuals within the workplace have different relationships with each other. To be able to analyse the nature of management relationships it is necessary to understand a number of important concepts.

- Power
- Authority
- Responsibility
- Accountability
- Empowerment
- Delegation

Power

Power is **the capacity to exert influence**, to make someone act according to your own preferences.

Types of power

French and Raven identified five possible bases of a leader's power:

- **Reward power** – a person has power over another because they can give rewards, such as promotions or financial rewards.
- **Coercive power** – enables a person to give punishments to others: for example, to dismiss, suspend, reprimand them, or make them carry out unpleasant tasks.

  Reward power and coercive power are similar but limited in application because they are limited to the size of the reward or punishment that can be given. For example, there isn't much a manager could get a subordinate to do for a $5 reward (or fine), but there are many, many things they might do for a $50,000 reward (or fine).

- **Referent power** – based upon the identification with the person who has charisma, or the desire to be like that person. It could be regarded as 'imitative' power which is often seen in the way children imitate their parents. Think of the best boss you've ever had – what did you like about them, did it encourage you to act in a similar way?

  Psychologists believe that referent power is perhaps the most extensive since it can be exercised when the holder is not present or has no intention of exercising influence.

- **Expert power** – based upon doing what the expert says since they are the expert. You will have a measure of expert power when you join CIMA. People will do as you suggest because you have studied and have qualified. However expert power only extends to the expert's field of expertise.

- **Legitimate power** – based on agreement and commonly-held values which allow one person to have power over another person: for example, an older person, or one who has longer service. In some societies it is customary for a man to be the 'head of the family', or in other societies elders make decisions due to their age and experience.

Case study style question 1

G, the senior partner of L, a medium sized accountancy firm, has worked for L for over twenty years and has a sound knowledge and understanding of the different activities of the firm's business. Over the years, G has become known for his fairness in how he manages staff. He is also well liked and respected for his enthusiastic approach. He always has time to encourage and mentor younger members of staff.

The firm has recently invested in new technology which will improve the effectiveness of its office systems, but will mean the roles and responsibilities of the support staff will change. G, has taken on the unenviable role of leading the project to introduce the technology and new working practices. He knows that the project will be met with resistance from some members of staff and he will need to draw on various sources of power to ensure the changes are successfully implemented.

Required:

Write an email to G explaining the different sources of power that he has which will help him in introducing the changes.

(15 minutes)

Authority

Authority is the **right to exercise power** such as hiring and firing or buying and selling on behalf of the organisation; the right that an individual has to require certain actions of others; the right to do or act.

Max Weber proposed that authority legitimises the exercise of power within the structure and rules of the organisation. Hence, it allows individuals within an organisation to issue instructions for others to follow. Weber defined three bases for such authority as follows:

Charismatic authority – Here the individual has some special quality of personality which sets the leader apart. Because the charismatic power in the organisation is so dependent on the leader, difficulties arise when he or she has to be replaced. Unless someone else is available, who also possesses the necessary charisma, the organisation either decays or survives in another form.

Traditional authority – This authority is based upon custom and practice. The personality of the leader is irrelevant: he or she inherits the status of leader because of the long-standing belief in the natural right to 'rule' which is sometimes handed down.

Rational-legal authority – This is Weber's classic bureaucracy. Power comes from the individual's position in the organisation chart. The ability to perform particular functions and their operations is based on following a set of written rules. This authority is not personal but is vested, impersonally, in the position held.

The link between authority and power bases

Weber's three types of authority (charismatic, traditional and rational-legal) can be linked to the French and Raven power bases as follows:

Power base	Authority base
Coercive and Legitimate	Traditional
Reward and Referent	Charismatic
Expert	Rational-legal

Responsibility

Responsibility involves **the obligation of an individual who occupies a particular position in the organisation to perform certain duties, tasks or make certain decisions**.

Responsibility means the right to hold subordinates accountable for personal performance and achievement of the targets specified by the organisation's plans. It is the obligation to use authority to see duties are performed.

The scope of responsibility must correspond to the scope of authority given

All managers should have both responsibility and authority appropriate to their role. If these are not in balance, it can cause serious problems.

Responsibility without authority – this may occur when a manager is held responsible for, say, timekeeping, but does not have the authority to discipline subordinates who are regularly late. The manager is likely to become frustrated and demotivated as they lack the power and authority needed to meet the targets they have been made responsible for.

Authority without responsibility – an HR department may have the authority to employ new members of staff, but are not held responsible for the quality of the employees that they have selected. Managers who are not made accountable for their decisions and actions may act irresponsibly, as they do not expect to suffer any negative consequences.

Accountability

Accountability describes **the need for individuals to explain and justify any failure to fulfil their responsibilities to their superiors** in the hierarchy. It refers to being called to account for one's actions and results.

Empowerment

Employee empowerment is where **employees are given autonomy and responsibility to undertake tasks without being directed at each step by management**. To be able to empower staff, management has to have trust in their capabilities and be willing to allow employees to make decisions, within set limits.

Companies can benefit from empowering staff as the managers will not feel the need to micro-manage every aspect of the employees behaviour, which should free up management time. From the point of view of the employees, they will feel valued and motivated.

To promote empowerment, managers should:

- Set clear boundaries and ensure employees know what is expected from them
- Actively encourage employee development
- Communicate openly with employees and adopt and open-door policy
- Allow employees to contribute and listen to their views
- Offer regular feedback
- Lead by example.

Delegation

Delegation is one of the main functions of effective management. It is the process whereby managers assign part of their authority to a subordinate to fulfil their duties. However, delegation can only occur if the manager initially possesses the authority to delegate. **Responsibility can never be delegated.** A superior is always responsible for the actions of his subordinates and cannot evade this responsibility by delegation.

Benefits of delegation

There are many practical reasons why managers should delegate:

- Without it the chief executive would be responsible for everything – individuals have physical and mental limitations.
- Allows for career planning and development, aids continuity and cover for absence.
- Allows for better decision making; those closer to the problem make the decision, allowing higher-level managers to spend more time on strategic issues.
- Allowing the individual with the appropriate skills to make the decision improves time management.
- Gives people more interesting work, increases job satisfaction for subordinates; increased motivation encourages better work.

Reluctance to delegate

Despite the benefits many managers are reluctant to delegate, preferring to deal with routine matters themselves in addition to the more major aspects of their duties. There are several reasons for this:

- Managers often believe that their subordinates are not able or experienced enough to perform the tasks.

- Managers believe that doing routine tasks enables them to keep in touch with what is happening in the other areas of their department.

- Where a manager feels insecure they will invariably be reluctant to pass any authority to a subordinate.

- An insecure manager may fear that the subordinate will do a better job that they can.

- Some managers do not know how or what to delegate.

- Managers fear losing control.

- Initially delegation can take a lot of a manager's time and a common reason for not delegating is that the managers feel they could complete the job quicker if they did it themselves.

Effective delegation

Koontz and O'Donnell state that to delegate effectively a manager must:

- define the limits of authority delegated to their subordinate.

- satisfy themselves that the subordinate is competent to exercise that authority.

- discipline themselves to permit the subordinate the full use of that authority without constant checks and interference.

In planning delegation therefore, a manager must ensure that:

- Too much is not delegated to totally overload a subordinate.

- The subordinate has reasonable skill and experience in the area concerned.

- Appropriate authority is delegated.

- Monitoring and control are possible.

- There is not a feeling of 'passing the buck' or 'opting out'.

- All concerned know that the task has been delegated.

- Time is set aside for coaching and guiding.

Case study style question 2

H has for some time been in charge of a department which was producing satisfactory results before he took over. However, recently, several of his staff have asked whether jobs in other similar departments are available. There have also been a number of unexpected mistakes, and information has not been transmitted properly.

You are H's manager. As a result of your concern you have been keeping an eye on the situation. You have found that H comes in early every day, stays late, takes large amounts of work home with him, and is showing definite signs of strain. In the meantime his staff appear bored and disinterested. You have arranged a meeting with H to discuss these issues.

Required:

Write briefing notes for the meeting covering the following:

(a) Describing the possible causes of this situation.

(10 minutes)

(b) Explaining the principles for effective delegation.

(10 minutes)

(c) Commenting on the advantages to both manager and subordinate of effective delegation.

(10 minutes)

Methods of delegation

There are different methods of delegation, which vary in effectiveness:

- *Abdication* – leave issues without any formal delegation, which is very crude and usually an ineffective method.

- *Custom and practice* – an age-old system, the most junior member of staff opens the mail, gets the coffee and so on.

- *Explanation* – manager's brief subordinates along the lines of how the task should be done. (not too little and not too much – a fine balance that requires judgement).

- *Consultation* – Prior consultation is considered to be important and very effective. People, if organised, are immensely powerful; by contributing or withholding their cooperation they make the task a success or failure. Managers admit that sometimes good ideas come from below. In fact the point of view of the person nearest the scene of action is more likely to be relevant.

4 Classical and contemporary theories of management

The study of management theory and development of ideas on effective management practice helps in providing an understanding of the principles underlying the process of management and which in turn influences management behaviour in organisations. The main schools of management thinking can be grouped according to their broad approaches as shown below:

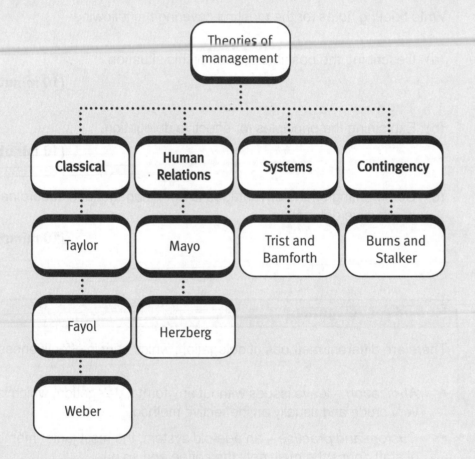

Classical theories

The classical approach to management emphasises the technical and economic aspects of organisations. It assumes that behaviour in organisations is rational and logical. There are different approaches within the Classical School which can be identified as Scientific Management (Taylor), Administrative Management (Fayol) and Bureaucracy (Weber).

The foundation on which the various theories developed was that management could be learnt and codified. These ideas were developed in an era when mass production and economies of scale were viewed as central to business success. Although some of these theories were developed over a century ago they do continue to inform management practice today.

There are some common interests that all these different perspectives focus on:

- The purpose and structure of organisations and planning of work.

- The technical requirements of each job.

- The principles of management.

Scientific management (Taylor)

The objective of management is to secure the maximum prosperity for both employer and employee:

- One best approach to the job, using work study methods

- Once employees were trained in the best approach then payment should be based on piece-rate (believed money to be a motivator)

- Well-trained employees delivered high productivity

- Win:win for both employee and organisation.

Taylor recognised that if specialised knowledge and skills were concentrated in the hands of well-trained and able employees, there would be an improvement in productivity. He therefore broke jobs down into separate functions and then gave each function to an individual. Taylor believed that it was only through the effective use of control by specialists that best use would be made of the resources available.

Administrative management (Fayol)

Fayol's approach was to view problems from the managerial aspects and to specifically analyse the work of management, stressing that most management features had universal application.

As well as the 5 main functions of management (planning, organising, coordinating, commanding and controlling), Fayol also proposed 14 principles of management:

(1) *Division of work* and specialisation should be encouraged since it leads to greater productivity.

(2) *Authority* to issue commands should be accompanied by responsibility.

(3) *Leadership.* Good leadership should be provided.

(4) *Unity of command.* There should be one person responsible to one boss. Wherever possible, a subordinate should be responsible to one superior. Divided authority and responsibility complicates delegation of duties, responsibilities and authority.

(5) *Unity of direction.* A single plan should be laid down for all employees engaged in the same work activities. In other words, one head and one plan for a group of activities with the same objective.

(6) *Remuneration.* The system of reward should be related where possible to the individual's wants and needs. Pay should be fair to both the employee and the firm.

(7) *Centralisation.* This is always present to a greater or lesser degree. The degree of centralisation or decentralisation should vary according to the circumstances of the organisation.

(8) *Scalar chain.* A clear line of authority is necessary to ensure that managers know who can delegate to them, who they can delegate to, and to whom they are accountable. It should be possible to trace the line of authority from top to bottom of an organisation and it is essential to have vertical and lateral communications.

(9) *Order.* There should be a place for everything and everything in its place. In order to minimise lost time and unnecessary handling of materials, it is essential to have material order and social order in an organisation.

(10) *Equity.* A combination of kindness and justice is required in dealing with employees.

(11) *Subordination of individual interests to the general interest.* The interests and goals of individual members of the organisation should be subservient to the overall organisational goals. The interest of one individual should not prevail over the general good.

(12) *Stability of tenure of personnel.* Successful businesses require stability of tenure. People need to be given time to settle into their jobs and management should avoid a 'hire and fire' mentality.

(13) *Initiative.* All employees should be given the opportunity to use their initiative. All staff need to be encouraged to show initiative within the limits of their authority.

(14) *Esprit de corps.* It is the task of management to foster *esprit de corps*, that is, to encourage harmony and teamwork.

Bureaucratic management (Weber)

Max Weber developed his model of the 'ideal type' of bureaucracy, in which he explored the characteristics of a rational form of organisation. Today, the term bureaucracy tends to have many negative connotations, but Weber used it to describe what he believed to be potentially the most efficient form of organisation.

Weber's bureaucracy is based on formalisation and standardisation.

- Based on hierarchy of authority
- Strict rules and regulations govern decision making
- Specialisation in duties, segregated 'offices' and levels.

Nowadays, most large organisations, will be bureaucratic. Because of the formal nature of this type of organisation, the main disadvantages are:

- slow response to change, as many rules have to be changed
- lack of speedy communication owing to the segregated 'offices' and levels
- little need for involving staff in decision-making
- rules stifle initiative and innovative ideas, preventing development
- no recognition of very important informal relationships.

This type of organisational culture is **not suitable if the firm operates in a dynamic changing environment.**

The main characteristics of bureaucracy

Weber listed the main characteristics of bureaucracy:

- *Specialisation.* Clear division of labour, so that each member has well-defined roles and responsibilities.
- *Hierarchy.* A hierarchy of authority, in which offices are linked through a clear chain of command.
- *Rules.* Strict rules and procedures govern decision-making and conduct.
- *Impersonality.* Objective and rational decisions rather than personal preferences.

- *Appointed officials.* Managers are selected by their qualifications, education or training.

- *Career officials.* Managers pursue their career within the bureaucracy and work within a defined salary structure.

- *Full-time officials.* Professionalism requires commitment.

- *Public/private division.* Money is used in a limited liability framework to prevent family money being used, as this creates conservatism because of personal risk.

5 The human relations school

In the 1930s researchers started studying the behaviour of people in groups. While the classical theories viewed workers as components in the system, and focused on processes and procedures, these researchers started looking at the effects of social interaction on motivation and productivity. This was the beginning of Human Relations School.

Mayo

Elton Mayo, together with several colleagues, carried out the famous Hawthorne investigations for the Western Electric Company at its Hawthorne works in Chicago during the 1920s and 1930s.

Over the course of five years, Mayo's team altered the worker's working conditions and then monitored how the working conditions affected the workers morale and productivity. The changes in working conditions included changes in working hours, rest breaks, lighting, humidity, and temperature. The changes were explained to the workers prior to implementation.

At the end of the five year period, the working conditions, reverted back to the conditions before the experiment began. Unexpectedly the workers morale and productivity rose to levels higher than before and during the experiments. This led to the conclusion that the need for recognition, security and sense of belonging is more important in determining workers' morale and productivity than the physical conditions under which he/she works.

Mayo's findings have contributed to organisational development in terms of human relations and motivation theory.

More on Mayo

From his experiments, Mayo concluded that workers were motivated by more than self interest and instead the following applied:

- There is an unwritten understanding between the worker and employer regarding what is expected from them; Mayo called this the psychological contract.

- A worker's motivation can be increased by showing an interest in them.

- Work is a group activity, team work can increase a worker's motivation as it allows people to form strong working relationships and increases trust between the workers.

- Workers are motivated by the social aspect of work, as demonstrated by the workers socialising during and outside work and the subsequent increase in motivation.

- The communication between workers and management influences workers' morale and productivity. Workers are motivated through a good working relationship with management.

Herzberg

Frederick Herzberg carried forward Mayo's emphasis on the identification of the motivational needs of individuals. His two factor theory describes motivational and hygiene factors.

- **Hygiene factors** – are based on a need to avoid unpleasantness. They do not provide any long-term motivating power. A lack of satisfaction of hygiene factors will demotivate staff.
- **Motivators** – satisfy a need for personal growth. Satisfaction of motivator factors can encourage staff to work harder.

Hertzberg believed that only motivators can move employees to action: the hygiene factors cannot. They can only prevent dissatisfaction.

In order to motivate the workforce management must avoid dissatisfaction and put in place motivators to encourage the staff.

Hygiene factors

To avoid dissatisfaction there should be:

- Policies and procedures for staff treatment.
- Suitable level and quality of supervision.
- Pleasant physical and working conditions.
- Appropriate level of salary and status for the job.
- Team working.

Motivational factors

In order to motivate staff managers should provide:

- Sense of accomplishment (achievement) through setting targets.
- Recognition of good work.
- Increasing levels of responsibility.
- Career advancement.
- Attraction of the job.

Herzberg felt that 'you can't motivate dissatisfied people'. Satisfiers or motivators will only generate job satisfaction if the hygiene factors are present.

Herzberg's theory of motivation illustration

C&G Local Authority employs around 8,000 members of staff. It operates as a traditional, formal governmental type of organisation. Over the last few years it has recognised a problem regarding its junior management level in that many of them are failing to meet the expected level of performance.

A team has been set up to investigate the problem and they have decided to hold a series of meetings with all levels of management. Initially they found that the junior managers were reluctant to participate in the meetings, saying that they could see no real value in them. 'We have seen it all before' was a typical response. After the meetings, the team produced a report which identified three main problem areas.

Firstly, it became apparent that the level of morale for all staff was low. Lack of facilities and pressure of work appeared to be the main grievance. There appeared however to be a deeper problem, that of mistrust between the staff as a whole and senior management. The reason for this was unclear.

The second problem appeared to be that junior managers were regarded by staff as poor at managing their sections. In response, the junior managers said that their positions in general were unclear; there were no clear lines of authority, command or responsibility which allowed them to make decisions for their departments. In addition many quoted their roles as being menial and highlighted funding shortages, unrealistic targets, little recognition of their position, no job descriptions and lack of training as problems.

Job security was the third issue. Financial cutbacks and changes in service levels had led to rumours of substantial cutbacks in staff. Rumours were especially strong amongst the junior management. It was felt that new, younger staff would be better trained and would be likely to replace them.

In all, the problems had shown themselves in high labour turnover, which in addition to the problems already outlined, were blamed on low salaries, little opportunity for personal advancement and poor working conditions.

Using Herzberg's theory of motivation, the attitude of the junior managers can be explained as follows:

The case illustrates Herzberg's motivation theory, which attempts to explain those factors which motivate the individual by identifying and satisfying the individual's needs, desires and the goals pursued to satisfy these desires.

This theory is based upon the idea that motivation factors can be separated into hygiene factors and motivation factors and is therefore often referred to as a 'two need system.' These two separate 'needs' are the need to avoid unpleasantness and discomfort and, at the other end of the motivational scale, the need for personal development.

A shortage of those factors which positively encourage employees (motivating factors) will cause those employees to focus on other, non job related factors, the so called 'hygiene' factors. These are illustrated in the case with the attitude of the junior management to senior management and their concerns for example with shortages, targets, recognition and training and 'we've seen it all before'.

The most important part of this theory of motivation is that the main motivating factors are not in the environment but in the intrinsic value and satisfaction gained from the job itself. It follows therefore that the job itself must have challenge, scope for enrichment and be of interest to the job holder. This is not the case in the scenario; there appears to be little or no intrinsic satisfaction from the junior manager's work, illustrated by them regarding themselves and their role as menial and their lack of responsibility and decision making powers within their own departments.

Motivators (or 'satisfiers') are those factors directly concerned with the satisfaction gained from the job itself, the sense of achievement, level of recognition, the intrinsic value felt of the job itself, level of responsibility, opportunities for advancement and the status provided by the job. Motivators lead to satisfaction because of the need for growth and a sense of self achievement. Clearly, none of this applies to the junior managers of C&G Local Authority.

A lack of motivators leads to over concentration on hygiene factors; that is those negative factors which can be seen and therefore form the basis of complaint and concern.

Hygiene (or maintenance) factors lead to job dissatisfaction because of the need to avoid unpleasantness. They are so called because they can in turn be avoided by the use of 'hygienic' methods i.e. they can be prevented. Attention to these hygiene factors prevents dissatisfaction but does not on its own provide motivation. Hygiene factors (or 'dissatisfiers') are concerned with those factors associated with, but not directly a part of, the job itself. These can be detected in the scenario; salary and the perceived differences with others, job security, working conditions, the quality of management, organisational policy and administration and interpersonal relations.

Understanding Herzberg's theory identifies the nature of intrinsic satisfaction that can be obtained from the work itself, draws attention to job design and makes managers aware that problems of motivation may not necessarily be directly associated with the work.

Maslow's hierarchy of needs

Maslow developed a hierarchy of needs, shown below.

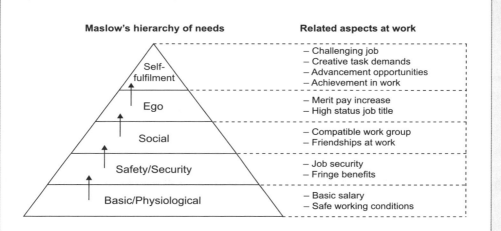

According to the model, each individual has a set of needs which can be arranged in a hierarchy. The above diagram has shown the hierarchy in a business context. The largest and most fundamental needs, such as basic pay and safe working conditions are shown at the bottom, and the need for self-fulfilment is at the top, moving through aspects such as job security, friendships at work and status.

The lowest needs must be satisfied first, only then can an individual move to the next level. This can be used as a motivational tool, if the management can determine where individuals are on the hierarchy, they will know that the next level can be used in motivating staff.

6 Systems theory

Systems theory is an approach to organisational work design which takes account of social aspects and technical aspects. It looks at the interaction between people and technology within the organisation.

Trist and Bamforth

Trist and Bamforth developed a socio-technical systems theory. While he was working at the Tavistock Institute, Trist's most famous research was into the structure and operation of the 'longwall' method of mining in County Durham in the 1940s as it highlighted the interaction between social needs and technological activities. The 'longwall' method introduced new cutting equipment which widened the narrow coal 'face' into a 'longwall'. But very soon the low morale, high absenteeism and deteriorating relationships were so serious that the Tavistock Institute was invited to investigate causes and possible solutions to the problems.

Trist and Bamforth diagnosed that although the new methods had been introduced 'scientifically':

- close-knit groups had been broken up
- communication was difficult because of the geographical spread of workers
- new payment schemes caused jealousy among the workforce
- too much specialisation and individuality was built into the jobs.

The mine owners had not considered the effects on the workforce, showing an ignorance of individual and group needs at work, especially in such a traditionally close-linked occupation as mining. The social and technological factors are interlinked and cannot be treated in isolation. Managers should note that this interaction between the technical and social aspects of work, if ignored, will inevitably bring problems.

7 Contingency theory

Managers, researchers and consultants often found that the methods suggested by the classical management schools did not always work. The idea of one approach being right, whether it be the school of scientific management, classical, human relations or systems, is rejected in favour of contingency. The contingency view suggests that the effectiveness of various managerial practices, styles and techniques will **vary according to the particular circumstances of the situation**.

Mechanistic versus Organic Organisations (Burns and Stalker)

Burns and Stalker (1961) distinguished between mechanistic and organic organisations. Burns is quoted as saying: 'The beginning of administrative wisdom is the awareness that there is no one best way of designing a management system.' Burns and Stalker studied the way in which high-technology industries were being introduced into Scotland. The difficulties experienced by low-technology companies in the conversion process to high technology highlighted many organisation structural problems.

Burns and Stalker's studies led them to distinguish between two major types of organisations – **mechanistic** and **organic**. However, they considered these two systems to be located at opposite ends of a continuum, with various combinations in between.

Features of a mechanistic organisation:

- High degree of task specialisation.

- Responsibilities and authority clearly defined.

- Coordination and communication – a responsibility of each management level.

- Selectivity in the release of top level information to subordinates.

- Great emphasis on the organisational hierarchy's ability to develop loyalty and obedience.

- Employees are often locally recruited.

- The mechanistic system was seen to be appropriate in fairly stable conditions where the management of change was not seen to be an important factor. The relationship with Weber's bureaucracy is obvious.

Features of an organic organisation

- Skills, experience and specialist knowledge recognised as valuable resources.

- Integration of efforts via lateral, vertical and diagonal communication channels.

- Leadership based on consultation and involvement in problem-solving.

- Commitment to task achievement, survival and growth more important than loyalty and obedience.

- Employees are recruited from a variety of sources.

- The organic system is seen to be more responsive to change, and is therefore recommended for organisations moving into periods of rapid changes in technology, market orientation, or tasks.

The appropriateness of organisational structure to its environment is a cornerstone of contingency theory.

Contingency theory – Joan Woodward's Essex Studies

Joan Woodward found that by knowing an organisation's primary system of production, you could predict their structure. This view states that all companies should be organised differently according to the underlying production process and product, with the external environment also being considered.

In her analysis of 100 companies (which ranged in size from 100 to 1000 employees), she identified ten types of technology which were condensed into three main groups.

These are:

- *unit and small batch production* – typical of 'craft' industries

- *large batch and mass production* – for example, cars

- *process production* – for example, cement, oil, and food processing.

Differences in production type accounted for many of the differences in organisation structure:

- *Unit and small batch production companies* were found to have short hierarchies, with no manager very far from production work, and a limited number of administrative controls. They tended to involve much smaller groups of more highly skilled workers and job satisfaction was higher.

- *Large batch and mass production companies* have shorter lines of command and thus fewer managers. There were a traditionally larger number of direct operatives. The large number of semi-skilled workers required for mass production means that the span of control of supervisors is very wide, and this may create an environment where human and industrial relations are strained. Job satisfaction was lowest.

- In *heavily mechanised process companies* taller hierarchies were found to exist, but with levels of committee rather than straight-line instruction. Since technical expertise is important, people were highly skilled, often graduates, with most of the organisation headcount being involved in administration. Control was far easier in these organisations. Satisfaction was middling.

Large batch and mass production systems, because of the high numbers of specialists involved, create more paperwork and demand clearer cut definitions of duties.

Woodward's studies indicated how four major factors in any company (task; technology; people; and structure) were inter-related, and that management needed to be aware that when one of these factors changed, it was vital to recognise the effects this change would have on the other factors. These studies contributed to the debate as to whether technology forced organisations to change their structure and culture.

Contemporary perspectives

Gareth Morgan has argued that we can view organisations in different ways as we try to understand them. We are rarely aware of the image of organisations we take for granted but, just like the photographs of the Parthenon from different perspectives, they fundamentally influence what we see and the explanations we put forward to make sense of it. However, the Parthenon can be approached from different directions, though not all are equally easy. Different angles will give different perspectives, and by arriving very early in the morning you could get a photograph with unusual lighting and fewer people in it.

The same is true of the way we look at organisations and the process of management.

From one perspective it is helpful to think of organisations as machines, in which the various jobs and departments are carefully designed to work smoothly together to perform certain functions effectively. This is certainly the view implicit in the early classical theories such as scientific management.

The view of organisations as machines provides some useful insights, but also imposes limitations, which in some circumstances can be severe. For example, the use of basic costing techniques in large multi-product firms may result in misleading information for decision-making. In this type of situation, more sophisticated models which recognise the more complicated nature of the organisation, may be more appropriate.

The limitations of mechanistic perspectives on organisations are as follows:

- They can create organisational forms that have great difficulty adapting to changed circumstances.

- They can result in mindless and unquestioning bureaucracy.

- They can have unanticipated and undesirable consequences as the interests of those working in the organisation take precedence over the goals the organisation was designed to achieve.

- They can have dehumanising effects upon employees, especially those at the lower levels of the organisational hierarchy (Morgan, 1986).

Morgan goes on to argue that there are other ways of viewing organisations that lead to different insights. It is not possible to go into all of those here, but two other perspectives he identifies are the view of organisations as organisms and organisations as cultures. It is important for managers to be able to examine organisational problems from more than one perspective in their search for effectiveness.

8 Leadership

Leadership is influencing others to do what he or she wants them to do; it involves human interaction and is often associated with the willing and enthusiastic behaviour of followers – the ability to influence needs the permission of those to be influenced. Leadership is related to motivation, interpersonal behaviour and the process of communication.

Leadership is a dynamic process and is very important at all levels within the organisation, from the board to the shop floor. It does not necessarily take place within the hierarchical structure of the organisation. A leader may have no formal title at all and may rely on personal traits and style to influence followers.

Leadership comes about in a number of different ways:

- Some leaders are **elected** – in politics and trade unions.

- Other leaders **emerge** by popular choice and through their personal drive and qualities.

- Within an organisation a manager is **appointed** to a position of authority. Leadership is a function of the position.

Types of leaders

- **Charismatic** – influence springs mainly from personality.

- **Traditional** – influence stems from social prejudice, such as the man at the head of the family.

- **Situational** – influence can only be effective by being in the right place at the right time.

- **Appointed** – influence arises directly from a position/status, e.g. most managers and supervisors. This is the bureaucratic type of leadership, where legitimate power springs from the nature and scope of the position within the hierarchy.

- **Functional** – secures the position by doing what he or she does well.

The benefits of leadership

There are many benefits from good leadership, including the following:

- Reducing employee dissatisfaction.
- Encouraging effective delegation.
- Creating team spirit.
- Helping to develop skills and confidence in the group.
- Helping to enlist support and co-operation from people outside the group or organisation.

The skills of a leader

The skill of leadership seems to be a compound of at least four major ingredients:

- The ability to use power effectively and in a responsible manner.
- The ability to comprehend that human beings have different motivation forces at different times and situations.
- The ability to inspire.
- The ability to act in a manner that will develop a climate conducive to responding to and arousing motivations.

Differences in attitudes between managers and leaders

There are differences in attitudes towards goals, conceptions of work, relations with others, self-perception and development between leadership and management.

- Managers tend to adopt impersonal or passive attitudes towards goals. Leaders adopt a more personal and active attitude towards them.

- In their relationships with other people, managers maintain a low level of emotional involvement. Leaders have empathy with other people and give attention to what events and actions mean.

- Managers perceive themselves as regulators of the existing order of affairs within the organisation. A leader's sense of identity does not depend upon membership or work roles. Leaders tend to search out opportunities for change.

- Management may be seen more in terms of planning, organising, directing and controlling the activities of subordinates. Leadership, however, is concerned more with attention to communicating with, motivating, encouraging and involving people.

- Management reacts. Leadership transforms – making a difference.

Theories of leadership

In the search to explain why some leaders are more effective than others, the following approaches can be identified:

- Personality, trait or qualities theories.
- Style theories.
- Contingency or situational theories.
- Transformational/transactional.

9 Personality, trait or qualities theories

Early studies focused on the qualities required by effective leaders. Lists were compiled of required leadership qualities including:

- physical traits, such as drive, energy, appearance and height
- personality traits, such as adaptability, enthusiasm and self-confidence; and
- social traits, such as co-operation, tact, courtesy and administrative ability.

Certain other writers selected other personal qualities which were thought to be desirable in leaders, who are '**born and not made**' Many great leaders were considered to have:

- above-average intelligence
- initiative – independence and inventiveness and the capacity to perceive a need for action
- motivation
- self-assurance and self-confidence
- the 'helicopter factor' – the ability to rise above the particulars of a situation and perceive it in relation to the surrounding context
- Other 'essential' qualities included enthusiasm, sociability, integrity, courage, imagination, determination, energy, faith, even virility.

The problem with personality or trait theories is that there are always counter-examples that can be given – for instance, when one theorist suggested a good leader must be tall, a short yet effective leader was identified; when one theorist suggested a leader must be tactful and courteous, a rude yet effective leader was found. Clearly good leadership is more than simply possession of particular physical or psychological attributes.

10 Style theories

The essence of leadership style theories is that a successful leader will exhibit a pattern of behaviour (i.e. 'style') in gaining the confidence of those they wish to lead. Style is a difficult factor to measure or define. The style of a manager is essentially how he or she operates, but it is a function of many different factors.

It is useful to start by looking at the three main styles of leadership:

Autocratic or authoritarian style. '*Do this*'

With this style the leader takes complete control, imposes all decisions on the group and neither asks for or listens to the opinions of others. Autocratic leaders tend to distrust the members of the group and as a result closely supervise and control the actions of the group.

While in many circumstances this style can cause resentment, in other situations it can be necessary. For example in the military, or where safety and security is paramount.

Democratic or participative style. '*Let's work together to solve this*'

With this style there is open discussion between the leader and the group. Ideas from the group are encouraged and while the leader will still ultimately make the decisions, the reasons for the decisions will be explained to the group.

This style is more likely to encourage innovation and creativity and group members are normally more motivated under a democratic leader.

Free rein or delegative style. '*You go and sort out the problem*'

With this style, the leader provides little or no leadership and expects the group to make decisions and solve problems on their own.

Like the autocratic style, this style of leadership can also lead to resentment within the group.

There are a number of theories dealing with style approaches to leadership. It is important that students have knowledge of a wide variety of theories.

- McGregor –Theory X and Theory Y
- Lewin
- Likert – four systems of management
- Tannenbaum and Schmidt – continuum of leadership styles
- Blake and Mouton – the managerial grid

As you go through these models, it can be useful to consider the similarities in each and identify if the positions in each model fit under the three main styles of leadership discussed above.

Model	Autocratic style	Democratic style	Free rein style
McGregor			
Lewin			
Likert			
Tannenbaum and Schmidt			
Blake and Mouton			

Douglas McGregor – Theory X and Theory Y

Independently of any leadership ability, managers have been studied and differing styles emerge. The style chosen by a manager will depend very much upon the assumptions the manager makes about their subordinates, what they think they want and what they consider their attitude towards their work to be. McGregor came up with two contrasting theories:

- **Theory X** – managers believe:
    - employees are basically lazy, have an inherent dislike of work and will avoid it if possible
    - employees prefer to be directed and wish to avoid responsibility
    - employees need constant supervision and direction
    - employees have relatively little ambition and wants security above everything else
    - employees are indifferent to organisational needs.

Because of this, most people must be coerced, controlled, directed and threatened with punishment to get them to put in adequate effort towards the achievement of organisational objectives. This results in a managerial style which is **authoritarian** – this is indicted by a tough, uncompromising style which includes tight controls with punishment/reward systems.

- **Theory Y** – managers believe:
  - employees enjoy their work, they are self-motivated and willing to work hard to meet both personal and organisational goals
  - employees will exercise self direction and self control
  - commitment to objectives is a function of rewards and the satisfaction of ego
  - personal achievement needs are perhaps the most significant of these rewards, and can direct effort towards organisational objectives
  - the average employee learns, under proper conditions, not only to accept, but to seek responsibility
  - employees have the capacity to exercise a relatively high degree of imagination, ingenuity and creativity in the solution of organisational problems.

This theory results in a managerial style which is **democratic** – this will be indicated by a manager who is benevolent, participative and a believer of self-controls.

Of course, reality is somewhere in between these two extremes.

Most managers do not give much conscious thought to these things, but tend to act upon a set of assumptions that are largely implicit.

Kurt Lewin

The first significant studies into leadership style were carried out in the 1930s by psychologist Kurt Lewin. His studies focused attention on the different effects created by three different leadership styles.

- **Authoritarian** – A style where the leader just tells the group what to do.
- **Democratic** – A participative style where all the decisions are made by the leader in consultation and participation with the group.
- **Laissez-faire** – A style where the leader does not really do anything but leaves the group alone and lets them get on with it.

Lewin and his researchers were using experimental groups in these studies and the criteria they used were measures of productivity and task satisfaction.

- In terms of productivity and satisfaction, it was the **democratic** style that was the most productive and satisfying.

- The **laissez-faire** style was next in productivity but not in satisfaction – group members were not at all satisfied with it.

- The **authoritarian** style was the least productive of all and carried with it lots of frustration and instances of aggression among group members.

Likert's four systems of management

An alternative model was put forward by Likert. Likert examined different departments in an attempt to explain good or bad performance by identifying conditions for motivation.

He found that poor performing departments tended to be under the command of '**job-centred'** managers. These tended to concentrate on keeping their subordinates busily engaged in going through a specific work cycle in a prescribed way and at a satisfactory rate (an approach similar to Taylor's scientific management).

Best performance was under '**employee-centred**' managers who tended to focus their attention on the human aspects of their subordinates' problems, and on building effective work groups which were set demanding goals. This finding appears to comply with Elton Mayo's findings that one of the components of success was the creation of an elite team with good communications, irrespective of pay and conditions. Such management regards its job as dealing with human beings rather than work, with the function of enabling them to work efficiently.

Likert concluded that the key to high performance is an employee-centred environment with general supervision, emphasis on targets, high performance goals rather than methods, and scope for input from the employee and a capacity to participate in the decision-making processes.

He summarised his findings into four basic leadership styles. He calls them 'systems of leadership':

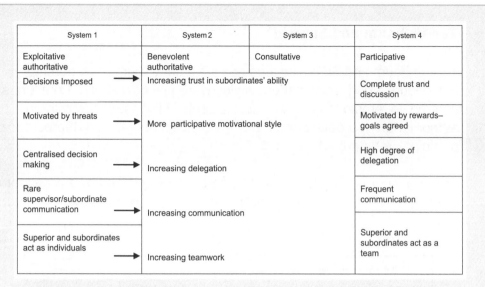

System 1	System 2	System 3	System 4
Exploitative authoritative	Benevolent authoritative	Consultative	Participative
Decisions Imposed ⟶	Increasing trust in subordinates' ability		Complete trust and discussion
Motivated by threats ⟶	More participative motivational style		Motivated by rewards– goals agreed
Centralised decision making ⟶	Increasing delegation		High degree of delegation
Rare supervisor/subordinate communication ⟶	Increasing communication		Frequent communication
Superior and subordinates act as individuals ⟶	Increasing teamwork		Superior and subordinates act as a team

- **Exploitative authoritative** – relies on fear and threats. Communication is downward only and superiors and subordinates are psychologically far apart, with the decision-making process concentrated at the top of the organisation. There are certain organisations that have no choice other than to exert exploitative authoritative leadership, such as the armed forces, where there must be little room for questioning commands.

- **Benevolent authoritative** – a step beyond System 1. There is a limited element of reward, but communication is restricted. Policy is made at the top but there is some restricted delegation within rigidly-defined procedures. Here, the leader believes that they are acting in the interest of the followers in giving them instructions to obey since they are incapable of deciding for themselves the right way to act.

- **Consultative** – rewards are used along with occasional punishment, and some involvement is sought. Communication is both up and down, but upward communication remains rather limited. The leader asks followers for their opinions and shows some regard to their views, but does not feel obliged to act upon them.

- **Participative** – management give economic rewards, rather than mere 'pats on the head', utilise full group participation, and involve teams in goal setting, improving work methods. Communication flows up and down. Decision making is permitted at all levels of the organisation. Leaders are often expected to justify their decisions to followers.

Likert recognised that each style is relevant in some situations; for example, in a crisis, a System 1 approach is usually required. Alternatively when introducing a new system of work, System 4 would be most effective.

His findings suggest that effective managers are those that adopt a System 3 or a System 4 style of leadership. Both are seen as being based on trust and paying attention to the needs of both the organisation and employees.

Tannenbaum and Schmidt

Tannenbaum and Schmidt came up with a continuum of leadership behaviours along which various styles were placed, ranging from 'boss centred' to 'employee centred'. Boss-centred is associated with an authoritarian approach and employee-centred suggests a democratic or participative approach.

The continuum is based on the degree of authority used by a manager and the degree of freedom for the subordinates, as shown below:

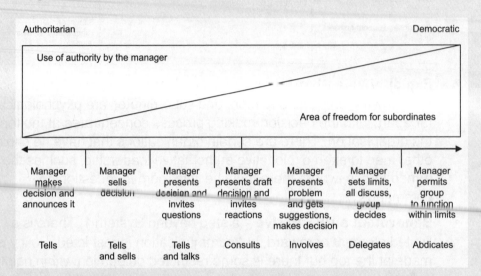

Blake and Mouton – The Managerial Grid

Effective leaders will have concern both for the goals ('tasks') of their department and for the individual ('people').

Blake and Mouton designed the managerial grid, which charts people-orientated *versus* task-oriented styles. The two extremes can be described as follows:

- **Task-centred leadership** – where the main concern of the leader is getting the job done, achieving objectives and seeing the group they lead as simply a means to the end of achieving that task.

- **Group-centred leadership** – where the prime interest of the leader is to maintain the group, stressing factors such as mutual trust, friendship, support, respect and warmth of relationships.

The grid derived its origin from the assumption that management is concerned with both task and people. Individual managers can be given a score from 1 to 9 for each orientation and then plotted on the grid.

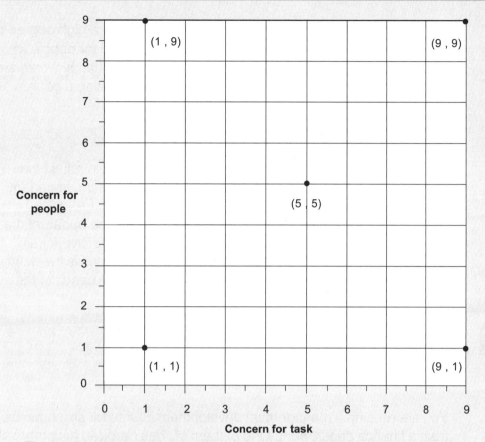

- The **task-orientated** style (9,1) is in the best Taylor tradition. Staff are treated as a commodity, like machines. The manager will be responsible for planning, directing, and controlling the work of their subordinates. It is a Theory X approach, and subordinates of this manager can become indifferent and apathetic, or even rebellious.

- The **country-club** style (1,9) emphasises people. People are encouraged and supported and any inadequacies overlooked, on the basis that people are doing their best and coercion may not improve things substantially. The 'country club' has certain drawbacks. It is an easy option for the manager but many problems can arise from this style of management in the longer term.

- The **impoverished** style (1,1) is almost impossible to imagine occurring on an organisational scale but can happen to individuals e.g. the supervisor who abdicates responsibility and leaves others to work as they see fit. A failure, for whatever reason, is always blamed down the line. Typically, the (1,1) supervisor or manager is a frustrated individual, passed over for promotion, shunted sideways, or has been in a routine job for years, possibly because of a lack of personal maturity.

- The **middle road** (5,5) is a happy medium. This viewpoint pushes for productivity and considers people, but does not go 'over the top' either way. It is a style of 'give and take', neither too lenient nor too coercive, arising probably from a feeling that any improvement is idealistic and unachievable.

- The **team** style (9,9) may be idealistic; it advocates a high degree of concern for production which generates wealth, and for people who in turn generate production. It recognises the fact that happy workers often are motivated to do their best in achieving organisational goals.

Style theories – is there one best style?

The difficulty with style theories, even when they attempt to reflect the multidimensional nature of leadership, is that they ignore the important influence of the **context** in which the leader is operating. From the discussions on the leadership styles theories, it should be apparent that there is no one best style of leadership that is equally effective for all circumstances. The best leadership style is the one that fulfils the needs of the group the most, while at the same time satisfying the needs of the organisation.

Case study style question 3

Management development

You are running a management development course for six supervisors from a finance department. One of them, A, has reported his proposals about a case, which they have been studying. The other five have rated A by placing crosses on Blake and Mouton's managerial grid. The results are as shown.

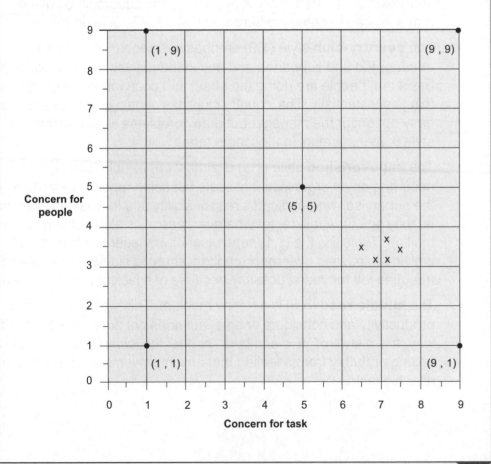

Required:

As part of the course discussion on this topic, what should you tell the group about the significance of the result and what suggestions could you make to A as to how he could improve his management style.

(15 minutes)

11 Contingency or situational theories

Contingency theory suggests that here is that there is no one best approach to leadership, either in terms of trait or style. A good leader will change their style to suit the situation. The best leadership style is the one that fulfils the needs of the individual, the group, and the organisation.

A more advanced version of simple trait theories is **situational leadership**. The theory here is that leaders are products of particular situations, e.g. Hitler in Germany of the 1930s, Churchill in England of the early 1940s and Mao in China after 1946. A given set of factors exists in certain situations, e.g. economic depression, weak government, high unemployment and a disenchantment with traditional politics. The theory suggests the emergence of a leader, who recognises the problems and has characteristics or traits that fit the needs of the situation.

Theories dealing with contingency or situational approaches to leadership:

- Adair – action centred leadership
- Fielder – contingency model
- Hersey and Blanchard – situational leadership

Adair – Action-centred leadership

Adair's action-centred leadership takes **Blake and Mouton's** ideas one step further, by suggesting that effective leadership regards not only task and group needs as important, but also those of the individuals making up the group:

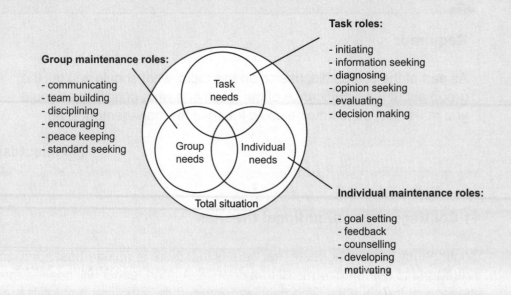

Adair's model stresses that effective leadership lies in what the leader does to meet the needs of task, group and individuals.

- Task achievement is obviously important for efficiency and effectiveness, but it also can be valuable for motivating people by creating a sense of achievement.

- Teams, almost by definition generate synergy out of the different skills and knowledge of individuals.

- Where individuals feel they have opportunities to satisfy their needs and develop, they are more likely to contribute to creativity and effectiveness.

The key task for the action-centred leader is to understand these processes and bond them together because otherwise there will be a tendency for the organisation to remain static.

However, the three elements can conflict with each other, for example, pressure on time and resources often increases pressure on a group to concentrate on the task, to the possible detriment of the people involved. But if group and individual needs are forgotten, much of the effort spent may be misdirected. In another example, taking time creating a good team spirit without applying effort to the task is likely to mean that the team will lose its focus through lack of achievement.

It is important that the manager balance all three requirements.

Case study style question 4

As part of your training, you have been sent on a leadership development course. Your manager P has worked for BL for over twenty years as the accounts partner. He has a sound knowledge and understanding of the different activities of the firm's business.

Over the years he has demonstrated fairness in how he manages staff and is well liked for his enthusiastic approach. P has decided that he needs to dedicate more time and energy managing the business and asked you to take over some of his leadership responsibility especially encouraging and leading the younger members of staff.

He has asked you to think about the different types of leader at BL whilst on the course.

During your time so far you have noted the following leadership styles from three of the partners:

L treats his staff like computerised machines and doesn't consider his employees views, feelings or ambitions.

J barely vacates his office and leaves his employees to get on with the workloads themselves.

A gives and takes. She is neither lenient nor too coercive.

Upon your return, P has asked for a report on certain matters.

Required:

Write a report to P, covering the following:

(a) Providing a definition of leadership.

(5 minutes)

(b) Describing the managerial grid and the five extreme scores identified by Blake and Mouton. Relating what you have learnt to the BL leadership styles.

(15 minutes)

(c) Briefly explaining Adair's action centred leadership theory.

(10 minutes)

(d) Explaining whether you feel one style of leadership is effective in all circumstances.

(10 minutes)

Fiedler – contingency model

The development of the contingency approach marked the bringing together of the personality and situational approaches. Fiedler's contingency model is the best example of an attempt to integrate individual characteristics with the structural and task properties of the situation.

First, he identified two distinct styles of leadership:

Psychologically distant managers (PDMs)

- seek to keep their distance from subordinates by formalising roles and relationships within the team
- are withdrawn and reserved in their interpersonal relationships
- prefer formal communication and consultation methods rather than seeking informal opinions
- are primarily task oriented

Psychologically close managers (PCMs)

- do not seek to formalise roles and relationships
- prefer informal contacts to regular staff meetings
- are primarily person oriented rather than task oriented

Fiedler suggested that the most effective style of leadership would be determined by the situation, which would be influenced by three factors:

- **Leader/member relations** – the nature of the relationship between the leader and the group
- **Task structure** – the extent to which the task is structured
- **Leader position power** – the degree of formal authority/responsibility allocated to the position

In terms of leadership style, Fiedler intimates that the leader can be high on only one aspect at a time – either people oriented or task oriented, but not both.

Fiedler suggested that a PDM approach works best when the situation is either very favourable or very unfavourable to the leader and the PCM approach works best when the situation is only moderately favourable for the leader.

Hersey and Blanchard – Situational leadership

Hersey and Blanchard's theory is based on three factors:

- Task behaviour – the extent to which the leader directs what has to be done, and how it should be done.

- Relationship behaviour – the extent to which the leader engages in two way communications.

- Level of maturity – the willingness of the follower to take responsibility for directing their own behaviour.

The leadership style is dependent on the maturity level of the follower. Maturity is not defined as age or psychological stability. The maturity level of the followers is defined as:

M1 – They generally lack the specific skills required for the job in hand and are unable and unwilling to do or to take responsibility for this job or task.

M2 – They are still unable to take on responsibility for the task being done; however, they are willing to work at the task.

M3 – They are experienced and able to do the task but lack the confidence to take on responsibility.

M4 – They are experienced at the task, and comfortable with their own ability to do it well. They able and willing to not only do the task, but to take responsibility for the task.

As the maturity of the follower increases, the leader should reduce the task behaviour and increase the relationship behaviour. They identified four levels of maturity and therefore four leadership styles:

Leadership style	Relationship behaviour	Task behaviour	Maturity
Delegating style	high	low	M4
Participating style	high	low	M3
Selling style	low	high	M2
Telling style	low	high	M1

Of these, no one style is considered optimal for all leaders to use all the time. Effective leaders need to be flexible, and must adapt themselves according to the situation.

12 Recent thinking on leadership

Transformational/transactional leadership

Bennis proposed that there were two types of leaders:

- **Transactional leaders** – these leaders see the relationship with their followers in terms of a trade: they give followers the rewards they want in exchange for service, loyalty and compliance.

- **Transformational leaders** – see their role as inspiring and motivating others to work at levels beyond mere compliance. Only transformational leadership is said to be able to change team/organisational cultures and move them in a new direction.

Transactional leaders tend to be more passive and transformational leaders more proactive. While a transactional leader would work within the confines of the organisational culture, the transactional leader would seek to change and improve the culture. Transformational leadership enhances the motivation, morale, and job performance of followers. They act as a role model and inspire others to develop and innovate. They would advocate empowerment, encouraging followers to take greater ownership for their work.

Transformational leadership has become more important in recent years. The dynamic nature of the environment facing many organisations today means that there is a constant need to innovate and change. It is suggested that to cope with this type of environment, leaders need to have vision and creativity, be innovative and capable of inspiring others. The distinguishing feature of transformational leadership is the ability to bring about significant change.

Skills required by transformational leaders

The new kind of transformational leader needs a different range of skills from those suggested by traditional management theories.

These new skills according to Boyd encompass:

- **anticipatory** skills providing foresight in a constantly changing environment

- **visioning** skills whereby persuasion and example can be used to induce the group to act in accordance with the leader's purpose or the shared purpose of a larger group

- **value-congruence** skills which enable the leader to be in touch with individuals' economic, psychological, physical and other important needs, in order to be able to engage them on the basis of shared understanding

- **empowerment** skills involving the willingness to share power and to do so effectively
- **self-understanding** so that the leader understands his or her own needs and goals as well as those of the followers.

Boyd believes that there is a need to develop such skills in organisations and to create the conditions in which this type of leadership can emerge.

Distributed leadership

Another more modern perspective on leadership is distributed leadership. While traditional leadership has been viewed as the role of one person in charge of others, a distributed, or shared, leadership perspective recognises that there are multiple leaders. This will be looked at in more detail in the building, leading and managing teams chapter.

Case study style question 5

Before taking up her position as Head of the Finance department of the S, T had enjoyed a career in the Army where she had attained the rank of major. The military style of command had suited T's personality. She is by nature an assertive kind of individual, so giving orders is something that comes naturally to her.

The start of her new post as Head of Finance has not been easy. She has found that her previous style of management has not been well received by her new staff. Her enthusiasm for improving the way things are done in the department is not matched by that of her staff. In fact, if anything, an air of resentment seems to exist in the department. More generally, T is finding it difficult to adjust to the whole way of operating in the S. In her view, so much time seems to be spent in meetings and in consultation generally that she wonders how the organisation manages to compete in the market place as successfully as it does.

Required:

Using any appropriate theory of management style, write an email to T explaining why she is experiencing the difficulties described in her new post, and recommend the kind of management style that might be more appropriate.

(15 minutes)

13 Summary diagram

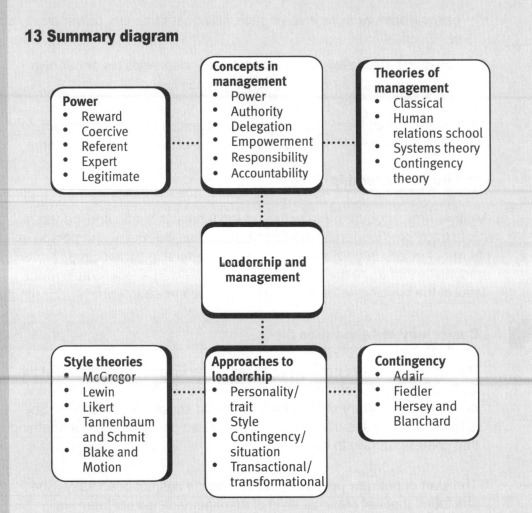

Power
- Reward
- Coercive
- Referent
- Expert
- Legitimate

Concepts in management
- Power
- Authority
- Delegation
- Empowerment
- Responsibility
- Accountability

Theories of management
- Classical
- Human relations school
- Systems theory
- Contingency theory

Leadership and management

Style theories
- McGregor
- Lewin
- Likert
- Tannenbaum and Schmit
- Blake and Motion

Approaches to leadership
- Personality/ trait
- Style
- Contingency/ situation
- Transactional/ transformational

Contingency
- Adair
- Fiedler
- Hersey and Blanchard

End of chapter questions

Question 1

Identify the correct definition for each of the following management concepts.

Accountability	Getting others to do things willingly
Delegation	Being called to account for one's actions and results
Responsibility	The right to exercise power
Power	The obligation to perform certain duties, tasks or make certain decisions
	The assignment of tasks or duties to another member of staff
	The ability to exert influence

Question 2

Insert the correct word into the sentences.

- Referent

- Coercive

- Reward

- Legitimate

- Expert

Where a member of staff undertakes a task because they believe their manager has knowledge about the subject, the manager is said to have _____ power.

A manager who uses threats to get compliance from staff is using _____ power.

Where a member of staff undertakes a task for their manager because they have respect for them, this would indicate _____ power.

Question 3

Authority which is based on custom and practice is known as?

A   Charismatic authority

B   Traditional authority

C   Expert authority

D   Rational-legal authority

Question 4

Which of the following statements are correct? Select all that apply.

- Authority can never be delegated.
- The scope of responsibility must correspond to the scope of authority given.
- Accountability is the ability to exercise influence.
- Responsibility is the right to exercise power.
- Responsibility can never be delegated.
- Authority is the right to exercise power.

Question 5

Which three of the following are common features of management as identified by Fayol?

- Contracting
- Commanding
- Communicating
- Co-ordinating
- Controlling
- Coercing

Question 6

Complete the sentences using the phrases provided.

- Psychologically distant managers
- Psychologically close managers
- Transformational leaders
- Transactional leaders
- Bureaucratic management
- Scientific management

The idea of there being one best approach to doing a job, arrived at from work study methods, comes from _____ theory.

Leaders who keep their distance from subordinates by formalising roles and relationships with their team are known as _____ .

_____ see their role as inspiring and motivating others.

_____ is based on a hierarchy of authority with strict rules and procedures.

Question 7

Using Herzberg's theory of motivation, match the items to whether they are hygiene or motivating factors.

- Team working
- Career advancement
- Increasing levels of responsibility
- Pleasant physical working conditions
- Suitable level and quality of supervision

Hygiene factor	Motivating factor

Question 8

With reference to Burns and Stalker's theory, match the following features to whether they relate to a mechanistic or an organic organisation.

- High degree of task specialisation
- Most suitable under stable conditions
- Employees recruited from a variety of sources
- Emphasis on loyalty and obedience
- Emphasis on task achievement
- More responsive to change

Question 9

Which of the following statements would relate to a Theory X manager? Select all that apply.

- Employees dislike work and will avoid it if possible
- Employees will exercise self direct and self control
- Employees accept and seek responsibility
- Employees need constant supervision
- Employees are indifferent to organisational goals
- Employees can exercise creativity to solve organisational problems

Question 10

In the Blake and Mouton managerial grid, shown below, match the styles to the correct place on the grid.

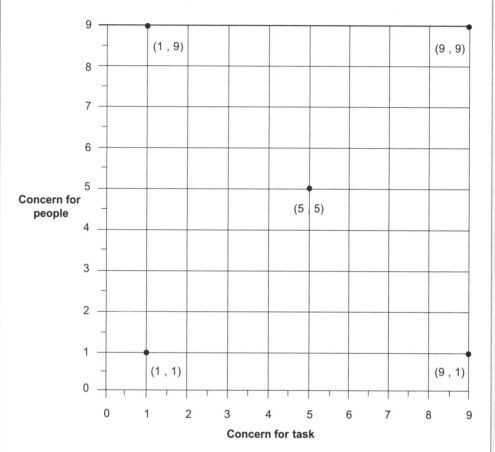

- Task orientated
- Country-club
- Impoverished
- Team style
- Middle road

Test your understanding answers

Case study style question 1

EMAIL

To: G

From: Management accountant

Date: today

Subject: Sources of power

A useful framework that can be used to discuss the different sources of power is that proposed by French and Raven and includes referent, reward, coercive, expert and legitimate power.

Referent power is sometimes termed charismatic power and is derived from one's admiration or respect for an individual that can inspire followers. This is gained by the personal qualities of the individual and when followers believe that the leader has desirable characteristics that should be copied, or has inspiration charisma. You are known for your fairness and are well liked and respected for your enthusiastic approach. It is therefore likely that you will have referent power which will help you in implementing the changes to working practices.

Reward power is where the leader is able to directly influence the intrinsic or extrinsic rewards available to followers. For example, the ability to provide incentives for individuals to behave in a particular manner and has control over the organisation's resources such as salary, bonuses or promotion. This type of power is usually used in a positive manner, although it can be used in a negative way through the threat of removal of rewards. As senior partner, you will have reward power that you could use to encourage people to adopt the new working practices. As well as financial rewards, you could use intrinsic rewards such as verbal praise and recommendation for promotion.

Coercive power, as the term implies, is the ability to punish or deprive people of things that they value and where the leader uses penalties or sometimes physical punishments to enforce compliance. It is based on fears and the use of the 'stick' or sanction, making life unpleasant for people. The receiver is unlikely to respond to this type of power. Whilst the immediate response might be compliance, it is unlikely to result in long term commitment. It is doubtful that you would want to resort to using this type of power, unless there is strong resistance to the changes, in which case you may have no choice.

Expert power is based on the followers' belief that the leader has certain expertise and knowledge relevant to a particular problem or issue. It will only work if others acknowledge that expertise. You will probably have this power given the time you has worked for the organisation and your sound knowledge and understanding of the firm's different business activities. This experience will be of great help in the drive to introduce new technology and working practices into the organisation and should encourage respect from staff.

Legitimate power, sometimes referred to as position power, is the power which is associated with a particular job. It is when followers accept that the leader has the right to influence them in certain areas or aspects of behaviour. This is often based on the individual's formal position in the organisation. Since you are a senior partner and leader of the project you will be deemed to have legitimate power in managing the changes and hence the right to issue instructions to staff.

I hope you have found the above helpful. Please do not hesitate to get in touch if you require any further information.

Case study style question 2

BRIEFING NOTES FOR MEETING WITH H

(a) **Causes of the situation**

- The main reason for the situation in H's department is his **inability or unwillingness to delegate work**.

- **What should he delegate?** – the day-to-day operational activities to his staff, instead of doing it himself.

- **Explain why**. This leaves his **time** free for organising and planning the medium-term activities of the department – putting the strategic decisions made by his superiors into place.

- **Why does H not delegate**? Whether he does not delegate because he **does not trust his staff** to do the work properly or he **does not know how to**, is a matter only H can clarify. As staff are trying to leave, H may even feel more pressure to carry most of the work load instead of having to pass it on to inexperienced staff in the future. There may have been changes or reorganisations in the department resulting in a higher workload for H, and thus inadequate time for managing his subordinates.

- **Any external factors?** The problems seem to have started recently, therefore, it must be established whether or not H is experiencing any external problems, domestic for instance, that are affecting his performance at work.

(b) **Principles of delegation**

- **Explain what delegation should be**. Delegation is the passing on to someone else of the freedom and authority to carry out a job for which the delegator is accountable.

- **Go through the process**. Ideally, the process should include a careful and thorough briefing of the subordinate by the senior covering the following points:

(i) the required performance levels

(ii) agreement of the actual tasks assigned

(iii) agreement of the resources allocated

(iv) delegation of authority to do the job

(v) recognition of the responsibility by the senior.

Although there is no single approach to delegation, it should be well planned and ensure that the content is appropriate and understood.

- **Explain the main principles**. The following principles are essential for delegation to be effective:

- The range of the authority delegated must be clearly understood by both parties and must be within the scope of the delegator's authority.

- It is the manager's responsibility to ensure that the subordinate has sufficient ability and experience to carry out the task. If necessary, training and an initial period of close supervision must be given.

- The manager must have the authority to delegate before he or she does so and must delegate sufficient resources to complete the task.

- The subordinate should have only one immediate superior, so that there is no confusion concerning his or her (space) accountability and responsibility.

(c) **Advantages of effective delegation**

In any large complex organisation, management must delegate some authority and tasks simply because of the limitation (physical and mental) of the workload on any individual and the need for specialisation of certain tasks.

- **Explain the Benefits**:

  (i) Workloads of managers and supervisors are relieved with the subsequent reduction in stress.

  (ii) Managers are left free to carry out non-routine tasks while passing on more routine activities to subordinates.

  (iii) Specialists are able to develop their specialisms.

  (iv) Training of subordinates is assisted by the delegation of tasks. The right opportunity to do a job is a very effective method of training.

  (v) Management succession is aided, as subordinates are able to gain experience and become accustomed to working at the higher level of management.

  (vi) Decisions can be made sooner by managers with delegated authority on the spot that can respond to changing events.

  (vii) The subordinate's work experience is enriched with subsequent increase in job satisfaction leading on to better work.

  (viii) The opportunity exists to evaluate the performance of a subordinate before being permanently promoted.

- **Explain the problems/disadvantages**:

  (i) Decisions taken at a lower level may not be to overall advantage of the organisation.

  (ii) The organisation must be able to meet the aspirations through eventual promotion of subordinates who accept delegated duties.

  (iii) There may be an increase in costs due to additional payments to the extra member of staff with delegated authority.

Case study style question 3

You should tell the group the following:

- That supervisor A is perceived to have a high 'concern for production'. In this context that could refer to the case they have been studying. It could also refer to insights others have gained into how A does their job. Either way this high concern for the job would be seen as a positive attribute of A.

- However, A is perceived to have a low 'concern for people'. Again this could refer to how the other supervisors felt they were treated on the course or how they feel A supervises his staff at work.

- This would be viewed as a potential problem with A being too task-orientated.

- These findings are reinforced by the fact that that everybody saw supervisor A in a similar light.

In terms of how A could improve his management style, you could suggest any of the following:

- Attending a further training course.

- Delegating more work to subordinates.

- Within this, using more trust rather than explicit control.

- Involving staff in more discussions.

- Asking staff for more feedback concerning his management approach.

- Treating staff more as adults.

- Using more group discussions to make decisions.

- Adopting an 'open door' policy.

- Adopting more 'management by walkabout'.

- Give staff more feedback on the quality of work done.

Case study style question 4

REPORT

To: Peter

From: Management accountant

Date: today

Subject: Management styles

Introduction

This report will cover the definition of leadership and look at two management models, namely the Blake and Mouton managerial grid and Adair's action centred leadership. It will also cover whether one style of leadership will be effective in all circumstances.

(a) **Definition of leadership**

Leadership is a conscious activity and in business is about setting goals and inspiring people to give a commitment to achieve the organisation's goals. It is a relationship through which one person influences the behaviour or actions of others.

Leadership is seen as 'a social process in which one individual influences the behaviour of others without the use or threat of violence'.

Leadership can be viewed from three standpoints:

- an attribute of a position e.g. your role at BL as Finance Director
- a characteristic of a person e.g. you are a natural leader, well liked by all
- a category of behaviour e.g. your enthusiastic approach to everything.

From the position of leadership at work, the latter standpoint is most applicable and can be considered as something one person does to influence the behaviour of others. It is all about moving people and things on, getting them from 'a' to 'b' by improving performance, changing the way things are done, making a new product or creating a new or better service.

There are different levels of leadership from the top down to small team leaders, but they will still share the same function – to get people to do the job. How they do that will depend on their attitudes, their perceptions of what motivates people and the prevailing culture of the organisation. If the designated leader cannot communicate the why, how and when of moving from 'a' to 'b' then he or she will neither behave like a leader, nor succeed in the task.

(b) Blake and Mouton's Managerial Grid

Blake and Mouton, observed two basic ingredients of managerial behaviour, namely: concern for production and concern for people. Concern for production includes the manager's attitude towards procedures, processes, work efficiency, and volume of output. Concern for people includes personal commitment, sustaining the esteem and trust of the group, maintaining interpersonal relationships and ensuring good working conditions.

They recognised that it was possible for concern for production to be independent of concern for people. It was therefore possible for a leader to be strong on one and weak on the other, strong on both, weak on both or any variation in between. They devised a series of questions, the answers to which enabled them to plot these two basic leadership dimensions as the axes on the following grid structure:

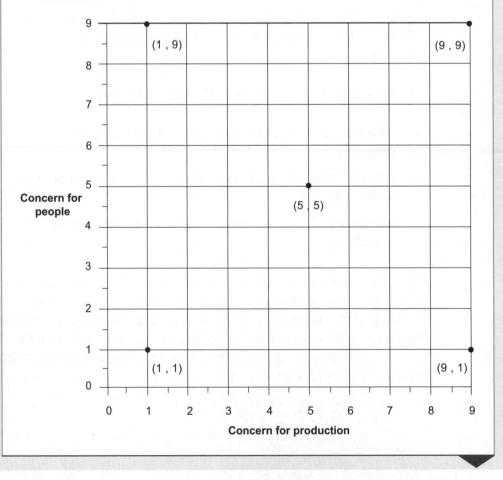

A high concern for production will score 9 and a high concern for people will also score 9, the two co-ordinates on the grid indicating the proportion of each concern present. Blake and Mouton picked out these two elements of a manager's job as characterising the leadership role. The implication is that managers should aim for the 9.9 combination; a goal-centred team approach that seeks to gain optimum results through participation, involvement, commitment and conflict solving where everyone can contribute. According to Blake and Mouton, individuals can adapt their style to become more effective personally and, working in a team, can build the synergy needed to raise output above the level that could be achieved individually.

Although there are 81 points of reference in the managerial grid, only five positions are precisely identified and described.

The task-orientated style (9,1) is almost totally concerned with production and has a low concern for people. Subordinates are treated as a commodity, like machines. Their needs are virtually ignored and conditions of work are arranged so that people cannot interfere to any significant extent. This is very similar to Alan Jones who treats his staff like computerised machines and fails to consider their views.

The country club style (1,9) emphasises people and pays little attention to achieving results. The manager is attentive to staff needs and has developed satisfying relationships. People are encouraged and supported, and any inadequacies are overlooked, on the basis that people are doing their best and coercion may not improve things substantially.

The impoverished style (1,1) is almost impossible to imagine, with a lazy manager showing little concern for production and low concern for staff or work targets. This type of manager only makes the minimum effort in either area and will make the smallest possible effort required to get the job done. John Claxton who very rarely leaves his office and makes no effort with his team is an example of this style of leader.

The middle road (5,5) is a happy medium. This viewpoint pushes for productivity and considers people, but does not go 'over the top' either way. It is a style of 'give and take', neither too lenient nor too coercive, arising probably from a feeling that any improvement is idealistic and unachievable. This manager is able to balance the task in hand and motivate the people to achieve these tasks. Alison Jacobs is a good example of this type of leader. She gives and takes and likes to be neither lenient nor coercive to her staff.

The team style (9,9) may be idealistic as it advocates a high degree of concern for production and for people. This manager integrates the two areas to foster working together and high production to produce true team leadership. Peter is the only manager that matches this description. He is the one to follow.

(c) **John Adair (1983)**

Adair put forward a model of action centred leadership, which is based on the premise that effective leadership requires a bringing together of task, team and individual needs. Adair's action-centred leadership takes Blake and Mouton's ideas one step further, by suggesting that effective leadership regards not only task and group needs as important, but also those of the individual subordinates making up the group.

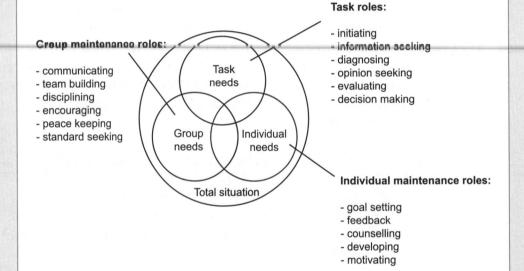

Group maintenance roles:

- communicating
- team building
- disciplining
- encouraging
- peace keeping
- standard seeking

Task needs

Group needs

Individual needs

Total situation

Task roles:

- initiating
- information seeking
- diagnosing
- opinion seeking
- evaluating
- decision making

Individual maintenance roles:

- goal setting
- feedback
- counselling
- developing
- motivating

Adair's model stresses that effective leadership lies in what the leader does to meet the needs of task, group and individuals.

Task achievement is obviously important for efficiency and effectiveness, but it can also be valuable for motivating people by creating a sense of achievement. Effective teams generate synergy out of the different skills and knowledge of individuals. Where individuals feel that they have opportunities to satisfy their needs and develop, they are more likely to contribute to efficiency and effectiveness.

The key is for us to understand these processes and bond them together because otherwise there will be a tendency for the organisation to remain static.

(d) **One best style**

From discussions of leadership it is clear that there is no one style that is equally effective in all circumstances and no one style has proved to be universally superior to the others. The best leadership style is the one that fulfils the needs of the group the most, whilst at the same time satisfying the needs of the organisation.

The variables that define the successful style include:

- The personality of the leader
- The situation of the group – calm or crisis
- The situation within the group – cooperative or militant
- The people within the group – intelligence and interest

Conclusion

This report has shown that there are many ways to look at leadership and a number of models available to help explain the different approaches. Styles of leadership should be adaptable to the situation to ensure that the leadership is always effective.

Case study style question 5

EMAIL

To: T

From: Management accountant

Date: today

Subject: Management style

Management style is concerned with how a manager deals with subordinates. There are a number of different models but one that is commonly used is that of Lewin.

Using Lewin's model, you could be described as adopting an autocratic style of management. This means that you are telling the subordinates what to do. This style of management probably comes naturally to you since it is the style adopted in the armed forces where subordinates are trained to not question their orders. Since you have spent a long time in this environment it is, understandably, the style you are used to.

The workers that you are supervising in the Finance department however may well be professionally qualified people used to carrying out tasks in their own way without a great deal of supervision.

With these kind of workers an autocratic style is unlikely to be successful, since the workers will resent the reduction in the amount of decision-making they are allowed. You may find it more useful to adopt a more democratic management style in which decisions are discussed with the employees rather than being imposed. This should lead to greater worker contentment with resulting gains in productivity and morale.

There will probably be a number of difficulties in changing your management style. You are used to doing things in 'the army way' (which you clearly did successfully having risen to the rank of major) and you are a naturally assertive person to whom an autocratic style of management is probably most comfortable.

Another factor that could cause problems is the potential for you feel that you are 'losing face' by changing to suit your subordinates. You might question the effect this will have on your authority both now and in the future, for example, what happens if they dislike something else, will you be expected to adapt to them again?

Although there are many practical difficulties surrounding this change in style they are not insurmountable. You may have to gradually change your style over time, perhaps by getting key subordinates more involved now and gradually extending this.

An alternative solution would be to involve another senior manager from a different department to help mentor you. This would involve working with a mentor who could help you discuss practical ways in which your style can evolve.

The above measures are likely to be unsuccessful unless you recognise that it is in your interests as well as that of your sub-ordinates and the company to change your style.

I hope you have found the above helpful. Please do not hesitate to get in touch if you require any further information.

Question 1

Power	The ability to exert influence
Accountability	Being called to account for one's actions and results
Delegation	The assignment of tasks or duties to another member of staff
Responsibility	The obligation to perform certain duties, tasks or make certain decisions

The right to exercise power is **authority**.
Getting others to do things willingly is **leadership**.

Question 2

Where a member of staff undertakes a task because they believe their manager has knowledge about the subject, the manager is said to have **expert** power.

A manager who uses threats to get compliance from staff is using **coercive** power.

Where a member of staff undertakes a task for their manager because they have respect for them, this would indicate **referent** power.

French and Raven suggested five sources of power:

* Expert power where the holder has specialist knowledge

* Coercive power where the holder has the ability to punish

* Reward power where the holder has the ability to reward

* Legitimate power where the holder has power du e to the position held

* Referent power where the holder has charisma and makes others desire to like them

Question 3

B   Traditional authority

According to Weber there are three bases for authority:

- Authority based on custom and practice is known as traditional authority.
- Charismatic authority is based on the individual's personality.
- Rational-legal authority comes from the individual's position in the hierarchy.

Question 4

- The scope of responsibility must correspond to the scope of authority given.
- Responsibility can never be delegated.
- Authority is the right to exercise power.

When delegating, authority must always be delegated but responsibility can never be delegated.

Accountability is being called to account for one's actions and results. The ability to exercise influence is power.

Responsibility is the obligation of an individual to perform certain duties, tasks or take certain decisions.

Question 5

- Commanding
- Co-ordinating
- Controlling

Fayol suggested five principles of management, the other two are Planning and Organising.

Question 6

The idea of there being one best approach to doing a job, arrived at from work study methods, comes from **scientific management** theory.

Leaders who keep their distance from subordinates by formalising roles and relationships with their team are known as **psychologically distant managers**.

Transformational leaders see their role as inspiring and motivating others.

Bureaucratic management is based on a hierarchy of authority with strict rules and procedures.

Question 7

Hygiene factor	Motivating factor
Team working	Career advancement
Pleasant physical working conditions	Increasing levels of responsibility
Suitable level and quality of supervision	

According to Herzberg, hygiene factors can avoid dissatisfaction and these factors must be in place before motivating factors will take effect.

Question 8

- High degree of task specialisation – mechanistic
- Most suitable under stable conditions – mechanistic
- Employees recruited from a variety of sources – organic
- Emphasis on loyalty and obedience – mechanistic
- Emphasis on task achievement – organic
- More responsive to change – organic

Burns and Stalker identified two major types of organisation which they felt were at the opposite ends of a continuum.

Mechanistic organisations show many of the features of Weber's bureaucracy and are seen as being more suitable under fairly stable conditions.

Organic organisations are more responsive to change and more suitable for organisations moving through periods of rapid change.

Question 9

- Employees dislike work and will avoid it if possible
- Employees need constant supervision
- Employees are indifferent to organisational goals

Theory X managers believe that people need to be coerced, controlled and directed. This results in an authoritarian approach to leadership. Theory Y managers would adopt a more democratic style of leadership.

Question 10

Task orientated – (9,1)

Country-club – (1,9)

Impoverished – (1,1)

Team style – (9,9)

Middle road – (5,5)

HRM approaches to managing and controlling performance

Chapter learning objectives

Discuss HRM approaches for managing and controlling individuals'
performance

1 Session content diagram

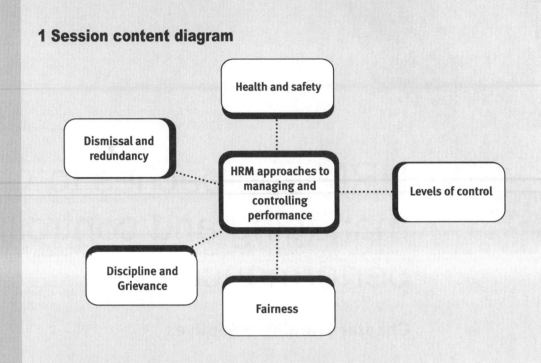

2 The purpose of human resources management

Fundamental to the achievement of organisational strategy is the contribution of the human element of the organisation. Hence, the effective management of human resources is a vital part of organisational success. Human resource management in its broadest sense is concerned with management decisions and practices associated with people. The management accountant needs to understand the importance of good managerial practices and how to make the best use of people. This encompasses, recruiting and selecting staff, development and reward, and performance management as well as ensuring that all legal requirements relating to human resources are adhered to.

Human resource management involves ensuring that the right people are recruited for the organisation and that they develop their knowledge, skills and experience so that they perform to the best of their abilities to help the organisation achieve its strategy. At the same time, they must control the behaviour of the people within the organisation to ensure that they are doing the right things in the right way within the rules of the organisation and any statutory rules imposed upon the organisation.

3 Management control

An underlying feature of the relationship between managers and their subordinates is management control. Most definitions of management include control as a function, it is essentially a means of ensuring that the objectives of the organisations are met. One definition of control is:

Control is a primary task and is the process of ensuring the operations proceed according to plan.

This chapter looks at the human resource management approaches to control. Behavioural aspects of control will be covered in the next chapter.

Within the context of human resources management, control will require to be exercised over the recruitment of staff, their performance and legal requirements connected with employment.

Note: all legal requirements referred to in this chapter are based on UK legislation.

Levels of control

Strategic

This is the level of control operating at board level. It will largely consist of the **setting of the control environment**:

- Strategic planning – determining course to be taken.

- Board procedures – appointment of directors, segregation of duties and so on.

- Setting and reviewing organisational structure.

- Policies on the conduct of the business, financial and other performance measures, risk assessments, environmental and ethical issues and so on.

- Monitoring compliance with plans and policies set.

At this level policies on recruitment, selection, appraisal, discipline, training and reward of employees will be set.

Tactical

This is control at the middle management level of the organisation. As an example, strategic control is the responsibility of the production director, tactical control is the responsibility of the production manager, the purchasing manager, and so on who report to the production director. At this level, controls should be in place to **implement the decisions and policies of the board**. Controls at this level include:

- Tactical planning, determining the production requirements and production schedule.

- Production budget.

- Procedures governing recruitment, training, and risk management to name but a few.

- Monitoring the achievement to plans and policies set.

At this level procedures for control the recruitment, selection, appraisal, discipline, training and reward of employees will be established and monitored.

Operational

This occurs at the lower levels of the organisation. Operational controls are designed to **control structured repetitive activities** according to preset rules. For example:

- computerised stock control systems

- production scheduling systems

- order processing systems.

At this level the controls established at the higher levels will be integrated into the day-to-day operations. Control failures will be highlighted and referred up to higher level management.

Control systems in practice

Internal control systems exist to enhance the achievement of organisational objectives. They promote the orderly and efficient conduct of business, help keep the business on course, and help it change safely.

In CIMA's framework of control, the control system is seen as consisting of:

- The control environment – management philosophy, operating style and management policies

- Control procedures – control mechanisms such as segregation of duties, authorisation, reconciliation and so on.

In today's organisations, one of the most important systems of control is the human resources system. The quality of an organisation's employees is fundamental to its success. It is essential for the organisation to get its people system right.

Human Resources are largely responsible for ensuring a number of employment practices are in place in the organisation. These should all contribute to the effectiveness of the organisation.

- Appraisal system
- Health and Safety
- Discipline and Grievance
- Dismissal and Redundancy
- Fairness in the workplace – Diversity and Equal Opportunities

Some of these, such as appraisal systems, are management controls, while others are legal requirements. Appraisal systems will be covered in the next chapter, while the rest of these control systems will be discussed in this chapter.

4 Health and Safety

A legal requirement which management must adhere to is health and safety legislation. Management have a responsibility to manage the health and safety risks in their workplace. They must think about what, in their organisation, might cause harm to people and ensure that they are doing enough to prevent that harm.

Management must identify the health and safety risks within their organisations and decide how to control them and put the appropriate measures in place.

Benefits of health and safety controls

- Employers' legal obligations for health and safety are being met.
- Cost savings – accidents and illness cost the employer money – legal damages and operating costs.
- Company image – company does not want to be associated with a poor health and safety record.
- To preserve the well-being of employees and others, improves employee morale, trust and motivation.

The Health and Safety at Work Act (HASAWA)

In the UK, the Health and Safety at Work Act 1974 (HASAWA) requires every organisation employing five or more persons to prepare and regularly revise a health and safety policy statement of:

- their policy for health and safety
- the organisation to enforce it
- the arrangements to implement it

and bring it to the attention of the employees.

The following are key areas:

- Provision and maintenance of risk-free plant and systems of work.
- Ensuring the safety in use, handling, storage and transport of articles and substances.
- Provision of information, training, instruction and supervision.
- Maintenance of a safe workplace.
- Provision of means of entry and exit.
- Provision of a safe working environment.
- Adequate facilities.

A **senior member** of the organisation should be responsible for implementing the policy and may be supported by safety officers.

Employees also have basic responsibilities in this regard.

Most companies have a **safety committee and representatives** who have some experience, are entitled to training and are consulted about arrangements to ensure the effectiveness of the health and safety policy implementation.

The Health & Safety Executive (HSE)

The Health & Safety Executive is an independent regulator with the duty to make adequate provision for the enforcement of the HASAWA. The main function of the HSE is providing workplace inspections to ensure compliance with the law and enforce the legal requirements, if necessary. The HSE also provides an advisory service to employers and unions.

Safety committee and meetings

One rule requires organisations to have a method of communicating and evaluating safety and health issues brought up by management or employees in their workplace. Larger employers must establish a safety committee. Smaller employers have the choice of either establishing a safety committee or holding safety meetings with a management representative present.

There is a difference between a safety committee and a safety meeting:

- A safety committee is an organisational structure where members represent a group. This gives everyone a voice but keeps the meeting size to an effective number of participants.

- A safety meeting includes all employees and a management person is there to ensure that issues are addressed. Typically, the safety committee is an effective safety management tool for a larger employer and safety meetings are more effective for a smaller employer.

Health and safety training

The Health and Safety at Work Act imposes a duty on employers to provide training to ensure a healthy and safe workplace. As well as being a way to obtain compliance with health and safety regulations, safety training enhances employees' knowledge, understanding and commitment.

Organisations implement safety training because it improves job knowledge and skills and ensures optimum employee performance at a specified level. In health and safety training, specified performance standards include attention to safety rules and regulations regarding safe work behaviour.

- First, problems or training needs are identified by inspection, by accident reports and through discussion at the health and safety committee.

- Next, the planning, execution and evaluation of the training takes place.

- Because training programmes only have a short-term effect on employee's behaviour, regular refresher courses should be organised.

- Top management support is a key ingredient in the availability and success of health and safety courses.

All new staff under **induction** must receive training that ensures their safety both in normal working conditions and in cases of emergency.

Monitoring policy

Safety specialists argue that the safety policy should reflect the employer's commitment to develop safe systems of work and to pursue a healthy work environment.

There is a growing awareness that, in practice, many employers are turning a blind eye to health and safety requirements.

Furthermore, many safety policies are not that helpful in practice because of the failure to monitor their relevance to workplace arrangements, inadequate training, and supervisors and safety officers lacking authority to make decisions.

A proactive approach would involve Human Resources regularly checking to ensure that safety policies, management procedures and arrangements are working and are changed to suit new developments or work structures in the workplace.

Case study style question 1

P has recently been taken over by R. R has always been very concerned about health and safety, however this is not an area that P has paid much attention to. The previous managing director of P has always said that as they are not a manufacturing company, then they don't really have to comply with health and safety. The management team of R have arranged a presentation about health and safety for the managers and staff of P. You have been asked to present part of the presentation.

Required:

Write briefing notes for your presentation. These notes should cover:

(a) An outline of the main features of health and safety legislation.

(8 minutes)

(b) An identification of those responsible for ensuring that the organisation is a safe place in which to work.

(10 minutes)

5 Discipline

The word discipline is used and understood in several different ways. It brings to mind the use of authority or force. To many, it primarily carries the disagreeable meaning of punishment. However, there is another way of thinking about discipline, based on the meaning of the original Latin *distipulus* – a learner or pupil. **Discipline means learning**, as in the discipline of management.

Maintaining discipline (learning) among employees is an integral function of management. Discipline is present when the members of the enterprise follow goals or objectives sensibly without overt conflict and conduct themselves according to the standards of acceptable behaviour.

Discipline therefore can be considered as positive when employees willingly follow or go beyond the rules of the enterprise. Discipline is negative when employees follow the rules over-strictly, or disobey regulations and violate standards of acceptable behaviour.

The main purpose of taking disciplinary action is to achieve a change in behaviour of employees so that future action is unnecessary.

The stages involved in a disciplinary process

Employees need to be aware that certain actions will lead to disciplinary action.

There are several situations where work norms might not be adhered to and which would cause problems if there were no remedial action:

- leaving work early, lateness, absenteeism
- defective and/or inadequate work performance
- breaking safety or other rules, regulations and procedures
- refusing to carry out a legitimate work assignment
- poor attitudes which influence the work of others or which reflect on the public image of the firm, such as improper personal appearance.

Rules will normally cover issues such as absence, timekeeping and holiday arrangements, health and safety, use of the organisation's equipment and facilities, misconduct, sub-standard performance, discrimination, bullying and harassment.

Rules and procedures should be clear, and should preferably be put in writing. They should be known and understood by all employees.

Process for handling disciplinary procedures:

- The informal talk.
- The oral warning.
- The written or official warning – first; second.
- Suspension.
- Demotion.
- Dismissal.

Standards need to be set for the right to appeal against these procedures.

In a well-managed organisation disciplinary procedures may not be needed very often. But if a problem does arise then they are vital. Good procedures can help organisations to resolve problems internally – and avoid employment tribunal claims.

The statutory procedures and the Code of Practice

Although organisations can be flexible about how formal or extensive their procedures need to be, there is a statutory procedure they must follow as a minimum if they are contemplating dismissing an employee – or imposing certain kinds of penalty short of dismissal such as suspension without pay or demotion. Unless employers follow the statutory procedure, employment tribunals will automatically find dismissals unfair.

The statutory procedure involves the following three steps:

- A statement in writing of what it is the employee is alleged to have done.
- A meeting to discuss the situation.
- The right of appeal.

The statutory procedure is the minimum standard. Employment tribunals expect employers to behave fairly and reasonably.

Disciplinary procedures are an aid to the effective management of people, and should not be viewed primarily as a means of imposing sanctions or as leading to dismissal. Where dismissal does occur, employees may make a complaint to an employment tribunal if they believe they have been unfairly dismissed, although ordinarily the employee must have one year's service.

It is for the employer to show the reason for the dismissal and that it was a fair reason.

The tribunal will determine whether the dismissal was fair or unfair and will take into account the size and administrative resources of the employer in deciding whether they acted reasonably or unreasonably. The tribunal consider how far the statutory procedures have been followed. Employment Tribunals expect employers to behave fairly and reasonably.

ACAS code of practice

In the United Kingdom, there exists a set of advisory booklets about various employment practices published by the Advisory Conciliation and Arbitration Service (ACAS). These are often used as yardsticks against which internal disciplinary procedures are judged to be fair or reasonable. The disciplinary code of practice states that disciplinary procedures should:

- be in writing
- specify to whom they apply
- provide for matters to be dealt with quickly
- indicate the disciplinary actions which may be taken
- specify the levels of management which have the authority to take the various forms of disciplinary action
- provide for individuals to be informed of the complaints against them and to be given an opportunity to reply
- give individuals the right to be accompanied by a trade union representative or by a fellow employee
- ensure that, except for gross misconduct, no employees are dismissed for a first breach of discipline
- ensure that disciplinary action is not taken until the case has been carefully investigated
- ensure that individuals are given an explanation for any penalty imposed
- provide a right of appeal and specify the procedure to be followed.

Handling discipline

Encourage improvement

The main purpose of operating a disciplinary procedure is to encourage improvement in an employee whose conduct or performance is below acceptable standards.

Act promptly

Problems dealt with early enough can be 'nipped in the bud', whereas delay can make things worse as the employee may not realise that they are below standard unless they are told. The manager should arrange to speak to the employee as soon as possible – the matter may then be able to be dealt with in an informal manner and not as part of the disciplinary process.

Gather the facts

Whilst maintaining satisfactory standards and dealing with disciplinary issues requires firmness on the part of the manager, it also requires fairness. The manager must be as objective as possible, keep an open mind, and do not prejudge the issues.

Having gathered all the facts, the manager or supervisor should decide whether to:

- drop the matter – there may be no case to answer or the matter may be regarded as trivial.

- arrange counselling/take informal action – this is an attempt to correct a situation and prevent it from getting worse without using the disciplinary procedure.

- arrange a disciplinary meeting – this will be necessary when the matter is considered serious enough to require disciplinary action.

Stay calm

All enquiries, investigations and proceedings must be conducted with thought and care.

Be consistent

The attitude and conduct of employees may be seriously affected if management fails to apply the same rules and considerations to each case.

Consider each case on its merits

While consistency is important, it is also essential to take account of the circumstances and people involved.

Follow the disciplinary procedure

The disciplinary procedure must be followed and the supervisor or manager should never exceed the limits of his or her authority.

If the employee is dismissed or suffers a disciplinary penalty short of dismissal – such as suspension without pay – the statutory minimum procedures must have been followed.

Suspension with pay

Where there appears to be serious misconduct, or risk to property or other people, a period of suspension with pay should be considered while the case is being investigated.

Self-discipline

Self-discipline is based upon socialisation, producing norms which follow reasonable standards of acceptable behaviour. Positive self-discipline is based upon the premise that most employees want to do the right thing. Most people accept the idea that following instructions and fair rules of conduct is part of the work ethic.

Once employees know what is expected of them and feel that the rules are reasonable, self-disciplined behaviour becomes a part of collective attitudes and group norms (i.e. the way in which employees behave as a work group), enabling 'responsible autonomy'. When new rules are introduced, the manager must try to convince employees of their purpose and reasonableness. If the work group as a whole accepts change, a strong sense of group cohesiveness on the employees' part will usually exert group pressure on possible dissenters, thus reducing the need for corrective action.

Douglas McGregor's 'hot stove rule'

This rule draws a comparison between touching a hot stove and experiencing discipline. When one touches a hot stove, the reaction is immediate, consistent, impersonal and with warning. The burn is immediate, with no questions of cause and effect. There is a warning, because everyone knows what happens if one touches a stove when the stove is hot. The result is consistent; every time a person touches a hot stove, he is burned. The result is impersonal; whoever touches a hot stove is burned. One is burned because of what he or she does, because the stove is touched, not because of who the person is. The comparison between the 'hot stove rule' and disciplinary action is that discipline should be directed against the act and not against the person.

Immediacy means that after noticing the offence, the supervisor proceeds to take disciplinary action as speedily as possible, normally the preliminary informal investigation.

For example, emotional incidents such as arguments in public or insubordination often require immediate response.

Case study style question 2

F was established three years ago. Since then, the company, which provides online financial advice, has experienced rapid growth, and the management has not really had the time to get all management systems and procedures into place.

The chief executive officer has recruited you to look at the way in which the company deals with its disciplinary problems and procedures.

Required:

Write a report to the CEO covering the following:

(a) Explaining why F should have a formal disciplinary procedure.

(5 minutes)

(b) Recommending guidelines for drawing up a disciplinary procedure.

(10 minutes)

6 Grievance procedures

Grievance procedures are not the same as disciplinary procedures. A grievance occurs when an employee feels superiors or colleagues are wrongly treating him or her; e.g. unfair appraisal, discrimination, prevented from advancing, being picked on, etc.

The grievance procedure often follows this sequence:

- The employee discusses the grievance with a colleague, staff or union representative.

- If the grievance is warranted, it is taken to the employee's immediate superior.

- If that superior cannot help, then it is referred to the superior's manager, at which stage the HR or Personnel department should be informed.

- Distinction should be made between an individual and a collective grievance.

- The colleague, staff or union representative should be permitted to be involved.

- Time-frames and deadlines should be stated to resolve the issue or submit an appeal.

Tribunals

A company may find that an employee is not happy with the outcome of a grievance procedure and that the individual wants to make a claim to an employment tribunal.

Employment tribunals are independent judicial bodies, less formal than a court, established to hear and determine claims to do with employment matters. Their aim is to resolve disputes between employers and employees over employment rights.

Examples include:

- unfair dismissal
- breach of contract
- discrimination
- equal pay.

Resolving disputes without a tribunal

In some cases it is possible to resolve disputes without the need for a tribunal. The following techniques may be used:

Arbitration

With arbitration, an independent arbitrator hears the case and delivers a legally binding decision in favour of one party. It is used to decide cases of alleged unfair dismissal or claims under flexible working legislation.

Benefits include:

- Speedy private informal hearing.
- No cross-examination.
- Limited grounds for review of the arbitrator's decision.

Mediation

With mediation an impartial third party facilitates discussion between the parties and encourages them to reach a mutually satisfactory conclusion.

Benefits include:

- Speedy resolution
- Avoid s the stress of a formal hearing
- Parties can express their views directly to each other

Conciliation

This can be used to settle a dispute before it gets to a tribunal hearing. It involves trying to build a positive relationship between the disputing parties.

Benefits include:

- Confidentiality.
- Avoid time, stress and cost of attending a tribunal.
- Lessening damage to the employment relationship.
- Reaching an agreement that satisfies both parties.

Benefits of discipline and grievance procedure

- Employer's legal obligations are being met.

- Cost savings – fewer costs for legal damages and lower operating costs.

- Company image – company does not want to be associated with a discipline and grievance record.

- To preserve the well-being of employees and others, improves employee morale, trust and motivation.

Case study style question 3

PA has worked in the customer services department of LMR company for two years. Last week he was sent to meet with MJ, a senior Human Resources manager.

At the meeting, which lasted less than ten minutes, PA was told that the company were very unhappy with his performance and that his attitude was 'not as it should be'. He was informed that, in accordance with the company's discipline code, he was being demoted to a lower graded role in the credit control department and that this was with immediate effect.

PA was shocked by this as he had never been informed of the company's unhappiness with him before and he was confused about the comment about his attitude. He had always enjoyed his job, and thought he got on well with his colleagues. He had also never heard of the company's discipline code.

Required:

Write an email to PA discussing what LMR have done wrong in the handling of his case and explain the actions which are available to him regarding this decision.

(20 minutes)

Case study style question 4

S, who was recently been appointed as Head of Human Resources (HR) in a small but growing business, reviewed the company HR policies and decided that they need updating. The company has existing documents covering Equal Opportunities, a Company Code of Conduct, Disciplinary Procedures and Grievance Procedures. Several members of staff did not know the difference between grievance and disciplinary procedures and were unaware that the company had policies on these matters.

Required:

Write an email to be sent to all members of staff explaining the difference between 'grievance' and 'discipline' and briefly describing the disciplinary process.

(20 minutes)

7 Dismissal and redundancy

What is dismissal?

Under UK law, dismissal is described as **termination of employment** with or without notice by the employer, or in the case of constructive dismissal, resignation by the employee because the conduct of the employer was sufficient to be deemed to have terminated the contract by the employer's actions. Dismissal without notice is usually wrongful dismissal, that is breach of the contract of employment; it may or may not also be unfair dismissal.

Dismissal is normally fair only if the employer can show that it is for one of the following reasons:

- a reason related to the employee's **conduct**.

- a reason related to the employee's **capability** or qualifications for the job.

- because a **statutory duty** or restriction prohibited the employment being continued.

- some **other substantial reason** of a kind which justifies the dismissal and that the employer acted reasonably in treating that reason as sufficient for dismissal.

- because the role was **redundant**.

Types of dismissal

- Constructive dismissal – resignation by the employee because the conduct of the employer was sufficient to be deemed to have terminated the contract by the employer's actions.

- Wrongful (unfair) dismissal – dismissal without notice, a breach of the contract of employment.

  For a dismissal to be fair, the employer must show that the reason for the dismissal is of a type acceptable under statute.

What is redundancy?

Redundancy is a dismissal. The grounds of redundancy may be justified on any of the following grounds:

- cessation of business
- cessation of business in the place where the employee was employed
- cessation of the type of work for which he or she was employed.

The law relating to redundancy

For the purposes of the right to be consulted, which applies when an employer proposes to make 20 or more employees redundant over 90 days or less, the law defines redundancy as: 'dismissal for a reason not related to the individual concerned or for a number of reasons all of which are not so related'. This definition might include, for example, a situation where dismissals are not related to the conduct or capability of the individuals but are part of a reorganisation.

Case study style question 5

D, a national airline carrier, has made a net loss for the last five years. While its major competitors have pursued programmes of modernisation, D has been left behind and is reported to have administrative costs and average salary costs that are, respectively, 35% and 25% higher than those of its competitors. The use of outdated and fuel-inefficient aircraft, as well as a reluctance to make use of modern Internet systems for online reservation, have been among the factors that have contributed to D's decline.

The board of D has produced a restructuring plan that includes 5,000 job cuts out of a workforce of 50,000; new, more demanding employment conditions; the sale of non-core assets; the establishment of twelve profit centres; a reduction in routes flown; replacement of its ageing fleet with fewer but more fuel-efficient aircraft and a complete overhaul of its reservation system.

Fierce confrontation is expected with the fourteen airline unions, but the board of D is committed to the implementation of the restructuring plan.

Required:

Your manager, the Finance Director, has asked you to prepare some notes for her on this matter for the next board meeting. Your notes should identify the key problems associated with making large-scale redundancies. and discuss the ways in which redundancies can be managed to minimise these problems for D.

(15 minutes)

8 Fairness and equality

Globalisation has changed the nature of companies in many ways. In terms of staff, it has meant:

- The end of the "job for life" ideal.
- A move from employee's effort due to loyalty to the company towards effort expecting appropriate rewards.
- Employees willing to look outside of the company for advancement opportunities.

Obtaining employee commitment is often seen as the key to competitive performance, but due to the above factors, commitment from employees is becoming more difficult for companies to obtain.

Rosseau and Greller looked into the relationship between what the employees believed was expected of them and what they expected in return from the employer. They called this the **psychological contract**. They defined three types of psychological contract:

- **Coercive** – employees feel forced to contribute and view rewards as inadequate.
- **Calculative** – employee acts voluntarily and works in exchange for an identifiable set of rewards.

- **Cooperative** – employees contribute more than would normally be expected from them. They actively seek to contribute further to the achievement of company goals.

In coercive contracts, motivation and commitment would be low, or even negative. In calculative contracts, motivation and commitment could be increased if the rewards were increased. In cooperative contracts motivation and commitment would be linked to achievement. Motivation was found to be highest when the contract was viewed in the same way by the organisation and the individual, that is where the employee perceived the practices of the company towards them to be fair.

Adam's equity theory

Employees judge fairness in two main ways:

- By comparing what they receive compared to what they contribute.
- By comparing their situation to that of others.

For example, suppose all employees in a company are given a bonus of $500, except one team which is given $600. All were probably happy with the $500 bonus, until they discovered that some got $600 and now they feel they are being treated unfairly.

Solomon

Solomon looked at the difficulty in achieving equity in relation to pay, there are many considerations:

- A living wage (compare employee needs and their income)
- Rate for the job (compare employees carrying out the same role)
- Output reward (compare the output of employees working in the same area)
- Responsibility (compare the responsibilities of employees at different levels of the organisation)
- Differentials (compare employees carrying out different roles within the organisation)
- Comparability (compare employees carrying out the same roles in different organisations)
- Status (compare employees carrying out different roles in different organisations)

- Contribution (compare the employee's pay to the profitability of the organisation)
- Supply and demand (compare the organisation's ability to pay and its need for labour)

Equality

In the UK, **The Equality Act** (2012) is the most significant piece of equality legislation to be introduced for many years. It is there to strengthen protection, advance equality and simplify the law. The Equality Act brings together, and significantly adds to and strengthens, a number of previous existing pieces of legislation, including race and disability. One of the key changes is that it extends the protected characteristics to encompass:

- age
- disability
- gender reassignment
- marriage and civil partnership
- pregnancy and maternity
- race
- religion or belief
- sex
- sexual orientation.

Diversity

Every business wants the best person for the job. Unequal treatment, prejudice or harassment discredits businesses and can be very costly. The owner or manager of a business may also be held responsible for discriminatory action by its employees.

Under the Equality Act (2012) it is unlawful to discriminate on the grounds of someone's sex, sexual orientation, status as a married person or a civil partner, race, colour, nationality, ethnic origin, religion, beliefs or because of a disability, pregnancy or childbirth, or subsequent maternity leave or because they are a member or non-member of a Trade Union. It is also unlawful to discriminate against part-time workers.

Equal opportunities

The object of providing equal opportunities on the workplace is to:

* ensure fair and non-discriminatory treatment is given by management to all job applicants and existing employees.

A positive approach to equal opportunities should:

* secure the best recruits from the widest available range of candidates.

* ensure the best use is made of the skills and abilities of all employees.

* reinforce the professionalism and image of the organisation itself.

The implementation of equal opportunities policies is important to all organisations. Unfair or unlawful discriminatory practices not only lead to resentment on the part of those who suffer from them: they also adversely affect public perceptions of the organisation and a career. A genuine belief in equal opportunities, couple with the knowledge that unfair or unlawful discriminatory practices will not be tolerated, should yield benefits within the organisation itself and lead to a more positive public belief in its fairness and professionalism and an improved relationship with its stakeholders.

Equal Opportunities Policy

The main points of a typical Equal Opportunities Policy should be as follows:

* Equal opportunities shall mean fairness for all; the recognition, development and use of everyone's talents.

* This fairness will run through recruitment, selection, training, promotion, specialisation and career development generally. It should also govern the relationship of all employees to each other.

* Equal opportunity does not just relate to sex or marital status, but the fact that people can be particularly disadvantaged for those reasons is reflected in legislation.

* No job applicant or employee shall receive unfavourable treatment directly or indirectly on the grounds of gender, sexual orientation, marital status, race, nationality, ethnic origin, religious beliefs and, where applicable, trade union membership, age or disability.

* Selection criteria and procedures will be frequently reviewed to ensure that individuals are selected, promoted and dealt with on the basis of merit, fitness and competence, subject only to the restrictions imposed by law.

- Training is an important part of the implementation of the Equal Opportunities Policy. Training programmes will be arranged to ensure that staff are fully aware of their roles and responsibilities and have the opportunity to develop and progress within the organisation.

The differences between equal opportunities and diversity:

Equal opportunities	Diversity
Removing discrimination	Maximising potential
Issue for disadvantaged groups	Relevant to all employees
A Human Resources role	A managerial role
Relies on proactive action	Does not rely on proactive action

9 Summary diagram

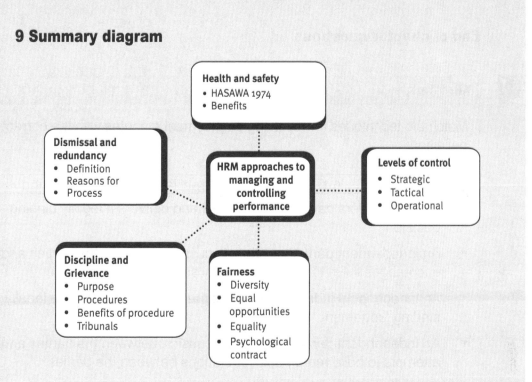

End of chapter questions

Question 1

Match the techniques for resolving employment disputes with the correct definition:

Tribunal	Arbitration	Conciliation	Mediation

- An independent party hears the case and delivers a legally binding decision

- An independent party facilitates discussion between the parties and encourages them to reach a mutually satisfactory conclusion

- An independent judicial body hears the claims and passes a legally binding judgement

- An independent party facilitates discussion between the parties and attempts to build more positive relations between the parties

Question 2

Match the activity to the correct level of control.

Strategic	Tactical	Operational

- Setting and reviewing the organisational control structure

- Setting production budgets

- Establishing procedures for control of recruitment, selection and appraisal of staff

- Monitoring the compliance with plans and policies

Question 3

Human Resources are largely responsible for ensuring a number of employment practices are in place in the organisation. One of these is health and safety. Health and safety legislation is a legal requirement in the UK.

Which of the following statements are true in relation to health and safety? Select all that apply.

- Health and safety is solely the responsibility of management
- The Health and Safety at Work Act 1974 applies to all organisations in the UK
- Organisations can save costs through health and safety compliance
- Health and safety issues should be covered during the induction of new members of staff
- Adhering to health and safety legislation can improve a company's reputation
- All large organisations in the UK must have an up to date health and safety policy statement

Question 4

Insert the correct words in the sentences below (words can be used more than once).

- Discipline
- Grievance
- Dismissal
- Tribunal
- Redundancy

A _____ occurs when a member of staff feels they are being treated unfairly.

The objective of _____ is to change behaviour.

Where an employee has been subject to _____ they may wish to take their case to a _____.

Unfair _____ would be grounds to take a case to a _____.

_____ is a form of _____ which would be allowed if the business ceased trading.

Question 5

Which of the following statements about discipline are true? Select all that apply.

- There are no legal requirements regarding disciplinary procedures; organisations can be flexible about how formal their disciplinary procedures are.

- Where a member of staff feels that they are being unfairly treated by colleagues or mangers, they may initiate disciplinary action.

- Douglas McGregors's 'hot stove rule' suggests that disciplinary action should be taken immediately after the offence is noticed.

- Persistant lateness or absenteeism would be unfair grounds for disciplinary action.

- Disciplinary action will normally follow a process including verbal and written warnings before dismissal would be considered.

- The purpose of a disciplinary procedure is to change behaviour.

Question 6

Using Rosseau and Greller's model of psychological contract, match the words to the definitions.

Calculative	Cooperative	Coercive

- Employees feel forced to contribute and view rewards as inadequate
- Employees contribute more than would normally be expected from them
- Employee acts voluntarily and works in exchange for an identifiable set of rewards

Question 7

Which of the following is NOT covered by the Equality Act 2012?

A   Pregnancy and maternity

B   Sexual orientation

C   Physical appearance

D   Religion or belief

Question 8

Which of the following would be seen as fair grounds for dismissal? Select all that apply.

- The member of staff was known as a troublemaker
- Company restructuring
- The role had become redundant
- Gross misconduct, such as theft or violence
- Long term absenteeism due to ill health
- Statutory restriction prohibiting continued employment

Question 9

Match the statements to whether they relate to equal opportunities or diversity.

	Equal opportunities	Diversity
A Human Relations role		
Objective of maximising potential		
Objective of removing discrimination		
Relevant to all employees		
A management role		

Question 10

Which of the following three statements regarding equality are correct.

- It is unlawful to discriminate against part-time workers

- Equal Opportunities is a managerial role

- Diversity is about removing discrimination

- Equal opportunities is an issue for disadvantaged groups

- The UK Equality Act 2012 makes it illegal to discriminate on the grounds of age.

Test your understanding answers

BRIEFING NOTES

Presentation on Health and Safety for P

(a)

– The **Health & Safety at Work Act (HASAWA)** was designed to have far-reaching consequences upon employers' premises and methods of work. The main provisions of the Act require an employer to provide a safe and healthy working environment in which to work. This includes the duty to provide training and appoint individuals responsible for maintaining safety at work, for example, safety representatives and trained safety officers.

– The **Health & Safety Executive (HSE).** The Commission, together with the Secretary of State makes appointments to the Health & Safety Executive whose duty it is to make adequate provision for the enforcement of the HASAWA. The main function of the HSE is providing workplace inspections to ensure compliance with the law and enforce the legal requirements, if necessary. The HSE also provides an advisory service to employers and unions.

(b)

– **Managerial responsibilities.** Health and safety at work is the responsibility of both employers and employees. Legislation can only provide the underpinning to safe working practices, ultimately, it is how the legislation is translated in practice that determines whether a workplace is safe, or not. There are a number of ways in which managerial responsibility can be discharged to make work safe. The management of an organisation carry the prime responsibility for implementing a policy they have laid down, and they also have responsibility under the Act for operating the plant and equipment in the premises safely and meeting all the Act's requirements whether these are specified in the policy statement, or not. Management has a duty to provide a safe and healthy working environment, which is hazard free, and to train others so that they are able to operate and maintain a safe and healthy working environment for themselves.

- **Employee responsibilities.** For the first time in health and safety legislation a duty is placed on employees while that are at work to take reasonable care for the safety of themselves and others. The employee is, therefore, legally bound to comply with the safety rules and instructions that the employer requires. Employers are also fully empowered to dismiss employees who refuse to obey safety rules on the grounds of misconduct, especially if the possibility of such a dismissal is explicit in the disciplinary procedure. Employees need to be enabled by management to carry out their duties and responsibilities. This might take the form of communicating policies and procedures about health and safety issues, appointing safety representatives, setting up committees and providing training.

- **Safety representatives.** To reinforce the employees' role in the care of their own health and safety, provision has been made for the appointment of safety representatives by trade unions. Safety representatives have a legal duty of consultation with employers and are entitled to paid time off for training to enable them to carry out their function. Under the HASAWA employers' are expected to set up safety committees and consult with safety representatives about the membership of that committee.

- **Safety committees.** Although the Act does not specifically instruct employers to set up safety committees, it comes very close. Safety representatives and training officers have to be consulted about the membership of the committee, and detailed advice on the function and conduct of safety committees is provided by the Health and Safety Commission. Since the Act there has been a great increase in the number of Safety Committees in operation. It has also been noted that the effectiveness of committees has been very much dependent on the employment of trained safety officers.

Case study style question 2

REPORT

To: CEO

From: Consultant

Date: today

Report on the need for a formal disciplinary procedure for F.

Introduction

In this report, the need for F to introduce a formal disciplinary procedure will be explained and guideline for drawing up this procedure will be recommended.

Need for a formal disciplinary procedure

(a) At its most fundamental level, the existence of a written disciplinary procedure is designed to protect both the employer and the employee.

Employer perspective

The employer should be protected from facing future actions (e.g. for unfair dismissal). If the company has clearly set out what it views as unacceptable behaviour and the actions that will be taken if this behaviour is undertaken, then it becomes very hard for the employee to claim they have been mistreated.

If an employee does undertake some action that is deemed unacceptable, the sliding scale of various different punishments should mean that the employee is less likely to repeat the action.

Looking at the big picture, the point of a disciplinary scheme is to deter employees from breaking the rules; in other words, to make sure that the scheme never has to be used.

Employee perspective

The employee of an organisation benefits from having a formal disciplinary procedure since it reduces the risk that they will be arbitrarily accused and punished for their actions.

This is becoming more important as more individuals are left to their own devices at work, rather than being given detailed rules and procedures (as organisations move from a mechanistic to an organic approach). This is likely to be particularly important in a company, such as finad.com which is growing and changing rapidly.

Guidelines for drawing up a disciplinary procedure

(b) Any disciplinary procedure must take account of local legislation. In the case of F.com, there are a number of steps that should be followed.

The company should write down the procedures to avoid misunderstandings, and provide all members of staff with a copy.

It should be very clear which sections apply to which staff (e.g. some parts may only be relevant to senior executives).

The procedures should state very clearly the forms of disciplinary action which can occur, e.g. verbal warnings, written warnings, etc.

The procedures should also state which levels of management are able to use certain kinds of action (e.g. only senior executives being able to issue written warnings).

Detail the steps that will be taken to investigate complaints that might lead to action being taken.

Detail the procedures of how the employee will be notified of any complaint and of any action being taken against them.

Detail the appeal procedures for workers who feel that the action taken is unmerited.

Conclusion

The establishing of a disciplinary procedure is important for F as it would protect the company and the employees of the company.

Case study style question 3

EMAIL

To: PA

From: Management accountant

Date: today

Subject: Grievance

Dear PA,

I feel that LMR have acted against the statutory procedures laid down for companies in the way they have treated you.

Companies are expected to follow the ACAS code of practice in all disciplinary and grievance procedures.

The purpose of disciplinary procedures should be to improve the behaviour of the individual before action such as suspension, demotion or dismissal takes place. These actions should only occur in cases of gross misconduct or after a number of other courses of action have been taken first. This is clearly not the case here.

The stages which would normally be undertaken in this sort of case before a demotion would be:

- Informal chat
- Oral warning
- Written warning – first then second
- Suspension

It would appear that none of these stages had been undertaken as the meeting notifying you of the demotion was the first you knew of the company's unhappiness with your performance. You also do not appear to have been given any details, or shown any evidence about the source of their unhappiness and it would appear that you has been given no opportunity to respond to their claims.

It is also significant that you were not aware of the company's discipline code. All employees should be made aware of this code when they join the company. The code should be clear about the expectations of the company and about actions which would be taken as a result of these expectations not being met.

You have obviously never had any sort of appraisal since joining the company or these matters would have been raised, and hopefully resolved, sooner.

In this case, you would have the right to appeal the decision at tribunal. As the company have not followed the statutory rules, it is likely that you would win your case.

I hope you have found the above useful. Please do not hesitate to get in touch if you would like any more information or would like to discuss any of these issues further.

Case study style question 4

EMAIL

To: all staff

From: Management accountant

Date: today

Subject: Grievance and discipline

It has come to the attention of Human Resources management that staff may be unclear about the difference between grievance and discipline and may not be aware of the disciplinary process within the company. The purpose of this email is to clarify the differences between grievance and discipline and to outline the disciplinary process within the company.

Grievance procedures are used for considering problems or concerns that employees wish to raise with their employers.

Discipline is not about punishment, but about correcting inappropriate behaviour. When an employee breaks the company code of conduct, a disciplinary process starts so that the employee becomes aware of their mistakes and can take the opportunity to improve their behaviour. Disciplinary offences may include, but are not limited to, persistent lateness, refusal to carry our reasonable work, poor work performance, harassment of colleagues and/or misuse of company assets.

A code of conduct should be established and documented. Staff should have access to the document and be made aware of its importance and the consequences of a breach.

The disciplinary process is progressive in nature. A disciplinary offence does not automatically lead to dismissal.

The stages of the disciplinary process are:

- informal talk
- formal talk
- verbal warning
- written warning
- decision – suspension, demotion, dismissal.

At each stage of the process, the employee must be made aware of the following:

- the section of the code that has been breached
- how the behaviour can be rectified
- what will happen if there is no improvement.

In many instances an informal talk can rectify problems without the need to progress through the formal stages. It is also important to establish if there are any mitigating circumstances that might be causing problems at work. Additionally all staff should be treated in the same manner with regard to discipline in accordance with the Equal Opportunities Policy.

I hope you have found the above useful. Please do not hesitate to get in touch if you would like any more information or would like to discuss any of these issues further.

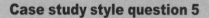

Case study style question 5

NOTES

To: Finance Director

From: Management Accountant

Date: today

Subject: Problems associated with large-scale redundancies

The key problems in any redundancy situation include that of deciding which personnel shall be made redundant, carrying out the redundancy process in a way that is fair and within the law, deciding what the redundancy package will consist of, and how to maintain the morale and motivation of the remaining workforce.

Selection for redundancy must be fair, carried out according to an agreed procedure laid down beforehand and consistently applied. This procedure does not have to be the last in first out' principle, although this is a popular method because of its ease of application.

In the United Kingdom, the ACAS Code of Practice provides a useful checklist that helps ensure that companies operate within the law and that individuals are treated fairly in the redundancy process. Other countries have similar codes of practice and these should be followed where available.

The ACAS code suggests that management should stop recruitment, reduce overtime, consider retraining or transfer of people to other jobs, retire those over normal retirement age and introduce short-time working. Where the redundancy is inevitable, as in the case of D, employers should give as much warning as possible, use voluntary redundancy and early retirement, and offer help in finding other work. Employers must also ensure that individuals are informed before any news leaks out, and should try to run down establishments slowly.

The redundancy package offered needs to be considered for a number of reasons. First, a basic legal minimum sum based on the number of years of employment can result in a substantial sum, and this has to be budgeted for. Second, D might consider paying over the legal minimum as a way of indicating to the remaining employees and the world more generally that it is a 'good' employer.

The needs of the remaining staff should also be considered. Their morale and confidence in the organisation will need to be boosted. In the case of a partial redundancy, those remaining at work may well have to change their work patterns by operating new machinery, coping with bigger jobs or changing their job location. This will need to be discussed with the trade union(s), the employees concerned and their supervisors.

The term 'outplacement' has come to be used to describe the efforts of management to place redundant employees in other economically active positions. Some consultants have become expert in revising curriculum vitae (CVs) of staff and 'selling' them to a network of contacts.

Please do not hesitate to get in touch if you would like me to prepare any additional notes on this topic.

Question 1

The correct definitions are:

- An independent party hears the case and delivers a legally binding decision – **Arbitration**

- An independent party facilitates discussion between the parties and encourages them to reach a mutually satisfactory conclusion – **Mediation**

- An independent judicial body hears the claims and passes a legally binding judgement – **Tribunal**

- An independent party facilitates discussion between the parties and attempts to build more positive relations between the parties – **Conciliation**

Question 2

- Setting and reviewing the organisational control structure – **Strategic**
- Setting production budgets – **Tactical**
- Establishing procedures for control of recruitment, selection and appraisal of staff – **Tactical**

The policies for these would be set at the strategic levels but the procedures would be set at the tactical level.

- Monitoring the compliance with plans and policies – **Strategic**

Monitoring the achievement of plans and policies would be carried out at the tactical level

Question 3

The correct statements are:

- Organisations can save costs through health and safety compliance – as they will avoid compensation payments and will avoid losing working hours through accidents and the will enjoy greater efficiency.
- Health and safety issues should be covered during the induction of new members of staff – this is a requirement of the HASAWA
- Adhering to health and safety legislation can improve a company's reputation – bad health and safety records can lead to the loss of investors, customers and employees.
- All large organisations in the UK must have an up to date health and safety policy statement – this is a requirement of the HASAWA

All employees have responsibility for health and safety, not just management.

The HASAWA applies to all organisations which employ five or more people.

Question 4

A **grievance** occurs when a member of staff feels they are being treated unfairly.

The objective of **discipline** is to change behaviour.

Where an employee has been subject to dismissal they may wish to take their case to a **tribunal**.

Unfair **dismissal** would be grounds to take a case to a **tribunal.**

Redundancy is a form of **dismissal** which would be allowed if the business ceased trading.

Question 5

The correct statements are:

- The purpose of a disciplinary procedure is to change behaviour.
- Douglas McGregors's 'hot stove rule' suggests that disciplinary action should be taken immediately after the offence is noticed.
- Disciplinary action will normally follow a process including verbal and written warnings before dismissal would be considered.

There are no legal requirements regarding disciplinary procedures; organisations can be flexible about how formal their disciplinary procedures are. This is incorrect as disciplinary procedures are set by law.

Where a member of staff feels that they are being unfairly treated by colleagues or mangers, they may initiate disciplinary action. This is incorrect as in this case they would initiate grievance procedures.

Persistant lateness or absenteeism would be unfair grounds for disciplinary action. This is incorrect as this would be grounds for disciplinary action.

Question 6

The correct definitions are:

Coercive – Employees feel forced to contribute and view rewards as inadequate

Cooperative – Employees contribute more than would normally be expected from them

Calculative – Employee acts voluntarily and works in exchange for an identifiable set of rewards

Question 7

The Equality Act 2012 covers:

- Pregnancy and maternity
- Sexual orientation
- Religion of belief
- Age
- Disability
- Gender reassignment
- Marriage and civil partnership
- Race
- Sex

But it does not cover physical appearance.

Question 8

Fair grounds for dismissal would be

- The role had become redundant
- Gross misconduct, such as theft or violence
- Statutory restriction prohibiting continued employment

A member of staff being known as a troublemaker is not grounds for dismissal but should be dealt with through the disciplinary process if there is evidence of troublemaking.

Company restructuring may result in redundancy but is not in itself grounds for dismissal.

Employees cannot legally be dismissed on the grounds of ill health.

Question 9

The correct matching is:

Equal opportunities	Diversity
A Human Relations role	A management role
Objective of removing discrimination	Objective of maximising potential
	Relevant to all employees

Question 10

- It is unlawful to discriminate against part-time workers
- Equal opportunities is an issue for disadvantaged groups
- The UK Equality Act 2012 makes it illegal to discriminate on the grounds of age.

Equal opportunities is a Human Resources role.

Equal opportunities is about removing discrimination.

Diversity is about maximising potential.

Behavioural aspects of control

Chapter learning objectives

Discuss behavioural aspects of management control

Discuss HRM approaches for managing and controlling individuals' performance

1 Session content diagram

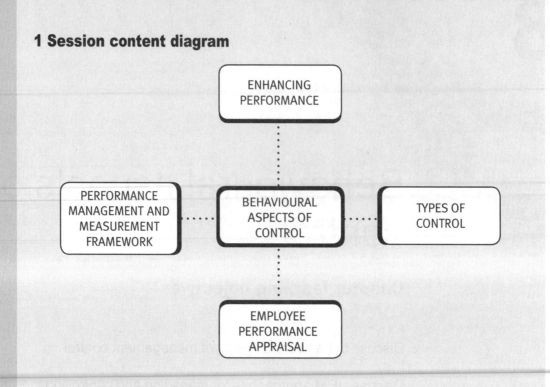

2 Approaches to control

In the previous chapter a number of control techniques were looked at. While these were the responsibility of HR they were all legal requirements. In addition to these legal requirements, organisations need to consider what other controls are necessary to manage and control the behaviour of their employees and to ensure that the organisation performs effectively.

The role of management includes trying to get the best performance from their employees as possible. This includes using control to modify the behaviour of employees. The leadership and management chapter covered a number of concepts which are used by management to control the behaviour of employees. The use of power and authority, the style of management adopted, the use of delegation and the empowerment of staff all contribute to behavioural control.

Types of organisational control

There are different types of control which can be implemented by organisations. The type of control used within organisations is largely dependent on the nature of the organisation, and will be influenced by the size and structure of the organisation, the number and types of employees and the work carried out within the organisation. There are four main types of organisational control.

- **Personal centralised control**. This approach is likely to be found in small owner-managed organisations where there is centralised decision-making by the owner. Control is carried out by the owner through personal supervision.

However, as the organisation grows in size and complexity, owners may find increasing external demands on their time and will need to employ others to undertake supervision of day-to-day tasks. In this phase of growth, control moves away from personal centralised control to more bureaucratic control or output control.

- **Bureaucratic control**. Controls will be based on formalised rules, procedures, standardisation and hierarchy. This is achieved through specifications of how employees should behave and carry out their work using formal job descriptions and specification of standard methods for performance of tasks. Reward and punishment systems can be used to reinforce this control strategy.

- **Output control**. This approach is a form of control that is based on the measurement of outputs and the results achieved. It is most appropriate where there is a need for quantifiable and simple measures of organisational performance since it requires a specification of output standards and targets to be achieved. This approach facilitates delegation without the need for bureaucratic controls, because once output standards have been agreed, employees can work semi-autonomously to carry out tasks.

- **Clan or Cultural control**. This form of control requires the development of employees' strong identification with management goals, for example through professional identification and acceptance of the values and beliefs of the organisation. If employees have the necessary skills, experience and ability, they can be given freedom in deciding how to undertake their tasks. This leads to semi-autonomous working with few formal controls. This approach depends on the common agreement of objectives and shared cultural values. It will require careful selection, socialisation and development of employees.

Trust and control

Trust is the belief that someone reliable and honest.

In an organisational context this suggests that management believe that employees can be depended upon to act ethically, with integrity and in the best interests of the organisation.

Where there is a high level of trust, management may reduce the level of formal control as they will have confidence that employees will always take the correct action. In essence, management have to find the right balance between trust and control within their organisation.

In the past, control systems within organisations were formal in nature. The system would rely on the required behaviour being specified in detail, with predictable outcomes expected. This type of approach could be seen in the classical theories of management where there was a high degree of specialisation, a hierarchical structure of authority and each employee was tasked with very specific roles.

A key feature of the scientific management school is the use of job, process analysis and time study to establish the optimum production methods and targets as to how long each task should take. The worker is not left with any discretion. The principles of scientific management make the workplace much simpler for managers to control. It is easier to measure inputs and outputs and compare the performance of workers. This approach can also be seen in McGregor's theory X model where the view held by the manager is that the employee is basically lazy and cannot be trusted. This opinion leads to an authoritarian approach to leadership.

The problem with this type of approach to management control, like the problem with the classical management theories, is that it fails to take account of the human element. A focus on this type of control could lead to:

- Motivation problems. Lack of morale; little worker commitment; no interchangeable skills (people are only trained to do one small part of the job); high staff turnover.

- Quality problems. No overall responsibility; no intrinsic satisfaction from work.

- Little understanding of people. People at work are not necessarily rational, for example they do not always work harder to earn more money and they are sometimes less inclined to work well if closely supervised; budgets sometimes cause problems, for example people might be inclined to purchase poor quality raw materials to stay within budget, thus causing production problems.

Today's business climate requires a far greater degree of flexibility and employees need to be more empowered to accommodate this flexibility. This suggests that an approach closer to McGregor's Theory Y approach, which was covered in the leadership and management chapter, should be adopted and managers should recognise that employees want to work and can be trusted.

The human relations approach emphasises the social organisation and the importance of informal relationships. Elton Mayo's studies on how to improve productivity revealed that work groups impose their own controls on members, such as the rate of work, working conditions and the members' interaction with managers. This control was imposed through a series of 'punishments', for example ostracising members who were persuaded to comply with the objectives of management rather than the norms set by the group.

Control is, therefore, a feature of interpersonal influences rather than close and constant supervision, recognising that people do not behave as unfeeling robots. This has an impact on control systems. There still needs to be control over the work being carried out and the manger must put in place regular reviews so that they have confidence that the objective will be met as required. Any possibility that the objective will not be met must be highlighted as soon as possible so that corrective action can be taken.

Allowing trust in controls works well for both the company and the employee. The employee is allowed to work on their own initiative and feels valued, this leads to increased motivation and increased productivity which benefits the company.

In order for control based on trust to work a number of factors must be in place.

- The manager must be confident that the employee has the knowledge and the skills to undertake the task.

- The objective must be clear and agreed by both parties.

- The employee must be motivated to work hard and use initiative to achieve the objective.

Case study style question 1

S develops accountancy software for small-to medium-sized businesses. S was established 15 years ago by a graduate in accounting. Despite an increasingly competitive environment, it has grown and diversified to become a global provider of specialised accountancy software.

In order to cope with the increasing size and diversity of the business, additional levels of management and control systems have been introduced, including additional policies, rules and procedures. Unfortunately, the increase in bureaucracy is having the effect of slowing down decision-making processes and limiting ideas for new software development.

The Chief Executive Officer is aware of the conflict between the structural changes and the need for continuous creativity and innovation that are critical to new software development and the future success of the business, but is not sure how to overcome the problem.

Required:

Write an email to the CEO explaining why formal control systems are increasingly necessary as an organisation grows and diversifies and why the use of bureaucratic forms of control in S might limit creativity and innovation.

(20 minutes)

3 Employee performance appraisal

An important management control system used in most organisations is the employee performance appraisal system.

A performance appraisal system involves the regular and systematic review of performance and assessment of potential, with the aim of producing action programmes to develop both work and individuals. It aims to improve the efficiency of the organisation by ensuring that the individual employees are performing to the best of their abilities and by developing their potential for improvement.

A performance appraisal system can bring many benefits to both the individual and the organisation.

Benefits to individuals

- Feedback about performance at work and an assessment of competence through comparison of performance against established standards and agreed targets
- Identifies work of particular merit done during the review period
- Provides a basis for remuneration
- May be used as an opportunity to discuss future prospects and ambitions
- Identifies training and development needs.

Benefits to organisation

- Provides a system for assessing competence of employees and identifies areas for improvement
- Provides a fair process for reward decisions
- Helps identify and formulate training needs
- Improves communication between managers and subordinates
- Provides clear targets linked to corporate objectives
- Provides a basis for HR planning
- Monitors recruitment and induction process against results.

The formal process of performance appraisal

Set targets – It is important that employees understand and agree to these targets. If they do not 'buy into' them, they will not put any effort in to accomplishing them – especially if they do not feel that the targets are achievable. This can lead to demotivation.

Monitor – during the period, the manager should monitor employee performance and provide regular feedback. Managers can offer rewards for good performance and support and help where it looks as though the employee is failing to meet their targets.

Review – at the end of the period, the manager and employee will usually have a formal appraisal interview where they discuss the employee's performance and investigate how successful the employee has been at meeting the pre-agreed targets.

Action plan – the manager and employee then agree on new targets that will be set for the coming period.

Approaches to performance appraisal

There are a number of approaches to performance appraisal, including:

The Ranking System – This is a formal structured approach which consists of the individual being assessed and analysed in terms of objectives, tasks, workflows and results achieved. These are then compared with previously agreed statements of required results and performance levels. For each of the set targets, the manager will provide a ranking as to the individual's performance. The rankings are usually based on an agreed scale, for example 1–5, with 1 being unsatisfactory and 5 being excellent.

The Unstructured Format – The unstructured format is another common approach where evaluators use an essay or short answer to grade employees. The benefit here is that any and all variables are used, from the most quantitative to the most informal. This approach tries to capture all aspects of employee performance rather than being restricted to the pre-agreed targets used in the more structured approach. Unstructured appraisals are meant to be open ended and all encompassing.

Self Rating – This approach is where the individual rates themselves on certain agreed criteria. This is then fed back to the manager who can review the individual's assessment and make their own assessment. The advantage of this approach is that that the individuals get the opportunity to consider their performance and in some cases remind management of what they have achieved in the period. It also forms the basis for the appraisal interview where both parties get the opportunity to discuss the ratings they have given and try to reach a consensus.

360 approach – In most appraisal approaches the manager appraises the individual. The individual may get some say in the appraisal, but ultimately the outcome will be decided by the manager. The 360 approach allows more participation by the individual. While the manager will appraise the individual, the individual is also given the opportunity to appraise the manager. In some systems, individuals will also appraise their colleagues. Every member of staff can be asked to give confidential and anonymous assessments on their colleagues and their manager. These assessments will help senior management to build up a more accurate pictures of the performance of departments. It also encourages individuals to work together for the good of the department.

Effective performance appraisal

To be effective, the system must:

- Be applied fairly and consistently
- Have the commitment and support from senior managers
- Be carried out with serious intent
- Relate to the main objectives of organisation
- Be clearly understood by all parties
- Be cost effective to operate

Barriers to effective performance appraisal

One aspect of the typical performance appraisal system that can reduce its effectiveness is the appraisal interview. Poor performance appraisal interviews can be confrontational, judgemental, just a chat, a paper exercise, a substitute for the management process that should be undertaken during the year and/or out of date and irrelevant because it is only held annually.

Barriers to effective appraisal may be overcome if:

- There is commitment from all parties involved
- There is a system of follow up and feedback
- Recorded agreement between manager and employee about future training and development. Training should be arranged within an agreed time period.
- Alternative methods of appraisal, such as self rating or 360 approach could be used.

Case study style question 2

H joined the finance department of M a year ago. He is surprised that in that time, he has never been given any clear targets or objectives and he has had no opportunity to discuss his performance with his line manager, G. Other members of the department feel the same so they have discussed this with G. G was surprised and stated that if something was wrong with their work, he would have told them about it by now. G has confided in you that he has never undertaken performance appraisal in the department because he felt that it would take up a lot of his time and he was not really sure what it would achieve.

Required:

Write an email to G, explaining the benefits that M and the individual members of staff would obtain from having a formal staff appraisal system.

(15 minutes)

Reward systems

Linked to behavioural control is the reward system used within the organisation. In developing a reward system, organisations hope to support the goals of the organisation by aligning the goals of employees with these. Reward systems can be used to motivate employees to work in the best interest of the organisation.

A reward is something given, to an individual or group, in recognition of their services, efforts or achievements. The rewards that an organisation offers to its employees can either be intrinsic or extrinsic. Note that extrinsic rewards are closely linked to Herzberg's hygiene factors, while intrinsic factors tie in to Herzberg's motivators.

- **Intrinsic rewards** – these arise from the performance of the job itself. Intrinsic rewards include the feeling of satisfaction that comes from doing a job well, being allowed to make higher level decisions or being interested in your job.

- **Extrinsic rewards** – these are separate from (or external to) the job itself and are dependent on the decisions of others (i.e. the workers have no control over these rewards). Pay, working conditions and benefits are all examples of extrinsic rewards.

The offering of positive rewards to employees is a key motivational issue for most organisations. However, rewards systems should be carefully designed in order to ensure that they:

- are fair and consistent for all employees, even for those workers with different job sizes or required levels of skill

- are sufficient to attract and retain staff

- maintain and improve levels of employee performance

- reward progression and promotion

- comply with legislation and regulation (i.e. minimum wage laws)

- control salary costs.

Employees can be rewarded in a number of ways, including through ongoing development and training (which will boost their future career prospects). This links back to Maslow's hierarchy of needs, as continuous development will help to meet self fulfilment and ego needs. However, most employees will be particularly interested in their remuneration. One way that businesses tie the performance of their employees to their pay is through the use of incentive schemes. There are a number of incentive schemes:

- **Performance related pay** (PRP) – part of the payments received by the individuals relates to the performance of the company.

- **Piecework** – reward related to the pace of work or amount of effort. The faster the employee works, the higher the output and the greater the reward.

- **Points system** – a range of rewards is available based on a point system derived from the scale of improvement made, such as the amount of cost reduction achieved.

- **Commission** – paid on the performance of an individual and typically paid to salaried staff in sales functions, where the commission earned is a proportion of total sales made.

- **Bonus schemes** – usually a one off as opposed to PRP schemes which are usually a continual management policy. Bonuses may also be awarded to teams or groups that have met or beaten certain targets. Group bonuses can help the team to pull together and work as a cohesive unit, but may lead to conflict if some members of the team are seen to be doing less work than others.

- **Profit sharing** – usually available to a wide group of employees (often company wide) where payments are made in the light of the overall profitability of the company. Share issues may be part of the scheme.

4 Performance management and measurement systems

While a staff performance appraisal system can offer many benefits to an organisation, one of its main objectives is to manage and measure performance. Within organisations, performance can be measured at divisional, departmental and individual level, as well as at the overall organisation level.

Target setting

In order to measure performance, a target must be set to measure performance against. To be acceptable a target must be viewed as fair, measurable, achievable and controllable by the person or people being measured.

A well set target can influence behaviour in a positive way and can lead to increased level of commitment and motivation, which in turn can lead to increased productivity. It is therefore important for organisations to carefully consider the targets they set to ensure that they obtain the behaviour they desire.

Setting targets for individuals is made more complex because most jobs have many dimensions, meaning that the targets must look at a number of different criteria in order to accurately reflect the employee's performance. Targets may include the following:

- Volume of work produced

- Knowledge of work

- Quality of work

- Management skills

- Personal skills

Drucker's Management by objectives

A model which can expand on the setting of targets within the appraisal system is Drucker's Management by objectives. Management by objectives can be defined as a type of control strategy which focuses on controlling outputs. Within this model Drucker emphasised that if corporate objectives are to be effective, they must be stated in behavioural or measurable terms, so that any deviation can be highlighted at an early enough stage to permit corrections to be made.

This is a process whereby individual goals are integrated with the corporate plan, as part of an ongoing programme of goal setting and performance review involving all levels of management.

Many people have responsibility in an organisation, but managers are held accountable for the work of others as well as their own. Managers, when setting objectives, have a responsibility to:

- agree their own departmental targets with their superiors

- discuss and agree targets for their staff that are achievable

- ensure that all targets set are measurable and possible, and that resources are made available together with some setting of priorities

- ensure that there is a balance between the goals and needs of departments and individuals

- apply the control system and discuss progress with staff at regular intervals. Where staff jointly set objectives with their manager they achieve valuable feedback on performance, a motivating factor acknowledged by Herzberg

- ensure continual review and appraisal of results.

Drucker's key objectives

Drucker argues that the nature of the business organisation requires multiple objectives to cover every area where performance and results affect the business.

Drucker suggested the following eight key objectives:

(1) **Profitability** – Growth in earnings per share. At some stage in the planning procedure, probably at the time of developing the strategic plan, this objective will need to be translated into targets for control linking sales, profit and capital employed.

(2) **Innovation** – The board must determine whether it intends to lead in developing technology and products, to follow other companies or to design to meet customer needs.

(3) *Market standing* – Overall marketing policies and objectives such as which products to sell and in which markets.

(4) **Productivity** – Productivity targets will be set in terms of output in relation to manpower, plant, material yields and costs.

(5) **Financial and physical resources** – Financing both working and long-term capital requirements through debt and shares. Physical resource objectives will include the location and acquisition of physical resources over the planning period, whether to lease or buy the assets, etc.

(6) **Managerial performance and development** – Policies and objectives will cover matters such as organisation and development; measures of performance; training and development; reward systems and organisational culture.

(7) **Worker performance and attitude** – Policies and objectives will cover the development of management and worker relationships.

(8) **Public responsibility** – There may well be objectives relating to social responsibility and business ethics.

Not all of these will apply to all organisations, and emphasis could change in response to environmental changes. The need for balancing objectives is obvious. There has to be a balance between profit and the demands of the future (short-, medium-, and long-term).

The Balanced Scorecard

Another commonly used performance management tool is Kaplan and Norton's Balanced Scorecard. In developing the balanced scorecard.

The balanced scorecard provides a framework which can be utilised to develop a multidimensional set of performance measures for strategic control of the overall organisation. These measures should be in line with the overall strategic objectives and vision of the organisation.

Once the balanced scorecard has been set at an organisational level, it can be cascaded down to departmental and individual levels. This way individuals can see how their efforts contribute to the overall goals of the organisation.

Kaplan and Norton recognised that when measuring performance, organisations tended to focus almost exclusively on short-term financial measures. They recognised that this did not reflect the complexity and diversity of business circumstances and that organisations should use a variety of measurements, many of them non-financial to give managers a broader perspective of their business performance. Measures used should attempt to address all relevant issues of performance in an objective and unbiased fashion and should cover areas such as profitability, customer satisfaction, internal efficiency and innovation.

Kaplan likened running a business to flying a plane in that airspeed, altitude, heading and fuel level are just a few of the pieces of information needed. Yet, in many businesses, managers have to rely on a narrow set of financial indicators to support their decision making – and this in an environment with many more complexities than a plane.

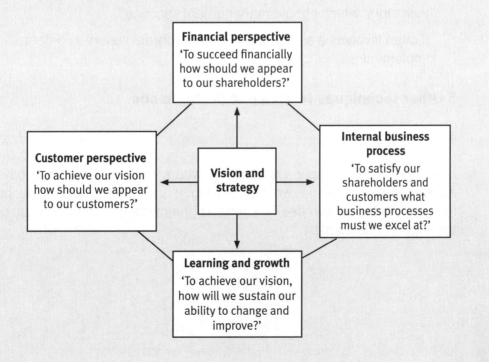

This is a powerful tool that assists in the running of an organisation. Gains in one area need to be considered with the losses that may arise in other areas and vice versa. Thus the manager's view is broadened and the tendency to concentrate on one measure is reduced, hopefully removed.

The main benefits are:

- It avoids management reliance on shorttermist or incomplete financial measures.

- By identifying the non-financial measures, managers may be able to identify problems earlier. For example, managers may be measuring customer satisfaction directly as part of the balanced scorecard. If this changes, steps can bo takon to improvo it again bcforc customers leave and it starts to impact on the company's finances.

- It can ensure that divisions develop success measures for their division that are related to the overall corporate goals of the organisation.

- It can assist stakeholders in evaluating the firm if measures are communicated externally.

The drawbacks are:

- It does not provide a single overall view of performance. Measures like ROCE are popular because they conveniently summarise 'how things are going' into one convenient measure.

- There is no clear relation between the balanced scorecard and shareholder analysis.

- Measures may give conflicting signals and confuse management. For instance, if customer satisfaction is falling along with one of the financial indicators, which should management sacrifice?

- It often involves a substantial shift in corporate culture in order to implement it.

5 Other techniques to enhance performance

Mentoring

Mentoring is quite simply a relationship where one person helps another to improve their knowledge, work or thinking. It is a very valuable development tool for both the person seeking support (the mentee) and the person giving the support (the mentor).

The benefits of mentoring include:

- Faster career progress.

- Excellent value for money for the organisation as the financial cost is relatively small.

- Enhances company image. The company does not want to be associated with a poor turnover record and encouraging learning helps staff to achieve their full potential and not look for new employment.

- Improved motivation. Employees often feel that real improvements in competences are delivered from the mentoring process. This can preserve the well-being of employees and others, improves employee morale, trust and motivation.

Who is a mentor?

A mentor should be someone who:

- Can give practical support and advice.

- Can give technical, ethical and general business guidance.

- Can help with development of interpersonal and work skills.

- Is an impartial sounding board – a mentor would generally have no direct reporting responsibility.

- Is a good guide, counsellor.

- Is a role model who can help improve career goals.

Quite often a mentor is from the same function (i.e. finance), it is unusual for them to be a direct line manager. The mentor is normally a role model, having already achieved a status (and possibly qualification) to which the subordinate aspires.

For a mentoring system to be successful, relationships should not be based on authority but rather a genuine wish by the mentors to share knowledge, advice and experience and should be one of mutual trust.

Mentoring works alongside more formal control mechanisms, such as appraisal, and is intended to provide the employee with a forum to discuss development issues which is relaxed and supportive. Mentors often discuss such issues as training, the choice of qualification, interpersonal problems and career goals.

The role of a mentor is to encourage and assist junior members of staff to analyse their performance in order to identify their strengths and weaknesses. The mentor should give honest but supportive feedback and guidance on how weaknesses can be eliminated or neutralised. The mentor could also act as a sounding board for ideas. The process should help junior staff to question and reflect on their experiences.

A mentoring system has both career-enhancing and psychological functions. The career function is concerned primarily with enhancing career advancement through exposure, visibility and sponsorship. The psychological function is more concerned with aspects of the relationship that primarily enhance competence and effectiveness in management roles. A mentoring system should help junior staff in expanding their network of contacts and gain greater exposure in the organisation.

Examples of the benefits of mentoring

Mentoring has many benefits for those involved:

Mentees will find a safe environment where they can admit gaps in knowledge and skills, raise queries and consider their strengths. Below you can see how some of our mentees felt they have gained from their mentoring relationships.

'I gained a better vision of what I want to do in the future, and what steps I must take in order to achieve my goals.'

'I gained a great deal. It was good to talk with someone who was independent of my work, college and home circumstances. I gained an alternative and dispassionate view and I have been able to make a more rational assessment of my priorities.'

'I learned about self belief, having respect for others, becoming more assertive, when to listen and when to ask questions, planning and decision making.'

'I gained a great insight into the practice of running your own business, which is what I would like to achieve myself.'

'My mentor gave a good sounding board and plenty of encouragement towards my impending exams.'

Mentors get a unique opportunity to put something back into their profession while enjoying a fresh challenge and personal and professional development of their own. Richard Garnett MAAT explains why he volunteered as a mentor:

'I felt it was time to give something back to the AAT. I think I have experience I can usefully share with those newer to the AAT. I really hope I helped my mentee to develop. I also think the scheme had some great learning for me too.'

Article by the AAT (Association of Accounting Technicians)

Case study style question 3

P is a senior manager in the finance department of LPM. He has worked for LPM for 25 years and is well respected throughout the company. LPM have decided to implement a mentoring scheme to help new recruits to the company fit in more quickly and P has been asked to be a mentor to K, who is a new management accounting trainee. K has just left university and his first placement is in the production department, but he will be moved to different areas of the company on a six monthly basis.

P has never mentored anyone before and is unsure about what would be expected of him, he is also concerned about spending time on this task as he is unsure of the benefits of mentoring.

Required:

Write an email to P, explaining what would be expected of P as a mentor and how a mentoring scheme would benefit K in his new role.

(20 minutes)

Coaching

Coaching is another method which can be used to enhance performance. Unlike mentoring, coaching focuses on achieving specific objectives, usually within a defined time period. It is more about improving the performance of someone that is already competent, rather than establishing competency in the first place.

- It is usually on a one to one basis and is set in the everyday working situation.

- It involves gently encouraging people to improve their performance, to develop their skills and increase their self confidence in order to develop their career prospects.

- Most coaching is carried out by a more senior person or manager, however the key issue is that whoever carries out the coaching must have sufficient expertise, experience and judgement to help the person being coached.

6 Summary diagram

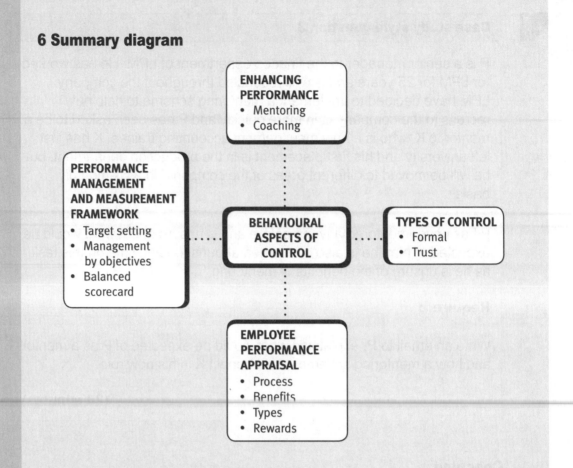

End of chapter questions

Question 1

There are a number of approaches to performance appraisal, such as:

- Ranking system
- 360 approach
- Self rating
- Unstructured format

Match the approach to performance appraisal to the correct description.

- This approach tries to capture all aspects of employee performance rather than being restricted to pre-agreed targets.
- This approach is where the individual rates themselves on certain agreed criteria.
- A structured approach where the performance is compared to previously agreed targets.
- The manager will appraise the individual and the individual is also given the opportunity to appraise the manager.

Question 2

Complete the following sentences regarding rewards:

Intrinsic	Extrinsic

- Rewards which arise from the performance of the job itself are known as _____ rewards.
- Herzberg's hygiene factors are closely linked to _____ rewards.
- Recognition or higher levels of responsibility would be classed as _____ rewards.
- _____ rewards would include pay and working conditions.

Question 3

There are a number of financial incentive schemes available for employers to motivate their staff, such as:

- Piecework
- Commission
- Profit sharing
- Bonus schemes
- Performance related pay

Match the incentive scheme to the description.

- Reward related to the pace of work or amount of effort. The faster the employee works, the higher the output and the greater the reward.
- Payments are made in the light of the overall profitability of the company.
- Paid on the performance of an individual and typically paid to salaried staff in sales functions.
- Key results are identified for which rewards will be paid on top of salary.
- One off rewards which can be paid to individuals or groups if they meet certain targets.
- Part of the payment received by individuals relates to the overall performance of the company.

Question 4

Which of the following are key objectives as suggested by Drucker? Select all that apply.

- Customer satisfaction
- Innovation
- Productivity
- Public responsibility
- Employee satisfaction
- Ethical behaviour

Question 5

In the balanced scorecard, one of the perspectives is the financial perspective. What are the other three perspectives?

- Customer
- Training and development
- Product
- Internal Business
- Employee
- Learning and growth

Question 6

Which of the following statements relating to mentoring are true? Select all that apply.

- Mentoring can lead to faster career progress.
- A mentor will generally be the mentee's line manager.
- A mentor can give technical, ethical and general business guidance.
- A mentor is a role model who can help improve career goals.
- Mentoring is used as a means of measuring performance.
- Mentoring focuses on achieving specific objectives, usually within a defined time period.

Question 7

Complete the sentences to suggest the most appropriate type of control for each organisation.

- Personal centralised
- Bureaucratic
- Clan or Cultural
- Output

Small, owner managed organisations which rely on key individuals are likely to use _____ control.

Large manufacturing companies would be most likely to use _____ control.

A professional firm of lawyers would most likely use clan or _____ control.

A large hierarchical organisation would be likely to use _____ control.

Question 8

The balanced scorecard model provides a framework which can be utilised to develop a multidimensional set of performance measures for strategic control of the overall organisation. The model is shown below:

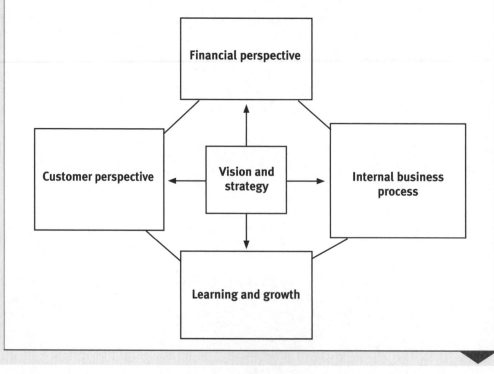

Within each perspective of the model, key metrics are used to measure the performance of the organisation.

Drag the following metrics to the most appropriate perspective on the balanced scorecard model.

- Number of complaints
- ROCE
- New products launched
- Operational efficiency
- Repeat purchases

Question 9

To achieve our vision, how will we sustain our ability to change and improve?

The above statement relates to which of the perspectives of Kaplan and Norton's balanced scorecard?

A   Financial perspective

B   Customer perspective

C   Internal business process

D   Learning and growth

Question 10

Which of the following statements regarding target setting are correct? Select all that apply.

- A well set target can improve motivation.
- Targets can only be set using financial measure.
- Volume of work would be a suitable target.
- To be accepted, target should be viewed as controllable and achievable.
- Ideally, each individual will be set just one main target.

Test your understanding answers

Case study style question 1

EMAIL

To: CEO of S

From: Management accountant

Date: today

Subject: The necessity of formal control systems

For any organisation like S, the growth and diversification of the business poses an increasing problem of control. As the number of levels in the organisation is increased and the number of different kinds of tasks to be carried out multiplies, the division of labour becomes more complex. In this changing situation, it becomes increasingly difficult to ensure that members of an organisation are doing what they are supposed to be doing.

Without some attempt to control what people do in organisations, there is a danger of staff beginning, intentionally or unintentionally, to do 'their own thing' by working towards their own personal goals and perceived self-interests.

To counteract the tendencies created by the processes of differentiation, and to ensure goal congruence, there is a need to create a 'common focus' in an organisation, which will control and integrate members' diverse activities. This is why organisations introduce a variety of formal controls.

In small, simple organisations it is possible for the owner manager or senior management to supervise subordinates' activities personally and systematically. Often, in such organisations, it is possible to achieve control in an informal way by setting employees tasks and then checking that they have been carried out. Any deviations from the accepted standard of performance can be communicated directly by the owner manager to particular employees and the necessary corrective action taken. In larger organisations, however, with a complex division of labour, and a taller hierarchy of responsibility, it is not physically possible to control people in such a simple manner. In such situations, formal policies, rules and procedures have to be put into place together with a system of rewards and punishments to ensure that the policies, rules and procedures are observed.

In such hierarchical organisations, policies and objectives are typically set, or at least confirmed, by occupants of higher-level positions and are then communicated to lower-level staff, who are then charged with the responsibility to carry out the necessary actions. It is up to the higher-level managers to determine whether or not the objectives have been met and, if not, to take the appropriate steps. This is the process of control.

It is important to note, however, that there are a number of different ways of exercising control in organisations and that the effectiveness of a particular type of control system depends on a number of factors including the organisation's strategy, culture, structure, environment and the type of goods or services produced.

In the case of S, it chose to use bureaucratic (administrative) forms of control, but as the CEO realised, such a form of control is not conducive to creativity and innovation.

Creativity, which can be defined as 'the generation of new ideas, and innovation, which is the transformation of creative ideas into tangible products or processes' varies considerably between one organisation and another. Some organisations have a reputation for creativity and innovation while other organisations hardly ever seem to generate new products or new ways of doing things.

The generation of new ideas and their translation into commercial use is a particularly important issue for an organisation like S because its future depends on a continuous supply of innovative software products. There are many factors influencing the rate of innovation in organisations, but research suggests that one reason has to do with how an organisation is structured and controlled.

Studies have found that excessive bureaucracy with its allegiance to central control and to rules and procedures discourages creativity and innovation. The focus on rules and procedures and the accompanying sanctions designed to ensure compliance means that employees 'play safe' by sticking to the rules rather than risk trying out new ideas. Rules can become 'ends in themselves'.

The division of labour that often accompanies the growth of an organisation also affects creativity and innovation because it restricts the sharing of ideas between individuals and between different units, departments or divisions. The case of S illustrates well the problems facing all large organisations at some time in their development – that of balancing the need to ensure adequate direction and control of staff and yet allowing sufficient freedom and discretion of middle managers and other employees to contribute their particular knowledge and expertise to the organisation. Too little direction and control can result in wasted effort and inefficiencies as the departments and divisions into which an organisation is subdivided pursue their own particular goals. Too much central control and lower level staff become frustrated by rules and procedures forced upon them from on high by those who are too far from the action to make informed decisions.

I hope you have found the above useful. Please do not hesitate to get in touch if you would like any more information or would like to discuss any of these issues further.

Case study style question 2

EMAIL

To: G

From: Management Accountant

Date: today

Subject: Performance appraisal system

You are right in saying that a performance appraisal system can be time consuming, but the time spent on this can bring many benefits to both the company and to the individuals within your department. Performance appraisal can help to improve efficiency and effectiveness of a company. It should be used to review, change, inform, examine and evaluate employees.

From the company point of view, a formal appraisal system can:

- Provide a means for assessing employees and identifying areas for improvement. The system would encourage you to review the work of the individuals within your department, which would benefit you in allowing you to get to know their capabilities.

- Provide a fair basis for reward decisions.

- Aid in succession planning by identifying candidates for promotion.

- Help to plan for training needs.

- Link targets to company's strategic plans.

- Aid in human resource planning

From the employee's point of view it can:

- Provide a fair and understandable basis for remuneration.

- Provide feedback about performance and allow an opportunity to discuss future prospects. H, and others within the department are unhappy with the lack of feedback from you. A formal appraisal system would give both you and H the opportunity to discuss his work.

- Identify training and development needs.

- Help to highlight work of high quality carried out in the period.

I hope you have found the above useful. A performance appraisal system can be very beneficial to both you as a manager, the individual members of your team and the company as a whole. Please do not hesitate to get in touch if you want to discuss any of these aspects more fully.

Case study style question 3

EMAIL

To: P

From: Management Accountant

Date: today

Subject: Mentoring

A mentor is a person who helps another person to develop. A mentor is usually a more experienced person within the organisation and they are appointed to mentor a more junior member of staff who will usually come from another part of the organisation. If the mentor is from the same department, they would not usually be a direct line manager. In this case, you are an experienced, well respected manager in the finance department, and have been asked to mentor K who is a management accounting trainee in the production department. This is a fairly typical mentoring arrangement whereby the mentor is from the same function, but not the same department.

As a mentor, you would be expected to arrange regular meetings with K, or allow K to contact you as required. When you meet, you should make it clear to K that he can discuss any issues of concern he has. Topics discussed could include study support and advice, technical or business guidance, training advice, interpersonal problems or career advice. K may also wish to use you as a sounding board for decisions he has to make. You should be able to give K impartial and independent advice.

Discussions between you and K should be confidential so that K feels that he can discuss any areas of concern he has in a safe environment.

There are many benefits from mentoring. There are career-enhancing benefits and personal developmental benefits. From a career-enhancing perspective, you can provide technical help and study support. K would be able to discuss openly areas of weakness within their role and you may be able to provide practical advice as to how to overcome these weaknesses. Going forward you could also advise K on routes for career development.

You may also be able to help K get to know other members of staff within the organisation. You have been with LPM for 25 year, so you are very likely to know many of the other managers that K will be dealing with. This is especially helpful to K as he will be moving round the organisation every six months. You may be able to give K information about the managers and staff he will be dealing with in each of the departments. As he moves around the organisation, K may come across new situations which he finds difficult to deal with. you may be able to him general advice to help build his confidence in dealing with new situations, or may be able to help identify suitable training courses which would help him.

In addition, K would also gain from a personal point of view. He is just out of university and is not used to this working environment. You will be able to help K understand the culture of LPM which would help him to settle in more quickly. A better understanding of LPM will improve K's confidence which would help him to perform better in his role.

Over time, as he develops in his role, K may contact you less about how to handle situations and more for advice on career development.

I hope you have found the above helpful. Please do not hesitate to get in touch if you want to discuss any of these aspects more fully.

Question 1

The correct descriptions are:

The Ranking System – A structured approach where the performance is compared to previously agreed targets.

The Unstructured Format – This approach tries to capture all aspects of employee performance rather than being restricted to pre-agreed targets.

Self Rating – This approach is where the individual rates themselves on certain agreed criteria.

360 approach – The manager will appraise the individual and the individual is also given the opportunity to appraise the manager.

Question 2

- Rewards which arise from the performance of the job itself are known as **intrinsic** rewards.

- Herzberg's hygiene factors are closely linked to **extrinsic** rewards.

- Recognition or higher levels of responsibility would be classed as **intrinsic** rewards.

- **Extrinsic** rewards would include pay and working conditions.

Intrinsic rewards arise from the performance of the job itself while extrinsic rewards are external to the job and rely on the decisions of others.

Question 3

The correct descriptions are:

Piecework – reward related to the pace of work or amount of effort. The faster the employee works, the higher the output and the greater the reward.

Commission – paid on the performance of an individual and typically paid to salaried staff in sales functions.

Profit sharing – payments are made in the light of the overall profitability of the company.

Bonus schemes – one off rewards which can be paid to individuals or groups if they meet certain targets.

Performance related pay – part of the payment received by individuals relates to the overall performance of the company.

Question 4

- Innovation
- Productivity
- Public responsibility

The others are:

- Profitability
- Market standing
- Financial and physical resources
- Management performance and development
- Worker performance and attitude

Question 5

- Customer
- Internal Business
- Learning and growth

The complete diagram is shown below:

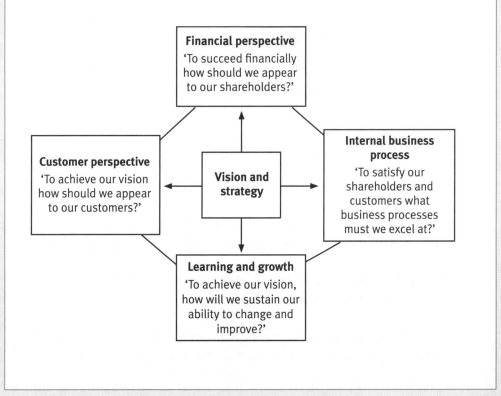

Question 6

The correct statements are:

- Mentoring can lead to faster career progress.
- A mentor can give technical, ethical and general business guidance.
- A mentor is a role model who can help improve career goals.

A mentor will generally be the mentee's line manager is incorrect. It is generally accepted that it is better for the mentor to come from a different department.

Mentoring is used as a means of measuring performance is incorrect. Mentoring is used to enhance performance.

Mentoring focuses on achieving specific objectives, usually within a defined time period is incorrect. Mentoring an ongoing activity.

Question 7

Small, owner managed organisations which rely on key individuals are likely to use **personal centralised** control.

Large manufacturing companies would be most likely to use **output** control.

A professional firm of lawyers would most likely use clan or **cultural** control.

A large hierarchical organisation would be likely to use **bureaucratic** control.

Personal centralised control is used where there is centralised decision making by a key individual. This is usually found in small, owner run companies.

Bureaucratic control is usually found in large hierarchical organisations with formalised rules and procedures and detailed job descriptions.

Clan or Cultural control is found where employees have a strong identification with management goals.

Output control is based on the measurement of outputs and results achieved and is often used in manufacturing organisations.

Question 8

The completed model is shown below:

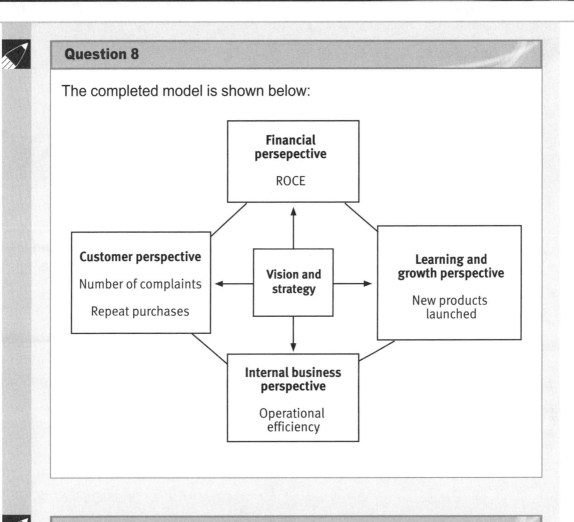

Question 9

D   Learning and growth

The learning and growth perspective looks at how an organisation manages change through development and innovation.

Question 10

The correct answers are:

- A well set target can improve motivation.

- Volume of work would be a suitable target.

- To be accepted, target should be viewed as controllable and achievable.

Targets can only be set using financial measure is incorrect. Targets can also use non-financial measures. In fact, in many cases, these are better measures than financial measures.

Ideally, each individual will be set just one main target is incorrect. Most jobs have a number of dimensions meaning that multiple targets are normally required to actually assess an employee's performance.

9

Organisational culture

Chapter learning objectives

Explain the importance of organisational culture

1 Session content diagram

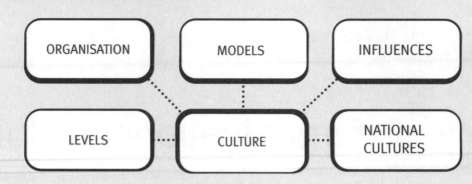

2 What is culture?

Organisational culture is an important concept since it has a widespread influence on the behaviours and actions of employees. It represents a powerful force on an organisation's strategies, structures and systems, the way it responds to change and ultimately, how well the organisation performs.

Culture may be defined as:

'the way we do things around here' – by Handy

By this Handy means the sum total of the *belief, knowledge, attitudes, norms* and *customs* that prevail in an organisation.

3 Levels of culture

According to Edgar Schein (1992)

Culture exists at a three of different levels:

(1) **Artefacts and creations** – the things that can be seen, heard and observed. This is largely the view of the organisation that the public experience. It can include items such as:
    – Dress codes – formal or informal, are uniforms worn.
    – Patterns of behaviour – the way people within the organisation are seen as acting.
    – Physical symbols – could include logos and branding.
    – Office layout – including the facilities and furnishings.

(2) **Espoused Values** – these can be identified from stories and the opinions of those within the organisation. It can include items such as:

– Language – the way people communicate both within and outside the organisation.

– Behaviour – shows what the people in the organisation feel is important.

– How people justify what they do – values can be deep rooted, many will take for granted that their behaviour is acceptable without questioning it.

(3) **Basic assumptions** – beliefs so deeply embedded in a culture that members are no longer consciously aware of them. It can include:

– Beliefs on environmental issues – if this is important, it will be part of every aspect of the work done.

– How people should be treated – human relations policies, customer relationships etc.

As you go through the levels, the elements become less visible and more ingrained. At the third level, those within the organisation may not even be aware of their beliefs, they have become so fundamentally part of their way of being.

For an organisation, understanding this helps them to anticipate problems with their culture and allows them to see how difficult it may be to change. Changing level one items, such as dress codes or office layouts, is relatively easy, but changing values and beliefs can be very difficult. This may also lead to differences between the levels, for example what the organisation says and does may be different to the how is perceived by the outside world. The public may view certain acts as superficial and often do not believe that the underlying beliefs of the organisation have really changed.

The cultural iceberg

The organisational iceberg

The idea of hidden elements in culture is often referred to as the organisational iceberg.

The iceberg describes two levels at which culture operates:

- Formal aspects (visible) above the water
- Behavioural aspects (hidden) below the water

The elements of culture above the surface would include:

- goals

- technology

- procedures

- structure

- skills

The hidden elements represent the larger part of the iceberg which is below the water, and that would include:

- attitudes

- style

- communication patterns

- values

- feelings

- beliefs

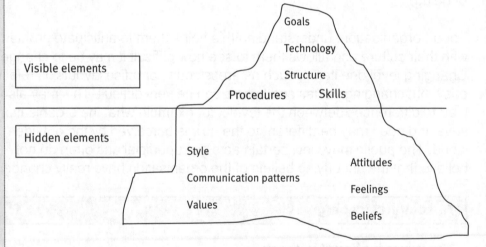

The diagram shows that what the public, customers, suppliers and others outside of an organisation see is only a small part of the picture. Much of what makes the organisation what it is, is intangible or hidden from view. It suggests that it is really only possible to fully understand the workings and culture of an organisation from within.

4 Why is culture important?

Culture is that invisible bond, which ties the people of a community together. It refers to the pattern of human activity. The importance of culture lies in its close association with the way of living of the people. The different cultures of the world have brought in diversity in the ways of life of the people inhabiting different parts of the world.

Culture is related to the development of one's attitude. The cultural values of an individual have a deep impact on his/her attitude towards life. They shape an individual's thinking and influence his/her mindset.

- It gives an individual a unique identity.

- The culture of a community gives its people a character of their own.

- Culture shapes the personality of a community – the language that a community speaks, the art forms it hosts, its staple food, its customs, traditions and festivities comprise the community's culture.

Advantages of having a strong culture

An organisation's culture has a significant bearing on the way it relates to its stakeholders (especially customers and staff), the development of its strategy and its structure. A strong culture will:

- facilitate good communication and co-ordination within the organisation.

- provide a framework of social identity and a sense of belonging.

- reduce differences amongst the members of the organisation.

- strengthen the dominant values and attitudes.

- regulate behaviour and norms among members of the organisation.

- minimise some of the perceptual differences among people within the organisation.

- reflect the philosophy and values of the organisation's founder or dominant group.

- affect the organisation's strategy and ability to respond to change.

Disadvantages of having a strong culture

A strong culture that does not have positive attributes in relation to stakeholders and change is a hindrance to effectiveness. Other disadvantages of a strong culture are:

- Strong cultures are difficult to change, beliefs which underpin culture can be deep rooted.

- Strong cultures may have a blinkered view which could affect the organisation's ability or desire to learn new skills.

- Strong cultures may stress inappropriate values. A strong culture which is positive can enhance the performance of the organisation, but a strong culture which is negative can have the opposite effect.

- Where two strong cultures come into contact e.g., in a merger, then conflicts can arise.

- A strong culture may not be attuned to the environment e.g., a strong innovative culture is only appropriate in a dynamic, shifting environment.

5 Influences on culture

The structure and culture of an organisation will develop over time and will be determined by a complex set of variables, including:

Size	How large is the organisation – in terms of turnover, physical size and employee numbers?
Technology	How technologically advanced is the organisation – either in terms of its product, or its productive processes?
Diversity	How diverse is the company – either in terms of product range, geographical spread or cultural make-up of its stakeholders?
Age	How old is the business or the managers of the business – do its strategic level decision makers have experience to draw upon?
History	What worked in the past? Do decision makers have past successes to draw upon; are they willing to learn from their mistakes?
Ownership	Is the organisation owned by a sole trader? Are there a small number of institutional shareholders or are there large numbers of small shareholders?

When analysing an organisation, look for clues given as to the culture of the organisation using these main areas, although there are many other influences, including the leadership style adopted.

Other influences on culture

As well as the main influences on culture listed above, there are other, more subtle influences:

- The degree of individual initiative – is it encouraged or are decisions always referred upwards?

- The degree of risk tolerance – are managers only allowed to follow low-risk strategies?

- Clarity of direction – is there a clear focus; are these clear objectives and performance expectations?

- The degree of integration between groups – are different units encouraged to work together? Are management aloof or approachable; is communication clear to lower level staff?

- The reward system – are individuals rewarded for succeeding, i.e. are rewards based on performance criteria?

- Conflict tolerance – are employees encouraged to air grievances?

- Communication patterns – is there a formal hierarchy or an informal network?

- Formalisation of clothing and office layout – are there strict rules over this?

- The kind of people employed (graduates, young, old, etc.).

6 The cultural web framework

Johnson and Scholes described a cultural web, identifying a number of elements that can be used to describe or influence organisational culture:

This can be shown in the diagram below:

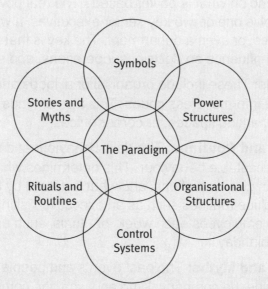

- **The Paradigm:** What the organisation is about; what it does; its mission; its values. The paradigm is influenced by the following six elements:

- **Stories and Myths:** The past events and people talked about inside and outside the company. Who and what the company chooses to immortalise conveys a message about what is valued within the organisation.

- **Rituals and Routines:** The daily behaviour and actions of people that signal acceptable behaviour. This determines what is expected to happen in given situations, and what is valued by management. This could include routines such as an executive visiting the factory floor to speak to employees each week, or rituals, such as buying a cake when it's your birthday

- **Symbols:** These include organisational logos and designs, and the formal or informal dress codes. This also extends to symbols of power such as parking spaces, or corner offices.

- **Organisational Structures:** Reporting lines, hierarchies, and the way that work flows through the business. This includes both the formal structure defined by the organisation chart, and the informal lines of power and influence that indicate whose contributions are most valued.

- **Control Systems:** The processes in place to monitor what is going on. These include internal control systems, performance measurement and reward structures.

- **Power Structures:** Who makes the decisions, how widely spread is power, and on what is power based? The real power in the company may involve one or two key senior executives, a whole group of executives, or even a department. The key is that these people have the greatest influence on decisions, operations, and strategic direction.

- **Power Structures:** Who makes the decisions, how widely spread is power, and on what is power based? The real power in the company may involve one or two key senior executives, a whole group of executives, or even a department. The key is that these people have the greatest influence on decisions, operations, and strategic direction.

- **Symbols:** These include organisational logos and designs, and the formal or informal dress codes. This also extends to symbols of power such as parking spaces, or corner offices.

- **Rituals and Routines:** The daily behaviour and actions of people that signal acceptable behaviour. This determines what is expected to happen in given situations, and what is valued by management. This could include routines such as an executive visiting the factory floor to speak to employees each week, or rituals, such as buying a cake when it's your birthday.

- **Stories and Myths:** The past events and people talked about inside and outside the company. Who and what the company chooses to immortalise conveys a message about what is valued within the organisation.

This model can be used to analyse the current organisational culture and to identify changes that could be made to improve it.

More detail on the cultural web framework

To analyse the current culture using the cultural web framework, the following are examples of questions which could be asked under each of the headings. Once all areas have been considered, it should give a good understanding of the culture of the organisation. From this any necessary changes can be made to improve the culture of the organisation.

Stories and Myths

- What do people say about our organisation?

- What is the reputation of the organisation?

- What do current staff tell new staff about the organisation?

- What do employees talk about when asked about the company?

Rituals and routines

- What do customers expect when they use our services or buy or products?

- What do our employees expect when they come to work?

- What core beliefs are suggested by these behaviours?

Symbols

- Is there a dress code within the organisation?

- Is jargon used which people outside the organisation would not understand?

- Do all branches, offices look the same no matter where they are located?

- Does the organisation have a recognisable corporate image?

Organisational Structures

- Is there a formal organisational structure?

- What type of structure is in place – a tall or flat structure?

- Are there any informal reporting lines?

Control systems

- Are there obvious controls in place within the organisation?

- Is the organisation well controlled?

- Are all employees aware of the controls, and of any implication of non compliance?

Power structure

- Who has the power to make decisions within the organisation?

- Is power concentrated at the top of the organisation?

- Is the power used appropriately?

7 The McKinsey 7-S Model

McKinsey, a US management consultancy, produced a framework for understanding organisations (the McKinsey 7-S framework). This model highlights the 'hard' and 'soft' aspects of organisations which can influence the culture. Similar to the cultural web framework, it also recognises the inter-relationships between the elements. In the cultural web, you saw that all the elements overlapped, in the 7-S model, lines are drawn between each of the elements to show that each element will have an impact on every other element. If one element is changed, then changes in all the other elements will have to be considered.

When public sector monopolies in the UK, such as British Telecom and the utility companies were privatised, the resulting shift to profit orientation created a dramatic change in their cultures and in management attitudes. This also necessitated the recruitment of new management. The change of strategy required a new culture and structure.

The seven factors referred to are:

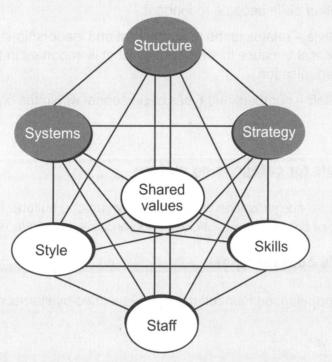

- The hard elements are: strategy, structure and systems
- The soft elements are: shared values, skills, style and staff

The hard elements are more visible from outside the organisation, while the soft elements are usually only completely understood from within the organisation.

More detail on the McKinsey 7-S model

The 7-S's – an overview of the seven elements:

- Strategy – The actions that are planned in response to environmental change in order that the organisation achieves its long term goals.

- Structure – how people and tasks are organised. This will consider the way the organisation's departments and divisions relate to each other.

- Systems – the information flows and processes of an organisation. This includes formal and informal procedures that ensure the organisation operates. For example, accounting systems, budgetary systems information technology systems and so on.

- Shared values – also known as super-ordinate goals. These identify what the organisation believes in and stands for, they are the guiding concepts, values and aspirations of the organisation.

- Skills – distinctive capabilities and competencies. A change in strategic focus may mean that new skills need to be acquired as other skills become redundant.

- Style – relates to the management and leadership style which will be critical because this will convey what is important in the organisation.

- Staff – numbers and types of personnel within the organisation.

8 Models for categorising culture

Whilst every organisation will have its own unique culture, there are a number of different ways of classifying organisation culture.

Handy's cultural types

Handy popularised four cultural types identified by Harrison:

(1) Power

(2) Role

(3) Task

(4) Person.

- *Power culture* **– Here, the ego of a 'key person' comes first.**

  Power culture is based on one or a few powerful central individual(s), often dynamic entrepreneurs, who keep control of all activities and make all the decisions. The structure is perhaps best depicted as a web whereby power resides at the centre and all authority and power emanates from one individual. The organisation is not rigidly structured and has few rules and procedures. This type of culture can react well to change because it is adaptable and informal and decision-making is quick.

  This is likely to be the dominant type of culture in small entrepreneurial organisations and family-managed businesses.

- *Role culture* – **Here, the job description of the actor comes first.**

Role culture tends to be impersonal and rely on formalised rules and procedures to guide decision-making in a standardised, bureaucratic way (e.g. civil service and traditional, mechanistic mass-production organisations). Everything is based on a logical order and rationality. There is a clear hierarchical structure with each stage having clearly visible status symbols attached to it. Each job is clearly defined and the power of individuals is based on their position in the hierarchy. The formal rules and procedures, which must be followed, should ensure an efficient operation.

Decisions tend to be controlled at the centre, this means that whilst suitable for a stable and predictable environment, this type of culture is slow to respond and react to change.

- *Task culture* – **Here, getting the job done right and on time comes first.**

Task culture is typified by teamwork, flexibility and commitment to achieving objectives, rather than an emphasis on a formal hierarchy of authority (perhaps typical of some advertising agencies and software development organisations, and the desired culture in large organisations seeking total quality management). It can be depicted as a net with the culture drawing on resources from various parts of the organisational system and power resides at the intersections of the net. The power and influence tends to be based on specialist knowledge and expert power rather than on positions in the hierarchy. Creativity is encouraged and job satisfaction tends to be high because of the degree of individual participation and group identity.

A task culture can quickly respond to change and is appropriate where flexibility, adaptability and problem solving is needed.

- *Person culture* – **Here, actors fulfil personal goals and objectives whether or not they are congruent with those of the organisation.**

People culture can be divided into two types. The first type is a collection of individuals working under the same umbrella, such as that found in architects' and solicitors' practices, IT and management consultants, where individuals are largely trying to satisfy private ambition. The organisation is based on the technical expertise of the individual employees.

Other types of organisation with people cultures exist for the benefit of the members rather than external stakeholders, and are based on friendship, belonging and consensus (e.g. some social clubs, informal aspects of many organisations).

Each of the different types of culture described has advantages and disadvantages and in reality, organisations often need a mix of cultures for their different activities and processes.

Cultural types and levels of management

Handy also matched appropriate cultural models to the levels of managerial activity:

Strategic management	Concerned with direction setting, policy making and crisis handling	Power culture
Tactical management	Concerned with resources and establishing means to meet the corporate goals	Task culture
Operational management	Concerned with routine activities	Role Culture

Case study style question 1

Up until two years ago, E enjoyed a monopoly position in the energy industry. However, a change in government policy has meant that new competition has been encouraged to move into the industry with E losing its monopoly. The company now finds itself facing severe difficulties.

E has developed a strong culture over the years which can be typified as a role culture. This is now acting as a barrier to the organisation's ability to change, to become more flexible and to be able to respond more quickly to changes in the environment and initiatives by its competitors.

E is falling behind its competitors when it comes to innovations in energy services. Developments in new services require staff to work together across functional boundaries. However, this is unheard of in E where people fiercely protect their functional specialism and will only work on the tasks specified in their job descriptions.

Required:

You have been brought in as a consultant by the Operations Director of E. He has asked you to draft a report for him covering the following:

(a) Discussing why the characteristics of a role culture may no longer be appropriate for E.

(10 minutes)

(b) Recommending, with reasons, the type of culture to which the company should now move.

(8 minutes)

9 Managing in different cultures

As many organisations operate at a global level and face international competition, an understanding of national culture has become increasingly important. Cultural practices vary between different countries and will impact on how organisations operate.

The features of a country's culture have important implications for managing cross border mergers, where problems can arise because of the different ways companies are run as a result of cultural differences. This point is very relevant to organisations who seek to grow through mergers and acquisitions with foreign companies. However, it is important to remember that cultures in society are not permanent and as mentioned earlier, all cultures have sub-cultures and a range of complex and interrelated factors influence organisational culture. The national culture is just of one of these influences.

Hofstede (1990) developed a model to explain national differences by identifying five 'key dimensions' along which national culture seems to vary:

(1) Power Distance

This dimension covers how much society accepts the unequal distribution of power, for instance the extent to which supervisors see themselves as being above their subordinates. In countries with high power distance, managers tend to make autocratic decisions and subordinates do what they are told rather than being involved in decision-making. This kind of culture was found, by Hofstede, to be particularly strong in Malaysia, China, Philippines, and Russia. Low power distance means people expect equality in power, such as in Denmark, Austria and Israel.

- High Power Distance means people accept inequality in power.

- Low Power Distance means people accept equality in power.

(2) Uncertainty Avoidance

Uncertainty avoidance is the degree to which members of society feel uncomfortable with risk, uncertainty and ambiguity, and feel threatened by unusual situations. High uncertainty avoidance will mean risk taking is discouraged and organisations will tend to rely heavily on rules and regulations so that people know what they are doing. This type of attitude is found in Greece, Japan, and Russia. Low uncertainty avoidance means people have high tolerance for the unstructured and unpredictable, this was found in Singapore, Taiwan and Thailand.

- High Uncertainty Avoidance means people are uncomfortable with uncertainty and ambiguity.

- Low Uncertainty Avoidance means people have high tolerance for the unstructured and unpredictable.

(3) **Individualism and Collectivism**

Individualism is the extent to which people are supposed to take care of themselves and be emotionally independent from others and reflects the values of a loosely knit social framework. This tends to be true for the United States, Canada, Britain and Australia. Collectivism is a preference for a tightly knit social framework in which individuals look after one another and organisations protect their members' interests. This was found to be particularly the case in China, Mexico, Chile, and Peru.

- Individualism means that individuals are expected to take care of themselves.
- Collectivism means that individuals look after one another and organisations protect their members' interests.

(4) **Masculinity/Femininity**

Masculinity relates to the degree to which masculine values predominate. For example, a focus on power, achievement, assertiveness, and material success as opposed to the stereotypical feminine values of relationships, modesty, sensitivity and concern for others. Masculine values are strong in Japan, Austria, Italy and Germany. Feminine cultural values were found in Sweden, Norway, Finland and Denmark. Both men and women subscribe to the dominant value in masculine and feminine cultures.

- Masculine orientation values achievement, heroism, assertiveness and material success important.
- Feminine orientation values relationships, caring for the weak and quality of life.

(5) **Time Orientation**

Time orientation is also known as **Confucian v Dynamism**. In this instance Hofstede examined how much society values long standing rather than short term values and traditions. Short term orientation means that people expect fairly rapid feedback from decisions, expect quick profits, frequent job evaluations and promotions, and so on.

- Long Term Orientation means valuing tradition, loyalty, education and training.
- Short Term Orientation means valuing fast promotions and quick profits.

It is important to see that Hofstede was attempting to model aspects of culture that might influence business behaviour, rather than produce national stereotypes or explain the differences he found in historical or socio-geographic terms.

Case study style question 2

X is a manufacturer of non-alcoholic soft drinks and has a well-established position and brand recognition in country Z. The potential for future growth in country Z is however limited, with the market reaching saturation. One option for expansion is to move into new markets in other countries offering their existing product range.

The business development team are evaluating this option and are currently working on proposals to sell their range of drinks in country Y. One possible method of achieving market entry development that the team is investigating is through a joint venture with a company that is already established in country Y and is in the drinks distribution business.

The board of X has given the business development team the task of undertaking a feasibility study to explore the viability of the proposed strategy. As part of the feasibility study there needs to be some assessment of industry competition and the attractiveness of the market in country Y. The feasibility study also needs to assess the cultural compatibility of the ways of doing business in country Y compared to how X currently operates in country Z.

Required:

Write an email to the head of the business development team discussing how Hofstede's research on national cultures could be used to assess the cultural compatibility of X's market development strategy to form a joint venture with a company in country Y.

(20 minutes)

Cultural differences in work-related attitudes

Hofstede also looked at cultural differences in work-related attitudes. These include:

- **Leadership** – in some countries, such as those in Latin America, leaders are expected to take a strong personal interest in employees and appear at private social functions such as weddings. In other countries such as Germany such social contact is discouraged. In yet other countries, notably in Asia and Africa, public criticism is intolerable as the loss of self-respect brings dishonour to the employee and his family.

- **Motivation** – the incentives for effective performance must match the culture. It is pointless offering individual bonuses to workers where there are strong group and company loyalties, as in Japan, or where loyalty to an individual's superior is paramount as in Turkey and the Near East.

- **Structure** – research showed that French firms are bureaucratic with orders and procedures set from above, whereas German firms rely more on the professional expertise from the trained knowledge and skill of the more junior employees.

Managing in a multi-cultural environment

In any situation, where you are required to manage in a cross-cultural or multi-cultural environment, there are a number of guidelines that you should follow:

- Always show respect and listen, do not be in a hurry.

- Try to gain an appreciation for the differences between Hofstede's 'masculine' and 'feminine' cultures.

- Do not feel your way is the best way.

- Emphasise points of agreement.

- Discern the perceived definitions of words.

- Do not embarrass anyone in front of others.

- Know or take someone who knows the culture.

- Understand that leadership may mean different things to different countries.

- Do not lose your temper.

- Avoid clique-building.

- Leave your own 'domestic' management style at home.

- Eliminate stereotypes.

- Learn to tolerate a high degree of unpredictability.

Managers may also have to modify their approach to take account of the following:

- Language

- Religion

- Attitudes

- Social organisation

- Education

- Ethnocentrism (a tendency to regard one's own culture as superior to others).

Case study style question 3

GH operates hotels in most of the developed countries throughout the world. The directors of GH are committed to a policy of achieving 'growth' in terms of geographical coverage and are now considering building and operating another hotel in Portland. Portland is a developing country which is situated 3,000 kilometres from the country in which GH's nearest hotel is located.

The managing director of GH recently attended a seminar on 'the use of strategic and economic information in planning organisational performance'. He has called a board meeting to discuss the strategic and economic factors which should be considered before a decision is made to build the hotel in Portland.

GH has always used local labour to build and subsequently operate hotels. The directors of GH are again considering employing a local workforce not only to build the hotel but also to operate it on a daily basis.

Required:

Prepare a briefing note for the managing director. The note should cover:

(a) The strategic and economic factors which should be considered before a decision is made to build the hotel.

(15 minutes)

(b) The ways in which the possibility of cultural differences might impact on the performance of a local workforce in building and operating a hotel in Portland.

(5 minutes)

Are culture and conflict connected?

Culture is always a factor in conflict, whether it plays a central role or influences it subtly and gently.

Conflicts between teenagers and parents are shaped by generational culture, and conflicts between spouses or partners can be influenced by gender culture.

In organisations, conflicts arising from different disciplinary cultures escalate tensions between co-workers, creating strained or inaccurate communication and stressed relationships.

Though culture is intertwined with conflict, some approaches to conflict resolution minimise cultural issues and influences. Since culture is like an iceberg – largely submerged – it is important to include it in our analyses and interventions. Icebergs unacknowledged can be dangerous, and it is impossible to make choices about them if we don't know their size or place.

It is important to recognise that there is no one-size-fits-all approach to conflict resolution, since culture is always a factor. Cultural fluency is therefore a core competency for those who intervene in conflicts or simply want to function more effectively in their own lives and situations.

This involves:

- understanding that roles vary across cultures
- acting respectfully
- communicating well
- trying to tame the conflict

10 Summary diagram

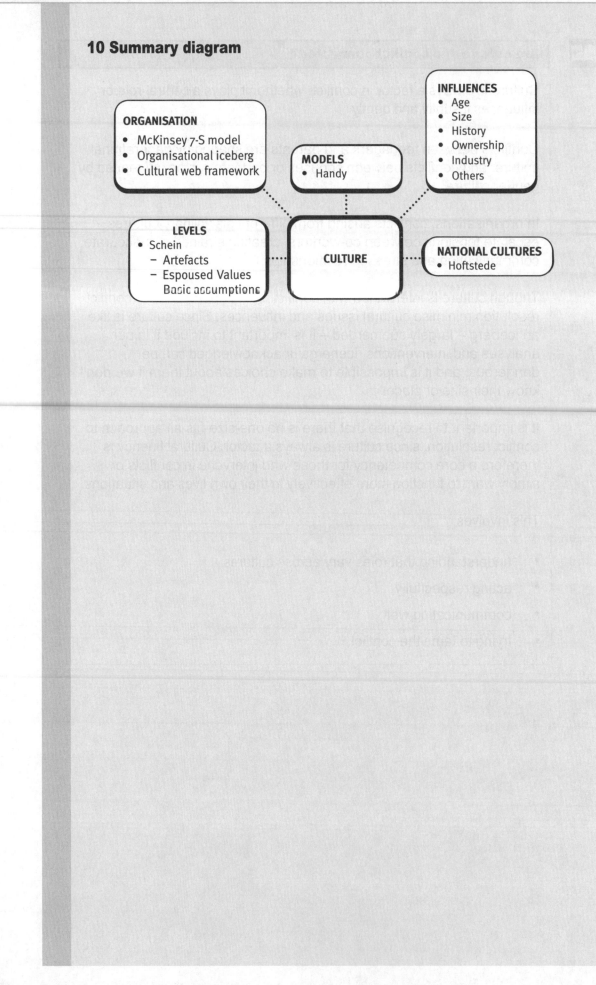

ORGANISATION
- McKinsey 7-S model
- Organisational iceberg
- Cultural web framework

MODELS
- Handy

INFLUENCES
- Age
- Size
- History
- Ownership
- Industry
- Others

LEVELS
- Schein
  - Artefacts
  - Espoused Values
    Basic assumptions

CULTURE

NATIONAL CULTURES
- Hoftstede

End of chapter questions

Question 1

According to Schein, there are three levels of culture. Insert the correct words to complete the sentences about the levels of culture.

- Artefact and creations
- Espoused Values
- Basic assumptions

_____ can be identified from stories and the opinions of those within the organisation.

_____ are things which can be seen, heard and observed.

_____ are so deeply embedded that members are no longer consciously aware of them.

Question 2

In the cultural iceberg model, elements are either visible or hidden. Insert the elements of culture under the correct heading.

- Structure
- Attitudes
- Skills
- Goals

Visible	Hidden

Question 3

Which of the following are elements from Johnson's cultural web framework? Select all that apply.

- Artefacts and creations
- Uncertainty avoidance
- Stories and myths
- Power structures
- Values
- Control systems

Question 4

The office layout would come under which heading from Schein's levels of culture model?

A   Basic assumptions

B   Values

C   Mission

D   Artefacts and creations

Question 5

Using the McKinsey 7S model, match the element to whether it is a hard or soft.

	Hard	Soft
Shared values		
Style		
Structure		
Skills		
Staff		
Strategy		
Systems		

Question 6

Match the item to the description from Schein's model on the levels of culture.

Values	How people justify what they do
Basic assumptions	Dress codes and patterns of behaviour
Artefacts and creations	Beliefs on how people should be treated

Question 7

Which element of the cultural web is explained by the following?

'The processes in place to monitor what is going on'.

A   Organisational structures

B   Power structures

C   The paradigm

D   Control systems

Question 8

Which three of the following descriptions are associated with Handy's Task culture?

- Typified by teamwork and flexibility
- Based on a one or a few powerful central individuals
- Relies on formalised rules and procedures
- Getting the job done right and on time comes first
- There would be a clear hierarchical structure
- Encourages creativity
- Centralised decision making

Question 9

With reference to Hofstede's model on national cultures, match the definitions to the element.

Power distance	The extent to which people are expected to take care of themselves
Individualism/Collectivism	How much society values long standing values and traditions
Uncertainty avoidance	The extent to which society accepts the unequal distribution of power
Time orientation	The degree to which members of society are uncomfortable with risk

Question 10

Small entrepreneurial organisations and family run businesses would tend to demonstrate which cultural type?

A   Power culture

B   Role culture

C   Task culture

D   Person culture

Test your understanding answers

Case study style question 1

REPORT

To: Operations Director

From: Consultant

Date: today

Report on the characteristics of role culture and its appropriateness for E

Introduction

In this report, the characteristics of role culture will be explained and it will be discussed why this may no longer be appropriate for E. The report will also contain a recommendation as to the type of culture which would be more suitable for E.

(a) **Types of culture**

The concept of organisational culture is an important one for E because it can exert a strong influence on business performance. It can shape the behaviours and actions of individuals in the workplace and is often referred to as the 'glue' that holds the organisation together.

There are different types of culture which are determined by an organisation's structures, processes and management methods. Currently, E is typified as having a role culture which can be very efficient and successful in a stable environment when work is predictable and the organisation can control its own environment, often by maintaining a monopoly position. However, this type of culture now appears to be having an adverse effect on E's performance as the company now faces very different operating conditions since losing its monopoly position. The reasons for this can be explained by examining the characteristics of a role culture.

Role culture

Role culture works by rationality and logic, and is usually associated with a formal structure with well established rules and procedures. Job descriptions are clearly defined, tightly describing the tasks of an individual's job. This leads to a strict division of labour with people often reluctant to take on wider responsibilities. Rather, they are obsessed by fulfilling narrow job duties, with a preoccupation on day-to-day administration rather than longer term issues. These characteristics would make it difficult for the organisation to be flexible and adapt to the more competitive operating environment, acting as a barrier to the developments needed in E.

Within a role culture the organisation is dependent upon various functions, each of which has their own areas of strength and influence, with an emphasis on internal processes. This type of culture is also impersonal, relying on formalised rules and procedures for work routines and communication and to guide decision making in a standardised and bureaucratic way. Relations between staff are dominated by hierarchy and authority with formal and rigid control systems. Individuals are selected for particular roles on the basis of their ability to complete a particular task to the required level: over achievement is not actively pursued. However, these characteristics of a role culture can mean that it is more resistant or very slow to adapt to change and getting people to work together across boundaries is difficult.

Innovation can be stifled, since the culture is one which insists people go through layers in the hierarchy to gain approval. Decisions are made at senior level with little involvement from other members of the organisation. In fact new ideas from below may be regarded with suspicion from above. Individuals are required to perform their job and not to overstep the boundaries of authority. This is occurring in the case of E, and would seem to be partly responsible for the lack of flexibility, responsiveness and problem solving capability.

(b) **Recommendation**

It is apparent that the culture of E needs to change and it is recommended that a task culture would be more appropriate given the changes in business conditions.

This type of culture is typified by teamwork, flexibility and commitment to achieving objectives rather than emphasising a formal hierarchy of authority. The task culture is often reflected in a matrix structure or project teams, where the focus is on completing a job or project.

Staff become loyal towards the work rather than towards formal rules. The principal concern is to get the job done, breaking down rigid hierarchies and functions. Therefore, the individuals who are important are those with the skills and ability to accomplish a particular task. Skill and expertise are more important than length of service and position in the organisation, as is currently the case in E. People are not hindered in terms of their contribution by tight job descriptions associated with the role culture. Hence, a task culture tends to encourage greater flexibility, with people working together across functional boundaries to achieve organisational objectives.

Team work is fundamental to a task culture, rather than the achievement of individuals. The result is that influence is spread throughout the organisation. By nature a task culture fosters creativity and is adaptable, responsive and able to change very quickly.

Conclusion

E has traditionally adopted a role culture, but given the changes experienced in the market place, it is recognised that this type of culture may no longer be appropriate for E. The recommendation in this report is that a task culture should be adopted.

Case study style question 2

EMAIL

To: Head of business development team

From: Management accountant

Date: today

Subject: Hofstede's research on national cultures

Just as an organisation develops its own corporate culture which will influence its strategy and its way of doing business, countries show international differences in how they view the world and develop their own cultures in terms of values and basic assumptions. This is an important concept since it will impact on the ways in which people behave at work and the way things are done in organisations. The effect of different environments is a key factor in determining the cultural compatibility of organisations moving into new territories. A mutual understanding of the different cultures will influence the effectiveness of working relationships and the management styles adopted.

Hofstede's research was developed to explain national culture by mapping different cultural characteristics. The outcomes from the research suggest that countries can be classified according to the four dimensions in which national culture varies and that might influence business behaviour. The dimensions are power distance; uncertainty avoidance; individualism; and masculinity. A country can be classified on these dimensions on a continuum from high to low.

Power distance is the extent to which a society accepts that power in organisations is distributed unequally. In countries with high power distance, managers tend to make autocratic decisions and subordinates do what they are told rather than being involved in decision making.

Uncertainty avoidance is the degree to which members of a society feel uncomfortable with risk, uncertainty and ambiguity and feel threatened by unusual situations. High uncertainty avoidance will mean risk taking is discouraged and organisations will tend to rely heavily on rules and regulations so that people know what they are doing.

Individualism versus collectivism is the extent to which people are supposed to take care of themselves and be emotionally independent from others (individualism), to one where people prefer a tight-knit social framework based on involvement (collectivism).

Masculinity relates to the degree to which masculine values predominate. For example, focus on power, achievement, assertiveness, and material success as opposed to the stereo-typical feminine values of relationships, modesty, sensitivity and concern for others.

These factors need to be considered when developing strategies in a cross cultural context since Hofstede argues that countries differ significantly in their 'score' on these dimensions. For instance, on the basis of Hofstede's work it has been argued that the Japanese are more collective, cautious, and authoritarian than Anglo Saxon countries. The implication of this is that Japanese methods of management may not work well in these countries and vice versa.

X could use Hofstede's work to help in the appraisal of cultural compatibility of the proposed strategy to enter country Y through joint venture. The comparison should not only take account of the two organisations but also the cultural differences between consumers in X's existing markets and the consumers in Country Y. If the two countries have significant cultural differences along all four dimensions, the joint venture might not be an attractive proposition.

Market development strategies often fail because whilst financial assessments are sound, insufficient attention has been placed on cultural factors.

I hope you have found the above useful. Please do not hesitate to get in touch if you would like any more information or would like to discuss any of these issues further.

Case study style question 3

BRIEFING NOTE

To: Managing director

From: Management accountant

Subject: Factors which should be considered before a decision is made to build the hotel

(a) Of vital importance is the need for reliable information on which to base the decision regarding the potential investment within Portland, since the lack of such information will only serve to increase the risk profile of GH.

The **strategic factors** that ought to be considered prior to a decision being made to build and operate a hotel in Portland are as follows:

The competition

The key notion here is that of the position of GH relative to its competitors who may have a presence or intend to have a presence in Portland. The strategic management accounting system should be capable of coping with changes that can and will inevitably occur in a dynamic business environment. Hence it is crucial that changes such as, the emergence of a new competitor, are detected and reflected within strategic plans at the earliest opportunity.

The government

The attitude of the government of Portland towards foreign organisations requires careful consideration as inevitably the government will be the country's largest supplier, employer, customer and investor. The directors need to recognise that the political environment of Portland could change dramatically with a change in the national government.

Planning and control of operations within Portland

Planning and control of operations within Portland will inevitably be more difficult as GH might not possess sufficient knowledge of the business environment within Portland. Indeed their nearest hotel is at least 3,000 kilometres away. It is vital the GH gain such knowledge prior to commencing operations within Portland in order to avoid undue risks.

The sociological – cultural constraints

While it is generally recognised that there is a growing acceptability of international brands this might not be the case with regard to Portland. In this respect it is vital that consideration is given to recognition of the relationships in economic life including demand, price, wages, training, and rates of labour turnover and absenteeism.

Resource utilisation

The attitude towards work, managers (especially foreign nationals) and capitalist organisations could severely impact on the degree of success achieved within Portland.

A primary consideration relates to whether or not to use local labour in the construction of the hotel. The perceived 'remoteness' of Portland might make it an unattractive proposition for current employees of GH, thereby presenting the directors of GH with a significant problem.

Communication

Consideration needs to be given to the communication problems that arise between different countries and in this respect Portland is probably no exception. Language barriers will inevitably exist and this needs to be addressed at the earliest opportunity to minimise any risks to GH.

The **economic factors** that ought to be considered prior to a decision being made to build and operate a hotel in Portland are as follows:

Resource availability

The hotel should be designed having given due consideration to the prevailing climatic conditions within Portland which might necessitate the use of specific types of building materials. It might well be the case that such building materials are not available locally, or are in such scarce supply in which case local supply would prove to be uneconomic.

Another consideration relates to local labour being available and reliable in terms of its quality.

Currency stability/restrictions

The stability of the currency within Portland assumes critical significance because profit repatriation is problematic in situations where those profits are made in an unstable currency or one that is likely to depreciate against the home currency, thereby precipitating sizeable losses on exchange. Any currency restrictions need to be given careful consideration. For example, it might be the case that hotel guests would be prohibited from paying accommodation bills in a foreign currency which would be problematic if the local currency was weak.

Legislation

All local and International legislation should be given careful consideration. It might be the case that local legislation via various licences or legal requirements favour local hotels.

Demand

The potential demand within Portland will be linked to the local economy. It is a developing economy and this may bode well for GH. However, again the need for reliable information about the size of the market, the extent of competition, likely future trends etc is of fundamental importance.

Financing

An important decision lies in the availability and associated costs of financing in Portland which might not have mature enough capital markets due to its developmental state. Hence GH might need to finance using alternative currencies.

Note: Other relevant comments would be acceptable.

(b) The directors of GH should be mindful that the effectiveness of a locally employed workforce within Portland will be influenced by a number of factors including the following:

The availability of local skills

If Portland is a lower wage economy it is quite conceivable that a sufficient number of employees possessing the requisite skills to undertake the construction of a large hotel cannot be found. If there are insufficient local resources then this would necessitate the training of employees in all aspects of building construction. This will incur significant costs and time and needs to be reflected in any proposed timetable for construction of the hotel. As far as the operation of the hotel is concerned then staff will have to be recruited and trained which will again give rise to significant start-up costs. However, this should not present the directors of GH with such a major problem as that of training construction staff. Indeed, it is highly probable that GH would use its own staff in order to train new recruits.

Attitudes to work

The prevailing culture within Portland will have a profound impact on attitudes to work of its population. Attitudes to hours of work, timekeeping and absenteeism vary from culture to culture. For example, as regards hours of work in the construction industry in countries which experience very hot climates, work is often suspended during the hottest part of each day and recommenced several hours later when temperatures are much cooler. The directors of GH need to recognise that climatic conditions not only affect the design of a building but also its construction.

A potentially sensitive issue within regarding the use of local labour in the construction of the hotel lies in the fact that national holidays and especially religious holidays need to be observed and taken into consideration in any proposed timetable for construction of the hotel. As regards the operation of a hotel then consideration needs to be given to the different cultures from which the guests come. For example, this will require a detailed consideration of menus to be offered. However, it might well be the case that the local population might be unwilling to prepare dishes comprising ingredients which are unacceptable to their culture due to, for example, religious beliefs.

Question 1

Espoused Values can be identified from stories and the opinions of those within the organisation.

Artefact and creations are things which can be seen, heard and observed.

Basic assumptions are so deeply embedded that members are no longer consciously aware of them.

Question 2

Visible	**Hidden**
Structure	Attitudes
Skills	
Goals	

Visible elements also include technology and procedures. Hidden elements would also include style, communication patterns, values, feeling and beliefs.

Question 3

- Stories and myths
- Power structures
- Control systems

The other elements of the cultural web are:

- The paradigm
- Symbols
- Organisational structures
- Rituals and routines

Question 4

D   Artefacts and creations

This level relates to the things which can be seen, heard or observed.

Question 5

Hard	**Soft**
Strategy	Shared values
Systems	Style
Structure	Skills
	Staff

The full model is shown below:

Question 6

The correct matches are:

Values		How people justify what they do
Basic assumptions		Beliefs on how people should be treated
Artefacts and creations		Dress codes and patterns of behaviour

Question 7

D   Control systems

Control systems include internal controls, performance measurement and reward structures.

Question 8

- Typified by teamwork and flexibility
- Getting the job done right and on time comes first
- Encourages creativity

Based on a one or a few powerful central individuals – this relates to power culture

Relies on formalised rules and procedures – this relates to role culture

There would be a clear hierarchical structure – this relates to role culture

Centralised decision making – this relates to role culture

Question 9

The correct definitions are:

Power distance	The extent to which society accepts the unequal distribution of power
Individualism/Collectivism	The extent to which people are expected to take care of themselves
Uncertainty avoidance	The degree to which members of society are uncomfortable with risk
Time orientation	How much society values long standing values and traditions

Question 10

A   Power culture

With power culture the 'ego' of the key person comes first. This is often seen in small, family run or entrepreneurial businesses. With power culture the power remains with the ley person and they tend to make all of the decisions.

Building, leading and managing teams

Chapter learning objectives

Evaluate the issues associated with building, leading and managing effective teams

1 Session content diagram

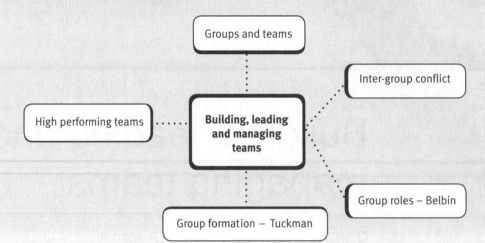

Definition of groups

There are many different definitions available to explain what constitutes a group. **Schein** suggests that a group is any number of people who:

- interact with one another

- are psychologically aware of one another; and

- perceive themselves to be a group.

Groups have power structures, leadership structures, role structures, communication structures and sociometric structures. They develop norms, ideologies, characteristic atmospheres, degrees of cohesiveness and morale.

Whereas teams are a kind of group, all groups are not teams.

2 Groups and teams

People rarely work in isolation at work, since most activities need some coordination through groups of people. Groups provide security and social satisfaction for their members. They support individual needs and promote communication, formally or informally.

What is a team?

A team is a **formal group**. It has a leader and a distinctive culture and is geared towards a final result.

An effective team can be described as 'any group of people who must significantly relate with each other in order to accomplish shared objectives'.

In order to ensure that the team is truly effective, team members must have a reason for working together. They must need each other's skills, talent and experience in order to achieve their mutual goals.

Multiskilled teams bring together individuals who can perform any of the group's tasks. These can be shared out in a flexible way according to availability and inclination.

Multidisciplinary teams bring together individuals with different specialisms so that their skills, knowledge and experience can be pooled or exchanged.

Types of groups

- **Formal groups** – organisations use groups to carry out tasks, communicate and solve problems. Membership is normally formal, often determined or constrained by the organisation into departments or divisions.

- **Informal groups** – individuals join groups to meet their social and security or safety needs. Membership is normally voluntary and informal. Individual members are dependent on each other, influence each other's behaviour and contribute to each other's needs.

- **Reference groups** – is a group the individual does not currently belong to but wants to join, for example a particular work group or committee.

- **Self directed and autonomous groups** – The ideas of these evolved from the work of Trist and Bamforth and through experiments carried out in the 70s by Swedish car manufacturers Volvo and Saab. A self directed or autonomous group is one which is encouraged to manage its own work and working practices.

Informal groups

Managers need to pay attention to the formation of, and support for, formal groups and also realise that they cannot ignore or suppress informal groups. In relation to informal groups, it is important:

- to let employees know that managers understand and accept them while discouraging dysfunctional behaviour in such groups

- to try to anticipate how decisions will influence informal groups; and

- to keep formal decisions from unnecessarily threatening informal groups.

Benefits and problems with groups

Benefits of groups

Within organisations there has been an implicit belief that people working as members of a group or team perform more effectively than if they are organised as individuals. There are a number of benefits from team working:

- **Increased productivity** – working as part of a group can result in a better overall result than could be achieved if each person worked independently. By breaking a task up into its component parts, different members of the group, with different skills, can be working on different aspects of the task at the same time.

- **Synergy** – One person cannot do everything, but a team can combine all the main areas of skill and knowledge that are needed for a particular job. Synergy describes the phenomenon in which the combined activity of separate entities has a greater effect than the sum of the activities of each entity working alone – often described as a way of making **2 + 2 = 5**.

- **Improved focus and responsibility** – each member can be given the responsibility for specific tasks, avoiding overloading one person with too much responsibility which may result in a loss of focus.

- **Improved problem solving** – having a group made up of members with different abilities will mean a higher likelihood of having the appropriate knowledge and skills to solve problems.

- **Greater creativity** – the idea that two (or more) heads are better than one. Group discussions can generate and evaluate ideas better that individuals working alone.

- **Increased satisfaction** – working as part of a group can bring social benefits and a sense of belonging to its members. In addition the group will offer support to its members and provide a facility for individual training and development needs.

- **Increased motivation** – members will work hard for the other members of the group. They will feel a collective responsibility and will not want to let the other members down.

- **Improved information flows** – there will be more effective communication through participation in group discussions.

Problems with groups

Unfortunately groups can also have negative as well as positive effects. Subsequent research has identified a number of these negative effects, some of which are discussed below:

- **Conformity** – individuals can be persuaded by group pressures to agree with decisions which are obviously wrong, and which the person must know to be wrong.

- **The Abilene paradox** – this is a famous case, which demonstrates that the group can end up with an outcome that none of the members wanted. The story was written up as a case by a sociologist whose family all ended up in Abilene, Texas, driving 100 miles through desert heat, though none of them actually wanted to go. They all thought each other wanted to go, and no one wanted to disturb the 'consensus'.

- **'Risky shift' or group polarisation** – this is the tendency for groups to take decisions which are riskier than any that the individual members would take on their own. It now appears that there is also a tendency, under certain circumstances, for groups to take excessively cautious decisions.

- **Groupthink** – this occurs within deeply cohesive groups where the members try to minimise conflict and reach consensus without critically testing, analysing, and evaluating ideas.

In a group, there is a high level of mutual interaction and awareness which are responsible for powerful forces, which cause the individual to behave, sometimes, rather differently from the way they would behave on their own. It is important to the organisation that these forces work for the organisation and not against it.

Clearly, managers must attempt to minimise these potential problems while harnessing the many benefits of groups and teams.

Groupthink

Some symptoms of groupthink are:

- the raising of protective barriers and the illusion of impregnability.
- a negative attitude towards competing projects.
- an unwavering belief in the group and its decisions.
- a sectarian emphasis on agreement.

Groupthink can lead to disastrous results. After the initial 'Bay of Pigs' disaster, when the United States encouraged an abortive 'invasion' of Cuba via the Bay of Pigs, John F Kennedy saw clearly how to try to avoid 'groupthink' and planned his leadership accordingly by insisting on:

* critical evaluation of alternatives

* independent sub-groups to work on solutions

* external testing of proposed solutions

* the leader avoiding domination of the group (which can be unconscious)

* the avoidance of stereotypes of the opposition.

Group cohesiveness

There are a number of factors which affect the integration of organisational and individual objectives in groups, and hence the cohesiveness of the group. They include:

Membership factors

* **Homogeneity**. Similarity of members is preferred for simple tasks; it leads to easier working but less creative problem-solving. A variety of skills and knowledge is more effective for complex tasks. Homogeneity of status, both internally and externally, leads to a more cohesive group.

* **Alternatives**. If the individual has alternatives, that is he or she can leave the group easily, his or her dependence on the group is reduced. Similarly, if turnover of membership is high, the group will tend to lack cohesion. Management may, of course, deliberately keep changing the membership of awkward groups.

* **Size of group**. The importance of this factor depends on the nature of the particular task. Groups solve problems more quickly and effectively than individuals, but one should also consider cost-effectiveness. As the size of the group goes up, the average productivity of the members goes down; there is less opportunity to participate; individuals' contributions are less obvious; cliques or factions may form; less work is done; and 'social loafing' or 'social noise' may increase.

* **Membership in other groups**. This may detract from the cohesion and effectiveness of the original group.

Environmental factors

- **Task**: the nature of the task and its organisation must be compatible.

- **Isolation of the group**: external threats and incentives are lower the more isolated the group is.

- **The climate of management and leadership**: the leadership style adopted should be appropriate to the task. For example in organisations where management adopt McGregor's Theory X approach, this can lead to anti-management groups forming, even if only informally.

Dynamic factors

- **Groups are continually changing**. It should be recoginsed that groups are changing all the time, not just in membership but also in understanding each other and of the task.

- **Success and failure**. There can be a tendency for groups to persist in failure.

3 Team development

The level of group performance is affected by the manner in which teams come together. According to Tuckman, teams typically pass through four stages of development: The stages are:

- **Forming**
- **Storming**
- **Norming**
- **Performing**

These development stages can be seen clearly in project management where teams are put together to undertake a specific project.

- **Forming** – at this initial stage, the team members are no more than a collection of individuals who are unsure of their roles and responsibilities until the project manager clearly defines the initial processes and procedures for team activities. The project manager must then provide clear direction and structure to the team by communicating the project objectives, constraints, scope, schedules and budget.

- **Storming** – most teams go through this conflict stage. As tasks get underway, team members may try to test the project manager's authority and team preconceptions are challenged. Conflict and tension may become evident. The conflict resolution skills and the leadership skills of the project manager are vital at this stage and he or she needs to be more flexible to allow team members to question and test their roles and responsibilities and to get involved in decision-making.

- **Norming** – this stage establishes the norms under which the team will operate and team relationships become settled. Project procedures are refined and the project manager will begin to pass control and decision-making authority to the team members. They will be operating as a cohesive team, with each person recognising and appreciating the roles of the other team members.

- **Performing** – once this final stage has been reached the team is capable of operating to full potential. Progress is made towards the project objectives and the team feels confident and empowered. The project manager will concentrate on the performance of the project, in particular the scope, timescales and budget, and will implement corrective action where necessary.

Not all teams automatically follow these four stages in this sequence. Not all teams pass through all the stages – some get stuck in the middle and remain inefficient and ineffective.

He added a fifth stage:

- **Dorming** (Adjourning) – If a team remains for a long time in the performing phase, there is a danger that it will be operating on automatic pilot. 'Groupthink' occurs to the extent that the group may be unaware of changing circumstances. Instead, maintaining the team becomes one of its prime objectives.

In this situation it may be necessary for the group to 'dorm' or be suspended. With project teams, they are disbanded or adjourned at the end of the project.

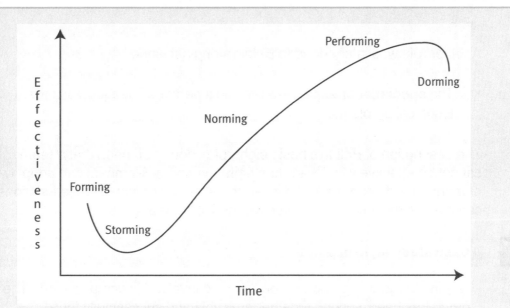

4 Belbin's team roles

Belbin suggests that the success of a group can depend significantly upon the balance of individual skills and personality types within the group. A well-balanced group should contain the following eight main character types:

- **coordinator** – co-ordinating (not imposing) and operating through others, delegates well. Tends to be mature and confident.

- **shaper** – committed to the task, may be aggressive and challenging, will also always promote activity.

- **plant** – thoughtful and creative and generates ideas.

- **monitor-evaluator** – analytically criticises others' ideas, brings group down to earth. Tends to be a stable, introverted type of individual with a high IQ.

- **resource-investigator** – not a new ideas person, but tends to pick up others' ideas and adds to them; is usually a social type of person who often acts as a bridge to the outside world. Tends to be outgoing and enthusiastic.

- **implementer (company worker)** – turns general ideas into specifics; practical and efficient, tends to be an administrator handling the scheduling aspects. Tends to be practical, reliable and efficient.

- **team worker** – concerned with the relationships within the group, is supportive and tends to defuse potential conflict situations. Tends to be cooperative, perceptive and diplomatic.

- **completer finisher** – unpopular, but a necessary individual; the progress chaser who ensures that timetables are met. Tends to be an anxious and conscientious.

Another role was later added to Belbin's original work:

- The **specialist** or **expert** – a technical person, if needed, to solve technical problems.

The description of Belbin's basic eight roles does not mean that a team cannot be effective with fewer than eight members. Members can adopt two or more roles if necessary. However, the absence of one of these functions can mean a reduction in the effectiveness of the team.

Case study style question 1

N is in charge of a group of twelve people involved in complex work. The group has been working together amicably and successfully for a considerable time. Its members value N's leadership and the back-up given him by O. She often elaborates on N's instructions and deals on his behalf with group members' queries, especially when he is absent on the group's business.

Much of the success of the group has been due to P, who is very creative at problem solving, and R who has an encyclopaedic knowledge of sources of supply and information. Q is an expert on all aspects of product development, and S is invaluable at sorting out disagreements and keeping everyone cheerful. The remaining members of the group also have roles which are acceptable to themselves and to the others.

Recently O resigned for family reasons. Because the workload has been increasing, N recruited four new people to the group. N now finds that various members of the group complain to him about what they are expected to do, and about other people's failings. P and R have been unusually helpful to N but have had several serious arguments between themselves and with others.

N recently attended a presentation about effective work groups and would like to understand the issues his group is experiencing better. The presentation covered models by Tuckman and Belbin and N thinks that of he understood these models better, he could improve the performance of his team.

Required:

Write an email to N explaining the causes of these changes in the group and recommending how he can ensure that the group reverts to its former cohesiveness. The email should refer to the theories of Belbin and Tuckman.

(20 minutes)

Role theory

Role theory is concerned with the roles that individuals adopt. Developing a group means identifying distinct roles for each of its members. Any individual can have several roles, varying between different groups and activities. The role adopted will affect the individual's attitude towards other people.

Role theory assists in the understanding of how productive teams are formed and operated.

There are several terms associated with role theory.

- **Role ambiguity** arises when individuals are unsure what role they are to play, or others are unclear of that person's role and so hold back co-operation. For example this can arise when a new member joins an established group.

- **Role conflict** arises when individuals find a clash between differing roles that they have adopted. A company finance officer who uncovers fraud by senior management may feel a conflict between the roles of professional confidentiality and honest citizenship.

- **Role incompatibility** occurs when individuals experience expectations from outside groups about their role that are different from their own role expectations.

- **Role signs** are visible indications of the role. Style of dress and uniform are clear examples of role signs. These may be voluntary (a male accountant wearing a grey or blue suit and a tie) or mandatory (in military, police and hospital occupations).

- **Role set** describes the people who support a lead person in a major role, e.g. the clerk and junior barristers would form part of a senior barrister's role set.

- **Role behaviour** where certain types of behaviour can be associated with a role in an office or works. For instance, the 'crown prince' behaving as if they are heir apparent to a senior position.

5 High performance teams

Vaill: high-performance teams

Vaill said that high-performing teams may be defined as human systems that are doing dramatically better than other systems. He claimed that they have a number of common characteristics:

- Clarification of broad purposes and near-term objectives.
- Commitment to purposes.
- Teamwork focused on the task at hand.
- Strong and clear leadership.
- Generation of inventions and new methods.

Peters and Waterman – successful teams

Peters and Waterman identified five key aspects of successful teams as:

- The numbers should be **small**, inevitably each member will then represent the interest of their section/department. Larger teams would be slower and harder to manage.
- The team should be of **limited duration**, and exist only to achieve a particular task.
- Membership should be **voluntary**. Where members do not want to be part of the group, they are unlikely to participate fully.
- **Communication should be informal and unstructured**, with little documentation and no status barriers.
- It should be **action-oriented**. The team should create a plan for action not 'just a form of words'.

Building the team and improving effectiveness

Teams are not always able to achieve their goals without some outside intervention or support from management. As such, managers may attempt to create 'teambuilding' exercises for workers. Team building exercises are tasks designed to develop group members and their ability to work together. Team building exercises tend to be based around developing the team in several areas, including:

- **improved communication**, such as through the use of problem solving exercises which force all team members to discuss a problem the group is facing.
- **building trust** between team members, which will help the individual members work as a group.

- **social interaction** between the individuals in the team can help to reduce conflict and increase the cohesion of the group.

In addition to formal teambuilding exercises, managers can attempt to reinforce the individual identity of the team, strengthening team members' sense of belonging and improving the efficiency of the group. This can be accomplished in a number of ways, including giving the team its own name, its own office/space or its own uniforms.

Measuring team effectiveness

There are many possible ways of measuring team effectiveness, including:

- the degree to which the team achieved its stated objectives and the quality of its output.

- team member satisfaction

- the efficiency of the team which can be measured by the resources used to achieve team objectives.

Management could measure these by using labour turnover or absenteeism rates or through the use of questionnaires for team members, interviews, or direct observation of the team. Team rewards could then be designed to not only motivate the individuals within the group, but also encourage cooperation and responsibility sharing between the team as a whole.

6 Distributive leadership

A distributed leadership perspective recognises that there are multiple leaders. From the leadership and management chapter it can be seen that traditionally leadership has been viewed as the role of one person in charge of others, but this view is changing.

Distributive leadership is also known as shared, or collective leadership and involves the sharing of the power base between a number of individuals. With distributed leadership, leadership is shared so that team members effectively interact with and lead each other. This form of leadership is more horizontal in nature, compared to traditional leadership which tends to be more vertical or hierarchical. This can be seen in the self directed and autonomous groups mentioned earlier in the chapter. With these group, individuals are encouraged to manage their own work and working practices.

Carson et al proposed that shared leadership is facilitated by an overall team environment that consists of three dimensions:

- **Shared purpose** – when team members have similar understandings of their team's main objectives and take steps to ensure a focus on collective goals.

- **Social support** – extent to which team members actively provide emotional and psychological strength to one another.

- **Voice** – the degree to which a team's members have input into how the team carries out its purpose.

The three dimensions are highly interrelated. If team members are encouraged to voice their opinions and get involved, they are more likely to start demonstrating leadership traits. If all members do this, there will be a greater focus on collective goals. This in turn leads to increased motivation within the team which encourages members to voice their opinions and get involved.

This suggests that a consequence of distributive or shared leadership is improved team performance and many studies have found a positive relationship between shared leadership and team effectiveness.

7 Inter-group and intra-group conflict

Inter-group conflict within organisations can be defined as the behaviour that occurs between organisational groups when participants identify with one group and perceive that other groups may block their group's goal achievement. While intra-group conflict occurs when there are disagreements or misunderstandings between members of a team. Conflict between team members can lead to a reduction in team productivity.

Inter-group conflict requires three ingredients.

(1) **Group identification.** Employees have to perceive themselves as part of an identifiable group or department.

(2) There has to be an **observable group difference** of some form. The ability to identify oneself as a part of one group and to observe differences in comparison with other groups is necessary for conflict.

(3) **Frustration.** Frustration means that if one group achieves its goal the other will not; it will be blocked. Frustration need not be severe and only needs to be anticipated to set off intergroup conflict. Intergroup conflict will appear when one group tries to advance its position in relation to other groups.

Managing inter-group conflict

Faced with inter-group conflict, the purpose of any managerial strategy will be to turn the conflict into fruitful competition or, if this is not possible, to control the conflict.

There are a number of approaches which can be used to manage inter-group conflict.

These include:

- **Confrontation.** Occurs when parties in conflict directly engage one another and try to work out their differences. Negotiation is the bargaining process that often occurs during confrontation and that enables the parties to systematically reach a solution. Confrontation is not always successful as there is no guarantee that discussions will focus on a conflict or that emotions will not get out of hand.

- **Third-party consultants.** When conflict is intense and enduring, and department members are suspicious and uncooperative, an expert third-party consultant can be brought in from outside the organisation to meet with representatives from both departments.

- **Inter-group training.** A strong intervention to reduce conflict is intergroup training. This technique has been developed by psychologists such as Robert Blake, Jane Mouton and Richard Walton. When other techniques fail to reduce conflict to an appropriate level, or when other techniques do not fit the organisation in question, special training of group members may be required.

- **Member rotation.** It means that individuals from one department can be asked to work in another department on a temporary or permanent basis. The advantage is that individuals become submerged in the values, attitudes, problems and goals of the other department. In addition, individuals can explain the problems and goals of their original departments to their new colleagues. This enables a frank, accurate exchange of views and information.

- **Superordinate goals.** Another strategy is for top management to establish superordinate goals that require cooperation between departments. Conflicting departments then share the same goal and must depend upon one another to achieve it.

Confrontation, third-party consultants and some training methods could also be used to manage intra-group conflict.

e.g

Illustration 1 – Rivalry generated by inter-group competition

The intensity of rivalry generated by inter-group competition can be seen in the well-known case documented below.

Sherif and Sherif divided boys at a summer school camp into two teams and established clear identities for each with a rivalry between the two. The immediate result was that inter-group competition increased group cohesion. Each group regarded the other as the enemy, and fraternisation and communication between the groups ceased.

Within each group it was found that:

- conformity was demanded, and group requirements outweighed individual needs

- group members encouraged a move from informal to formal and from a leadership approach of participation to an autocratic one

- the group became better organised.

At the end of the exercise a winning team and losing team resulted. The friction existing between the teams resisted concentrated efforts to remove it. Attempts to run joint teams and act against an outside team were of limited success. It was noted that the winning team retained its spirit and cohesion but became complacent and sought to satisfy the needs of individuals. On the other hand, the losing team sought to allocate blame both inside and outside the group. Its cohesion fell and it ignored the needs of individual members.

In summary, some degree of competition may prove beneficial but the long-term result of excessive competition is likely to result in conflict and a reduction in efficiency.

Managing Intergroup conflict – training

Training is a method for managing inter-group conflict.

This training requires that department members attend an outside workshop away from day-to-day work problems. The training workshop may last several days, and various activities take place. This technique is expensive, but it has the potential for developing a company-wide cooperative attitude. The steps typically associated with an intergroup training session are as follows:

- The conflicting groups are both brought into a training setting with the stated goal of exploring mutual perceptions and relationships.

- The conflicting groups are then separated and each group is invited to discuss and make a list of its perceptions of itself and the other group.

- In the presence of both groups, group representatives publicly share the perceptions of self and other that the groups have generated, while the groups are obligated to remain silent. The objective is simply to report to the other group as accurately as possible the images that each group has developed in private.

- Before any exchange takes place, the groups return to private sessions to digest and analyse what they have heard; there is great likelihood that the representatives' reports have revealed to each group discrepancies between its self-image and the image the other group holds of it.

- In public session, again working through representatives, each group shares with the other what discrepancies it has uncovered and the possible reasons for them, focusing on actual, observable behaviour.

- Following this mutual exposure, a more open exploration is permitted between the two groups on the now-shared goal of identifying further reasons for perceptual distortions.

- A joint exploration is then conducted of how to manage future relations in such a way as to encourage cooperation between groups.

After this training experience, department employees understand each other much better. The improved attitudes lead to better working relationships for a long time.

Case study style question 2

L is a firm which undertakes road reconstruction and maintenance. The work is carried out by teams which operate independently of each other. The team members have worked together for years and are well integrated. Each team includes a salesman who is responsible for getting additional work, ideally in the area where the team is already working. The teams draw their materials and road-surfacing and other machinery from the company pool, and obtain information on potential customers from a central sales office.

Although the firm's performance has been satisfactory, the operations manager has decided to try to improve productivity by introducing competition between the teams. This will be done by drawing half of the wages of each team member from a single bonus pool for which all the teams compete.

The finance manager is concerned about these proposals as she feels that while this could improve team performance, it could also adversely affect the behaviour of the teams. She has requested a meeting with the operations manager to discuss the proposals. She has asked you to prepare some discussion points for her to use in the meeting.

Required:

Prepare a paper containing discussion points for the finance manager. The points should cover how such a policy is likely to affect the behaviour of these teams.

(15 minutes)

8 Summary diagram

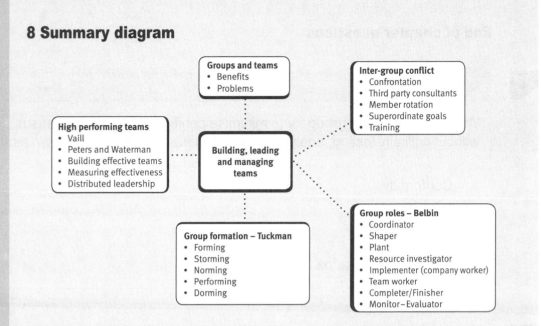

Groups and teams
- Benefits
- Problems

Inter-group conflict
- Confrontation
- Third party consultants
- Member rotation
- Superordinate goals
- Training

High performing teams
- Vaill
- Peters and Waterman
- Building effective teams
- Measuring effectiveness
- Distributed leadership

Building, leading and managing teams

Group roles – Belbin
- Coordinator
- Shaper
- Plant
- Resource investigator
- Implementer (company worker)
- Team worker
- Completer/Finisher
- Monitor–Evaluator

Group formation – Tuckman
- Forming
- Storming
- Norming
- Performing
- Dorming

End of chapter questions

Question 1

When members of a group try to minimise conflict and reach consensus without critically testing, analysing and evaluation ideas, this is known as:

A   Conformity

B   Risky shift

C   Groupthink

D   The Abilene paradox

Question 2

Using Tuckman's model, match the descriptions to the stage of team development.

Storming	Members start to operate as a team and appreciate the roles of others
Performing	Team members test the manager's authority, and conflict can arise
Forming	The team is capable of operating to full potential
Norming	Team members are a collection of individuals unsure of their roles

Question 3

Using Belbin's team roles, insert the correct character type in the sentences below.

- Shaper
- Team worker
- Monitor-evaluator
- Resource-investigator
- Plant
- Coordinator
- Implementor (Company worker)
- Completer/Finisher

The _____ is concerned with the relationships within the group.

The _____ will promote activity within the group.

The _____ analyses others' ideas and brings the group down to earth.

The _____ chases progress and ensures timetables are met.

Question 4

Consider the following types of group behaviour:

According to Peters and Waterman, which of these would be characteristics of a successful group? Select all that apply.

- Avoidance of conflict
- Small number of members
- Informal and unstructured communication
- Strong pressure for group members to conform
- Voluntary membership
- Dominant individual members

Question 5

Which of the following are the three requirements for intergroup conflict?

- The groups have to have superordinate goals.

- Employees have to perceive themselves as part of an identifiable group or department.

- There has to be dominant personalities within the groups

- The has to be weak leadership within the groups.

- There has to be an observable group difference of some form.

- There has to be a degree of frustration between the groups.

Question 6

Which of the following statements about distributed leadership are true?

- Distributed leadership is facilitated by the team members having a shared purpose, social support and a voice.

- Distributed leadership is also known as transformational leadership.

- Distributed leadership tends to be more vertical in nature while more traditional leadership tends to be more horizontal.

- Distributed leadership has been found to improve motivation and team performance.

- Distributed leadership involves the power base for a team being shared between a number of team members.

Question 7

Team X is successfully run by A and has six members including A. A has been in the team for over 20 years and is very good at analysing new ideas and at keeping the group focused.

D has been in the industry for 20 years but only joined the team two years ago. She has a lot of contacts with suppliers and customers and is very good at networking.

E is very good at sorting out disputes and conflicts between team members. The main disputes happen between B, who can be aggressive and pushes people to get the job done, and F who is stable and deals with the administration and the scheduling for the team.

C tends to generate the ideas for the team and is very creative at problem solving.

Match the team members to the Belbin's tam role which they would be most suited to. A team member can have more than one role.

- coordinator.

- shaper

- plant

- monitor-evaluator

- resource-investigator

- implementer (company worker)

- team worker

- completer finisher

Question 8

Match the approach for managing inter-group conflict to its description.

| Superordinate goals |
| Member rotation |
| Third-party consultants |
| Confrontation |

- Parties directly engage with each other to attempt to work out their differences

- An expert is brought in from outside to meet with both parties

- Conflicting parties are set the same goal and must depend on each other to achieve it

- Individuals from one department can be asked to work in another department

Question 9

Which of the following statements about types of groups are true?

- Organisations should try to discourage informal groups.

- A group that an individual does not belong to but would like to join is known as a reference group.

- Organisations use informal groups to carry out tasks, communicate and solve problems.

- When making business decisions managers should always consider how these decisions will impact on informal groups.

- Individuals join informal groups to meet social and security needs.

Question 10

According to Valll, which of the following are key characteristics of high-performance teams? Select all that apply.

- Commitment to purpose
- Functional specialism
- Eight main character types
- Strong and clear leadership
- Super-ordinate goals
- Teamwork focused on the task at hand

Test your understanding answers

EMAIL

To: N

From: Management Accountant

Date: today

Subject: Team performance

Neville,

Your group of twelve people is a long established and successful group. It would therefore be operating in Tuckman's fourth and final stage, which he terms 'performing'. In this stage the group is mature and individuals have evolved the roles that each will discharge and the norms of behaviour for group sessions. Such a settled group will be comfortable and familiar with each other, encouraging each individual to fulfil his/her role.

Belbin has devised a series of questionnaires whereby a person's natural role within a group can be defined. His theory further explains that a successful group has a balance of types.

Prior to the recent changes in the team, you were fulfilling the 'coordinator' role; P was the 'plant', capable of innovative solutions but may be low on practical follow through. R would have been the 'Resource Investigator', Q was an 'implementor (company worker)', but may also have functioned as a 'Monitor Evaluator', providing an organising, dutiful, unemotional aspect to the group's work. S was the 'Team Worker', defined by Belbin as important in promoting team spirit. O seems to have been the 'Completer/Finisher', ensuring that matters are followed through; also during your absence she may have acted as 'Shaper' in providing the drive and momentum for completion of the work. This analysis suggests that this group was well balanced in having all major team roles present.

The resignation of O could cause an imbalance within the group unless another individual develops into the 'Completer/Finisher' and 'Shaper' roles. Belbin explains that people can adopt different roles in different groups and amend their behaviour to fill a vacant role. However, there will be a temporary imbalance. Furthermore, the resignation of O and her replacement by four new people means that the group reverts to the earlier stages of Tuckman's group formation i.e., forming, storming and norming.

As the group seeks to absorb new unknown people and strange roles are adopted it is inevitable that some people conflict will emerge. This could be aggravated by the increased size of the group. When the group had twelve members, a degree of cohesiveness is possible; however, this is less likely in a group of fifteen, especially when four members are new.

Since P and R have been unusually helpful, they are probably aware of this difficulty and are trying to cover O's role gap. However, the friction between them and with others highlights the need for you to take action.

To recapture group cohesiveness and efficiency you could:

- let the group evolve over time through the four stages until the performing stage is reached when group cohesiveness would be restored. This would incur the intermediate stages when the group members get to know each other, when roles develop and are accepted by others, when disagreements arise. This may feel like a safe option since eleven of the fifteen members are long standing and extra support is coming from P and R. However, you need to remember that the personality of the new group will be different from the old team – there are new people and roles involved. Also, the size of the group is significantly larger and could not operate in the same way.

- break the group into smaller teams, which may progress through the four stages of formation more quickly. A smaller team can be managed in a more personal manner and this may suit you.

- become directly involved in structuring the progression of the group through each stage of formation. You could, for example, influence the development of roles and behaviour norms through your own behaviour in recognising a particular person as the 'Shaper' in the team.

- change the group structure through delegation, assigning individual responsibilities, making some tasks team based instead of personal based. Since the tasks are complex, this may be a current practice.

- emphasise the change and need for a new approach by altering the physical layout of the office. A revised desk seating plan could create its own team influences and separate potential conflict staff.

- introduce a series of team building training sessions in which the group could analyse its own behaviour. This could involve understanding the value that each person brings to the team as well as ensuring that everyone understands the group tasks that must be completed. In the final resort this could lead to the payment of team bonuses based on team, rather than individual, performance.

- you may also have to consider whether there is a need to change your management style. Likert emphasises that the effective manager can adapt his/her management style in response to changes in staff, tasks and situation. For example, you may find it necessary to be less participative in the early stages of group formation. Or even adopt two different styles if he chooses to split the group into two smaller teams.

I hope you have found the above useful. Please do not hesitate to get in touch if you would like any more information or would like to discuss any of these issues further.

Case study style question 2

Discussion points for meeting re team bonus structure

Prepared by Management Accountant

Date: today

Introduction

Road reconstruction and maintenance work will consist of contracts where each contract is different in nature, size and location. The techniques and materials used may be common but the application will be variable. Under this pattern of work there is considerable initiative available to the work team while central control cannot be detailed.

The present teams are cohesive, successful and operate independently of each other. The introduction of competition between groups will heighten the cohesive aspect and reduce the co-operation overall, this can be concluded by the Boys Camp experiments of Sherif and Sherif. This will be accentuated in this example because the change in wage system means that teams are competing for a share of a single bonus pool. The operations manager's introduction of competition will change the attitude and behaviour of the teams. Some of these changes will be beneficial while others will be negative.

The positive changes in behaviour are likely to be:

- An improvement in productivity within the teams. Each team will endeavour to safeguard or increase its share of the bonus pool. The team will concentrate its attention on improving its own productivity through streamlining working practices, ignoring trade demarcation boundaries and working outside normal hours to complete the job.

- The bonus element of the wages can be calculated on a basis of contract profitability as contract time targets. If profitability is the measure then the team will be cost conscious and material wastage, equipment abuse etc will be minimised. However, if the measure is time targets then wastage and machinery abuse will be irrelevant to the team's bonus and management will need a central system to check team behaviour and operations.

- An improvement in timekeeping and attendance should occur. Mayo, in the Hawthorne Experiment, was the first researcher to point out the strong pressure of group colleagues upon the behaviour of any individual within a group. The more cohesive the group, the stronger its peer pressure. Group names will be clearly evident covering areas of attendance, timekeeping, 'breaktimes' and individuals will be pressurised to fulfil their role within the team. As Mayo discovered, if the behaviour of an individual usurps a team name then team members exact a penalty and the offender is subjected to ostracisation, sneering comments and similar social pressure.

- Local sales effort is likely to be increased. If potential customers are logged with a central sales office then once a team has commenced work with a customer, they are likely to 'sell' extra services and develop sales to a maximum. There could be a situation where this is damaging to the organisation. For instance a major customer operating several sites could employ more than one team from the road reconstruction company. If one team disparages the work of another team or causes it to miss a deadline, in order to gain the next slice of work, then the overall company reputation is damaged. This is the potential danger in all situations of local rivalry.

- There will be a change in internal working relationships as group members become less social in behaviour and more task centred. This will increase pressure on newcomers or poor-performers, as time spent in coaching or supporting by other team members becomes resented.

The negative changes in behaviour are likely to be:

- Competition will breed selfishness and the bonus shareout will create winners and losers encouraging envy and recriminations between teams and their members.

- Teams will be selective in the jobs that they undertake. A difficult or potentially low bonus job is likely to be avoided. An additional temptation would arise when a team developed a major customer and was unable to handle all the work generated in the timescale required by the customers. The team may seek to postpone the work and so safeguard future bonuses but would damage customer services in doing so.

- Fluctuating wages and internal group pressure to perform could have harmful consequences for individuals and reduce loyalty.

- There will be severe pressure on the sales person to put the interests of his team first and the company second. Sub-optimising of performance is likely as each team seeks to direct its sales person's efforts for the team's benefit. This selfishness of behaviour could extend to other areas such as machines being drawn from the company pool and not returned promptly for other teams to use. A further example could arise where one team learns of a contract which is in the immediate vicinity of a rival team's current working. The overall benefit of the company dictates that disruption and travelling costs would be minimised by the team in that locality fulfilling that work. But selfish team behaviour may block this.

In summary competition between teams will deeply affect the behaviour of individuals within groups and inter group behaviour.

Question 1

C   Groupthink

Conformity is where individuals are persuaded by team pressure to agree with decisions which are obviously wrong.

Risky shift is the tendency for groups to take riskier, or more cautious, decisions than the individuals would take.

The Abeline Paradox refers to the situation where the outcome achieved was not what any of the members wanted but they all thoughts the others did.

Question 2

The correct match is:

Norming	Members start to operate as a team and appreciate the roles of others
Storming	Team members test the manager's authority, and conflict can arise
Performing	The team is capable of operating to full potential
Forming	Team members are a collection of individuals unsure of their roles

Question 3

The **team worker** is concerned with the relationships within the group.

The **shaper** will promote activity within the group.

The **monitor-evaluator** analyses others' ideas and brings the group down to earth.

The **completer/finisher** chases progress and ensures timetables are met.

Question 4

- Small number of members
- Clear objectives
- Voluntary membership

Paters and Waterman also suggested that successful teams should be of a limited duration and be action orientated.

Question 5

- Employees have to perceive themselves as part of an identifiable group or department.

- There has to be an observable group difference of some form - individuals must identify themselves as part of one group.

- There has to be a degree of frustration between the groups - frustration means that one group achieving its goals will block another group from meeting its goals. Frustration only has to be anticipated to cause conflict.

Question 6

- Distributed leadership is facilitated by the team members having a shared purpose, social support and a voice.

- Distributed leadership has been found to improve motivation and team performance.

- Distributed leadership involves the power base for a team being shared between a number of team members.

Distributed leadership is also known as transformational leadership. This is false, it is also known as collective leadership.

Distributed leadership tends to be more vertical in nature while more traditional leadership tends to be more horizontal. This is false as distributed leadership tends to be more horizontal.

Question 7

A   is coordinator and monitor-evaluator

B   is completer/finisher

C   is plant

D   is resource-investigator

E   is team worker

F   is implementer (company worker)

Question 8

The correct matching is:

- Parties directly engage with each other to attempt to work out their differences – **Confrontation**

- An expert is brought in from outside to meet with both parties – **Third-party consultants**

- Conflicting parties are set the same goal and must depend on each other to achieve it – **Superordinate goals**

- Individuals from one department can be asked to work in another department – **Member rotation**

Question 9

- A group that an individual does not belong to but would like to join is known as a reference group.

- When making business decisions managers should always consider how these decisions will iImpact on informal groups.

- Individuals join informal groups to meet social and security needs.

Organisations should try to discourage informal groups. This is false, they have to be aware of them and understand the need for them.

Organisations use informal groups to carry out tasks, communicate and solve problems. This is incorrect. While informal groups may contribute to these outcomes, they would generally use formal groups for these purposes.

Question 10

- Commitment to purpose
- Strong and clear leadership
- Teamwork focused on the task at hand

In addition Vaill suggested that high performing teams would also exhibit:

- Clarification of broad purpose and near term objectives
- Generation of inventions and new methods

Techniques for managing organisational relationships

Chapter learning objectives

Discuss the roles of communication, negotiation, influence and persuasion in the management process

Discuss approaches to managing conflict

1 Session content diagram

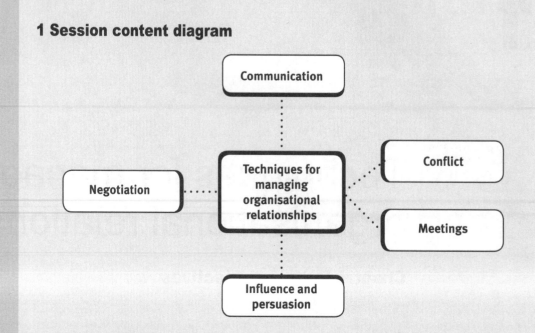

2 Communication

An important aspect in all relationships within an organisation is communication. Most organisations will depend to some extent on the speed and accuracy of communication to maintain their competitive edge, and the management function relies on effective communication. Good communication skills are often included as an essential management competence, since people with good communication skills have been found to make better decisions and tend to be promoted more frequently.

Effective and regular personal communication is vital to ensure coordination and to identify problems quickly.

Types of communication

Most communication within an organisation can be classified as either formal or informal.

Formal communication

This helps to provide management structure, so that individuals know what is expected of them and how they have actually performed. It could include plans, procedures, policies and performance reports and meetings, as well as the formal communication of management decisions.

Informal communication

This is communicated informally by means of face-to-face conversations, telephone conversations, emails and text messages. It does not follow the lines of authority, instead being a feature of co-operation between individuals.

The process of communication

The communication process can be defined as a process that is used to transmit a message from a sender to a receiver by using a medium of communication. A message can be words, numbers, gestures or non verbal cues such as body language.

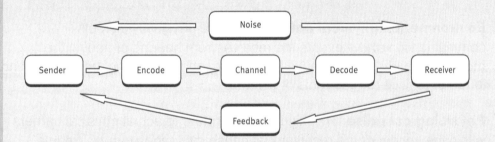

The message goes through several stages when it is sent by the sender to the receiver. These stages are as follows:

(1) **Sender**. The sender is the entity that conveys or sends the message.

(2) **Encoding**. Encoding is a process through which the message is symbolised.

(3) **Channel**. Channel is the medium through which message is being sent. (email, conversations, meetings, memos etc).

(4) **Receiver**. The receiver is the entity that receives the message.

(5) **Decoding**. Decoding is the process in which the message is translated and meaning is generated out of it. (problems can occur here due to interpretation).

(6) **Feedback**. Is the process through which receiver sends their response.

The importance of feedback

When a message is sent, it is important that the sender receives feedback from the receiver to let them know that the message was successfully received. Feedback can be verbal, for example acknowledgements, questions or comments or it can be non-verbal such as a smile (or a frown). Feedback can also be written, for example in replying to a text or email.

Feedback is a very important part of the communication process as it gives the sender the knowledge that the message has been received as intended, or can allow the sender to clarify the message where it appears that the receiver is confused or doesn't understand the message.

It is important that the sender asks for feedback. Assuming a message has been received and understood can be a dangerous assumption to make.

Noise

Another feature of the communication process is noise. Noise is anything which interferes with the communication process and stops the message being received and understood by the receiver as it was intended. There are many types of noise, including:

Environmental/physical noise: This noise physically disrupts communication and prevents the receiver from hearing or seeing the message clearly. For example, loud music, phones ringing, people chatting loudly or difficult-to-read fonts or colours.

Physiological noise: This kind of noise refers to actual physical barriers within the sender or the receiver that cause messages to have trouble getting through. For example, hearing loss, poor eyesight or the sender having a speech impairment.

Semantic noise: This noise occurs when the sender and receiver have a different understanding of words. This could include different dialects or languages, using jargon, or words with several possible meanings.

Psychological noise: The attitude of the sender and receiver can also make communication difficult. For example anger or sadness may cause someone to lose focus, being preoccupied with a problem or feelings of prejudice can all affect the communication process.

Barriers to communication

Sender:

- not being clear as to what has to be communicated
- omitting information
- choosing words in coding the message that do not accurately reflect the idea/concept, and or choosing words that the intended receipts cannot understand
- choosing words that provoke an emotional response
- using technical jargon
- choosing an inappropriate medium
- sending too much information
- sending mixed messages.

Receiver:

- not in an appropriate state to receive the message
- not wishing to receive the message
- filtering out elements that he or she does not wish to deal with
- information overload
- mindset that does not admit the substance of the message.

Ways to overcome the barriers:

the **sender** should:

- have a definite, clear objective
- plan the communication
- think about the receiver and their situation
- anticipate reactions to the message and cater for these
- practise using the channels of communication
- seek and work with the feedback.

the **receiver** should:

- consider their contribution
- listen attentively
- check out anything that is vague
- give feedback.

Non verbal communication

Not all communication is verbal – a great deal of communication can take place without any words at all. The raised eyebrow, the smile, the frown and the glare all say a great deal; so can more obvious physical gestures such as the hand shake, pat on the back or an arm around the shoulders.

Body language is about:

- appearance
- eye contact
- facial expression
- posture and distance
- tone

Non verbal actions can vary across countries and cultures.

According to Druker: **"The most important thing in communication is hearing what isn't said."**

Studies by Mehrabian suggested that only around 7% of a message is transmitted through the actual words said, with the other 93% being conveyed through the way the words are said and other non-verbal elements.

3 Meetings

Meetings can be an effective communication method for the manager. In order to ensure that meetings are effective and useful it is important to adopt the following steps:

- determine the purpose of the meeting
- establish who needs to attend
- determine the agenda in advance
- make suitable arrangements for location and time
- facilitate discussion
- manage the plan of action
- summarise
- publish results/minutes

A rule of thumb of facilitation is that successful meetings are:

80% preparation and **20% execution**.

Roles of team members in meetings:

- The manager should act as a **facilitator** in the meeting process, setting the agenda and ensuring the meeting achieves its objectives.

- One person needs to act as a **chairperson**, to ensure the agenda is followed.

- The meeting will require a **secretary or administrator** to take minutes.

- Team members will play various roles:
    - protagonists – positive supporter.
    - antagonists – challenging and disruptive.

All meeting members must be listened to with respect, but it is the responsibility of the manager to make the whole team aware of the overall project objective, and the role that each team member plays in its achievement.

If the meeting is designed to solve problems, individual team members will be called upon to offer their own expertise and advice on the situation. Other team members will take a more passive role, but will be important in providing an objective perspective on the solutions generated. It is important that a variety of skills are represented at a meeting so that those present can provide varying expert opinions upon the same problem.

Problems with meetings and their solutions

Problems with meetings	Actions to avoid problem
Inappropriate chairperson.	Selection should be based on someone with the requisite range of communication skills.
The objectives of the meeting are undefined and so unclear.	Ensure that an agenda is produced and circulated prior to the meeting. During the meeting, the chairperson should state the objective(s) and must return the focus of the meeting to the points on the agenda.
Lack of enthusiasm or interest in the meeting	For future meetings, ensure that only those with an interest in the meeting, or whose view is required, are actually invited to the meeting. For the current meeting, suggest a short break or stress the need to reach a conclusion.

Attendees talk too much without regard to the chairperson's requests.	The chairperson must impose some order on the meeting. Possible solutions include asking the participants to speak in accordance with meeting protocols such as a time constraint if necessary, or (worst case) asking them to leave the meeting altogether.
Attendees cannot reach an agreement concerning issues on the agenda.	The chairperson will need to exercise negotiation skills to try to bring the meeting to some agreement. If this is not possible, then attendees may have to agree to differ. However, some action points may be required to ensure that more information is obtained so agreement can be achieved at the next meeting.
Action points from previous meetings have not been carried out.	Assuming that minutes were issued correctly, in the current meeting, the chairperson should obtain reasons for actions not being completed. For future action points, ensure that each has a person identified as responsible for completing it. Check the minutes of the meeting to ensure that all action points are included.
Minutes are either too long (information overload) or too brief (do not include appropriate points).	Ensure that the minutes are either minutes of resolution (which contain agreed outcomes) or, if minutes of narration, that they are sufficiently edited to provide the flavour of the discussions, but not small detail.

Case study style question 1

QB has experienced significant success over the last year and is expanding rapidly. B, the founder and managing director, feels that changes to the way the company is being run will have to be made in order to ensure future success. One area he has identified which needs improving is the communication between managers.

The main means of communication between mangers is via a monthly managers' meeting, however these meetings are generally unproductive. B feels this is due to the following reasons:

- Lack of participation – During the meetings, some managers do not contribute, many feel they have better things to do with their time, so keep quiet to speed the meeting up.

- Non-attendance – not all managers turn up for the monthly meetings, and on some occasions the operations manager has sent a junior member of staff on his behalf.

- Decisions are rarely made at the meeting as the managers don't usually know what will be discussed at the meeting so rarely bring any documentation. Discussions can be held at the meeting, but managers can leave the meeting unclear as to what will happen next.

- The manager of the sales department is a formidable character and the others managers are usually reluctant to disagree with him. He usually takes over the discussions within the meeting.

B has employed you as a consultant for advice as to how to improve these areas.

Required:

Write a report for B discussing the problems which have been experienced in the monthly meetings and suggesting what should be done to make future meetings more productive.

(15 minutes)

4 Influence, persuasion and negotiation skills

Influence, persuasion and negotiation are all aspects of communication skills. They are linked and can often be used together, but they are different:

Influence is the ability to change others' attitudes, opinions or behaviour. Influence can be direct or indirect. Direct influence is when the person attempting to change the attitude of another speaks directly to the other person. This type of influence would be used within sales or customer services roles. Indirect influence is where the message attempts to reach its target via a third party. For example organisations may pass messages to public relations firms or analysts, in the hope that these parties will in turn influence potential customers.

Persuasion is the ability to deliberately influence others to change an attitude, opinion, or behaviour. Therefore persuasion differs from influence in that it is always direct and deliberate, while influence can also be indirect.

Negotiation is the ability to discuss an issue with one or more other people in the attempt to establish ways to reach agreement.

Influence

Influencing techniques are used frequently by sales people to encourage us to purchase goods and services. There will also be many situations within organisational relationships where it will be important to influence other people, for example, attempting to gain support for a new product or process. When attempting to influence others it is important to consider the objective and the reasons why influencing the other party is necessary as forceful influence may be seen as manipulative.

Cialdini came up with six principles of Influence (or the six weapons of influence). These can be used whenever there is a need to influence others.

(1) **Reciprocity** – Human nature can lead us to feel obliged to return favours. Therefore we may influenced to support someone who has supported us in some way in the past.

(2) **Commitment** (and Consistency) – As humans, we desire consistency and don't like to be seen to be changing our minds. Therefore we may be influenced to follow through with our support for something if we had shown some initial interest in it .

(3) **Social Proof** – This principle relies on the fact that humans tend to be influenced by peer pressure. If we see others acting in a certain way, it is likely to influence us to act in the same way

(4) **Liking** – This principle is based on the fact that as humans we are more likely to be influenced by people we like, people who are nice and friendly towards us or people who are similar to us.

(5) **Authority** – Another principle of influence is based on the premise that we are more likely to be influenced by people in positions of authority. This comes from a sense of trust and respect for the position held.

(6) **Scarcity** – This principle suggests that we are more likely to want something if its availability is limited. We are more likely to support something if we fear losing out if we don't.

Using the six principles of influence

Reciprocity – Identify what you want to achieve and what you need from the other person. You can then identify what you may be able to offer them, or remind them of what you have done for them in the past.

Commitment – Try to get some commitment from others at an early stage on the process. This makes it more difficult for them to withdraw their support later on.

Social Proof – Use the opinions of those already supporting you to influence others to join that support. If others are talking about your project, new people will want to be part of it.

Liking – Build relationships with those you want to influence so that they trust you. This can be difficult and can take some time, also different approaches may be required for different people.

Authority – Use your own authority and the authority of others, as influencers. Getting the backing of senior, powerful people will encourage others to back you.

Scarcity – People need to know that they could miss out if they don't act quickly. Imposing deadlines to enhance urgency can encourage people to give their support.

It is worth recognising these principles so that you can be aware when others are trying to use them to influence you.

Persuasion

Persuasion is a stronger form of influence. While influence can be direct or indirect, intentional or unintentional, persuasion is always direct and intentional. The aim of persuasion is to change a person, or group's attitude or behaviour towards something or someone. The person using persuasion has a clear objective and is set on achieving it by getting others to support them. Persuasion falls short of telling or ordering someone to do something, as it attempts to get the other person to agree.

The six principles of influence can be used in persuasion, albeit they may be used in a stronger form.

Negotiation

Negotiation is another important communication skill required within organisations. Negotiation can be used by managers in their relationships with not only subordinates but with other stakeholders such as suppliers and customers.

The aim of negotiation is to settle differences between people or groups, and to allow them to come to an agreement which both parties accept.

Negotiation is defined by three characteristics:

(1) Conflict of interest between two or more parties. What one wants is not necessarily what the others want.

(2) No established set of rules for resolving conflict, or the parties prefer to work outside of an established set of rules to develop their own solution.

(3) Parties prefer to search for an agreement rather than to fight openly, to have one side capitulate, to break off contact permanently, or to take their dispute to a higher authority.

Examples of negotiations managers might need to undertake:

- on **his/her own behalf** when securing a pay rise, for instance, or an improvement in the terms and conditions of employment.

- on **behalf of a department or functional area**, e.g. securing an acceptable departmental budget.

- with the **external environment** on behalf of the organisation, e.g. obtaining planning permission for an extension to the warehouse.

The skills required by a negotiator can be summarised under three main headings:

- **Interpersonal skills** – the use of good communicating techniques, the use of power and influence, and the ability to impress a personal style on the tactics of negotiation.

- **Analytical skills** – the ability to analyse information, diagnose problems, to plan and set objectives, and the exercise of good judgement in interpreting results.

- **Technical skills** – attention to detail and thorough case preparation.

The process of negotiation

The negotiation process can be divided into four distinct stages:

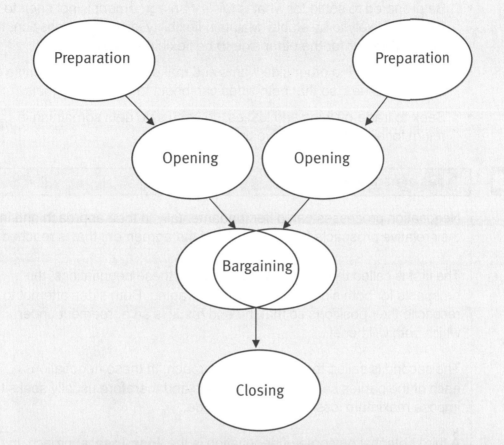

- **Preparation** – information gathering – knowing the background to the problem, and the likely constraints acting on each participant.
- **Opening** – both sides present their starting positions, good opportunity to influence the other party.
- **Bargaining** – purpose is to narrow the gap between the two initial positions, persuade other party of the strength of your case. In order to do this, you should use clearly thought out, planned and logical debate.
- **Closing** – agreement is reached, looking for a mutually beneficial outcome.

Guidance for successful negotiation

- Focus initially on each side's primary objective – minor negotiating points can become a distraction in the early stages.

- Be prepared to settle for what is fair – if an agreement is not seen to be fair it is unlikely to be stable. Maintain flexibility in your own position, this makes it easier for the other side to be flexible as well.

- Listen to what the other side wants and make efforts to compromise on the main issues, so that both sides can begin to attain their goals.

- Seek to trade-off wins and losses, so each side gets something in return for everything they give up.

Types of negotiation

Negotiation processes can differ fundamentally in their approach and in their relative prospects for the stability of the agreement that is reached.

The first is called the '**win-win**' approach. In these negotiations, the prospects for both sides' gains are encouraging. Both sides attempt to reconcile their positions so that the end result is an agreement under which both will benefit.

The second is called the '**win-lose**' approach. In these negotiations, each of the parties seeks maximum gains and therefore usually seeks to impose maximum losses on the other side.

A third potential outcome of negotiation is the '**lose-lose**' approach. In this scenario either both parties concede more than they initially intend, or no agreement is actually reached. Both parties can end up in worse positions than they were in before the negotiation.

It is clear that a win-win solution is more likely to lead to a stable solution and a successful business relationship in the long run.

Case study style question 2

D is a manufacturer of building materials, supplying the house building industry. As a result of the downturn in the demand for its products and in response to difficult operating conditions in its existing market, the company is currently going through a major restructuring. It is anticipated that the restructuring plan will involve the consolidation of some business activities which will result in a number of staff having to move to different areas of the company. This could mean re-location to different sites, and other staff being made redundant.

While employee relations have in the past been good, the management of the company is aware that employees and the trade unions which represent their interests will be resistant to the changes that need to be made. The first stages of change will require skilful negotiation between the management and unions on a range of issues relating to the movement of staff jobs, the proposed job losses and, specifically, the criteria for redundancy and the redundancy package.

K, the operations director has been asked to lead the negotiations on behalf of D. He is not confident about this as he has never been involved in negotiations of this kind before. He has asked you for some advice.

Required:

Write an email to K, explaining the role of negotiation in the management of change in D, making reference to the different stages involved in the negotiation process.

(15 minutes)

Why are these communication skills important?

In any organisation there will frequently be conflicting demands on time, or differences of opinion or attitude for which these skills are key in trying to reach agreements where all parties are happy and can work together towards the organisational goals. In certain job roles they will be more important than others, for example in any role with responsibility for customer or supplier relationships, or for managing others, these communication skills are essential.

The importance of effective communication for Chartered Management Accountants

For Chartered Management Accountants (CMAs) who are required to deal with a variety of parties, both internal and external, these skills are fundamental.

CMAs are an integral part of any business and hold a variety of positions within organisations, often senior management positions. Their roles are varied and can include (amongst others):

- formulation of policy and setting of corporate objectives
- acquisition and use of finance
- generation, communication and interpretation of financial and operating information for management and other stakeholders
- derivation of performance measures
- improvement of business systems

To undertake these roles, they often work as part of multi-skilled management teams. They will be required to deal with other employees throughout the organisation, at all different levels, and external parties such as customers, suppliers, contractors and advisors. Effective communication skills are therefore vital for the CMA as they will be required to deal with a variety of people in order to carry out a variety of roles. Influencing, persuasion and negotiation skills will be particularly important.

5 Conflict

Conflict is a disagreement, and is when one party is perceived as preventing or interfering with the goals or actions of another. Conflict can occur in a variety of forms and at different levels, for example organisational, group or individual level.

Inter-group conflict was looked at in the previous chapter.

Conflict can arise for many different reasons, these are known as the **causes of conflict**. When conflict occurs certain behaviours can develop, these are known as the **symptoms of conflict**. There are also two main **types of conflict**. It is important that that you can distinguish between these different elements of conflict.

Causes of conflict

Mainwaring suggested that the causes of conflict generally include:

- **History**. Conflicts have a tendency for being self-perpetuating.
- **Differences**. Mainly of interests, objectives, priorities and ideologies.
- **Limited resources**. Where there are limited resources, there may be a battle for what is available.
- **Win/lose situations**. Success for one group often involves failure for others.
- **Interdependencies**. Where relationships, responsibilities or boundaries are not clearly defined, and/or where they are perceived to be unfair.
- **Misunderstandings**. These include communication failures and are common where there already exists some sort of conflict or threat.
- **Conviction beliefs**. If one group is convinced of their essential rightness or goodness, then there may be tendencies to 'enlighten' others, causing resistance.
- **Stress and failure**. If an individual, a group, or an organisation feels unable to cope with pressures and problems, then this is likely to generate fault finding, reality denial and seemingly irrational acts.
- **Change**. Individual, group, organisational and societal change creates new relationships, objectives, perceptions, problems and possibilities.

Symptoms of conflict

Certain behaviours and attitudes can manifest themselves when conflict exists. Sometimes these behaviours are overt, as when it emerges in the form of a strike, or individuals refusing to communicate with each other at all. However, the management of conflict is likely to be easier and more effective if these symptoms of conflict can be recognised and dealt with at an earlier stage. Such symptoms would probably include some of the following:

- Problems, even trivial ones, being passed up the hierarchy because no one wants to take responsibility for them.

- Hostility and jealousy between groups.

- Poor communications up and down the hierarchy, and between departments.

- Widespread frustration and dissatisfaction because it is difficult to get even simple things done efficiently.

- Problems constantly being polarised around people, usually in different groups, and personalities rather than issues.

Types of conflict

Horizontal conflict

The first type of conflict is horizontal. Horizontal conflict occurs between groups and departments at the same level in the hierarchy. The main sources of horizontal conflict are:

- **Environment** – each department or group becomes tailored to 'fit' its environmental domain and, thus, is differentiated from other groups or departments.

- **Size** – as organisations grow, members of departments begin to think of themselves as separate, and they erect walls between themselves and other departments.

- **Technology** – interdependency creates opportunity for conflict as technology determines task allocation.

- **Structure** – divisionalisation and departmentalisation create competition which can lead to conflict.

- **Goal incompatibility** – each department's operative goals interfere with each other or the achievement of goals by one department may block achievement of the goals of other departments.

- **Task interdependence** – dependence on each other for materials, resources and information. Generally, as interdependence increases, the potential for conflict increases.

- **Reward system** – if departments are rewarded only for departmental performance, managers are motivated to excel at the expense of the rest of the organisation.

- **Differentiation** – functional specialisation causes differences in cognitive and emotional orientations.

Vertical conflict

A second type of conflict is vertical. Vertical conflict occurs among individuals and groups at different levels in the hierarchy. Individual employees may have conflicts with their bosses. Managers of international divisions often experience conflict with senior executives located at domestic headquarters. Many of the sources of horizontal conflict above may apply here as well. The other primary sources of vertical conflict are often about power and powerlessness and differences in status and power. Some example are:

- **Power and status** – at the bottom of the hierarchy, workers often feel alienated.

- **Ideology** – different values, e.g. free enterprise *versus* the right to industrial action.

- **Psychological distance** – workers feel isolated from the organisation.

- **Scarce resources** – financial resources affecting remuneration and working conditions, and costs.

More on horizontal conflict

The potential for horizontal conflict exists in any situation in which separate departments are created, members have an opportunity to compare themselves with other groups, and the goals and values of respective groups appear mutually exclusive. The main sources of horizontal conflict are:

- **Environment** – each department is geared to fit its external dynamic environment. As the uncertainty and complexity of the environment increase, greater differences in skills, attitudes, power, and operative goals develop among departments. Moreover, increased competition, both domestically and internationally, have led to demands for lower prices, improved quality, and better service. These demands exert more intense goal pressures within an organisation and, hence, greater conflict among departments.

- **Size** – as organisations increase in size, subdivision into a larger number of departments takes place. Employees feel isolated from other people in the organisation. The lengthening hierarchy also heightens power and resource differences among departments.

- **Technology** – groups that have interdependent tasks interact more often and must share resources. Interdependence creates frequent situations that lead to conflict.

- **Structure** – Pay incentives may be based on competition among divisions. Organisation structure defines departmental groupings and, hence, employee loyalty to the defined groups.

- **Goal incompatibility** – goal incompatibility is probably the greatest cause of intergroup conflict in organisations. A typical example of goal conflict may arise between marketing and manufacturing departments. Marketing strives to increase the breadth of the product line to meet customer tastes for variety. A broad product line means short production runs, so manufacturing has to bear higher costs.

- **Uncertainty** – when departments do not know where they stand because activities are unpredictable. When factors in the environment are rapidly changing, or when problems arise that are poorly understood, departments may have to renegotiate their respective tasks. Managers have to sort out how new problems should be handled. The boundaries of a department's territory or jurisdiction become indistinct.

- **Reward system** – the reward system governs the degree to which subgroups cooperate or conflict with one another. When departmental managers are rewarded for achieving overall organisation goals rather than departmental goals, cooperation among departments is greater.

- **Differentiation** – functional specialisation requires people with specific education, skills, attitudes, and time horizons. The underlying values and traits of personnel differ across departments, and these differences lead to horizontal conflicts.

Destructive and constructive conflict

Management thinking and writing has generally viewed conflict as negative, unhelpful and undesirable. However it is accepted that not all conflict is harmful and a certain degree of conflict is positive, beneficial, desirable and often inevitable. The terms destructive and constructive conflict are used to differentiate between negative or positive outcomes.

Constructive conflict

Constructive conflict is considered useful, positive and beneficial to the organisation as it does not revolve around personality and:

- creates an environment of innovation and change

- facilitates bringing problems to the surface so that they can be dealt with

- settles and defines boundaries of authority and responsibility.

Destructive conflict

Destructive conflict tends to be *ad hoc* and personal:

- harmful for the organisation and its involved members

- causes alienation between groups, within groups and between individuals

- can be demoralising for those involved.

Some companies have sought to promote team spirit by creating competition between work teams. In some instances this has been successful in reducing absenteeism and bad timekeeping but, when extended to include poor productivity, working relationships have tended to deteriorate. It was found that work teams concentrate on rivalry instead of the tasks to be achieved. A group would take greater interest in impeding the progress of the competing group than in achieving a better result.

Consequences of conflict

Daft (1989) noted that several **negative consequences** for organisations that may arise from conflict are as follows:

- diversion of energy – time and effort wasted

- altered judgement – judgement becomes less accurate

- loser effects – the loser may deny or distort the reality and may seek scapegoats

- poor coordination – under intense conflict co-ordination does not happen. Co-operation across groups decreases and groups may actively attempt to jeopardise the goals of other groups.

6 Managing conflict – the Thomas-Kilmann Conflict Mode Instrument

A useful framework for classifying different ways of handling conflict is the **Thomas-Kilmann Conflict Mode Instrument (TKI).** It is based on two conflict-management dimensions. These are the degree of assertiveness in pursuit of one's interests and the level of co-operation in attempting to satisfy others' interests. The strength of each of these in a particular situation can suggest the ways the conflict may be resolved, as shown:

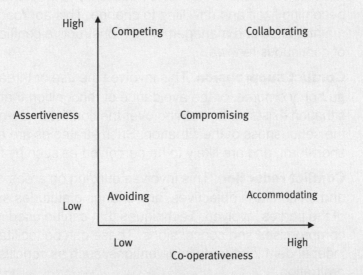

This results in five conflict-handling strategies:

- **Competing:** High assertiveness and low co-operativeness – the goal is to **'win'**. All or both parties seek to maximise their own interest and goals. They do not co-operate, creating winners and losers as well as causing damage to the organisation and one of the parties.

- **Avoiding:** Low assertiveness and low co-operativeness – the goal is to **'delay'**. One or more of the parties seeks to ignore or suppress the conflict.

- **Collaborating:** High assertiveness and high co-operativeness – the goal is to **'find a win-win solution'**. A 'win-win' situation is achieved through joint confrontation of the problem and using problem-solving techniques with creative solutions.

- **Accommodating:** Low assertiveness and high co-operativeness – the goal is to **'yield'**. One party puts the other party's interests first.

- **Compromising:** Moderate assertiveness and moderate co-operativeness – the goal is to **'find a middle ground'**. Negotiation results in each party giving up something and 'meeting half way'. The problem is each party may lose something when there may be a better alternative.

Mainwaring – strategies for managing conflict

Mainwaring (1991) suggested four broad strategies for managing conflict in organisations:

- **Conflict stimulation and orchestration**. This approach actively encourages conflict as a means of generating new ideas and new approaches or of stimulating change. There are obvious dangers in generating conflict, not least that they will escalate in a destructive way. However some conflict is necessary to prevent organisations becoming fixed and unwilling to change. This approach involves the maintenance and management of constructive conflict as a means of continuous renewal.

- **Conflict suppression**. This involves the use or threatened use of authority or force, or the avoidance of recognition that a conflict situation exists, or smoothing over the conflict by de-emphasising the seriousness of the situation. Such strategies are essentially short-term, and are likely to be perceived as such by those involved.

- **Conflict reduction**. This involves building on areas of agreement and on common objectives, and changing attitudes and perceptions of the parties involved. Techniques that can be used include compromises and concessions. These can be facilitated by independent third party interventions, such as conciliation and arbitration.

- **Conflict resolution**. This seeks to eliminate the root causes of conflict by establishing a consensus. Attitude change is a key element, particularly regarding the possibility of 'win-win' situations where the parties involved are aware of the mutual gains to be derived from co-operation and collaboration.

The mix of strategies used will depend not only on the situation, but also on the assumptions that managers make about conflict.

Important methods to apply when dealing with organisational conflict are altering:

- The context, e.g. new procedures, reducing interdependency, changing work allocation.

- The issue in dispute by separating into smaller issues, separating people- and task- related issues.

- Proximity, i.e. physically separating the persons or groups involved.

- The individuals involved including relocation and dismissal, or changing behaviour through training or organisational development techniques.

Dealing with industrial relations conflict

Although vertical conflict can take place without the presence of trade unions, Unions highlight vertical conflict as they try to equalise power differences between workers and management where the ground rules for conflict are formalised by laws and regulations. The sources of vertical conflict reflect the reasons why workers join unions.

The first priority for representatives is loyalty to their group. These can create strategies for avoidance or individualistic approaches:

- **Union avoidance strategies** including 'double-breasting' (setting up new plants in areas of high unemployment, or low union activity), devolving collective bargaining to factory level, removing unions from annual pay rounds whilst giving the right of the union members to be consulted and represented.

- **Individualistic approaches** away from third party involvement using appraisal systems, training and development schemes, performance-related pay systems, share schemes and the same pension and health schemes for all.

- **Collective bargaining** using procedural methods (a prescribed format) ultimately leading to the substantive agreement (defining each party's rewards and responsibilities for the next two to three years) in collective negotiations between workers and management.

New approaches tend to be more co-operative including:

- **Partnership agreements.**

- **Gain sharing** based on bonuses and profit rather than fixed-rate increases.

- **Labour-management teams** based on Japanese quality circles at shop-floor levels, middle management and union leader teams, and at top management, long-term policies to avoid layoffs.

- **Employment security** rather than job security where workers are reassigned to different positions and jobs are dependent on the firm's success.

Case study style question 3

Textile company, T, is in a troubled state. The weavers have just been awarded a pay increase, and this has led to a claim by the mechanics, who maintain the machinery, for a similar percentage pay increase. T is seeking to resist the mechanics' claim on the grounds that the weavers' extra payment can be justified by increases in productivity, while the maintenance work carried out by the mechanics has not changed. The response of the mechanics has been to threaten industrial action.

The problems for T have been made worse by a dispute between the Weaving Department and the Cloth Inspection Department. All members of the Weaving Department receive a bonus based on the productivity of the whole department. Employees in the Cloth Inspection Department are paid a fixed salary based on proven competence and experience.

The conflict between the departments has heightened recently by the decision of the new manager of the Cloth Inspection Department to tighten up of the inspection standards. He insists that the quality of output has to improve if the company is to remain competitive. This has resulted in weaving machines standing idle more frequently than in the past while faults detected during cloth inspection are investigated.

The sight of idle machines has resulted in intense frustration among management and employees in the Weaving Department as every idle machine means a reduction in their bonus payments. The weavers' frustration is now being taken out on the Cloth Inspection Department by adopting a policy of not cooperating.

The CEO has become aware of these issues and is concerned about the effect they are having on productivity.

Required:

The CEO has asked you to write a report for him:

(a) Explaining the causes of the conflicts within T.

(10 minutes)

(b) Discussing how each type of conflict within T might be resolved.

(10 minutes)

7 Summary diagram

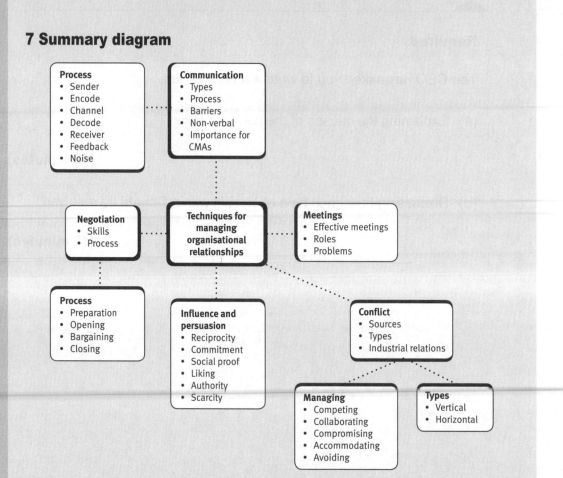

End of chapter questions

Question 1

The element in the communication process which makes it a cycle rather than a series of send-receive events is called_____.

The process through which the message is symbolised is known as _____.

_____ is anything which stops the message being received and understood as intended.

Supply the term that most accurately fills the gaps.

- Message
- Encoding
- Noise
- Feedback

Question 2

Which of the following is most likely to cause vertical conflict within an organisation?

A   Psychological distance
B   Goal incompatibility
C   Task interdependence
D   Functional specialisation

Question 3

Mainwaring suggested four strategies for managing conflict.

Match the strategy to the correct description.

Stimulation and orchestration
Suppression
Reduction
Resolution

- This approach actively encourages conflict as a means of generating new ideas and stimulating change.

- The approach seeks to eliminate the root cause of the conflict by establishing consensus.

- The approach involved building of areas of agreement and on common objectives.

- The approach involves the use, or threatened use of authority or force.

Question 4

X is trying to communicate with all the staff within his department. He has placed the information on the business intranet, but after a week very few staff members have seen the information. X has been told by several of his colleagues that they 'never really look on the intranet' and so they had failed to see X's message.

Which aspect of the communication process has caused this problem?

A   X has chosen the wrong channel

B   X has encoded the message poorly

C   X's communication has suffered from too much noise

D   X's communication has not been accurately decoded

Question 5

Match the description to the stage in the negotiation process.

Bargaining
Preparing
Closing
Opening

- Getting to know the background to the problem and the likely constraints
- Attempting to narrow the gap between the two initial positions
- Reaching agreement which is mutually beneficial
- Presenting starting positions and attempting to influence the other party

Question 6

Two key roles in a meeting are that of the chairperson and the secretary. Match the responsibilities shown to the correct role.

Chairperson	Secretary

- Ensuring all agenda items are discussed
- Preparing minutes of the meeting
- Summing up the issues discussed at the meeting
- Preparing and issuing the agenda before the meeting

Question 7

According to Cialdini, which of the following are principles of Influence. Select all that apply.

- Reciprocity
- Accountability
- Commitment
- Trust
- Assertiveness
- Authority

Question 8

Three important concepts in communication are Negotiation, Influence and Persuasion.

Match each of these to their correct definition.

- The ability to deliberately manipulate others to change an attitude, opinion, or behaviour.
- The ability to change others' attitudes, opinions or behaviour and can be direct or indirect.
- The ability to discuss an issue with one or more other people to determine ways to reach agreement and mutual satisfaction.

Question 9

The conflict management strategy recommended as a means to benefit all parties in a dispute is:

- compromising
- competing
- collaborating
- accommodating
- avoiding

Question 10

Place the conflict resolution strategies on the Thomas-Kilmann conflict managing grid.

- Avoiding
- Competing
- Collaborating
- Compromising
- Accommodating

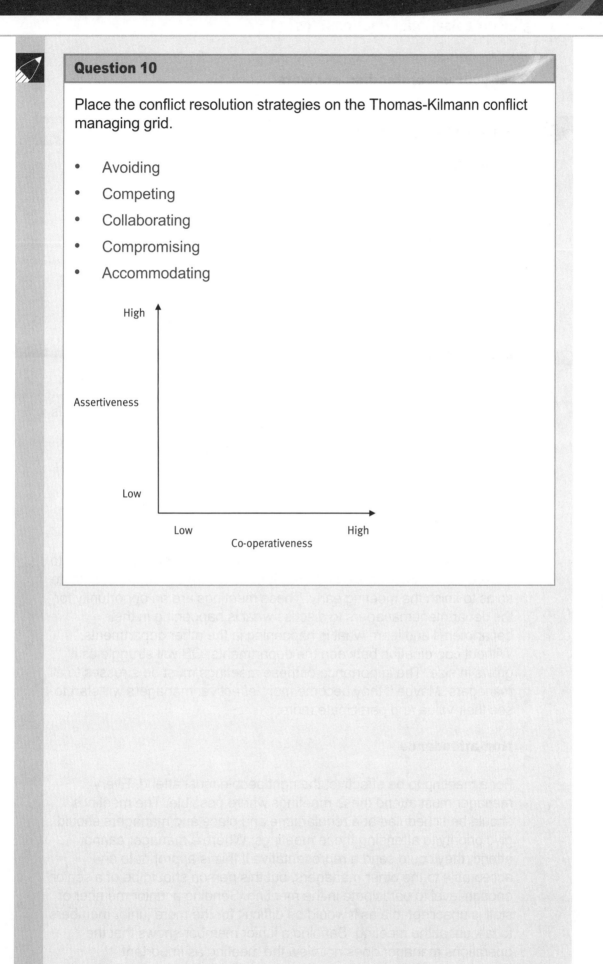

Test your understanding answers

Case study style question 1

REPORT

To: B

From: Consultant

Date: today

Subject: Management communication within QB

Introduction

There is a need for good communication between the mangers in QB, especially as the company is growing. To this end, a monthly meeting is held with the departmental managers however the meetings are not effective. This report will look at the issues affecting the effective communication at the management meetings and will suggest improvements.

Lack of participation

The first problem with the meetings is that the managers do not seem to appreciate the importance of them. Some deliberately do not contribute so as to finish the meeting early. These meetings are an opportunity for the department managers to discuss what is happening in their departments and learn what is happening in the other departments. Without coordination between the departments, QB will struggle as it grows in size. The importance of these meetings must be stresses to all managers. Maybe if they become more effective, managers will start to see their value and participate more.

Non-attendance

For a meeting to be effective, the right people must attend. Every manager must attend these meetings where possible. The meetings should be scheduled at a regular time and place and managers should give priority to attending these meetings. Where a manager cannot attend, they could send a representative if this is appropriate and acceptable to the other managers, but this person should be of a senior enough level to participate in the meeting. Sending a junior member of staff is unacceptable as it would be difficult for the more junior members to talk out at the meeting. Sending a junior member shows that the operations manager does not view the meeting as important.

No agenda

Managers do not know what is going to be discussed at the meeting which suggests that there is no agenda. For a meeting to be successful, all participants must prepare for the meeting and bring along any relevant documentation. This is only possible if an agenda is drawn up and circulated in advance of the meeting. This also gives managers the opportunity to add items to the agenda which they would like discussed.

Action points not recorded

Decisions must be made at the meetings. Attendees should leave the meeting with a clear understanding of what has been agreed and any action points which they have to take away with them. It appears that there is no secretary at the meetings as nothing appears to be being recorded. A secretary should attend the meeting taking notes of proceedings and documenting decisions made. The minutes of the meeting should be sent to all attendees soon after the meeting to ensure that everyone is aware of the decisions made.

No Chairperson

There appears to be no one chairing the meetings. The sales manager is domineering and others are not contributing. A chairman should be selected to chair each meeting. The chairman must be a strong character and must be able to keep all attendees in line, they must ensure that all attendees are given the opportunity to speak at the meeting. The chair should ensure that an agenda is available for the meeting and that it is followed. This would avoid the meeting becoming unproductive and going off topic.

Conclusion

The monthly management meetings held at QB important in terms of communication between the managers, however a number of improvements are required in order to make this form of communication more effective.

Case study style question 2

EMAIL

To: K

From: Management Accountant

Date: today

Subject: Negotiation

Negotiation is an activity that seeks to reach agreement between two or more conflicting starting positions. The aim in any negotiation is to achieve a settlement that is acceptable to the other parties concerned but which also comes as close as possible to one's own desired outcome.

In the case of D the two parties involved and their objectives are as follows:

- Management is seeking to restructure the organisation to ensure business survival and long-term profitability. This will involve cutting costs through redundancies and staff relocations.

- Trade unions will represent employees' interests and will thus be acting to minimise job losses, and to enhance relocation and redundancy packages.

There is thus a clear conflict over job cuts and how much the company will pay to the employees affected. Negotiation is essential in this situation as the alternative is likely to be a strike, which would benefit neither party in the short term. Such a scenario could precipitate a collapse of the company, ultimately affecting all employees' jobs.

Most writers on negotiation argue that the aim is to achieve a 'win-win' situation where both parties feel that they have gained from the negotiation process.

Most negotiation processes go through four stages: preparation, opening, bargaining and closing. These can be applied to D as follows:

Preparation: The preparation stage involves each side gathering information to gain insights into the conflict. This could include trying to understand the other party's key concerns and finding out who will be involved in the negotiating process. In the case of D, the union will seek to understand the business case for redundancies, explore possible alternative strategies that the firm could undertake and will ensure it is are fully up to date on employment law. This will help it see how strong its bargaining position is.

Similarly management will try to obtain details of how many employees will be affected, their ages and likelihood of getting other jobs. For example, the option of early retirement sounds better than redundancy, even though it is still a job cut. The time for negotiation will also be agreed.

Opening: During this stage each party presents its position to the other, hoping to gain influence early on. Management will presumably want to emphasise that redundancies are inevitable to save the company. It will try to move the negotiation onto what support is given rather than whether job cuts are needed. Similarly the union may present the case that it wants to prevent any job cuts and will initially reject all management proposals in this respect.

Bargaining: During the bargaining phase both parties will try to narrow the gap between the two positions and to seek a win-win solution. Usually this will involve a degree of compromise by each party. The main focus during this phase is the ability to argue and persuade the other side that your arguments are stronger than theirs to ensure that they compromise more than you. Given the circumstances involved, it is likely that the negotiations for D will end up with a reduction in the overall number of planned redundancies and detailed discussion focusing on the size of redundancy payouts and the level of support for employees to gain new jobs.

Closing: The closing phase gives the opportunity to capitalise on the work done during the previous stages. During the closing phase agreement is reached and the results are publicised and implemented.

I hope you have found the above useful, please do not hesitate to contact me if you require any additional information.

REPORT

To: CEO

From: Management accountant

Date: today

Report on the conflict within T

Introduction

In this report, the causes of the current conflict within T will be explained and recommendations will be made for how each type of conflict could be resolved. The report will also cover the factors which might influence the likelihood of a successful outcome for each type of conflict.

(a) **The causes of conflict**

The conflict in T encompasses both vertical and horizontal conflict.

Horizontal conflict

Horizontal conflict happens between groups of staff or between departments at the same level in the hierarchy. The conflict between the Weaving Department and the Cloth Inspection Department could be classified as horizontal conflict. The cause of the conflict is due to the fact that the tightening of standards in the inspection process has had the knock-on effect of machines standing idle. This has affected the productivity of weavers and reduced their bonus payments. At a more fundamental level, there is a conflict in the goals of the Departments, the weavers are focused on producing cloth to maximise output and hence receive bonuses. On the other hand, the key objective of the Cloth Inspection Department is the quality standard of the material. The two groups are rewarded in different ways.

Vertical conflict

Vertical conflict occurs between individuals or groups who are at different levels in the hierarchy, and often arises because of status and power differences amongst groups. In the case of T, conflict has arisen between mechanics and management over status and pay. Mechanics want the same percentage pay increase as weavers but management argues that weavers can justify the increase by increasing productivity, whereas the work carried out by mechanics has not changed. This has led to industrial unrest.

(b) **Managing conflict**

A useful framework for classifying different ways of handling conflict is known as the TKI. It is based on two conflict-management dimensions. These consist of the degree of assertiveness in pursuit of one's interests and the level of cooperation in attempting to satisfy others' interests. The relative strength of each of these produces five conflict-handling strategies.

It is difficult to determine the degree of assertiveness and the level of cooperation that exist in the case of T, so we cannot come to a conclusion here and now but the framework does provide a useful means of considering alternatives if we can gather the necessary information.

The five conflict-handling strategies are:

Avoidance – one or more parties in conflict may seek to avoid, to suppress or to ignore the conflict. This is not recommended as it does not resolve the conflict and may break out again when the parties meet in the future.

Accommodation – this involves one party putting the other's interests first and suppressing their own interest in order to preserve some form of stability and to suppress the conflict. Again, if the causes of conflict are endemic or lasting, the accommodation strategy may not resolve the differences. Also, the accommodating party may well lose out as a result.

Compromise – often seen as the optimum solution. Each party gives something up, and a deal somewhere between the two is accepted after negotiation and debate. However, in compromise, both parties lose something and there may be a better alternative. This approach could be used to resolve the conflict between mechanics and management.

Competition – this is a state where both or all parties do not cooperate, instead they seek to maximise their own interests and goals. It creates winners and losers. The resultant conflict can prove damaging to the organisation as well as to at least one of the parties. So it is not recommended.

Collaboration – from the perspective of all parties, this is likely to be the optimum solution. Differences are confronted and jointly resolved, novel solutions are sought, and a win/win outcome is achieved. This is the proposed strategy to deal with the conflict between weavers and the cloth inspection staff.

Managing horizontal conflict

The best approach to managing horizontal conflict in T would be collaboration where differences are confronted and jointly resolved. The desired outcome is a win:win for both groups. This could be achieved by holding meetings between the two Departments, including the managers, weavers and inspection staff. Solutions to how quality standards could be maintained while minimising the down time of machines could be discussed. Communications between the different Departments, sharing an understanding of each other's goals and objectives should assist the process. Perhaps, the organisation could look at some of the techniques associated with total quality management in resolving the problems.

Managing vertical conflict

The vertical conflict in T is an example of industrial relations conflict over pay claims. This type of conflict may be resolved through negotiation between management and representatives of the mechanics through collective bargaining. The representatives of the mechanics could present a proposal for consideration by management, followed by counter-proposals and concessions.

Conclusion

The outcome will depend on the relative power held by the mechanics (for example, withdraw labour, gain support from other workers and willingness to take industrial action) and the power of management (ability to replace mechanics, ability to switch production to other factories). A win/win situation is desirable but often industrial relations conflict is resolved through compromise.

Question 1

The complete sentences are:

The element in the communication process which makes it a cycle rather than a series of send-receive events is called **feedback**.

The process through which the message is symbolised is known as **encoding.**

Noise is anything which stops the message being received and understood as intended.

Question 2

A   Psychological distance

Psychological dsitance refers to the situation where workers feel isolated from the organisation.

Goal incompatibility, task interdependance and functional specialisation are all examples of horizontal conflict.

Question 3

The correct matching is:

Stimulation and orchestration – This approach actively encourages conflict as a means of generating new ideas and stimulating change.

Resolution – The approach seeks to eliminate the root cause of the conflict by establishing consensus.

Reduction – The approach involved building of areas of agreement and on common objectives.

Suppression – The approach involves the use, or threatened use of authority or force.

Question 4

A   X has chosen the wrong channel

The channel is the medium through which the message is sent. It is important for the sender to select the correct channel to ensure the message gets through to the receiver as expected.

Question 5

The correct matching is:

Bargaining – Attempting to narrow the gap between the two initial positions

Preparing – Getting to know the background to the problem and the likely constraints

Closing – Reaching agreement which is mutually beneficial

Opening – Presenting starting positions and attempting to influence the other party

Question 6

The correct matching is:

Chairperson	Secretary
Ensuring all agenda items are discussed	Preparing minutes of the meeting
Summing up the issues discussed at the meeting	Preparing and issuing the agenda before the meeting

Question 7

- Authority
- Commitment
- Reciprocity

The other principles of influence are:

- Social proof
- Liking
- Scarcity

Question 8

The correct definitions are:

Negotiation – The ability to discuss an issue with one or more other people to determine ways to reach agreement and mutual satisfaction.

Influence – The ability to change others' attitudes, opinions or behaviour and can be direct or indirect.

Persuasion – The ability to deliberately manipulate others to change an attitude, opinion, or behaviour.

Question 9

C   collaborating

The approaches of competing, collaborating, compromising, accommodating and avoiding come from the Thomas-Kilmann conflict mode instrument. The collaborating approach attempts to find a win-win solution.

Question 10

The complete diagram is shown below:

12

The finance function and managing its relationships

Chapter learning objectives

Discuss the effectiveness of handling relationships between the finance function and other parts of the organisation and the supply chain

Discuss the effectiveness of handling relationships between the finance function and external experts and stakeholders

1 Session content diagram

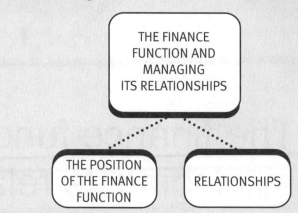

2 The finance function

The importance of the finance function

Historically, the role of the finance function was cost control, variance analysis and reporting on past performance. This role has steadily developed over the years into a more proactive, value adding role. The role has changed from reporting performance to enhancing performance.

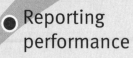

Current roles of the finance function include:

- assisting in the formulation of corporate objectives and strategy

- strengthening management and understanding of the risks and funding costs associated with particular products and strategies.

- dealing with increasing product complexity, unprecedented market instability and ever more exacting regulatory requirements.

- coming under pressure from senior management to cut costs, while providing more effective advice.

- turning data into a genuinely valuable source of information. For example analysing customer sales over a period in order to highlight the customers which add the most value to the organisation.

The changes in the finance function

The recent financial crisis and recession has highlighted the need for organisations to get the most value from their finance functions. It is important for organisations to ensure that they have properly staffed and trained finance functions to help add value and drive their organisation through the uncertain times ahead.

There is a focus on efficiency for organisations today. They are striving to ensure that all expenditure incurred can be seen to add value, this is known as lean operations. With lean operations, all unnecessary activities, expenditure or waste is eliminated. The finance function is expected to play an important role in this business transformation. Finance is expected to contribute to the strategic decision-making process to help drive the business forward.

Many organisations are now focusing on a more sustainable long-term approach to profitability and value creation. Finance functions are set to play a critical role in promoting this more balanced approach to risk and reward.

Companies are never too big or too small to begin strategising the finance function, particularly important when the business is considering major changes in the organisation intended to make the company stronger. A few examples of changes which are dependent on a strong finance function include going public, acquiring a business loan and seeking growth through acquisition. These activities rely on thorough knowledge of the core of the business and relate to the longer-term strategic success of the company. Accordingly a company should consider whether the responsibility for these aspects of financial service operations remain in-house, or are carried out by a third party.

Decision-making is becoming the basis of competitive advantage and value creation. If markets give all organisations access to similar resources globally and competition causes many routine business processes to converge on world-class standards, the quality of information could become a key differentiator. Enhancing the value of accounting in financial management processes requires a shift in focus away from transaction processing and reporting to a role which is fully integrated into the strategic and daily business activities of the organisation.

3 Relationship between finance and other parts of the organisation

Given the role that finance now plays in an organisation, it is necessary for it to coordinate with many other areas of the organisation, for example Procurement, Production and Marketing.

Finance relationship with Procurement

Procurement is responsible for placing and following up orders for goods and services required by the organisation. It coordinates with finance as follows:

Establishing credit terms – Finance will work with the procurement department to liaise with suppliers to obtain a credit account and to negotiate credit terms which are acceptable.

Prices – Finance can advise the procurement department on the maximum price that should be paid to maintain margins.

Payments – Payments may be approved by procurement but are made by finance.

Data capture, e.g. orders – Order details will be input by procurement and details passed to finance.

Inventory – Procurement will consult with finance to determine the quantity of items already in stock and therefore the quantity required to be ordered.

Budgeting – Finance will consult with procurement on likely costs in preparing budgets.

Finance relationship with Production

The production department plans and oversees the production of goods. It liaises with finance as follows:

Cost measurement, allocation, absorption – The production department measures quantities of materials and time used; the management accountant gives a monetary value to them. Costs are then allocated and absorbed to calculate production costs based on advice given by the production department.

Budgeting – The production department will decide how many items of what type are to be produced. The cost of producing these will be determined by the accounting and production departments together, and incorporated into the overall budget.

Cost v quality – The production and finance departments will discuss the features that can be included in products and the raw materials that should be used. They should agree which better quality materials and features justify the extra cost, and discuss how to maximise quality and profit.

Inventory – The production department will liaise with finance to ensure that there are sufficient raw materials in inventory for the production that is planned.

Finance relationship with Marketing

The marketing department will attempt to identify, anticipate and supply customer needs efficiently and profitably. The marketing department coordinates with finance as follows:

Budgeting – Finance will discuss the likely sales volume of each product with the marketing department, in order to produce the sales budget.

Advertising – Finance will help the marketing department in setting a budget, and in monitoring whether it is cost effective. For example, they could help in measuring new business generated as a result of different advertising campaigns.

Pricing – Finance will have input into the price that is charged. Often products are priced at cost plus a percentage. Even if the marketing department determines the price based on market forces they need to consult with finance to ensure that costs are covered.

Market share – Finance can provide the marketing department with information on sales volumes for each product, to help the marketing department in determining market share.

The above examples are by no means exhaustive. Finance will also have to deal with IT in terms of capital spend on new equipment and HR in terms of budgeted headcount and costs of recruitment and training.

In the modern business, finance is involved with all areas and in this way plays an integral part in decision making and adding value to the business.

The position of the finance function in organisations

When deciding on their structure, organisations need to decide where to position the finance function to allow them to play the fullest role in driving the business forward. There are several options available:

- The finance function is **embedded within the business area** as a business partnering role.

- The finance function is consolidated as part of a **shared service centre (SSC)**.

- The finance function is carried out by an external party – **business process outsourcing (BPO)**.

Business partnering role

A dedicated finance function may be set up within each business area. This brings many benefits to both the accountants and the management of the area.

The finance function plays a critical role in providing information for decision-making. In the new business environment where competition is global and fierce, companies need better information than ever before in order to remain competitive. Organisations and their chief executive officers now expect finance directors and management accountants to add value to the business by becoming more involved in matters of production, distribution and sales and to play a fuller role at a strategic management level, in particular helping to decide which markets to serve with which products.

Benefits of business partnering:

- The finance function is part of the business area it serves. Information can be provided as and when required for business decision making. As a dedicated resources the accountant will be able to play a stronger role within the business.

- Increased knowledge of the business area and its needs. The accountant will be involved in all decisions being made within the business and will build up detailed local knowledge and understanding of the business and its information needs.

- Strong relationships can be built up between the accountants and the management of the business area. Trust is required within this relationship. Accountants that are dedicated resources are expected to act as full business partners.

Drawbacks of business partnering:

- Duplication of effort across the organisation. Similar work will be carried out across various business areas.

- Lack of best practice. There is no sharing of knowledge which can happen within a larger, more diverse team. Best practice may not be being employed and practices within some business areas may become outdated.

- The accountants can feel isolated within the business. Within the business there may only be one or two dedicated accounting resources, leaving them to work more or less alone. Without a larger team around them, they may not be able to develop the required skills or knowledge.

Shared service centres (SSC)

The finance function across the organisation may be consolidated and run as a central unit, or a shared services centre (SSC).

A SSC refers to the provision of a service by one part of an organisation or group where that service has previously been found in more than one part of the organisation or group. An example would be a large multinational organisation with financial processing centres in several countries in which it operates, chooses to consolidate these activities at one site or shared service centre.

It is sometimes referred to as 'internal outsourcing'. It allows an organisation to investigate the potential benefits of consolidation of activities, whilst maintaining full internal control and thus minimising control risks.

Benefits of SSC:

- Headcount reductions. Economies of scale can be realised if all the finance personnel are gathered together to form one centre of excellence, rather than being spread across the business areas.

- Reduction in premises and associated costs. Linked with the headcount reduction, there would be associated savings in premises and other overhead costs.

- Potential favourable labour rates in the chosen geographical location. The location of the SSC can be carefully selected to ensure the lowest cost provision.

- Quality of service provision. Learning and sharing of knowledge will occur within the SSC which should lead to improved quality.

- Consistent management of business data. Standard approaches can be developed across the organisation, rather than each individual area developing their own methods.

Drawbacks of SSC:

- Loss of business knowledge. The finance function may not have a detailed knowledge of each part of the business.

- Further from the everyday decision making. The SSC will be unlikely to have day-to-day contact with the business areas which it supports, it may therefore lack the required knowledge to provide up to date information for decision making.

- Business relationships are not as strong. The SSC may not be able to build strong business relationships with the business areas, which may result in them not performing for the business area as well as they could.

Business process outsourcing (BPO)

The third option in the positioning of the finance function is business process outsourcing (BPO). Outsourcing is the act of giving a third-party the responsibility of what would otherwise be an internal system or service. BPO is contracting with a third party (external supplier) to provide part or all of a business process or function.

Many of these involve offshoring, when the outsourced function is in another country.

Benefits of outsourcing:

- Cost reduction through economies of scale. Suppliers can perform the finance function far more cheaply and efficiently than companies working on their own. For example a reduction in working capital or improvements in tax efficiency.

- Access to capabilities. A specialist provider can bring best practice expertise and new investment in resources.

- Release of capacity. Allows the retained finance function to concentrate on their role as business partners, in order to improve decision making.

Drawbacks of outsourcing:

- Loss of control. Business areas may not be able to dictate what information they need and when they need it.

- Over reliance on external providers. The outsourcing partner may dictate what information is to be provided and how it is to be provided. This may not tie in exactly with business needs. It can be difficult and expensive to bring the function back in house.

- Confidentiality and a risk to intellectual property. The outsourcing partner will have access to confidential information, and they may also process information for competitors.

- Risk of unsatisfactory quality. The quality of the information provided may not be as required for decision making purposes.

Case study style question 1

You have applied for a job as a senior management accountant for TP. Within the job description for the role was the following statements:

The finance function is continually evolving in line with the demands of the organisations they support. Finance functions are now expected to contribute to decision making at all levels of the organisation, including strategic decision making. Organisations are therefore under pressure to develop finance functions which meet their ever growing demands, but which are also cost-effective.

The finance function must be managed in a way which maximises its value to the organisation.

One of the questions on the application form asks for your views on this.

Required:

Discuss the advantages and disadvantages for the organisation of embedding finance in the business, setting up a shared services centre or outsourcing the finance function (business process outsourcing).

(15 minutes)

4 Outsourcing – Transaction cost theory

From the above, you can see that organisations make decisions about what activities to undertake in-house, and which to outsource to a third party. This is an important decision for organisation to make. Outsourcing requires careful consideration and monitoring, can be costly to set up and it can be problematic to reverse outsourcing decisions in the short term.

Transaction cost theory (Coase and Williamson) provides a means for making the decision about which activities to outsource and which to perform in-house.

Transaction cost theory suggests that organisations choose between two approaches to control resources and carry out their operations:

* **Hierarchy solutions** – direct ownership of assets and staff, controlled through internal organisation policies and procedures
* **Market solutions** – assets and staff are 'bought in' from outside under the terms of a contract (for example, an outsourcing agreement).

It may be helpful to think of this theory as a more complex version of the familiar 'make-or-buy' decision. Management will make in-house the things that cost them more to buy from the market and will adopt the market when transaction costs are lower than the costs of ownership. However, transaction cost theory looks beyond just the unit costs of the product or service under consideration. It is specifically interested in the costs of control that (together with the unit costs) make up transactions costs.

Hierarchy solutions – costs will include:

* staff recruitment and training
* provision of managerial supervision
* production planning
* payments and incentive schemes to motivate performance
* the development of budgetary control systems to coordinate activity
* divisional performance measurement and evaluation
* provision and maintenance of non current assets, such as premises and capital equipment.

Market solutions – costs:

Transaction costs = 'buy-in' costs + external control cost

External control costs will include:

- negotiating and drafting a legal contract with the supplier

- monitoring the supplier's compliance with the contract (quality, quantity, reliability, invoicing, etc.)

- pursuing legal actions for redress due to non-performance by the supplier

- penalty payments and cancellation payments if the firm later finds it needs to change its side of the bargain and draft a new contract with the supplier.

External control costs arise because of the following risk factors:

- **Bounded rationality:** the limits on the capacity of individuals to process information, deal with complexity and pursue rational aims.

- **Difficulties in specifying/measuring performance**, e.g. terms such as 'normal wear and tear' may have different interpretations.

- **Asymmetric information:** one party may be better informed than another, who cannot acquire the same information without incurring substantial costs.

- **Uncertainty and complexity.**

- **Opportunistic behaviour:** each agent is seeking to pursue their own economic self-interest. This means they will take advantages of any loopholes in the contract to improve their position.

Asset specificity

The degree of asset specificity, is the most important determinant of transaction cost. Asset specificity is the extent to which particular assets are of use only in one specific range of operations.

The more specific the assets required, the greater the transaction costs would be and hence the more likely the transaction will be internalised into the hierarchy. On the other hand, when assets are non-specific the process of market contracting is more efficient because transaction costs will be low.

Asset specificity

There are **six main types of asset specificity:**

(1) **Site specificity** – the assets may be immobile, or are attached to a particular geographical location, for example:

- locating a components plant near the customer's assembly plant
- building hotels near a certain theme park or tourist attraction
- building of pipelines and harbours to service an oilfield.

(2) **Physical asset specificity** – this is a physical asset with unique properties, for example:

- reserves of high-quality ores
- a unique work of art or building.

(3) **Human asset specificity** – where workers have particular skills or knowledge, for example:

- specific technical skills relevant to only one product
- knowledge of systems and procedures peculiar to one organisation.

(4) **Dedicated asset specificity** – a man-made asset which has been made to an exact specification for a customer and only has one application, for example:

- Eurotunnel; military defence equipment; Sydney Harbour Bridge.

(5) **Brand name capital specificity** – a brand and associations that belong to one family of:

- products and would lose value if spread wider, for example:
- Coca-Cola; McDonald's.

(6) **Temporal specificity** – the unique ability to provide service at a certain time, for example:

- the right to conduct radio broadcasts at an allotted time
- rights to exploit an asset for only a limited number of years.

Contractual relationships and service level agreements (SLAs)

One of the most important aspects for organisations to consider when outsourcing their finance function is how they will manage the relationship with the outsourcing party.

The agreement between the organisation and the outsourcing party is a contractual one. The organisation must set up a binding contract with the third party to undertake the required activities on their behalf. It is essential that these activities are done to the standards required by the organisation and that they have redress available to them in the event of the outsourcing party not performing as required.

Service level agreements (SLAs) will set out exactly what is required by the organisation. These SLAs should be agreed by both parties and should form part of the outsourcing contract. It is important that the SLAs are measurable and are measured on a regular basis. A relationship manager should be appointed by the organisation to oversee the work carried out by the outsourcing party and to monitor the compliance with the SLAs.

Transaction cost theory and strategy

Transaction cost theory approaches are being used in strategic considerations for a number of reasons:

(1) **Identification of distinctive competencies** – according to transaction cost theory this will be an operation or an asset that cannot be provided by another organisation without increasing the transaction costs or risks to the firm.

(2) **To support organisational restructuring** – organisations should sell off upstream or downstream divisions that can be provided at lower transaction costs by the market.

(3) **To predict the impacts of developments in information technology** – it is believed that the cost of searching for a supplier, maintaining the supplier/buyer relationship have been reduced by developments in Information Technology (IT). These are often put under the umbrella of ecommerce.

Case study style question 2

RS is a clothing manufacturer, which sells its designs exclusively via its website. The online fashion industry is becoming more competitive and RS's CEO is looking at how savings can be made in the company to make it more competitive. She is focusing her attention for saving on the finance department. She feels that savings could be made if she were to outsource some functions of the department.

The finance department currently employs 25 members of staff. The department is responsible for; payroll, invoice processing, budgeting, variance analysis and monthly management reports. She has asked for your advice as a consultant in this matter. The CEO feels that the payroll and invoice processing functions are more routine and they could more easily be outsourced.

Required:

Write an email to the CEO explaining what she has to consider in making the decision to outsource these finance functions. Use transaction cost theory in your answer.

(15 minutes)

5 Relationships with professional advisors

In order to meet organisational objectives and governance responsibilities, all organisation, regardless of size, will require expertise and support of a team or people with a variety of skills. Some of these will be internal to the organisation, while others may be external. Management must therefore build relationships with a variety of professional advisors who will be able to provide knowledge and advice to the organisation to aid decision making.

Here are examples of professional advisors which may be used by an organisation:

- Solicitors
- Accountants
- Tax Consultants
- Insurance Brokers
- IT specialists
- Environmental Advisors.

Why use professional advisors?

There are at least two reasons why it's important to have professional advisors:

(1) They're looking at your business with a dispassionate and unbiased perspective.

(2) As professionals, they can take what they see and help you turn problems into opportunities.

An organisation should always be open to reaching out to others for advice.

Dealing with professional advisors

Often an experienced solicitor for example can also recommend other advisors such as accountancy and insurance professionals. Some of them will become important components in your ongoing business, even if you only need to consult them occasionally. It is extremely important to have most of them in place before you make important strategic decisions.

When dealing with professional advisors, it is very important to:

- Have a good working relationship with all of them. Organisations may need to call on them at short notice, and will require the advisor to give full commitment to their issues or concerns.

- Allow them to get to know your business. Advisors are unable to provide correct and worthwhile advice if they do not know all the facts about the situation.

Keep them up to date with new developments and potential future projects. They may be able to give advice which will set the business on the right track going forward.

When do you seek professional advice?

Advice from experts should be sought when:

- Sales are low – the economy and your competitors are doing well but you're not, it's time to turn to experts for advice.

- Profits are low – often, sales can be good while profits may still be down. You may need to consult with an expert to find out what's eating up your money and causing low profit margins.

- Profits are high – don't lose an opportunity. Contact experts who can help you make the most of this precious money.

- Entering into important contracts/projects – an experienced solicitor will read every important contract you sign and get involved during the negotiation period and the creation of any contracts.

- Your company is being sued – at the first sign of a potential lawsuit, consult legal advice.

- You're considering bringing in new finance – anytime you are considering changing the ownership structure of your company. Always consult with your business adviser, accountant and solicitor when borrowing.

- Initial environmental reviews show the need to improve performance, identify immediate cost savings and improve resource efficiency.

Professional advisors can be very helpful to organisations and can assist them in making strong strategic decisions. It is important that management foster good relationships with a range of professional advisors.

6 Relationships with external stakeholders

Relationships with auditors

The finance function can support organisations in delivering results and meeting externally imposed rules. Both are important in order to stay in business. External audit's work relates to the financial statements, they are concerned with the financial records that underpin these. The external auditors will review the system of internal control in order to determine the extent of the substantive work required on the year-end accounts. The auditors will identify the areas of weakness and recommendations for improvement.

It is important that the management of the finance function know that they are properly managing the risk of any internal control failures. (The growing recognition by management of the benefits of good internal control, and the complexities of an adequate system of internal control have led to the development of internal auditing being recognised as an important form of control.) The finance function should implement any recommendations from internal and external audit to enhance the efficiency and effectiveness of the information sent to management. It is important therefore that the finance function as decision makers fully understand the benefits of a good audit and should be extracting the maximum benefit from the company's audit service.

Relationships with financial stakeholders

We have seen the importance of the finance function in terms of its contribution to internal decision making. Another of its primary purposes is to provide transparency and usefulness to external stakeholders. Stakeholders such as lenders, shareholders and the government are external to the company but still take an interest in the company's performance.

Investors and financiers:

In spite of their absence on a day to day basis, investors and financiers (those lending money to the company) often rely exclusively on the legally mandated reporting requirements of the organisation to gain an understanding of company performance. They rely on the accuracy and predictability of the data coming from the companies in which they invest. They hold the company to performance predictions or forecasts and typically punish those companies that do not meet their expectations by selling their shares. This shows the importance of good data for external reporting and the important role the finance function can play in maintaining credibility with the external community.

Banks:

Financing the company's operations may be the single most important aspect of the finance function for the small and emerging business owner. Approaching banks is often a popular solution; the finance function will provide data on the health of the company and/or forecast its performance. Documentation provided to potential lenders must be robust; assembling sketchy documentation may mean that the business does not receive the finance it requires to start or stay in business.

Taxing and statutory authorities:

The finance function must be prepared to gather the necessary information and documentation to support remittances to taxing and statutory authorities. Finance need to be familiar with legal and statutory requirements prevailing in their respective locations and promote compliance throughout the organisation and then reporting to and filing returns with relevant authorities on a timely basis.

Contribution of finance to other functions:

- Finance people need to be trained not just to furnish and assemble information but to draw insights and communicate these effectively to support decision-making.

- Finance people will be expected to use their understanding of the numbers and metrics to evaluate opportunities and support decision making about investment opportunities and resource allocation.

- The role may need to emerge as a challenging sparring partner, able to challenge in a positive way and will require broader business understanding.

- The finance function is under pressure to enhance its value contribution to the business, deliver information and maintain effective controls in line with ever changing governance needs.

7 Corporate Governence

Corporate governance was covered in paper E1. Corporate governance can be described as 'the system by which companies are directed and controlled in the interests of shareholders and other stakeholders'. There has been an increased emphasis on governance regulations over the last 20 years as a result of a number of high profile scandals and corporate failures over that period.

Finance professionals play an important role in corporate governance.

Some of the main requirements of the UK Corporate Governance code are:

- Every company should be headed by an effective board.

- There should be a clear division of responsibilities at the head of the company between the running of the board (chairman) and the executive responsibility for the running of the company's business (CEO) so that no one individual should have unfettered powers.

- Boards should consist of a mix of executive and independent non-executive directors (NEDs).

- As part of their role, NEDs should scrutinise the performance of the executive directors and constructively challenge and help develop proposals on strategy. NEDs are there to balance the power on the board and to ensure that the company is run in the best interests of the shareholders.

Committees

Another important requirement of the UK Corporate Governance code is the development of various committees, within which NEDs play key roles. These committees are:

- Remuneration – to determine the remuneration packages for the individual executive directors.

- Nomination – to bring independence and objectivity to the selection and recruitment of board members.

- Audit – responsible for recommending the appointment and removal of the external auditors and overseeing the work carried out by the internal auditors. The audit committee helps to ensure the independence of both the external and internal auditors and provides a whistleblowing facility within the company where members of staff can report issues in a confidential manner. This committee is made up of 100% NEDs, one of which must have recent financial experience.

8 Summary diagram

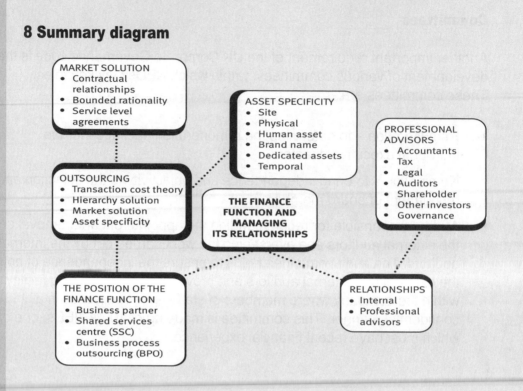

MARKET SOLUTION
- Contractual relationships
- Bounded rationality
- Service level agreements

ASSET SPECIFICITY
- Site
- Physical
- Human asset
- Brand name
- Dedicated assets
- Temporal

PROFESSIONAL ADVISORS
- Accountants
- Tax
- Legal
- Auditors
- Shareholder
- Other investors
- Governance

OUTSOURCING
- Transaction cost theory
- Hierarchy solution
- Market solution
- Asset specificity

THE FINANCE FUNCTION AND MANAGING ITS RELATIONSHIPS

THE POSITION OF THE FINANCE FUNCTION
- Business partner
- Shared services centre (SSC)
- Business process outsourcing (BPO)

RELATIONSHIPS
- Internal
- Professional advisors

End of chapter questions

Question 1

Using transaction cost theory, match the cost to whether it would come under market solution or hierarchy solution.

Hierarchy solution		Provision of managerial supervision
		Payment of incentive schemes to motivate performance
Market solution		Negotiating and drafting legal contracts
		Provision of non-current assets

Question 2

External control costs form part of the market solution within transaction cost theory. Which of the following could cause external control cost to arise? Select all that apply.

- Uncertainty and complexity

- Asymmetric information

- Untrained staff

- Bounded rationality

- High salary costs

Question 3

The finance function can be set up as a business partner, a shared services centre or business process outsourcing. Each setup has advantages and disadvantages. Identify the following advantages or disadvantages with each of the three set ups.

Business Partner	Shared Services Centre	Business Process Outsourcing

- Increased knowledge of business area
- Risk of unsatisfactory quality
- Release of capacity
- Confidentiality risk
- Learning and sharing of knowledge

Question 4

Finance can be positioned in different ways within an organisation. Match the descriptions to the three options.

Business partner	The finance function is consolidated and run as a central unit
Shared services centre	A third party is contracted to provide some or all of the finance functions
Business process outsourcing	A dedicated finance function is set up within each business unit

Question 5

Management may on occasion need to deal with professional advisors. Which three of the following statements regarding dealing with professional advisors is true?

- Professional advisors should only be given information on a selective basis in order to protect confidentiality.

- It is important for businesses to develop good working relationships with a range of professional advisors as they may need to call on them for help at short notice.

- Professional advisors can help businesses as they can look at the business from an unbiased perspective.

- Professional advice is only required when the business is being sued or suffering from low sales or low profits.

- It would be important to engage professional legal advice if the business was considering entering into an important contract or taking on new financing.

Question 6

Match the examples to the type of asset specificity it relates to:

Dedicated asset	a hotel built near a tourist attraction
Physical asset	a well known soft drink
Temporal	knowledge of an organisations systems
Site	the right to air a television show at a particular time
Brand name capital	a unique work of art
Human asset	specialised military equipment

Question 7

Asset specificity is the most important determinant of transaction cost. Which type of asset specificity is described as 'an asset which has been made to an exact specification for a customer and has only one application'?

A   Physuical asset specificity

B   Brand name capital specificity

C   Dedicated asset specificity

D   Site specificity

Question 8

Which of the following statements regarding transaction cost theory are correct?

- A transaction cost theory approach can assist in organisational restructing as companies sell off upstream and down stream divisions.

- Transaction cost theory suggests that where the market solution costs more than the hierarchy solution, the activity should be outsourced

- The more specific the assets required to undertake an activity are, the less likely a company is to internalise that activity.

- The costs of staff recruitment and training and the provision of managerial supervision would be included as hierarchy costs.

- Risk factors which would lead to external control costs in an outsourcing arrangement would include asymmetric information and bounded rationality.

Question 9

Finance may have to build relationships with a number of internal departments. Which of the following roles would generally be carried out by the finance department? Select all that apply.

- Advise procurement on the maximum price to be paid on a purchase.

- Run focus groups to establish the views of customers.

- Maintain inventory records and advise on optimum reorder levels.

- Advise marketing on the minimum price which should be charged for the product.

- Maintain relationships with suppliers.

Question 10

The limits on the capacity of individuals to process information, deal with complexity and pursue rational aims is known as which of the following?

A   Asset specificity

B   Bounded rationality

C   Asymmetric information

D   Opportunistic behaviour

Test your understanding answers

Case study style question 1

Embedding finance personnel in the business

The finance function plays a critical role in providing information for decision-making.

In the new business environment where competition is global and fierce, companies need better information than ever before in order to remain competitive. Organisations and their chief executive officers now expect finance directors and financial controllers to become more involved in matters of production, distribution and sales to play a fuller role at a strategic management level, in particular helping to decide which markets to serve with which products.

Decisions are only as good as the information on which they are based. Providing this information as and when required relies on thorough knowledge of the core of the business. It can therefore be argued that a company should consider retaining the finance function in-house and positioning it within the business units which it serves.

In this way, finance becomes a part of the business process in a role which is fully integrated into the strategic and daily business activities of the organisation.

An alternative to the embedded finance function is the **shared service centre (SSC)**. This refers to the provision of a service by one part of an organisation or group where that service had previously been found in more than one part of the organisation or group. An example would be a large multinational organisation with financial processing centres in all or several of the countries in which it operates, chooses to consolidate these activities at one site.

Benefits of SSC:

- Headcount reductions
- Cost savings through economies of scale, and reduced labour costs by locating the centre in an area with favourable labour rates
- Maintain internal control
- Best practice can be identified
- Consistency of approach throughout the organisation.

Disadvantages of SSC:

- Loss of business knowledge
- Further from the everyday decision making
- Business relationships are not as strong.

Business Process Outsourcing (BPO)

Business Process Outsourcing (BPO) is contracting with a third party (external supplier) to provide part or all of a business process or function. Many of these BPO efforts involve offshoring.

Offshoring is a type of outsourcing and simply means having the outsourced business function done in another country.

Benefits of outsourcing:

- Cost reduction through economies of scale by using standardised procedures and leading edge technology. Suppliers can perform finance and administration functions far more cheaply and efficiently than companies working on their own.

- Access to capabilities and expertise of the provider. The outsourcing partner will be a specialist provider and so can bring best practice expertise and new investment in resources.

- Outsourcing financial operations can encourage business to be more innovative and focused on value creation. It can free up the time of the remaining finance personnel to focus on value adding activities.

Drawbacks of outsourcing:

- Loss of control. External providers are now relied upon to input the right level of resource and skill required to meet the organisational needs.

- Risk to innovation. Over-reliance on external providers can lead to an erosion of internal knowledge and skills.

- Risk to competitive advantage. Confidentiality and risk to intellectual property are often cited as key reasons why companies choose not to outsource to an external provider.

- Unsatisfactory quality and service or even failure of supplier.

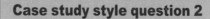

Case study style question 2

EMAIL

To: CEO

From: Consultant

Date: today

Subject: Outsourcing of the finance function

Transaction cost theory suggests that two solutions must be compared when making an outsourcing decision:

* The in-house or hierarchy solution.

* The outsourced or market solution.

As cost saving is the driver in this case, the cost of both solutions should be ascertained to determine which would be cheaper.

When considering the hierarchy solution, all internal costs associated with the running of the finance department must be considered. This will include the direct cost of employing the 25 members of staff plus the overheads associated with employees, such as office space, benefits and human resources. It will also include the cost of the assets needed for the department to function, such as desks, chairs, computer and telephone equipment. Other internal costs would be training, supervision, maintenance of equipment and IT support.

The market solution will principally be the transaction cost for the service provided by the outside company, plus the external control costs.

The level of transaction costs will be influenced by the specificity of the assets required for the contract. In this case the assets would have fairly low specificity as regards physical specificity as the assets needed (general IT equipment) would be fairly general and could be used for many different companies and industries.

There would also be low site specificity as the outsourcer could be located anywhere in the world in terms of the IT processing but consideration would have to be given to the potential contact required with employees or customers. Payslips would have to be dispatched and this may have to be coordinated locally. Likewise invoices would have to be sent to customers.

In addition, employees and customers may have queries relating to their pay or invoice. It is therefore important that the outsourcer was available during suitable hours (in the home country) to answer any queries.

Human asset specificity would be higher in that the outsourcer would have to build up the skills and knowledge relating to the product and designs of RS, but this would reduce over time.

Temporal specificity could also be high in that the customer services department would have to be available to answer calls from customers without delay. If customers are encouraged to correspond by email rather than telephone, then this could also reduce.

Overall the transaction costs for fairly general finance functions such as invoice processing and payroll is likely to be fairly low. However the external control costs can be significant and must be carefully considered. They include:

- Negotiating the contract, including tendering and legal costs in drafting the contract.

- Enforcing costs which will include setting up service level agreements, quality assurance testing and managing the relationship with the outsourcer.

RS would also have to consider the potential reputation risk it could face by outsourcing these finance functions particularly as the outsourcer would be required to deal with customers. Customers may be lost as a result of this decision and that has to be taken account of as part of the consideration.

I hope the above is helpful to you. Please do not hesitate to contact me if you wish to discuss any aspects of this further.

Question 1

The correct matching is:

Hierarchy solution	Provision of managerial supervision
Hierarchy solution	Payment of incentive schemes to motivate performance
Market solution	Negotiating and drafting legal contracts
Hierarchy solution	Provision of non-current assets

The Hierachy solution involves undertaking the activity in-house. Market solution in values outsourcing the activity to a third party.

Question 2

- Uncertainty and complexity

- Asymmetric information

- Bounded rationality

External control costs arise due to five main risk factors. The two others are:

- Difficulties in specifying and measuring performance

- Opportunistic behaviour

Question 3

The correct matching is:

Business Partner	Shared Services Centre	Business Process Outsourcing
Increased knowledge of business area	Learning and sharing of knowledge	Risk of unsatisfactory quality Release of capacity Confidentiality risk

Question 4

The correct matching is:

Shared services centre	The finance function is consolidated and run as a central unit
Business process outsourcing	A third party is contracted to provide some or all of the finance functions
Business partner	A dedicated finance function is set up within each business unit

Question 5

- It is important for businesses to develop good working relationships with a range of professional advisors as they may need to call on them for help at short notice.

- Professional advisors can help businesses as they can look at the business from an unbiased perspective.

- It would be important to engage professional legal advice if the business was considering entering into an important contract or taking on new financing.

Professional advisors should only be given information on a selective basis in order to protect confidentiality. This is incorrect. To get the most from professional advisors it is important to let them get to know the business well and know all the facts about the situation.

Professional advice is only required when the business is being sued or suffering from low sales or low profits. This is incorrect. Professional advice may also be required when profits are high, to ensure that the business makes the most of the opportunities this would present.

Question 6

The correct matching is:

Site	a hotel built near a tourist attraction
Physical asset	a unique work of art
Human asset	knowledge of an organisations systems
Dedicated asset	specialised military equipment
Brand name capital	a well known soft drink
Temporal	the right to air a television show at a particular time

Question 7

C   Dedicated asset specificity

Physical asset specificity refers to a physical asset with unique properties.

Brand name capital asset specificity refers to a brand and the associations that belong to that brand.

Site specificity refers to immobile assets or assets which must be sited at a particular location.

Question 8

- A transaction cost theory approach can assist in organisational restructing as companies sell off upstream and down stream divisions.

- The costs of staff recruitment and training and the provision of managerial supervision would be included as hierarchy costs.

- Risk factors which would lead to external control costs in an outsourcing arrangement would include asymmetric information and bounded rationality.

Transaction cost theory suggests that where the market solution costs more than the hierarchy solution, the activity should be outsourced. This is incorrect. Where the market solution costs more than the hierachy solution the activity would be done in-house.

The more specific the assets required to undertake an activity are, the less likely a company is to internalise that activity. This is incorrect. The more specific the asset, the more likely it is that the activity would be internaliised.

Question 9

- Advise procurement on the maximum price to be paid on a purchase.

- Maintain inventory records and advise on optimum reorder levels.

- Advise marketing on the minimum price which should be charged for the product.

The department which would run focus groups to establish the views of customers would be marketing department.

The procurement department would maintain relationships with suppllers.

Question 10

B   Bounded rationality

Bounded rationality is a risk factor which causes external control costs to arise in outsourcing.

Managing organisational change

Chapter learning objectives

Discuss the concept of organisational change.

Recommend techniques to manage resistance to change.

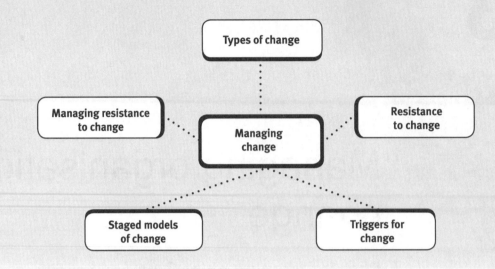

1 Organisational change

In the strategic management section of the text the need for organisations to carefully consider the strategic direction they want to take and how they develop that strategy was considered. The need for organisations to continually assess their environment and change their strategy to ensure that they retain their competitive advantage, particularly given the dynamic nature of today's business environments was covered in some depth.

Change is therefore an inevitable feature of all organisations. Organisations must continually assess their position within the environment and their performance compared to competitors, and be prepared to change their strategic direction in order to survive. Organisations which fail to change are unlikely to survive. Organisations therefore should not question whether or not they need to undertake change, instead they should question:

- **What to change?**
- **What to change to?**
- **How to successfully manage change?**

2 Triggers for change

Triggers for change can be divided into external or internal.

External triggers

Environmental pressure for change can be divided into two groups.

- General (indirect) environmental factors – these can be identified using the familiar PESTLE framework and
- Industry/competitive (direct) factors – these can be assessed using Porter's five forces model

Examples of external triggers

Environmental (indirect) triggers – PESTLE

Political	Changes in government
	Competition policy
	Import duties
Economic	Growth or recession
	Changes in currency and interest rates
	Local labour costs
	Regional prosperity/opportunities
	Disposable income
Social	Attitudes to work and leisure
	Environmentalism
	Attitudes to health/education
	Fashion trends
	Changing national/regional culture
Technological	Growth in Internet
	Public use of IT
	Global sourcing/call centres
	Innovations
Legal	New labour laws
	European directives
Environmental/Ecological	Emissions targets
	New environmental protection policies

Industry/competitive (direct) triggers – Porter's five forces

Competitive rivalry	Powerful rivals may force the firm to have to adapt to survive, either through innovation, if a differentiator, or cost cutting if a cost-leader.
Power of customers	Powerful customers could trigger a firm to consider forwards vertical integration
Power of suppliers	Supplier power could encourage a firm to redesign products in order to reduce the reliance on specialist components and thus facilitate multi-sourcing
Threat of new entrants	New entrants may force incumbent firms to improve quality to maintain market share
Threat of substitutes	New technologies may result in substitutes that render existing products obsolete. This could lead to factory closure and reorganisation.

Internal triggers

The internal triggers for change within the organisation could span any functional area of operation or level of control from strategic to operational.

Philosophy	New ownership
	New CEO
	New initiative/management style
Reorganisation	Takeover/merger
	Divisional restructuring
	Rationalisation/cost reduction
Personnel	Promotions/transfers
	Rules/procedures
	Training/development
Conditions	Location change
	Outsourcing
	Rosters/flexible working
Technology	New procedures/systems
	Changing information demands
	Integration of roles

Problem identification as a precursor to change

The above triggers can be reasons **why** change is considered or even necessary. However, further strategic analysis is needed to determine **what** needs changing.

For example, if a company has experienced falling profits, declining margins and a loss of market share over the last two years, it will try to identify the problems which have caused this situation. If it discovers that the main reason for this decline is increasing competition from overseas manufacturers, it can identify that external trigger for change is increased competitive rivalry, but it then has to address what needs changing?

The first step would involve analysing the company's cost base and determining customer perceptions regarding relative quality. This should help the company to see how it's competitive advantage is being eroded. Suppose poor quality is identified as the underlying problem.

Even then, it is not obvious what needs changing. "Poor quality" could be an underlying problem of customer perception related to brand or design flaws, the quality of raw materials, production problems or an underlying culture where quality is not valued highly enough. Determining the main cause(s) could involve discussions with customers, competitor analysis, Porter's value chain analysis, SWOT and /or benchmarking.

Only then will management have a clear idea of what needs changing.

3 Types of organisational change

Types of change can be classified by the extent of the change required, and the speed with which the change is to be achieved:

	Extent of change	
	(big) **Transformation**	**Realignment** (small)
(slow) **Incremental**	**Evolution:** Transformational change implemented gradually through inter-related initiatives; likely to be proactive change undertaken in anticipation of the need for future change. This results in a fundermentally different organisation once completed	**Adaptation:** Change undertaken to realign the way in which the organisation operates; implemented in a series of steps
Big Bang	**Revolution:** Transformational change that occurs via simultaneous initiatives on many fronts: This change is more likely to be forced and reactive because of the changing competitive conditions that the organisation is facing	**Reconstruction:** Change undertaken to realign the way in which the organisation operates with many initiatives implemented simultaneously: This is often forced and reactive because of a changing competitive context
(fast)		

Speed of change (row label on the left spanning vertically)

Incremental change is also known as "continuous" change while "discontinuous change" refers to the big bang above.

Transformation entails changing an organisation's culture. It is a fundamental change that cannot be handled within the existing organisational paradigm, while realignment does not involve a fundamental reappraisal of the central assumptions and beliefs

Strategic change is by definition far-reaching. We speak of strategic change when fundamental alterations are made to the business system or the organisational system. Adding a lemon-flavoured Coke to the product portfolio is interesting, maybe important, but not a strategic change, while branching out into bottled water was a major departure from Coca-Cola's traditional business system.

Evolution or revolution?

In selecting an approach to strategic change, most managers struggle with the question of how bold they should be. On the one hand, they usually realise that to fundamentally transform the organisation, a break with the past is needed. To achieve strategic renewal it is essential to turn away from the firm's heritage and to start with a clean slate. On the other hand, they also recognise the value of continuity, building on past experiences, investments and loyalties. To achieve lasting strategic renewal, people in the organisation will need time to learn, adapt and grow into a new organisational reality.

The 'window of opportunity' for achieving a revolutionary strategic change can be small for a number of reasons. Some of the most common triggers are:

- competitive pressure – when a firm is under intense competitive pressure and its market position starts to erode quickly, a rapid and dramatic response might be the only approach possible. Especially when the organisation threatens to slip into a downward spiral towards insolvency, a bold turnaround can be the only option left to the firm.

- regulatory pressure – firms can also be put under pressure by the government or regulatory agencies to push through major changes within a short period of time. Such externally imposed revolutions can be witnessed among public sector organisations (e.g. hospitals and schools) and highly regulated industries (e.g. utilities and telecommunications), but in other sectors of the economy as well (e.g. public health regulations). Some larger organisations will, however, seek to influence and control regulation.

- first mover advantage – a more proactive reason for instigating revolutionary change, is to be the first firm to introduce a new product, service or technology and to build up barriers to entry for late movers.

Case study style question 1

Historically the directors of Z Bank have resisted change, seeking to offer a traditional approach to its customers. However, recent problems within the banking industry and an increasingly competitive market has forced the Board to consider a number of important initiatives, including:

- enhancing its current services to customers by providing them with on-line internet and telephone banking services; and

- reducing costs by closing many of its rural and smaller branches (outlets).

In an attempt to pacify the employee representatives (the Banking Trade Union) and to reduce expected protests by the communities affected by branch closure, a senior bank spokesperson has announced that the changes will be 'incremental' in nature. In particular, she has stressed that:

- the change will be implemented over a lengthy time period

- there will be no compulsory redundancies

- banking staff ready to take on new roles and opportunities in the online operations will be retrained and offered generous relocation expenses.

For customers, the bank has promised that automatic cash dispensing machines will be available in all the localities where branches (outlets) close. Customers will also be provided with the software needed for Internet banking and other assistance necessary to give them quick and easy access to banking services.

The leader of the Banking Trade Union is 'appalled' at the initiatives announced. He has argued that the so-called 'incremental' change is in fact the start of a 'transformational' change that will have serious repercussions, not only for the Union's members but also for many of the bank's customers.

Required:

One of your colleagues in the finance department (J) is confused at the different terminology being used by the bank and the Union and has asked you to clarify this for him. Write an email to J distinguishing incremental change from transformational change. Your email should explain why the bank spokesperson and the trade union leader disagree over their description of the change.

(15 minutes)

4 The cultural process of change

The inherent culture of the organisation is important for two reasons:

Firstly the existing culture can become "embedded" and hence resistant to change. Overcoming this resistance can be a major challenge.

Secondly the existing culture can limit the types of strategy development and change that are considered.

- Faced with forces for change, managers will seek to minimise the extent to which they are faced with ambiguity and uncertainty by defining the situation in terms of that which is familiar.

- This can explain why some firms adopt incremental strategies and, worse, why some fail to address the impact of environmental triggers, resulting in strategic drift.

Faced with a change trigger such as declining performance, management are likely to react as follows:

(1) First managers will try to improve the effectiveness and efficiency of the existing strategy

   e.g. through tighter controls

(2) If this is not effective, then a change in strategy may occur but in line with existing strategies

   e.g. through market development, selling existing products into markets that are similar to existing ones and managing the process in the same way as they are used to.

(3) Even when managers know intellectually that more radical change is needed, they find themselves constrained by existing routines, assumptions and political processes.

5 Managing the change process

Understanding the factors that impact on change management can be complex. However, even when a manager has a good understanding of the context of change within their organisation, they still need to be able to successfully implement the change itself.

Given the conflicting views of different stakeholders – such as shareholders, employees and customers – achieving change within an organisation is often difficult and prone to failure. Due to this, a number of different theorists have examined the issue and identified possible approaches to managing the change process within the organisation.

In this chapter three of these models will be covered:

- Lewin's three-stage model
- Lewin's force field analysis
- Beer and Nohria's Theory E and Theory O

Lewin's three-stage model

The three-stage model of change, known as the ice cube model, was proposed by Kurt Lewin in the 1950's. He argued that, in order for change to occur successfully, organisations need to progress through three stages.

This process, shown in the following diagram, includes unfreezing habits or standard operating procedures, changing to new patterns and refreezing to ensure lasting effects.

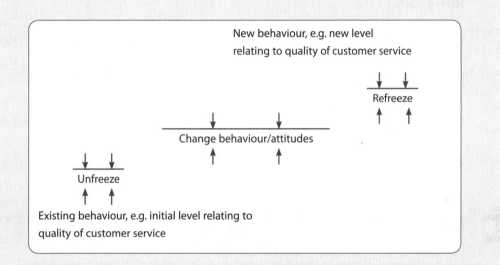

The process of change comprises three stages.

Unfreezing

In this stage, managers need to make the need for change so obvious that most people can easily understand and accept it. Unfreezing also involves creating the initial motivation to change by convincing staff of the undesirability of the present situation. Ways of destabilising the present stability could include:

- Identifying and exploiting existing areas of stress or dissatisfaction.
- Creating or introducing additional forces for change, such as tighter budgets and targets or new personnel in favour of the change.
- Increasing employee knowledge about markets, competitors and the need for change.

Change

The change process itself is mainly concerned with identifying what the new behaviour or norm should be. This stage will often involve

- Establishing new patterns of behaviour
- Setting up new reporting relationships
- Creating new reward/incentive schemes
- Introducing a new style of management

It is vital that new information is communicated concerning the new attitudes, culture and concepts that the organisation wants to be adopted, so that these are internalised by employees.

Refreezing

Refreezing or stabilising the change involves ensuring that people do not slip back into old ways. As such it involves reinforcement of the new pattern of work or behaviour by:

- Larger rewards (salary, bonuses, promotion) for those employees who have fully embraced the new culture
- Publicity of success stories and new "heroes" – e.g. through employee of the month

---

Criticisms of Lewin's three-stage model

Kanter et al suggest that Lewin's ice cube model is too simplistic.

They argue that the model is based on the assumptions that organisations are stable and static so change results only from concentrated effort and only in one direction.

Kanter et al argue that change is 'multi-directional and ubiquitous', that it happens in all directions simultaneously and is often a continuous process.

Case study style question 2

WW is a company specialising in industrial paint manufacturing. It has recently experienced significant growth in turnover and has opened two new factories to help it cope with the additional demand.

The managers of WW have become concerned that their current accounting software is no longer adequate for their needs. The current system is a basic one, which is mainly designed to record transactions and produce financial statements at the end of each period. Given the growth in the business, the managers of WW now need additional information, such as the production of monthly management reports and the ability to accurately cost each unit of their products.

The current accounting system does not support these functions, meaning the accounting department is required to produce the information manually, which is both complex and time-consuming. WW's managers are concerned that this delay in obtaining management information may be putting the firm at a disadvantage in the marketplace.

The managers are therefore currently considering the purchase of a new, more complex, accounting package that will easily allow the production of the management accounting information that they need.

The manager of the accounting department, N, has been asked to oversee the purchase of the new package. N is aware that he may face resistance to the move to the new system from members of his team.

The accounting department has six members of staff. All of these staff members have been employees of the company for many years. The current accounting package has been in use within WW for the last seven years.

Required:

Write a report to N explaining Lewin's three-stage model and explain how this could help him manage the changeover to the new accounting package.

(15 minutes)

Force field analysis

Lewin also emphasised the importance of force field analysis. He argued that managers should consider any change situation in terms of:

- the factors encouraging and facilitating the change (the driving forces)
- the factors that hinder change (the restraining forces).

Change will only be successful if the driving forces are larger than the restraining forces.

If managers want to bring about change they must change the equilibrium by.

- strengthening the driving forces
- weakening the restraining forces
- or both.

The model encourages managers to identify the various forces impinging on the target of change, to consider the relative strengths of these forces (shown by the length of the arrows) and to explore alternative strategies for modifying the force field.

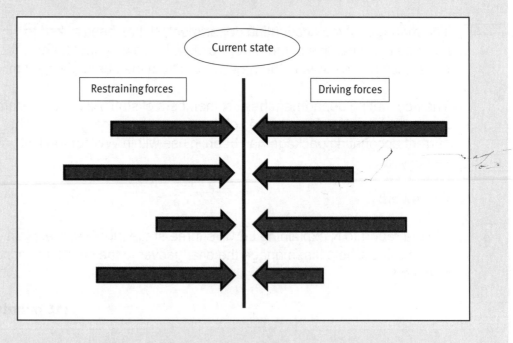

The above model can show driving and restraining forces from the point of view of employees or from the organisations point of view.

For employees faced with a change, driving forces could include fresh challenges, improved rewards or increased job satisfaction. Restraining forces could include anxiety about job security or fear of loss of power or status.

From an organisation's point of view, driving forces could be increased market share, customers demanding new products or increased efficiency while restraining forces could be lack of training, capital outlay or fear of disruption.

Beer and Nohria – Theory E & Theory O

Beer and Nohria (2000) identified that a large proportion of all business change initiatives fail. They believed that this was caused by managers becoming overwhelmed by the detail of the change management process and failing to focus on the overall goals of the change itself.

Beer and Nohria identified that every organisational change conforms to a variant of either:

- **Theory E strategies** – these are based on measures where shareholder value is the main concern. Change usually involves incentives, layoffs, downsizing and restructuring.

- **Theory O strategies** – these are 'softer' approaches to change, often involving cultural adjustment or enhancing employee capabilities through individual and organisational learning. This involves changing, obtaining feedback, reflecting and then making further changes. This requires involving employees in the change process.

Both approaches have drawbacks. A Theory E approach will tend to ignore the feelings and attitudes of their employees, which will often lead to a loss of motivation and commitment from staff members. This can damage the competitive advantage of the organisation.

Theory O organisations, on the other hand, will often fail to take the 'tough' decisions that may be needed.

To solve these problems, Beer and Nohria recommended that organisations should implement both Theory E and Theory O approaches simultaneously and try to balance the associated tensions.

e.g

Illustration 1 – Beer and Nohria

Due to the recent economic slowdown, many high-street retailers have seen a significant reduction in their profits, forcing them to consider a number of strategies to improve their results.

A **Theory E** approach means that the retailer is only concerned with the effect that falling profits has on shareholders – such as reduced dividends and share prices. The managers of the company will usually try to improve this quickly by laying off staff, reducing employee pay or closing stores that are seen as underperforming.

While this can have a positive impact on profits in the short-term, it fails to consider the needs of other stakeholders, such as employees. This can cause problems with employee motivation and commitment as staff members will not feel that the company is acting in their best interests. As such, the company may suffer from poor performance in the long-term.

A **Theory O** approach would see the retailer attempt to improve their profits by developing the organisation's capabilities and culture. For instance, a high-street retailer may train its staff to provide better customer service for shoppers. This will improve the customer experience and therefore, in the longer-term, should improve the profitability of the business. The retailer may well choose to involve staff in the decision-making process, asking for suggestions as to how customer service could be improved.

All of this is likely to make the employees feel more valued and should improve the commitment and motivation of the workforce. However, it may be insufficient in the short–term to deal with the fall in profitability and shareholders may expect more drastic, Theory E action in order to quickly improve their returns.

Beer and Nohria suggested that companies needed to be prepared to take both approaches simultaneously. This could, for example, involve some restructuring as well as a development of remaining employees. This would still need careful management as it would be easy to get the 'worst of all worlds' where staff are demotivated by the job losses while investors feel the cost cuts have not gone far enough.

Balance is needed!

6 Resistance to change

Resistance to change is the action taken by individuals and groups when they perceive that a change that is occurring is a threat to them.

Resistance is 'any attitude or behaviour that reflects a person's unwillingness to make or support a desired change'.

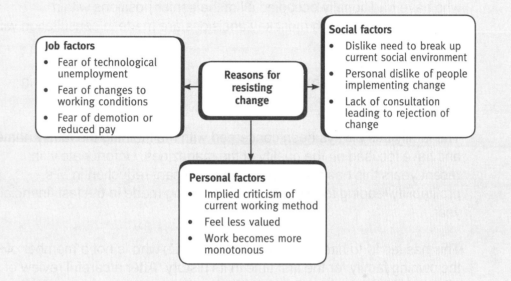

Resistance may take many forms, including active or passive, overt or covert, individual or organised, aggressive or timid. For each source of resistance, management need to provide an appropriate response, e.g.:

Source of resistance	Possible response
• The need for security and the familiar	• Provide information and encouragement, invite involvement
• Having the opinion that no change is needed	• Clarify the purpose of the change and how it will be made
• Trying to protect vested interests	• Demonstrate the problem or the opportunity that makes changes desirable

Case study style question 3

M publishes several major magazines in country A. M's best-selling title is a fashion magazine – Mean – although it also produces magazines on other topics, such as sport and technology.

The majority of M's shares are held by members of the founding family, who have traditionally occupied all of the senior positions within management, although most key decisions are made in consultation with the staff.

M currently employs around 2,500 staff in one large office building in country A's capital city.

The family has always been concerned with maintaining the family name and have focused on the quality of the magazines. Unfortunately, in recent years this has not prevented a significant reduction in M's profitability leading to M's first ever loss being made in the last financial year.

This has led M to hire a Finance Director (FD) who is not a member of the owning family for the first time in its history. After a careful review of M's expenditure he has discovered a large amount of unnecessary expenditure.

He has therefore proposed centralising a number of key functions, such as accounting, printing and proof-reading which are currently duplicated in each magazine. This will lead to around 300 job losses.

In addition he has suggested that the magazines should be produced using cheaper paper and inks, that the large expense accounts offered to senior managers should be cut and that M should start making use of intranets and groupware to allow staff to share ideas quickly and easily.

The FD's proposals have been met with significant resistance from M employees, as well as a number of members of the owning family. He is unsure as to why this is the case and has asked for your help.

Required:

Write an email to the FD discussing the reasons that his proposals are likely to have met with resistance.

(20 minutes)

7 Managing resistance

In order to determine the appropriate leadership approach to manage resistance Kotter and Schlesinger (1979) highlighted the need to understand why certain people resist change, for example:

- **Parochial self-interest** (some people are concerned with the implication of the change for themselves and how it may affect their own interests, rather than considering the effects for the success of the business).

- **Misunderstanding** (communication problems; inadequate information).

- **Low tolerance to change** (certain people are very keen on security and stability in their work).

- **Different assessments of the situation** (some employees may disagree on the reasons for the change and on the advantages and disadvantages of the change process).

Kotter and Schlesinger set out the following leadership approaches to deal with resistance to change:

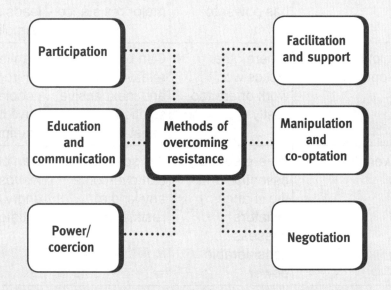

Key considerations when deciding upon a leadership style

- The speed at which change must be introduced

- The strength of the pressure for change

- The level of resistance expected

- The amount of power held by the manager

- How much information is needed before can be implemented the change and how long it will take to get that information

Approach/style	Situations used	Advantages	Disadvantages
Education and Communication	Where there is a lack of or inaccurate information and analysis	If persuaded, people will help with the implementation of change	Can be time consuming if many people are involved
Participation	Where initiators do not have all information to design change, and where others have power to resist	Participants are committed to implementing change including their relevant contribution	Can be very time consuming with possibly inappropriate changes made
Facilitation and Support	Where resistance comes from adjustment problems	Best approach for adjustment issues	Can be time consuming, expensive and still fail
Negotiation	Where one group will lose out and has power to resist	Can be an easy way to avoid major resistance	Can be too expensive if it leads to general compliance
Manipulation and Co-optation	Where other tactics won't work or are too costly	Can be a relatively quick and inexpensive solution to resistance	Can lead to future problems if people feel they have been manipulated
Power/Coercion	Where speed is essential, and the change initiators possess considerable power	It is speedy and can overcome any kind of resistance	Can be risky if it leaves people angry at the initiators

Explanation of the Kotter and Schlesinger styles

- Participation – aims to involve employees, usually by allowing some input into decision making. This could easily result in employees enjoying raised levels of autonomy, by allowing them to design their own jobs, pay structures, etc.

- Education and communication – used as a background factor to reinforce another approach. This strategy relies upon the hopeful belief that communication about the benefits of change to employees will result in their acceptance of the need to exercise the changes necessary.

- Power/coercion – involves the compulsory approach by management to implement change. This method finds its roots from the formal authority that management possesses, together with legislative support.

- Facilitation and support – employees may need to be counselled to help them overcome their fears and anxieties about change. Management may find it necessary to develop individual awareness of the need for change.

- Manipulation and co-optation – involves covert attempts to sidestep potential resistance. The information that is disseminated is selective and distorted to only emphasise the benefits of the change. Co-optation involves giving key people access to the decision-making process.

- Negotiation – is often practised in unionised companies. Simply, the process of negotiation is exercised, enabling several parties with opposing interests to bargain. This bargaining leads to a situation of compromise and agreement.

Case study style question 4

G is a conglomerate organisation with two major divisions: A and B. The two divisions are run as autonomous business units as they operate in completely different markets. Both are entering a period of organisational change and the directors of G are considering what style of management would be the most effective for each division.

Division A is currently highly profitable. However, it is looking at ways of increasing its efficiency. The managers of A have decided to centralise the accounting function within the business, which will reduce overheads and allow for a reduction in the number of employees. Division A has always had an excellent relationship with its relatively small number of highly skilled staff and is concerned about how these plans may affect that.

Division B is currently loss-making. It is also planning on reducing the number of staff it employs, but wishes to do so across all departments. B has a large number of workers and initial estimates are that 18% of all staff members will be made redundant. B has undertaken similar exercises in previous years, leading to significant conflict between the relatively unskilled staff and managers. The directors of G have informed the managers of B that if the division does not move back into profit in the near future, the division will be closed.

Required:

Write a report to the managers of A and B divisions suggesting which of Kotter and Schlesinger's leadership styles would be most appropriate for their division.

(15 minutes)

8 Change agents

Many organisations employ change agents to encourage and facilitate change. They can play a major role in helping deal with resistance to change. Usually change agents are figures who are familiar and non-threatening to other people.

The quality of the relationship between the change agent and key decision makers is very important, so the choice of change agent is critical.

Whether internal or external, the change agent is central to the process, and is useful in helping the organisation to:

- **Define the problem and its cause** – the change agent should be able to identify restraining forces or potential resistance and help management to understand the root causes behind them.

- **Diagnose solutions and select appropriate courses of action** – the change agent will be responsible for proposing ways in which these problems can be overcome and then helping management to select the most appropriate course of action.

- **Implement change** – once management have made their decision about which course of action to take, it will need to be implemented. Given that the change agent will be well informed about the proposed change and the reasons behind it, they are likely to be the best person to take the lead in implementing the change.

- **Transmit the learning process to others and the organisation overall** – the change agent should document the learning process and discussions which the company has undergone during the change process. They can then take the lead in spreading this information throughout the company.

Skills and attributes of change agents

The skills and attributes of the change agent would include:

Goals	• Clarity in defining the achievable
	• Sensitive to the impact of change on all stakeholders
	• Flexibility to adapt to internal and external triggers
Roles	• Team-building skills to establish work groups
	• Networking skills inside and outside the company
	• Tolerance of ambiguity and uncertainty
Communication	• Skills with colleagues and subordinates
	• Personal enthusiasm, stimulating commitment
	• Meeting management
Negotiation	• Creating vision and selling plans
	• Resolving conflict
	• Contract negotiation
Managing	• Political awareness and influencing skills
	• Balancing goals and perceptions
	• Helicopter perspective

"Power skills" of change agents (Kanter)

Kanter identified seven 'power skills' that change agents require to enable them to overcome apathy or resistance to change, and enable them to introduce new ideas:

- ability to work independently, without the power and sanction of the senior management hierarchy, providing visible support
- ability to collaborate effectively
- ability to develop relationships based on trust, with high ethical standards
- self-confidence, tempered with humility
- being respectful of the process of change, as well as the substance of the change
- ability to work across different business functions and units
- a willingness to stake personal rewards on results, and gain satisfaction from success.

Using external consultants as change agents

Advantages of using external consultants as change agents are as follows:

- They can bring a fresh perspective to the problem
- May have state-of-the-art knowledge of the required change – e.g. introducing TQM
- Being a dedicated resource they may be able to give it more time and energy
- They may have more experience and hence be better able to avoid traps and pitfalls
- Greater objectivity as they have no personal stake in the outcomes of the change.

MMM is a small company based in country A. It is currently considering the acquisition of a rival company, POR, which is based in country D. Unfortunately, the employees in country D speak a different language to staff members in country A. The directors of MMM are concerned about the effect that this could have on the viability of the acquisition.

They have decided to appoint a change agent to help control the process.

Required:

Write an email to the directors of MMM, explaining how a change agent could help in the acquisition of POR.

(15 minutes)

9 Managing decline

In reality, businesses are not always successful at expanding their business. Many managers may therefore find themselves having to manage decline rather than growth. The changes required during a period of decline pose particular dilemmas for managers as decisions often affect the organisation's workforce – its pay, conditions and job security.

When attempting to help a business recover from a period of decline, a manager's strategic priorities are likely to be:

- reducing costs to improve efficiency, and
- improving competitiveness in order to increase revenue.

Initially, when facing a downturn, the typical management response is to cut costs. While these can be cut from anywhere in the supply chain, the most obvious starting point is to reduce labour costs. At first, this may simply involve altering working patterns, such as the elimination of paid overtime or the replacement of full-time with part-time jobs. If this does not produce a sufficient cost reduction, management may move on to a program of voluntary or compulsory redundancies.

There is, however, a danger that if staff cuts are too severe then there will be reductions in the quality of the product and services provided to customers. There is also likely to be a serious impact on staff morale, potentially leading to a loss of commitment, a loss of skilled staff and an increase in conflict within the organisation.

It should be noted that many of the changes that a business may wish to make during a period of decline, such as compulsory redundancies or improving factory layout, may require some initial expenditure. The business may be unable to afford this if it is experiencing falling revenues.

In this case, managers may have to consider a fundamental change to the business strategy. This may involve:

- **Retrenchment** – this involves doing the same as before, but drastically cutting costs.

- **Turnaround** – the organisation repositions itself within the market to generate competitive advantage.

- **Divestment** – this involves the external sale of part of the organisation, or the internal closure of units as part of a rationalisation programme.

- **Liquidation** – the organisation is sold to one or more buyers. This is an admission of failure by the senior managers and is normally a last resort.

All four of these strategies require managers to make difficult decisions, which may have adverse effects on the organisation's stakeholders – especially employees. Whichever approach is taken, it is important that the business acts ethically towards its stakeholders when making tough decisions.

10 The importance of adaptation and continuous change

Many authors have argued that firms need to look beyond change as an event and develop a culture where change is embraced as an ongoing process. These include:

- change-adept organisations (Kanter)
- excellent firms that thrive on chaos (Peters)
- learning organisations (Senge)

Change-adept organisations – Kanter

Attributes of companies that manage change successfully.

- The imagination to innovate.
- The professionalism to perform.
- The openness to collaborate.

Skills for leaders in change-adept organisations – skills identified by Kanter.

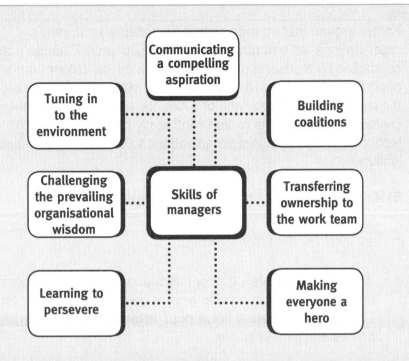

Change adept organisations

Rosabeth Moss Kanter looked at the characteristics of organisations that managed change successfully ('change-adept organisations'), and the qualities of their leaders and managers. She suggested that change-adept organisations share three key attributes:

- **The imagination to innovate.**

  Effective leaders help to develop new concepts, which are a requirement for successful change.

- **The professionalism to perform.**

  Leaders provide both personal competence and competence in the organisation as a whole, which is supported by workforce training and development. This enables the organisation to perform strongly and deliver value to ever more demanding customers.

- **The openness to collaborate.**

  Leaders in change-adept organisations make connections with 'partners' outside the organisation, who can extend the organisation's reach, enhance its products and services, and 'energise its practices'. 'Partners' will include suppliers working in close collaboration, joint venture partners, and so on.

Kanter argued that change should be accepted naturally by organisations, as a natural part of their existence. Change that is compelled by a crisis is usually seen as a threat, rather than as an opportunity for successful development. Mastering change means being the first with the best service or products, anticipating and then meeting customer requirements (which continually change) and applying new technology. This requires organisations to be 'fast, agile, intuitive and innovative'.

Skills for leaders in change-adept organisations

- Tuning in to the environment.

  A leader can actively gather information that might suggest new approaches, by tuning in to what is happening in the environment. Leaders can create a network of 'listening posts', such as satellite offices and joint ventures.

- Challenging the prevailing organisational wisdom.

  Leaders should be able to look at matters from a different perspective, and should not necessarily accept the current view of what is right or appropriate.

- Communicating a compelling aspiration.

  Leaders should have a clear vision of what they want to achieve, and should communicate it with conviction to the people they deal with. A manager cannot 'sell' change to other people without genuine conviction, because there is usually too much resistance to overcome. Without the conviction, a manager will not have the strength of leadership to persuade others.

- Building coalitions.

  Change leaders need the support and involvement of other individuals who have the resources, knowledge or 'political clout' to make things happen. There are usually individuals within the organisation who have the ability to influence others – 'opinion shapers', 'values leaders' and experts in the field. Getting the support of these individuals calls for an understanding of the politics of change in organisations.

- Transferring ownership to the work team.

  Leaders cannot introduce change on their own. At some stage, the responsibility for introducing change will be handed to others. Kanter suggested that a successful leader, having created a coalition in favour of the change, should enlist a team of other people to introduce the change.

- Learning to persevere.

  Something will probably go wrong, and there will be setbacks. Change leaders should not give up too quickly, but should persevere with the change.

- Making everyone a hero.

  A successful leader recognises, rewards and celebrates the accomplishments of others who have helped to introduce a change successfully. Making others feel appreciated for their contribution helps to sustain their motivation, and their willingness to attempt further changes in the future.

Thriving on Chaos (Tom Peters)

Tom Peters has written extensively on management theory. One of his ideas relates to 'excellent' companies that have succeeded by seeking to create a climate of continual and radical change. Peters called this 'thriving on chaos'. He suggested that:

- Incremental change is the enemy of true innovation, because it makes an organisation less willing to be truly innovative.

- Excellent firms don't believe in excellence, only in constant improvement and constant change.

- A constantly changing environment does not necessarily mean chaos: instead, it may mean that companies can handle the introduction of change successfully.

Peters suggested that the advantages of having a climate of change are as follows:

- Innovation and the introduction of new products and new methods are actively sought and welcomed.

- People who are used to change tend to accept it without resistance.

- Employees develop an external viewpoint, and are less insular and defensive in their outlook.

However, there are possible disadvantages:

- With a climate of change morale might be damaged
- Staff might become involved in office politics because of their concerns about the possible changes that might occur in the organisation.

Learning organisations – Senge

A learning organisation is an organisation skilled at creating, acquiring and transferring knowledge and at modifying its behaviour to reflect new knowledge and insights. It is an organisation that facilitates the learning of all its members and continuously transforms itself.

Learning organisations encourage questions and explicitly recognise mistakes as part of the learning process. They encourage testing and experimentation. Because they want to find new answers they recognise that failed answers are as important as successful ones.

Peter Senge outlines five disciplines that individuals and groups should be encouraged to learn to create a learning organisation.

- **Systems thinking** – is the ability to see particular problems as part of a wider whole and to devise appropriate solutions to them.
- **Personal learning and growth** – individuals should be encouraged to acquire skills and knowledge.
- **Mental models** – are deeply ingrained assumptions that determine what people think, e.g. a marketing group may think that price is more important than quality. Learning organisations can use a number of group techniques to make these models explicit and to challenge them.
- **A shared vision** – that does not filter knowledge which undermines learning.
- **Team learning** – teams must be trained to learn because there are factors in group dynamics that impede learning.

11 Summary

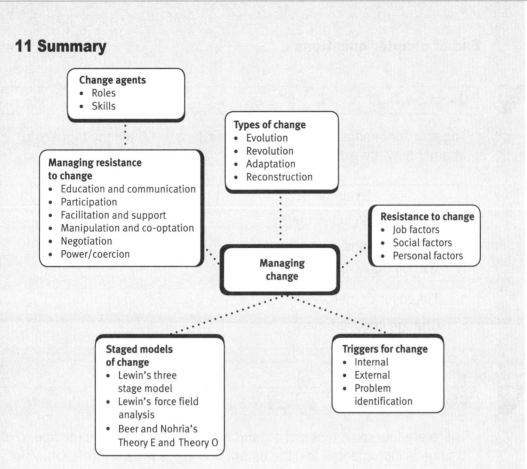

Change agents
- Roles
- Skills

Managing resistance to change
- Education and communication
- Participation
- Facilitation and support
- Manipulation and co-optation
- Negotiation
- Power/coercion

Types of change
- Evolution
- Revolution
- Adaptation
- Reconstruction

Resistance to change
- Job factors
- Social factors
- Personal factors

Managing change

Staged models of change
- Lewin's three stage model
- Lewin's force field analysis
- Beer and Nohria's Theory E and Theory O

Triggers for change
- Internal
- External
- Problem identification

End of chapter questions

Question 1

Triggers for change can be external or internal. Match the triggers to whether they are external or internal.

External	Internal

- New entrants to the market
- Fashion trends
- New procedures or systems
- Takeover or merger
- Change in government

Question 2

There are four main types of organisational change. Where the speed of change is incremental, and the extent of change is transformation, what type of change is suggested?

A   Reconstruction

B   Adaptation

C   Evolution

D   Revolution

Question 3

According to Kotter and Schlesinger, there are four reasons why people resist change. Which four of the following are those reasons?

- Parochial self-interest
- Dislike of the people implementing the change
- Misunderstanding
- Low tolerance to change
- Lack of consultation
- Disagreement on the reasons for change

Question 4

The three stages of Lewin's three stage model are:

- Unfreeze
- Change
- Refreeze

Match the activity to the stage at which it takes place.

- Identifying and exploiting existing areas of stress or dissatisfaction
- Publicising success stories and new 'heroes'
- Creating new reward or incentive schemes

Question 5

Three main reasons for resistance to change are:

- Job factors
- Social factors
- Personal factors

Insert the correct reason into the sentences below.

- Fear of reduced pay would be a _____ factor.
- Fear of feeling less valued would be a _____ factor.
- Dislike of people implementing the change would be a _____ factor.

Question 6

Beer and Nohria suggested that organisational change conformed to either Theory E or Theory O strategies. Which of these statements relate to Theory O? Select all that apply.

- With this approach, shareholder value is the main concern.
- This approach may result in poor employee performance in the long-term.
- This approach involves employees in the change process.
- Organisations adopting this approach may fail to take required 'tough' decisions.
- This is the approach recommended by Beer and Nohria.
- This approach suggests higher profits are gained from developing capabilities and culture.

Question 7

Kotter and Schlesinger suggested six methods for dealing with resistance to change, depending on the situation. These are:

- Participation
- Education and communication
- Power/coercion
- Facilitation and support
- Manipulation and co-optation
- Negotiation

Which of the above methods would be appropriate for the following situations?

- Where resistance comes from adjustment problems.
- Where speed is essential.
- Where one group will lose out and has power to resist.

Question 8

According to Kanter, which of the following are the key attributes of the change-adept organisation?

- The professionalism to perform
- The resources to develop
- The openness to collaborate
- The strength to succeed
- The imagination to innovate

Question 9

Which of the following statements about Lewin's force field model is true?

A Fear of loss of power or status would be a driving force

B Change will only be successful if the driving forces are larger than the restraining forces

C Weakening the driving forces can change the equilibrium and bring about change

D The factors which hinder change are known as driving forces

Question 10

During periods of decline organisations may have to make difficult decisions such as:

- Retrenchment
- Turnaround
- Divestment
- Liquidation

Match the following descriptions to the approach being described.

- This involves the external sale of part of the organisation or closure of business units
- With this approach the organisation repositions itself within the market to generate competitive advantage
- This involves continuing with the current operation but drastically cutting costs
- Normally a last resort, this involves the sale of the organisation to one or more buyers

Test your understanding answers

Case study style question 1

EMAIL

To: J

From: Management Accountant

Date: today

Subject: Change

Incremental change means step-by-step changes over time, in small steps. When incremental change occurs within an organisation, it is possible for the organisation to adapt to the change without having to alter its culture or structures significantly. Employees are able to adapt to the gradual changes, and are not unsettled by them.

In contrast, transformational change is a sweeping change that has immediate and widespread effects. The effect of transformational change is usually to alter the structure and culture of the organisation, often with major staff redundancies and the recruitment of new staff with new skills.

The spokesperson for the bank has argued that the change will be incremental. Since the change will take place over a long period of time, staff will have time to adapt to the new structure. There will be no compulsory redundancies and staff will be re-trained in new skills. Although some branches will close, others will remain open, and customers will be offered additional facilities through on-line banking.

The trade union leader believes that the change will be much more dramatic. He might believe that many employees will leave the bank because they are unable to adapt to the new service, or because they are unwilling to re-locate from the branches that are closed down. The bank might push through the branch closure programme more quickly than it has currently proposed, and staff redundancies could be made compulsory if there are not enough individuals willing to take voluntary redundancy.

Essentially, the two individuals take differing viewpoints because they are looking at change differently. The spokesperson for the bank wants to persuade employees to accept the change, and even welcome it. The trade union representative wants to warn employees about the potential consequences, and has therefore stressed the risks.

I hope you have found the above useful, please get in touch if you need any more information about this.

Case study style question 2

REPORT

To: N

From: Management Accountant

Date: Today

Subject: Lewin's three-stage model

Introduction

Lewin's model suggests that, in order to be successful, WW will need to follow three stages in the change-over to a new accounting package.

Unfreeze

Staff need to be convinced of the need for the new accounting package. This could be difficult within WW for several reasons.

WW's six employees have used the current accounting system for many years. This may mean that they are 'stuck in their ways' and unwilling to learn the new skills required for the new system.

In addition, currently management accounting information can only be produced after a time-consuming and complex process. If a new system improves the efficiency of this process, employees may fear that they will become redundant.

To help with this, WW need to convince them of the superiority of the new system. For instance, it appears that it will make the production of management reports much faster, easing the workload for the employees.

WW also needs to communicate well with its employees. Resistance is often caused by a fear of the unknown. Managers could discuss with staff about the level of training that they will be given on the new system and attempt to allay any fears they may have about potential redundancies.

Finally, WW's managers could also stress to staff members that it will benefit the business as a whole. The current system may cause WW to be less competitive in the marketplace, which could threaten the business as a whole.

Change

This involves actually moving staff onto the new accounting system.

This stage will involve training all members of the accounting department on how to use the new system. Enough time must be allowed for employees to be reasonably comfortable with the new system before the change-over is made.

Communication is also vital here – employees must know when the new system will be installed and what will be expected from them. For example, what new reports will the managers expect from the system and when they will need to be prepared.

Refreeze

Finally, WW's managers must ensure that employees do not slip back into old habits and start using the old systems again.

Clearly, if the old accounting system is entirely replaced by the new one, it should be easy to ensure that staff members do not continue to use the original accounting system. However, employees may still continue preparing the management reports manually.

To avoid this, managers could refuse to accept reports in the old, manual format – instead requiring that they be produced from the new system. Staff could be rewarded for using the new system and penalised if the old methods are still used.

Conclusion

Change is an inevitable function within organisations, but it can face resistance and can be difficult to manage. Using a model such as Lewin's three-stage model should help the change to be managed more effectively.

Case study style question 3

EMAIL

To: FD

From: Management Accountant

Date: today

Subject: Resistance to change

There may be many reasons why you are meeting resistance from M when trying to push through a change management process. I will try to cover the main ones in this email.

Job factors

Many employees may be resisting due to concerns about their jobs. For 300 employees, your proposals will mean unemployment, which means they are likely to be strongly resistant to them.

Many other employees will be affected by the plans to centralise key functions. Those members of staff who remain may be forced to take on a heavier workload to cover the roles of employees made redundant. This may also cause resistance.

Senior managers will be unhappy due to the reduction in their expense accounts as this will be perceived as a loss of their status within the business.

In addition, you are proposing increased use of intranets and groupware. Staff may well be unfamiliar with these systems and dislike the idea of having to learn how to use them. They may also have concerns over the impact they will have on their jobs.

Personal factors

The changes you have suggested may well be seen as an implied criticism of the long-standing methods of the business. This may well cause resistance from not only the staff, but the owners who have been heavily involved in running the business.

Senior managers may feel less valued under the proposals due to the cuts to their expense accounts, leading to further resistance.

The owners of the company have traditionally focused on the quality of the magazines as they feel this reflects on their family name. The proposals to reduce the quality of the paper and ink is therefore likely to be poorly received by them.

Social factors

The family has normally made key decisions within the company in full consultation with the employees. This does not seem to have been the case with your proposals, reducing the likelihood that employees will accept the changes.

You are also new in your role and, for the first time, not a member of the owning family. This may reduce his perceived authority, making it more likely that employees, managers and owners will feel that they do not have to follow your suggestions.

I hope you have found the above useful, please get in touch if you need any more information about this.

Case study style question 4

REPORT

To: Managers of A and B divisions

From: Management Accountant

Date: Today

Subject: Kotter and Schlesinger's leadership styles

Introduction

In this report, the approaches to managing the changes being planned by divisions A and B will be considered using Kotter and Schlesinger's model of leadership styles.

Division A

Division A appears to be making a relatively small change to its business. It is currently highly profitable – indicating that it is not currently experiencing a crisis.

As such, education and communication may be the best approach. This involves explaining the reasons behind the proposed centralisation of the accounting function and attempts to persuade the employees that this is a beneficial idea. While this is often time-consuming, A has a relatively small number of staff, which makes this approach more realistic. In addition, as the company currently has a good relationship with its workers (and likely needs to maintain this given that its staff are highly skilled and therefore very important to the company), this approach is most likely to keep the majority of staff happy.

It is possible that staff may not be convinced by the need to cut costs given that the division is highly profitable. In this case, A could choose facilitation and support – perhaps helping the staff who will be made redundant to find new jobs, such as by giving them time off for job interviews.

Finally, A could consider participation and involvement. This would see A getting its employees involved in the change process. Perhaps job losses can be avoided if employees are able to think of alternative ways of improving efficiency. This may be very time consuming, although there is no evidence of time-pressure in the scenario.

Division B

Division B is clearly in a crisis, with poor industrial relations and the potential threat of closure.

Given the serious nature of its situation, B could also adopt an education and communication style. If the alternative to job losses is a total closure of the division, this may be enough to convince employees of the need for the change. However, given the poor relations between staff and managers, as well as the tight time-constraints that B is under, this may not be realistic.

As an alternative, B could choose a manipulation and co-optation style. This involves undermining resistance in a more covert manner, perhaps by stressing the potential for the division to be closed, or down-playing the number of job losses that would be involved. It is a faster way of dealing with resistance than education and communication, but if employees feel that they are being manipulated, it may damage industrial relations further.

Finally, B could opt for coercion. This involves the managers of B forcing the staff to accept the changes. Any individuals who resist can be threatened with redundancy. Given the urgent nature of the needed change, this may be the easiest and most effective way of dealing with resistance. However, it will be likely to leave employees angry and may lead to demotivation and high employee turnover.

B may decide that its industrial relations are less important than its long-term survival, especially as employees are low skilled and will therefore be easy to replace.

Conclusion

Change must be carefully managed to ensure success. How change is managed depends on the individual circumstances of each case. Different approaches to managing change should be used in different situations.

Case study style question 5

EMAIL

To: Directors of MMM

From: Management Accountant

Date: today

Subject: Change agents

A change agent is a person, or group of people, who help an organisation to achieve its strategic change. If MMM appoints a change agent, he or she would carry out a number of useful functions, including:

Identify any problems and their causes

This is likely to be relatively straightforward for MMM. The biggest problem with their proposed purchase of POR is the language barrier between their staff. MMM and POR will find it almost impossible to work together as they do not understand each other's language.

This could cause the acquisition to fail.

Diagnose solutions and select appropriate courses of action

The change agent is responsible for proposing ways in which the problems that they have identified could be overcome.

For MMM, it could consider:

- sending key members of staff in both companies on external language courses, or

- hiring some additional staff members in both companies who are bilingual.

In many cases there will be a number of possible solutions. The change agent will be responsible for presenting these to management and helping them to decide which option is most appropriate for MMM.

Implement change

Once the management have selected an appropriate strategy, they will need someone to implement it. As the change agent has been part of the decision-making process, they will be the most logical choice to actually carry out the plan. In MMM, the change agent may, for example, investigate and book language courses for appropriate members of staff.

Transmit the learning process to others and the organisation overall

There may be some resistance to the proposed changes. A change agent can champion the proposals, explaining to employees why it is necessary and what the advantages will be.

The change agent will also document the decision-making process and communicate to all members of staff in both MMM and POR. This is a vital step, as employees in both businesses will need to be kept informed about the developments in the company.

I hope you have found the above useful, please get in touch if you need any more information about this.

Question 1

The correct matching is:

External	Internal
New entrants to the market Fashion trends Change in government	procedures or systems Takeover or merger

External triggers come from environmental factors and can be general (indirect) or task (direct) factors.

Internal triggers come from changes within the organisation.

Question 2

C   Evolution

The full model of organisation change is shown below:

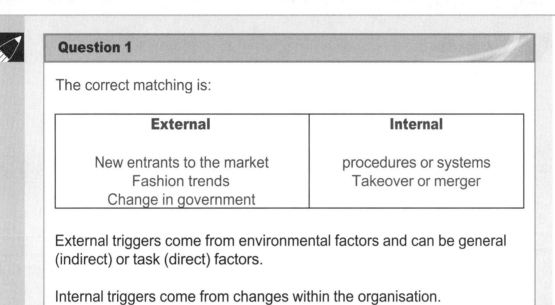

Extent of change

	(big) **Transformation**	**Realignment** (small)
(slow) **Incremental**	**Evolution:** Transformational change implemented gradually through inter-related initiatives; likely to be proactive change undertaken in anticipation of the need for future change. This results in a fundermentally different organisation once completed	**Adaptation:** Change undertaken to realign the way in which the organisation operates; implemented in a series of steps
Speed of change **Big Bang** (fast)	**Revolution:** Transformational change that occurs via simultaneous initiatives on many fronts: This change is more likely to be forced and reactive because of the changing competitive conditions that the organisation is facing	**Reconstruction:** Change undertaken to realign the way in which the organisation operates with many initiatives implemented simultaneously: This is often forced and reactive because of a changing competitive context

Question 3

- Parochial self-interest
- Misunderstanding
- Low tolerance to change
- Disagreement on the reasons for change

Dislike of the people implementing the change and lack of consultation are also reasons for resisting change but they are not the main four suggested by Kotter and Schlesinger.

Question 4

The correct matching is:

Unfreeze – Identifying and exploiting existing areas of stress or dissatisfaction

Change – Creating new reward or incentive schemes

Refreeze – Publicising success stories and new 'heroes'

Lewin's three stage model firstly involves 'unfreezing' the existing situation, then making the required changes, then 'refreezing' to reinforce the new situation.

Question 5

The complete sentences are:

Fear of reduced pay would be a **job** factor.

Fear of feeling less valued would be a **personal** factor.

Dislike of people implementing the change would be a **social** factor.

Question 6

- This approach involves employees in the change process.
- Organisations adopting this approach may fail to take required 'tough' decisions.
- This approach suggests higher profits are gained from developing capabilities and culture.

The following points relate to Theory E:

- With this approach, shareholder value is the main concern.
- This approach may result in poor employee performance in the long-term.

Beer and Nohria suggested that a combination of the two theories should be used at the same time.

Question 7

The correct matching is:

Facilitation and support – Where resistance comes from adjustment problems.

Power/coercion – Where speed is essential.

Negotiation – Where one group will lose out and has power to resist.

Question 8

- The professionalism to perform
- The openness to collaborate
- The imagination to innovate

Kanter suggested that change adapt organisations had the following attributes:

The professionalism to perform – competent leadership supported by workforce training and development.

The openness to collaborate – management have connections with 'partners' outside the organisation which can extend the organisation's reach and enhance its products, services and practices.

The imagination to innovate – Effective leaders help to develop new concepts which are required for successful change.

Question 9

B   Change will only be successful if the driving forces are larger than the restraining forces

Fear of loss of power or status would be a **restraining** force.

Weakening the **restraining** forces can change the equilibrium and bring about change.

The factors which hinder change are known as **restraining** forces.

Question 10

The correct matching is:

Divestment   This involves the external sale of part of the organisation or closure of business units.

Turnaround   With this approach the organisation repositions itself within the market to generate competitive advantage.

Retrenchment This involves continuing with the current operation but drastically cutting costs

Liquidation   Normally a last resort, this involves the sale of the organisation to one or more buyers.

Managing projects

Chapter learning objectives

Discuss the characteristics of the different phases of a project.

1 Session content diagram

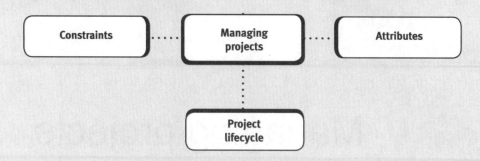

2 The importance of project management in delivering change

From the previous chapter it is clear that change is an inevitable part of today's organisations. Effectively managing this change is therefore critical to the ongoing success of the organisation.

Change will be delivered through projects, therefore understanding project management and being able to successfully complete projects is essential for organisations.

This and the following few chapters cover the project management process in detail.

3 Defining a project and project management

Project

A project has a number of key attributes which differentiates it from business as usual:

A project is a **unique** undertaking to achieve a specific **objective**.

A project has a **defined beginning and end**.

A project has **resources**, like staff and funding allocated specifically for the length of the project.

The project will also have **stakeholders**, i.e. all those who are interested in the progress and final outcome of the project.

A project will inevitably have some degree of **uncertainty** as the uniqueness of it will lead to some degree of risk in the deliverables and the activities to achieve the deliverables.

Once completed, it should then become integrated into the normal day-to-day activities of the business.

The Association of Project Managers defines a project as: '***A human activity that achieves a clear objective against a time scale.***'

Project management

Project management is about managing a specific group of specialists; the professional mix of this group is tailored specifically for the accomplishment of a project. This may be a year or less in some projects, and may run to five years and upward for long-range, high-budget projects.

Project management is not a long line of repetitive or similar functions stretching ahead, such as you would find within operations areas such as manufacturing or sales.

CIMA Official Terminology defines project management as '**the integration of all aspects of a project, ensuring that the proper knowledge and resources are available when and where needed, and above all to ensure that the expected outcome is produced in a timely, cost-effective manner**.'

4 Project constraints

Every project has constraints. Constraints are anything which restricts, limits, prevents or regulates activities being carried out. When running a project it is critical that the constraints are known, so they can be taken account of throughout the project.

The primary constraints are time, cost and quality. These are often referred to as the 'project triangle':

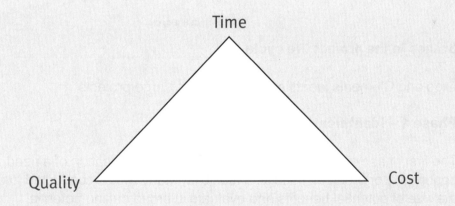

It is worth thinking about the conflicting nature of these constraints.

Time and cost tend to be positively correlated in projects (i.e. when time increases, so does cost), as taking longer to complete a project generally means that human resources are needed for longer. However, this is not always the case. If there is a degree of urgency in a project, it may be possible to reduce the timescale to completion by allocating additional resources, or by scheduling expensive overtime working. Both of these situations will increase cost while reducing time.

Project quality tends to be positively correlated with both cost and time, in that increasing the quality of the project will normally lead to an increase in both the cost of the project and its overall duration.

In additional to these three main constraints, there are a number of other constraints which will affect the project's delivery, such as legal, technological, political, environmental and ethical.

5 The project life cycle

Large-scale projects usually follow a life cycle made up of separate phases, which occur in sequence. There are a number of models which detail these phases. Regardless of which model is used, it is important to highlight the separate stages which the project goes through from beginning to end, and to understand what happens during each stage. A project life cycle is shown below:

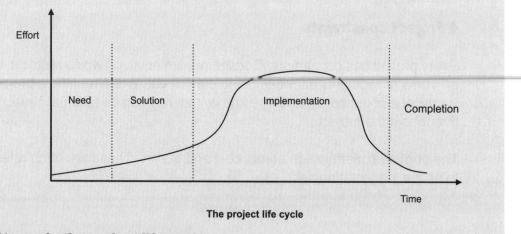

The project life cycle

Stages in the project life cycle

Gido and Clements identified four phases of large projects

Phase 1 – Identification of a need

The first phase of the project life cycle involves identification of a need, opportunity or problem. Initially, a feasibility study will be conducted to check the size of potential benefits and evaluate in broad outline potential alternative solutions and their lifetime costs. At the end of this phase, the company will decide whether to proceed with the project. If it does, then a project team is formed and a project initiation document (PID) is raised. This will include a vision and a business case for the project. The business case is an important guide to decision-making throughout the project, and the vision encourages motivation and congruent goals in the project team.

Phase 2 – Development of a proposed solution

The second stage of the project life cycle is the development of a proposed solution. All proposals for the solution will be submitted to the company, which then evaluates them and chooses the most appropriate solution to satisfy the need.

Phase 3 – Implementation

The third stage of the project life cycle is the implementation of the proposed solution. Once a proposed solution has been selected, the work to build the required product or service can commence. This phase is the actual performance of the project and will involve doing the detailed planning, and then implementing that plan to accomplish the project objective.

The overall solution is subdivided into separate deliverables to be achieved at fixed milestones through this stage of the project. Achievement of these deliverables may be linked to stage payments. The project's objectives of functionality, quality, cost and time are monitored regularly against each deliverable to ensure they are being met. Timely appropriate action can then be taken if any slippage has occurred.

Phase 4 – Completion

The fourth stage of the project life cycle is the completion or closure of the project. When a project closes, important tasks need to be carried out, such as confirmation that all deliverables have been provided and accepted, and all payments have been made and received. Project performance is evaluated and appraised in order to learn from the project for future reference. Obtaining customer feedback is important in improving the quality of future project provision. The business case is also revisited to check whether any subsequent actions are needed to ensure achievement of the anticipated benefits.

6 Five project management process areas

An alternative five stage project life cycle based on the Project Management Institute's 5 Project Management Process Areas identifies the stages as:

- Initiating
- Planning
- Executing (implementating)
- Controlling
- Closing/Completing

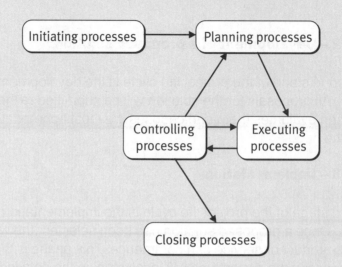

This model is very similar to the 'general' project life cycle above. However, it places greater emphasis on the 'planning' and 'controlling' activities, as is to be expected from a professional project management institute.

It is important to understand the purpose of each stage of the project life cycle and the activities which are carried out at each stage. Each of the stages will now be looked at in detail.

7 Initiating

Projects are initiated when a need or objective is defined.

Objectives are those things that the organisation wants to achieve. Typically, top-level objectives are profit-oriented, or in not-for-profit organisations objectives will be to improve the standard of living or education, and so on of members. It is usually a function of the board of directors to determine the high-level organisational objectives.

There are a number of reasons why a project would be initiated:

- To help meet the company's long term goals and objectives.
- Process/service enhancement.
- Solve problems identified internally or externally.
- To take advantage of new opportunities.
- Statutory/legal requirement.

Companies may have a number of potential projects they would like, or need to undertake, but they may not have the resources to carry them all out. They often have to go through a selection process to establish the most worthwhile projects. The purpose of the initiation stage is to identify the most worthwhile projects to undertake. Only these projects will be taken forward to the planning stage.

One of the main ways companies select the most worthwhile projects is by considering the **feasibility** of the proposed projects and the **risk and uncertainty** relating to the project.

Feasibility

The development of any new project requires careful consideration and planning. It will consume large volumes of resources, both financial and non-financial, and is likely to have a major effect on the way in which the organisation will operate.

Feasibility studies may be carried out on a number of potential strategies and the aim of the study is to decide on which proposal to choose.

Sometimes the potential project manager is involved in the feasibility study stage of a project, but not always. However, it is important for project managers to understand the process of feasibility assessment.

Types of feasibility

There are a number of types of feasibility which could be considered, including the following:

- Technical feasibility

- Social (operational) feasibility

- Ecological (environmental) feasibility

- Economic (financial) feasibility

Technical feasibility – can it be done?

There are a number of key aspects regarding technology which must be considered, for example:

- Is the technology available?

- Is the technology tried and tested?

- What performance do we require of the technology?

- Is the technology suitable to satisfy the objective of the project effectively?

Social (operational) feasibility – does it fit with current operations?

It is becoming increasingly necessary to assess operational/social factors affecting feasibility. These may include awareness of the social issues within a group or office (e.g. introducing a computerised system), or larger social awareness regarding the effect of projects or products on workers, employment or the environment. It is also important to ensure that the projects fits with business goals.

Social considerations include:

- Number of people required (during the project and after integration).
- Skills required – identify recruitment, training, redundancy.

Some of these issues can be directly costed (such as training costs). Others have less tangible effects that must be documented in the feasibility report.

Ecological (environmental) feasibility – how does it affect the environment?

Ecological considerations may be driven by the understanding that customers would prefer to purchase alternative products or services as they are more ecologically sound and less harmful to the environment.

Ecological considerations include:

- Effects on local community and what that might do to company image.
- What pollution could be caused by the project.

Economic (financial) feasibility – is it worth it?

The project (proposed system) must provide a benefit to the organisation. Economic feasibility will be assessed through a cost-benefit analysis. Cost-benefit analysis helps to identify and evaluate the costs of the proposal over its anticipated life. The other side to cost-benefit is the identification and evaluation of the benefits of the project over its life.

Cost-benefit analysis

When considering economic feasibility, the benefits and the costs of the project must be considered in detail.

Financial costs and benefits can be evaluated using investment appraisal techniques such as payback and discounted cash flow approaches.

You would not rely on a single measure to determine the financial feasibility of a project.

The types of costs and benefits involved in a project will depend upon the precise nature and scope of that project and can vary greatly.

Benefits

- Tangible – those benefits that can be evaluated financially (reduction of employees when processes are automated).

- Intangible – those benefits that are not easy to evaluate financially (a new computer system may provide better information to managers for decision making and control).

Remember that any intangible benefits will have been excluded in the financial evaluation process.

Costs

- *Capital Costs* – costs incurred in the acquisition of assets plus any additional costs of installation and maintenance.

- *Revenue Costs* – any costs other than for the purchase of assets. These costs are incurred on a regular basis and include repairs and consumables.

- *Finance Costs* – finance costs are usually incurred as interest charges. Sources of finance include banks, shareholders, retained profit from the business and grants or subsidies from the government.

Types of feasibility example

We will use the following example to explain the types of feasibility:

SMK, a manufacturer of car components, operates from a large industrial site in V town where it is the largest local employer. SMK is well respected in the town, and have always stated their commitment to the town and their employees. The current site is too small for the company's current needs and is in need of some upgrading. As such the board have been considering alternative courses of action to expand the current site.

Last week the board of SMK was approached with an offer to buy their current site for a substantial sum of money from a neighbouring mining company who have plans to develop the site as an open cast mine. As part of the deal, the mining company have offered to build SMK a new factory on land they own in H town, about 150 miles from SMK's current site. The board of SMK are considering the offer.

Technical feasibility – can it be done?

For SMK, this may involve considerations such as the ability to set up a fully functioning factory in H town. Given the nature of SMK's business, this may involve the moving and installation of large pieces of equipment. It will also have to be considered if all utilities required will be available at the new site, the ability to get planning permissions and so on. It seems likely that the project will be technically feasible.

Social (operational) feasibility – does it fit with current operations?

For SMK, they may have difficulty with the social and operational feasibility of the project. It will mean moving from V town where they are a respected employer (and the largest local employer) and the move will result in many people losing their jobs. It is unclear how many jobs the mining operation would bring to the area, but it unlikely that the mining company would be able to take on all of those affected by the move. It would seem that the project would not be socially feasible.

Ecological (environmental) feasibility – how does it affect the environment?

For SMK, there are some environmental implications of the proposal. Firstly for V Town, they would be losing a factory but gaining an open cast mine. This could have large adverse implications for the local environment. On the other hand, the new factory operated by SMK is likely to be more efficient and have less impact on the environment than the old factory, but the overall impact on the environment is likely to be adverse. How SMK's board feel about this will depend on their view of social responsibility. They have always stated their commitment to V town, but if the plan goes ahead they will cause unemployment and environmental damage to the area.

Economic (financial) feasibility – is it worth it?

For SMK, the cost of the project will include the cost of planning and building the new factory. The costs will also include kitting out the new factory and they will have to consider the employment costs. A number of current employees will not be able to move to work at the new site, therefore SMK may face redundancy costs and they will also incur costs in hiring and training a new workforce for the new factory. The costs will be high but a substantial sum of money will be received from the sale of their existing site.

Benefits should derive from the business case that identified the need to expand the current factory in the first place (e.g. capital growth, increased equity, increased capacity and income, profits). It seems likely that the project would be economically feasible.

Risk and uncertainty

Another important activity which is carried out at the initiation stage is to undertake a risk assessment to consider the risks associated with the proposed project and to consider how these risks can be managed.

Risk management process

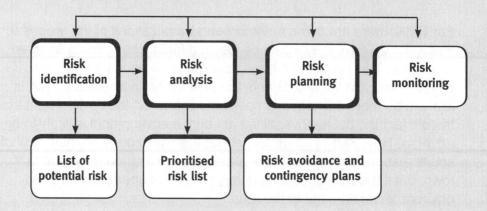

- Identify risk – produce a list of risk items.

- Analyse risk – assess the loss probability and magnitude of each item.

- Prioritise – produce a ranked ordering of risk items.

- Management – plan how to address each risk item, perhaps by avoiding, transferring or reducing the risk.

- Resolution – produce a situation in which risk items are avoided or reduced.

- Monitoring – continually monitor the progress towards resolving risk, and indentification of new risks.

Managing risk

Once the risks have been listed they should be plotted on the following grid to determine whether the project should go ahead.

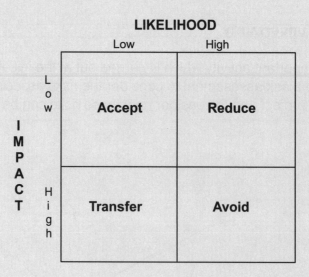

A useful way to remember the risk management approaches is **TARA (Transfer, Avoid, Reduce, Accept)**:

Transfer	• Subcontract the risk to those more able to handle it, such as a specialist supplier or insurer.
Avoid	• Abort the plan. • Escape the specific clause in the contract. • Leave the risk with the customer or supplier.
Reduce	• Take an alternative course of action with a lower risk exposure. • Invest in additional capital equipment or security devices to reduce risk or limit its consequences.
Accept	• Accept that some risks are an inevitable part of doing business. • Continue to monitor risks to ensure that their potential impact or likelihood have not increased.

Uncertainty

Unlike risk, uncertainty is impossible to evaluate because it is impossible to assign probability to an uncertain event. If the event is uncertain we cannot put in place management control to reduce the probability of its occurrence, simply because we do not know that probability. Instead we must use contingency planning.

Contingency planning

Contingency planning involves considering alternative actions should uncertain events occur.

Contingency plans may include:

* contacting lenders to discuss possible additional finance.

* re-planning the remaining project with a longer duration.

* identifying if required materials are available from other possible suppliers.

The purpose of contingency planning is to speed up the planning process. The contingency plans may never be used, but we can do our contingency planning when it suits us. If we wait for the uncertain event before doing any planning, this may further delay the project.

Project initiation document (PID)

A project initiation document (PID) is a reference document produced at the outset of a project – at the end of the initiation stage. There are two primary reasons for having a PID:

(1) For authorisation by the project steering committee or project board

(2) To act as a base document against which progress and changes can be assessed.

The PID can be used to ensure that the project team and project shareholders are in general agreement about the nature and parameters of the project.

This document therefore:

- Defines the project and its scope.
- Justifies the project.
- Secures funding for the project, if necessary.
- Defines the roles and responsibilities of project participants.
- Gives people the information they need to be productive and effective right from the start.

A project initiation document (PID) should contain at least the following sections:

- **Purpose statement** – explains why the project is being undertaken.
- **Scope statement** – puts boundaries to the project by outlining the major activities. This section is important in preventing 'scope creep', where additional activities are added making achievement of the cost and time objectives totally impossible.
- **Deliverables** – tend to be tangible elements of the project, such as reports, assets and other outputs.
- **Cost and time estimates** – it is a good idea for the project team to have some feel for the organisation's expectations in terms of the project budget. These estimates will be modified later in the project, but are necessary to give a starting point for planning.
- **Objectives** – a clear statement of the mission, CSFs and milestones of the project.
- **Stakeholders** – a list of the major stakeholders in the project and their interest in the project.
- **Chain of command** – a statement (and diagram) of the project organisation structure.

Case study style question 1

It is often claimed that all project management is risk management since risk is an inherent and inevitable characteristic of most projects. The aim of the project manager is to combat the various hazards to which a project may be exposed.

L is a new project manager and is about to undertake her first project. She is concerned about risk management as she knows it is an important part of her role as project management. She has come to you for advice.

Required:

Write an email to L explaining the concept of risk and the ways in which risk can be managed in a project.

(15 minutes)

---

8 Planning

The planning stage of a project is essential – it helps to:

- Communicate what has to be done, when and by whom.
- Encourage forward thinking.
- Provide the measures of success for the project.
- Make clear the commitment of time, resources (people and equipment), and money required for the project.
- Determine if targets are achievable.
- Identify the activities the resources need to undertake.

In the planning stage, a number of separate detailed plans will be drawn up. For example, separate plans for:

- **Time** – the time plan lists all the activities, who will do what and how long each is planned to take. This includes the milestone finish dates of each stage of the project life cycle, and the estimated completion date of the whole project.

- **Cost** – the cost plan uses a rate per hour for each activity in the time plan, plus cost of purchases from the resource plan, plus contingency costs to create a budget for the project. This will be time phased to provide a cash flow forecast.

- **Quality** – the quality plan includes identification of the customers, the key outcomes each expects, acceptance criteria that has been agreed with them, a test plan for how each outcome will be tested, and responsibility for each test. This may include safety and security planning. It will also include an audit plan for the project management process.

- **Resources** – the resource plan checks peaks and troughs of workload to ensure the plan is feasible and lists purchases to be bought.

- **Contingency** – contingency planning includes assessment of risk and decides what additional activities and buffer of cost and time need to be added to the plan to ensure a reliable budget and completion date. A risk register will identify contingency plans for each of the key risks and allocates responsibility for monitoring each.

- **Communication** – the communication plan identifies the key people in the project, their likely concerns, messages needed, planned method of communication and who will be responsible.

- **Deliverables** – the deliverables plan will detail exactly what has been agreed as the deliverables of the project. This must be agreed by the users and sponsors at the outset of the project.

The project manager and planning

It is important to understand the responsibilities of the project manager within the planning stage. The primary responsibility is to **define the project objective** clearly with the customer, then to **communicate** this objective to the rest of the project team, making it clear what constitutes a **successful project outcome**.

The project manager should involve the team members in the planning process, as this will encourage involvement, commitment and ownership of the project.

A project reporting information system should be set up to record and monitor the progress of the project against the plan. The comparisons between actual and plan should be communicated to team members on a regular basis. Responsibility structures may be used (i.e. ensuring that team members receive information on their own area of influence), but this must be carefully weighed against ensuring that project team members do not forget that their particular area of control is likely to affect other areas and will ultimately affect the overall achievement of the whole project objective.

Example of project planning

A project is to be undertaken to upgrade the computer system of E, a company which deals with examination results.. The deadline for completion is 30 September 2016. Key personnel in the project are the project manager, H and J (E's IT manager). As the system will deal with examination results, security of the system will be critical.

The plan below would be issued to stakeholders such as corporate management, customers and the project team. There may be 'commercial-in-confidence' elernents in it that would only be shown to the senior management. **There are no set layouts or contents of management plans**. Some illustrative examples have been used.

Section title	Contents
Overview or summary	Project objectives; organisation of the project team; schedule of work; especially the milestones; resources required including the budget and an assessment of significant risks.
Project name	For example, project for the upgrade of a computer system for E.
Project players and responsibility	The project authorisation document will identify roles and responsibilities such as the project board, the project manager, and the project team. For example: H, Project Manager. Responsible for: initiating the project; selecting the project team; preparing and implementing plans; managing the successful delivery of the project to time, cost and quality applications.
Project objectives	For example, to design and implement an upgraded examination system for E, the customer, maintaining pre-existent standards but catering for an increase in candidate applications.
Project scope and contract	This is identified in the project authorisation document. Reasons for undertaking this project, what is to be achieved in terms of the deliverables (e.g. the completion of the contract with all user training by 30 September 2016 at a cost of $x).
Methodology	The project team will use project management techniques consistent with accepted UK standards.

Assumptions	These may refer to site access, costs of supplies, the cost of borrowing money, inflation, the availability of particular staff and so on. A major assumption for the E project is that the system is accessible in the quiet period between major application periods or examination dates.
Technical plan	The technical features of the project are identified. They will include requirements, specifications, system diagrams, site plans, tools, techniques, support functions, standards and any relevant document relating to the provision of the new exam administration system. In-house or subcontracted provision of modules will be specified.
Quality and management	The quality plan identifies our customer, E, the key outcomes it expects, acceptance criteria agreed, a test plan of how each outcome is to be tested, and responsibility for each test. Safety and security planning will be essential, as this system must be 100 % secure. An audit plan will be included.
Communication plan	This will identify the key stakeholders in the project, what their interest in the project is and their concerns that will need to be addressed, what communication is planned and the responsible person. In our project, H will be responsible for communicating with J on a weekly basis to update her on the progress and to tackle any concerns she has. Monthly status projects, monthly resource reports (financial – critical to this project – and human resource reports) will be issued and any milestones will be reported on in writing. Should any critical status reports be needed, they will be made outside the weekly meeting.
Organisation and personnel	The organisation plan describes the structure of the project team and each person's responsibilities. Included will be any sub-contract staff and staff from E with any input to the project. Organisation charts will be drafted by position if staff need to be recruited. If so, recruitment methods, sources and training required will be identified with start times. In our project, we need to recruit one extra software engineer to bespoke the application.
Project schedule	This will describe the main phases of the project and highlight all key milestones. It is usually illustrated by a Gantt chart or with a network diagram.

Resources and facilities including budget breakdown	This includes checks on peaks and troughs of workload to ensure the plan is feasible and to ensure procurement is achieved by the provision of lists. The cost plan will give a rate per hour for all work and the costs of purchases. Contingency costs are included to give the project budget. Time phasing will give a cash flow forecast. E has made it clear that no extra project money will be available, so H must ensure as much as possible that his costings and time/resources management are accurately assessed. The contracting company will be bearing the risk of over-run and any other contingencies.
Risk assessment and risk management	The risks are identified and contingency plans made, including extra activities and cost and time buffers to be added to ensure reliable budget and completion date. The risk register identifies each contingency plan for each key risk and allocates responsibility for monitoring. In the E project, unauthorised access to candidate details or results is the greatest outcome risk. Security must be 100%. This may mean that the best encryption software will be needed for online applications. There will be cost implications which H has taken account of. He must also make contingency costing in line with his contingency plans.
Acceptance	The project manager will submit the final system for acceptance to the customer, in our example E. It may sign off the project or return it with a specific statement of requirements that will make it acceptable. Acceptance will be in writing. The managing director of E will sign off the project with J.
Change management	Requests for change may be initiated by H or E represented by J. These will be reviewed and approved by the project board with decisions in writing.

Post-implementation audit	After the project, when all change requests have been reviewed to ensure completion, input should be sought from the project team, any subcontractors, suppliers and the customer. It will include a summary of performance reviewing all aspects of the project, including the way it was managed, the tools used, the time it took, the delivery of quality as required, the costs incurred against estimates, the performance of the team and its relationship with all other project members. The lessons learned to prevent recurrence of any problems should be identified. An action plan with recommendations for prevention should be drawn up. All documentation should be reviewed after filing.

Project constraints – time, cost and quality

Project constraints were discussed earlier in the chapter. It was highlighted that the successful accomplishment of the project objective is usually constrained by three main factors: time, cost and quality. Recognising these, and the other constraints the project faces, is critical at the detailed planning stage as these constraints, and their interrelationships, will have to be taken into account of within each part of the project plan.

Project time

The schedule is the timetable for activities involved in achieving the project objective. The project will have a finite date for completion, either set by the customer or negotiated and agreed upon with the customer. For example, planning a wedding will require organisation of all activities to occur at a specific time and on a specific date.

Project cost

The cost is the amount the customer agrees to pay for the final project or product. The project cost is based on the budget, which includes a cost estimate of the resources that will be used in the project. This will include salaries of the people working on the project, project materials, equipment purchase or hire, subcontractors' or consultants' costs and facilities costs.

Quality (customer satisfaction)

The objective of any project is to complete the project within the budget and by the agreed date to the customers' satisfaction and quality requirements. It is important to ensure that prior to the project planning the project team has a clear understanding of the customer specifications and requirements, that the customer is kept informed of project progress throughout the project life, and that the plan includes progressive testing to ensure that quality requirements are fully met. Quality in computer systems can be measured in the number and type of errors ('bugs') it still contains, response times, fitness for purpose (i.e. matches the business process it is intended to support) and so on.

Another important constraint is **scope/functionality.**

The scope of the project is all of the work that must be carried out to satisfy the project's objective. The customer will expect the work to be carried out to completion and that there is nothing expected which is missing. For example, when building a house the project scope will include clearing the land, building the house and landscaping, all within the agreed quality standards expected by the customer. Leaving windows or walls unfinished, a hole in the roof, or a garden full of rubble, will be unlikely to satisfy the customer! In computer systems, the scope is often defined by all the functions that the system is expected to fulfil.

Project scope tends to be positively correlated with both cost and time, in that increasing the number of tasks to be performed within the project will normally lead to an increase in both the cost of the project and its overall duration. Managing variations to scope is one of the most complex aspects of project management. The manager must ensure that every time the customer asks for a change or addition to the scope of the project, the customer is informed of (and 'signs off') the cost and time consequences of that change. Such changes should also be fully recorded and documented to avoid arguments about what changes were required and authorised.

9 Executing and controlling

Once the project plan has been developed and agreed by the customer and project team, the project can commence. At this stage, the project manager must provide leadership and co-ordination to the project team members and other stakeholders with the aim of successfully delivering the project objectives. This is the stage where stakeholders need to be focused upon the project tasks and the project team will perform the tasks they are responsible for, as and when scheduled in the plan.

This stage can be weeks, months or years long.

The executing stage is closely linked with the controlling stage.

Configuration management and change control

Change is an inevitable part of any project and it must be managed carefully during the execution stage.

Change control

Change may arise from internal or external factors, and can often change the outcome of the project. It is therefore important to have an agreed **change management process** in place so that everyone involved in the project is aware of how change will be managed.

Change can be required at all stages of the project, very often during the execution phase as new factors emerge. It is important that the initial project documents, such as the PID and the detailed project plan, remain as "baselines" so that all changes can be carefully monitored and controlled.

A change control process is not to stop change happening, but to ensure that the changes, which will inevitably be required during the project, are agreed and communicated to all parties before they are implemented.

Problems if change is not managed:

- Team members may be working to the old plans which do not incorporate the changes. This can mean wasted time on aspects which may no longer be relevant.

- The project is unlikely to deliver the set objectives if change is not well managed.

- End users will be unhappy at the final product if their expectations have not been managed throughout the project and they have not been advised of changes.

- The project may end up costing more as costs may continue to be spent on aspects of the project which are no longer required, but that team members were unaware of.

- It can cause confusion and conflict for the project stakeholders.

Change process

At the outset of the project a change management process must be agreed. It should include the following:

- **Method for prioritising changes requested**. Changes requested will range from:
  - Must be done. Without these changes the project cannot succeed, to
  - Nice to have. These are changes requests suggesting enhancements to the current project plan. Not all changes of this nature are able to be incorporated into the final project.

- **Authorisation for changes**. It must be agreed who has the authority to agree to changes. This may be set as a sliding scale whereby the project manager is able to authorise small, low cost changes, but larger changes must be authorised at the highest level, for example the project committee or the project sponsor.

- **Agreement of a change budget**. It is likely that changes will result in additional cost to the project. A change budget may be set up for this purpose to avoid the project sponsor having to authorise every dollar of additional spend.

- **Recording of changes**. A set procedure should be agree for how all changes are to be recorded and who will manage this procedure.

- **Communication of changes**. The change management process must specify how changes to the project will be communicated to all interested parties.

Configuration management

Configuration management is an important element within projects. It involves tracking and controlling all aspects of the project and all documentation and deliverables from the project. The configuration management system for a project will specify how all aspects of the project are to be managed.

Included in configuration management will be:

- Version control for documentation

- Ownership and responsibility for documentation

- Authorisation and tracking procedures for any changes required to documentation

- Monitoring and control procedure to ensure only authorised documents and records are held

- Access control over project records

The change control process discussed above will be part of the configuration management system.

Without configuration management, several versions of documents or product may be being used and no one will be aware of which is the correct version. It also helps to ensure that the project runs smoothly, even when key personnel are unavailable.

Throughout the execution stage of the project the project manager is responsible for monitoring and controlling its progress towards successful completion. The most important aspect of project control is ensuring that monitoring progress is carried out and reported on a regular basis.

Effective project control will involve a system to regularly gather data on actual project progress, costs and performance, and compare these against the project plan. If a deviation is discovered (such as overspending or taking longer than anticipated), and the project manager considers that corrective action needs to be taken, the project manager must:

- report the deviation

- obtain authorisation if necessary

- take corrective action to get the project back on track

A regular project reporting period should be set up (e.g. daily, weekly or monthly), depending on the complexity or duration of the project. More complex projects are likely to require more frequent progress assessment and reporting.

What are the main purposes of a control system?

- Prevention of deviations.

- Correction of deviations.

- Prevention of any future deviations, by revising plans, target, measures etc.

- Implementation of recommendations from monitoring, reviewing and evaluating the project.

A project control system (Gido and Clements) is shown below:

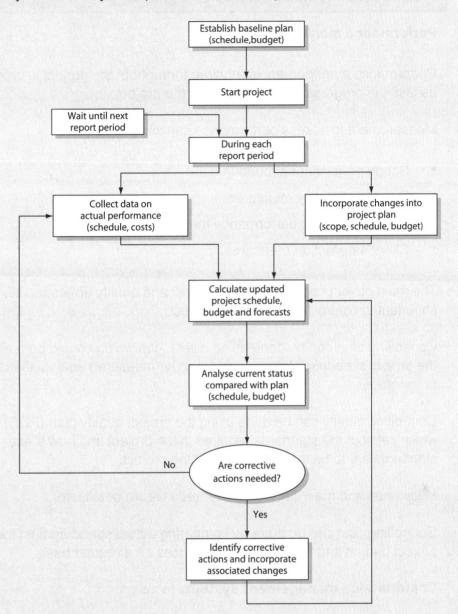

How elaborate a control system is depends on the size and scope of the task to be managed, as well as the size and distribution of the team working on it.

Performance and conformance management

Performance management

Performance management is required throughout the project in order to assess the progress of each aspect of the project.

Measurement to assess performance can include:

*   Scope performance measures.
*   Functional quality measures
*   Technical quality performance measures
*   Client satisfaction measures.

The main project constraints of time, cost and quality are especially important to control throughout the project.

Controlling time can be done using milestones which should be built into the project schedule. Progress can then be measured against these milestones.

Controlling quality can be done using the project quality plan (PQP) which sets out the standards required in the project and how these standards are to be tested throughout the project.

Milestones and the PQP will be covered in more detail later.

Controlling cost can be done by comparing actual spend against the project budget and by calculating variances on a regular basis.

Conformance management systems focus on:

*   inspection
*   quality control
*   quality assurance

Conformance quality depends upon compliance with technical specifications and relates to the use of superior operations management to reduce waste and costs, and increase uniformity.

For each element, control limits should be set at outset which can be used to assess the seriousness of any deviation from plan. Where non-conformance with the set standards are detected, any deviation larger than a specified limit should automatically trigger corrective action.

Reports and meetings

The two most important elements used in the control of projects are reports and meetings.

Project reports

To enhance and facilitate the communication of control and progress throughout the life of the project, the following main reports are produced:

Exception reports

This is when everything is in accordance with the plan. Only exceptions are reported.

Progress reports

Both formal and regular, these note what has happened in the report period and the project status to date. It normally includes:

- Status against plan in terms of cost, timetable, and scope.
- Status and progress of resolving issues identified to date.
- New issues.
- Corrective action plan. (Corrective action requires consideration of alternatives before implementation. For instance, adding extra resources in order to get a project back on time will incur extra costs and may therefore overrun the project budget. The project manager needs to consider very carefully the implications of any corrective action upon the project scope, budget and schedule).
- Expected achievement of milestones before next report.
- Next report date.

Reports from the project manager to the project board should be made on a regular and frequent basis. In most projects, written reports are made monthly, with a major summary report quarterly (or on completion of a life cycle stage). These reports should have a standard format, both within and between projects, so the recipients become familiar with their content. Areas covered by the report would obviously focus on progress in terms of cost, scope, and time, with any anticipated variances from plan highlighted.

Project meetings

Regular meetings are an essential part of control within a project. As well as communicating the progress of the project, they can also enhance relationships with the project team and with other stakeholders.

The main meetings which should be held throughout the project are:

Team meetings

The project manager should hold regular meetings with the members of the project team. These may be formal or informal and may be held periodically or when a specific issue needs to be resolved.

Team meetings can foster good working relationships with the project manager and the members of the project team and also between the team members.

Regular team meetings ensure that all team members are aware of the progress of the project and any issues which have arisen.

Project progress review meetings

These are regular, formal meetings involving the project manager, team members, and the customer or steering committee.

In many projects, such a meeting might take place quarterly, and the project manager would present their summary report. This will allow those involved with the project to ask questions that are not covered by the written report. The purpose of the meeting is to provide an update on the project status, identify any issues and establish action plans from that point.

Other meetings

A number of other meetings may be held by the project manager throughout the project, such as:

Project problem solving meetings – these would be held on an ad hoc basis as required to deal with problems which have arisen.

Meetings with external parties – the project manager will also have to arrange meetings with external resource providers such as suppliers and sub contractors.

Remember: meetings were covered in the techniques for managing organisations relationships chapter. All of the material covered earlier is equally applicable to project meetings.

Case study style question 2

G is about to undertake his second project in the role of project manager. In his last project he was criticised by the project sponsor for the lack of reporting throughout the project. G has commented that he does not see the need for reporting as long as the project is delivered as it would just take his time away from managing the project.

Required:

The new project has the same sponsor and he has asked you to email G to explain to him the benefits of a well-defined project reporting system.

(10 minutes)

10 Closing

The final stage of the project life cycle is the closure of the project once the project work is finished. A number of activities must be undertaken at this stage:

- Project is delivered to users
- End of project meeting
- Formal sign off of project
- Project review meetings
- Final report issued
- Project team disbanded

An end of project meeting confirms closure of the project by a formal sign-off. At this meeting or another shortly afterwards, a review evaluates how well the project was managed: if deadlines were met, quality standards maintained and budgets adhered to. Lessons learned from the review are used in future projects.

Project review meetings should be carried out both internally with project team members and externally with the customer.

End of project review meetings

The internal review (team)

This is:

- an opportunity to review the planning, management, reporting and control

- an opportunity to discuss the success and failures of the project process

- to establish what can be learned in future for the benefit of other projects

- an opportunity for the project manager to discuss with individual team members their role in the project and the means by which they could improve their own performance on future projects.

The external review (customer)

This is:

- a crucial aspect of project closure

- an important part of establishing whether the project has satisfied the customer's requirements

- to obtain feedback to help improve future projects

- when customers can voice any concerns regarding how the project was carried out.

The final report

The contents of the final project report will include:

- Brief overview of project.

- Customer original requirements and original project deliverables.

- List of deliverables which the customer received.

- Actual achievements re costs, schedules and scope.

- Degree to which the original objective was achieved.

- Future considerations.

To produce this report reference will be made to the following documentation:

- feasibility study and report
- PID
- project planning reports
- milestones and gates.

The purpose of this stage of the process is:

- To ensure that the project is finally completed and conforms to the latest definition of what was to be achieved.
- Formal comparison between PID and project outcomes.
- To evaluate performance of project against agreed levels of performance.
- Cost of the system in comparison with budgeted cost with an explanation of variances.
- Comparison of time taken with the budgeted time anticipated.
- Effectiveness of the management process.
- Significance of any problems encountered.
- To complete project termination activities:
    - Organising and filing all project documentation.
    - Receiving and making final payments to suppliers of resources.
    - Agreeing formally with the customer that all agreed deliverables have been provided successfully.
    - Meeting with project team and customers to report on project successes and failures.
    - Disbanding the project team.
- To provide continuous improvement and feedback – any improvement, even a small one, is important.
- To learn from the experience.

Post Completion Audit (PCA)

A meeting of managers, users and developers, held a few months after the project has been completed.

- Designed to review the success of the project as a whole as well as to receive the user's feedback on it.

- It may also highlight specific issues with the project and the review meeting may organise a set of actions to deal with these issues.

- It should also establish whether the project has helped the business to deliver the benefits defined in the original business case.

The primary benefit derived from the post-completion audit is to augment the organisation's experience and knowledge. This may be difficult to quantify, it may be necessary to justify the cost of the post-completion audit by carrying out a cost benefit analysis. In this case, the expected savings to future projects should be offset against the cost of the audit.

Other benefits of PCAs include more realistic forecasting of a project's costs and revenues, enhanced understanding of project failures, and improved future decision making and project management performance.

Post completion audit – key areas

Key areas to consider in the post completion audit:

- Technical performance review (was scope of project achieved?).

- Extent to which the quality has been achieved.

- Whether benefits have been achieved.

- Cost/budget performance.

- Schedule performance.

- The effectiveness of project planning and control.

- Team relationships.

- Problem identification process.

- Customer relationships.

- Communication.

- Risk evaluation and assessment of risk management policies.

- Outstanding issues.

- Recommendations for future management of projects.

Continuous improvement

Many organisations view project management as a strategic competence, from which they can gain a competitive advantage. This is particularly true of organisations in project-based industries, such as engineering and consultancy.

Such organisations have begun to see that using project management without continuous improvement to the methodology allows for the repetition of mistakes and poor practices. Excellence in project management requires the development of a methodology, a culture that believes in the methodology, and continues improvements to the methodology.

Elements of continuous improvement can be seen in the activities carried out during the completion and post-completion stages of the project. As part of the internal review at the end of the project and the post completion audit, an aspect of learning takes place whereby the project team review how well the project was carried out and considers lessons learned which could be taken forward to benefit future projects.

Case study style question 3

T is about to complete his first project as project manager. Prior to this project he spent six months as a member of a project team working on the development of an educational visitors centre for the company.

Reflecting on his experiences whilst working on the previous project, he feels that the final stages of the project were not dealt with effectively, with the project members going back to their functional jobs without any discussion or feedback on the project performance and outcomes.

He is determined that he will improve the experience for his project team, however most of the project team in his current project were members of the team in the last project so T feels that he will have to convince them of the need to undertake certain activities as the project draws to a close.

Required:

T has asked you to write a report for him to circulate to the team members explaining the importance of the activities to be carried out at the closure and post-completion stages of the project.

(15 minutes)

11 Summary diagram

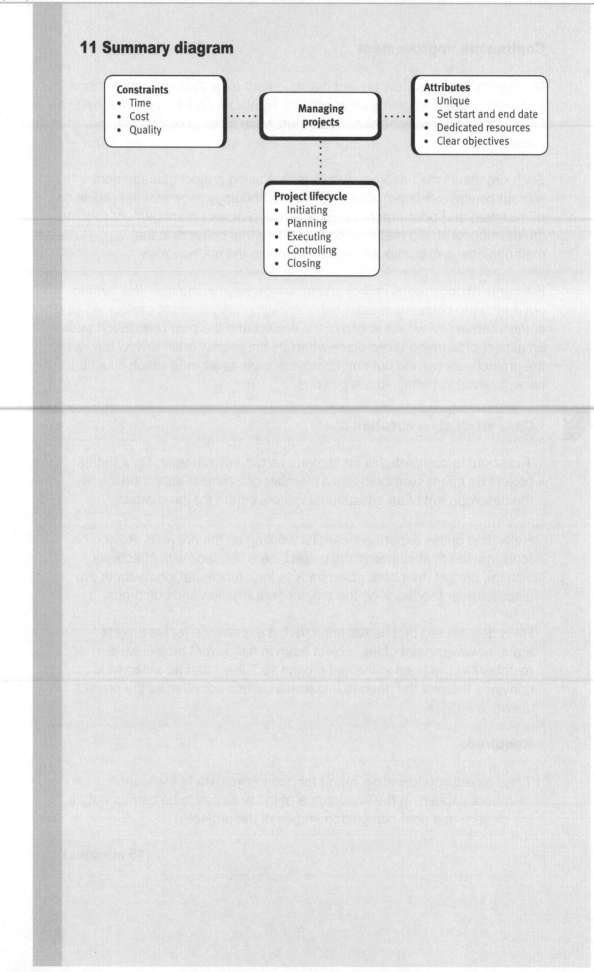

Constraints
- Time
- Cost
- Quality

Managing projects

Attributes
- Unique
- Set start and end date
- Dedicated resources
- Clear objectives

Project lifecycle
- Initiating
- Planning
- Executing
- Controlling
- Closing

End of chapter questions

Question 1

There are four main types of feasibility which should be considered when deciding to initiate a project, namely:

- Technical
- Social
- Ecological
- Economic

Match the descriptions to the types of feasibility.

- Does it fit with current operations?
- How will it affect the environment?
- Can it be done?
- Is it worth it?

Question 2

There are four risk management strategies:

- Transfer
- Avoid
- Reduce
- Accept

Complete the following sentences using the correct risk management strategy.

The most appropriate strategy to manage a risk with high likelihood and low impact is _____.

Taking out an insurance policy would be an example of the _____ strategy.

Management would tend to _____ risks with low impact and low likelihood.

Where a project risk is assessed as having high likelihood and high impact, the most appropriate strategy would be to _____ the risks.

Question 3

Which of the following are purposes of a project initiation document? Select all that apply.

- Acts as a base document against which progress can be assessed
- Assesses whether the project is technically feasible
- Justifies the project
- Defines the project and its scope
- Provides a method for prioritising change requests
- Considers alternative actions should uncertain events occur.

Question 4

Complete the following sentences relating to project constraints, using the following words:

- reduce
- increase

Part way through a project to install a new IT system, one of the finance providers announced that it could no longer support the project. It is likely that the quality of the project will _____ or the timescale of the project will _____.

It has now been made clear by the project customer that the system must be in place by the agreed date, or the company will lose a very valuable contract.

To get the project installed on time, it is likely that the quality of the project will _____.

Question 5

All projects have a number of constraints that which restrict their progress. The three main constraints are known as the project triangle. Which of the following constraints make up the project triangle?

- Legal
- Resources
- Quality
- Communication
- Time
- Cost

Question 6

Insert the correct word from the list to complete the sentences below:

- Completion
- Implementation
- Need
- Solution

The project stage where customer feedback would be obtained during an external review meeting is known as _____.

At the _____ stage, a project initiation document would be completed.

The phase when the actual performance of the project is undertaken is known as_____.

At the _____ stage, proposals are evaluated and the most appropriate is selected.

Question 7

Configuration management is designed to:

A   track deviation from proposed deliverables

B   track deviation from schedule

C   track product changes and versions

D   track co-ordination between different project teams

Question 8

Which of the following statements regarding project control are correct? Select all that apply.

- A project control system will ensure that the project meets its deadlines.

- Performance management is only required at the end of the project.

- Reports and meetings are important elements of control within projects.

- Project progress review meetings are regular, formal meetings involving the project manager, team members, and the customer or steering committee.

- The main purposes of a control system are to prevent and correct deviations.

Question 9

A number of activities are undertaken at the completion stage of a project. Further activities are undertaken a few months after the completion of the project, this is known as the post completion review. Match the statements below to whether they relate to the completion or the post completion stages.

Completion	Post completion

- The purpose of this stage is to establish whether the project helped the business to deliver the benefits defined in the original business case

- The project team will be disbanded.

- The purpose of this stage is to ensure that the project conforms to the latest definition of what was to be achieved.

- At this stage the final report is produced

Question 10

An important element in projects that is used to track and control all aspects of the project and includes version control and access over project records is known as:

A   Change control

B   Risk management

C   Configuration management

D   Project initiation document

Test your understanding answers

Case study style question 1

EMAIL

To: L

From: Management Accountant

Date: today

Subject: Risk management

Risk can be defined as the probability of an adverse or undesirable event occurring. Undertaking any project carries an element of risk and project management will be concerned with understanding what is risky about a particular project or activity within the project. Essentially this will involve identifying the different types of risk and then how to manage the risk. The first stage will require an assessment of the probability of risks occurring and their likely impact on the project. It will then require plans to be put in place to reduce or eliminate them. In other words, risk management which is what the project manager does to counteract or prepare for the risks.

The process of risk assessment involves obtaining a clear definition of the possible risks, for instance determining how important the risk is to the project, the likelihood of that risk occurring and what the severity of its occurrence would be, in other words its sensitivity. This can be achieved by some assessment of the likelihood and consequences of risks and then plotting the outcomes on a matrix which maps the potential impact of risk (low, medium, high) and the threat of likelihood (low, medium, high).

A number of stages are involved in the process of managing risk:

*   Identification of risks, producing lists of risk items in a risk register.

*   Analysis of the risks in terms of the impact of each risk item on project performance, schedule and quality.

*   Estimate of the probability of the risk occurring during the execution of the project (project exposure).

- Prioritise the risk according to exposure, effect and problems associated with the risks (sensitivity).

- Carry out risk management strategies, deciding how to address each risk item.

- Review and monitor, tracking the success of resolving the risk and the risk management approach.

These steps will enable the project manager to monitor risk factors and take appropriate action during the execution of the project. In deciding what to do about the risk, in other words risk management, this should be determined in terms of the level of impact (e.g. either high or low) and the probability of the risk (high or low).

There are different strategies for dealing with risk, for example:

- Avoidance of risk – where the factors which give rise to the risk are removed totally from the work to be done.

- Reducing the risk – where the potential for the risk cannot be removed but analysis has enabled the identification of ways to reduce the incidence or consequences.

- Transference of the risk to others, which is where the risk is passed on to someone else, for example through insurance.

- Acceptance – this is when the potential risk is accepted in the hope or the expectation that the incidence and consequences can be coped with if necessary, perhaps having contingency plans should the risk occur.

Risk management is a continuous process through the life of the project. Procedures are necessary to regularly review and reassess the risks documented in the risk register.

I hope you have found the above useful, please get in touch if you need any more information about this.

Case study style question 2

EMAIL

To: G

From: Management Accountant

Date: today

Subject: The benefits of a well-defined project reporting system

I have been asked by the sponsor of your latest project to write this email to explain to you the benefits of a well-defined project reporting system. I appreciate that your last project was a success and that you therefore see little point in spending time on reporting, but a well defined project reporting system will have the following benefits:

- It will enhance the communication throughout the project.

- It ensures that all team members are aware of the importance of regular monitoring and control. Everyone involved in the project will know that their progress will be monitored and reported on which will encourage hard work within the team.

- It ensures that all stakeholders can be kept informed of the progress of the project, which means that issues affecting the project are advised to the relevant parties on a timely basis.

- Corrective action can then be undertaken sooner to ensure that the project stays on track.

- It is necessary to compare with planned performance, although it must be done regularly to ensure progress is maintained. Reporting can be daily, weekly or monthly, depending on the complexity and timescales involved.

- Standard reports will make it easier for all parties to follow the progress of the project, and to compare the progress of projects against each other.

I hope that you have found the above useful and that you will see the benefit of implementing a project reporting system for this and all of your future projects. Please do not hesitate to get in touch if you want to discuss this further.

REPORT

To: Members of the project team

From: T

Date: Today

Subject: The importance of the activities at the closing and post-completion stages of the project.

Introduction

In this report, the importance of the activities at the completion and post-completion stages of the project will be considered.

Project closing

Project closing is the final stage of the project life cycle and occurs once the project work has finished. The purpose is to ensure benefits are gained in the final stages. It is important that all members of the team maintain commitment until all the work is completed since people tend to be more motivated to move on to new projects rather than tying up the loose ends. It is also important to evaluate the conduct of the project in order to learn from experiences which will help the company improve on its performance in future projects. The questions that could be asked include:

- Was the project completed to quality, on time and within budget?

- Did the project deliver according to the objectives set?

- Are there lessons to be learnt?

- Are there any follow up action on this project needed?

Project closing activities would involve practical tasks such as organising and filing all project documentation and ensuring that members of the project team have jobs to return to. It should also involve formally agreeing with the 'client' that all the agreed deliverables have been achieved. The business case should be reviewed to check that intended benefits are likely to be realised. In other words, examining project performance by comparing achievement with the original project plan to show that the project has delivered the outputs.

Post completion review and audit.

In addition, there should be a review of the project organisation and methods to recommend future improvements. This can be achieved through the post completion review and audit. The main purpose of the post completion review is to evaluate the overall project and to learn from the experiences gained before the project team is disbanded. This might involve debriefing meetings which enable all parties involved in the project to assess their own performance.

It provides a forum to discuss with individual team members their role in the project and how they could improve their own performance for the future. An evaluation from the client's perspective will establish if the project was successful in satisfying their requirements and has given them the opportunity to voice any concerns.

The review will provide an opportunity to discuss the successes and failures of the project process. The feedback should provide reinforcement of good skills and behaviours and the identification of areas for improvement or change in practice for the smooth running of future projects.

The post completion audit is the final stage and involves conducting a formal audit of the entire project against a checklist. This will include an assessment of the extent to which:

- the required quality of the project has been achieved; the efficiency of the solution compared with the agreed performance standards

- the actual cost of the project compared with budgets and reasons for over/under expenditure

- the time taken to develop the solution compared with target dates and reasons for any variances

- the effectiveness of project management methodologies.

Together, the review and audit can provide a case history of the project, providing a repository for the knowledge captured. The project manager should issue a report summarising project performance and advising on how it could be improved in the future. The reason that post project activities are not always undertaken is that it is often difficult to quantify in a tangible way the benefits derived, given the associated costs of review and audit.

Conclusion

The activities carried out at the closing of the project are important as they help to ensure that the project is completed successfully, they help to review not only what was delivered by the project but how it was delivered. This allows all parties to the project learn lessons which will help them improve the management of future projects.

Question 1

The correct matching is:

Technical – Can it be done?

Social – Does it fit with current operations?

Ecological – How will it affect the environment?

Economic – Is it worth it?

Question 2

The most appropriate strategy to manage a risk with high likelihood and low impact is **reduce**.

Taking out an insurance policy would be an example of the **transfer** strategy.

Management would tend to **accept** risks with low impact and low likelihood.

Where a project risk is assessed as having high likelihood and high impact, the most appropriate strategy would be to **avoid** the risks.

Question 3

- Acts as a base document against which progress can be assessed
- Justifies the project
- Defines the project and its scope

Assessing if the project is technically feasible would be done as part of the feasibility study.

A change process provides a method for prioritising change requests.

Contingency planning considers alternative actions should uncertain events occur.

Question 4

The complete sentences are:

Part way through a project to instal a new IT system, one of the finance provides announced that it could no longer support the project. It is likely that the quantity of the project will **reduce** or the timescale of the project will **increase.**

It has now been made clear by the project customer that the system must be in place by the agreed date, or the company will lose a very valuable contract.

To get the project installed in time, it is likely that the quality of the project will **reduce.**

Question 5

The 3 main constraints which make up the project triangle are:

- Quality
- Time
- Cost

Question 6

The complete sentences are:

The project stage where customer feedback would be obtained during an external review meeting is known as **completion**.

At the **need** stage, a project initiation document would be completed.

The phase when the actual performance of the project is undertaken is known as **implementation**.

At the **solution** stage, proposals are evaluated and the most appropriate is selected.

Question 7

C   track product changes and versions

Configuration management involves tracking and controlling all aspects of a project and all documentation and deliverables from the project.

It includes version control for documentation and all aspects of change management

Question 8

- Reports and meetings are important elements of control within projects.
- Project progress review meetings are regular, formal meetings involving the project manager, team members, and the customer or steering committee.
- The main purposes of a control system are to prevent and correct deviations.

A project control system will aim to reduce the risk within a project but cannot ensure that a project will meet its deadlines.

Performance management is required throughout a project to assess the progress of each aspect of the project.

Question 9

The correct matching is:

Completion	Post completion
The project team will be disbanded. The purpose of this stage is to ensure that the project conforms to the latest definition of what was to be achieved. At this stage the final report is produced	The purpose of this stage is to establish whether the project helped the business to deliver the benefits defined in the original business case

Question 10

C   Configuration management

Change control is used to ensure that all changes to the project are agreed and communicated before they are implemented.

Risk management considers how the risks associated with a proposed project can be managed.

A project initiation document is used to authorise the project and to act as a base document against which the project deliverables can be assessed.

Project management tools and techniques

Chapter learning objectives

Apply tools and techniques for project managers.

1 Session content diagram

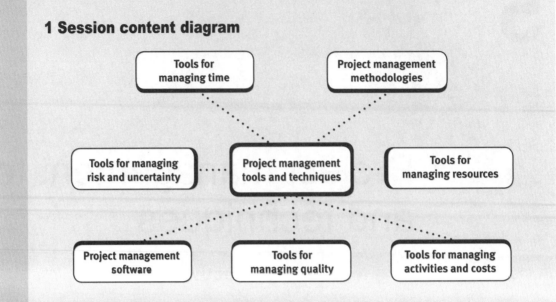

2 Tools and techniques

There are a number of tools, techniques and documents which are used throughout a project, particularly at the planning stage.

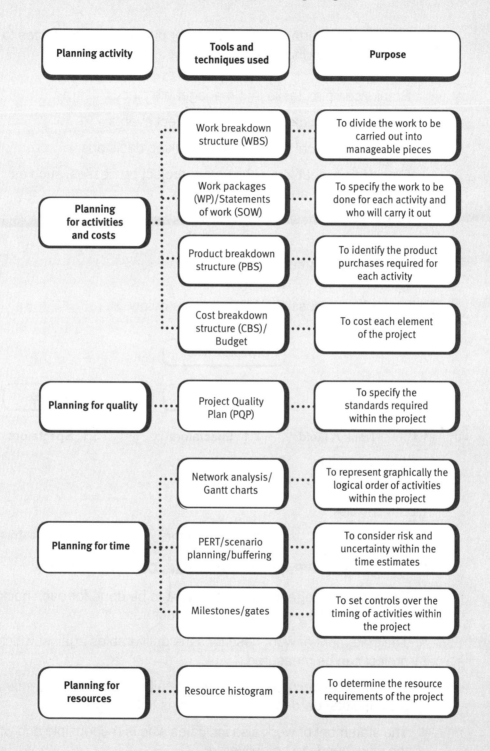

Planning activity	Tools and techniques used	Purpose
Planning for activities and costs	Work breakdown structure (WBS)	To divide the work to be carried out into manageable pieces
	Work packages (WP)/Statements of work (SOW)	To specify the work to be done for each activity and who will carry it out
	Product breakdown structure (PBS)	To identify the product purchases required for each activity
	Cost breakdown structure (CBS)/Budget	To cost each element of the project
Planning for quality	Project Quality Plan (PQP)	To specify the standards required within the project
Planning for time	Network analysis/Gantt charts	To represent graphically the logical order of activities within the project
	PERT/scenario planning/buffering	To consider risk and uncertainty within the time estimates
	Milestones/gates	To set controls over the timing of activities within the project
Planning for resources	Resource histogram	To determine the resource requirements of the project

3 Planning for activities and costs

Breakdown structures:

(1) Work Breakdown Structure (WBS)

The WBS is an important starting point for planning. It contributes to planning in the following ways:

- Breaks complex tasks into manageable pieces.
- Sets out the logical sequence of project events.
- Provides a logical framework for making decisions.
- Provides an input into subsequent project processes, such as estimating time and resources.
- Provides a framework for continuous assessment of the project progression.
- Provides a communication tool.

An extract from a possible WBS appears below.

```
                        ┌─────────────────┐
                        │  Olympic Games  │
                        └─────────────────┘

   ┌──────────────┐      ┌──────────────┐      ┌──────────────┐
   │ 1.  Events   │      │ 2. Facilities│      │ 3.  Security │
   └──────────────┘      └──────────────┘      └──────────────┘

   1.1    Track & Field    2.1 Spectators      3.1 Spectators

   1.1.1  Long Jump

   1.1.2  Javelin

   1.1.3  Hurdles

   1.2    Equestrian       2.2 Competitors     3.2 Competitors
```

(2) Work Packages (WPs) and Statements Of Work (SOWs)

- The work package specifies the work to be done for each package described in the work breakdown structure.
- The statement of work describes the deliverables against which the project can be measured.
- Both types of document identify in detail work to be done and may state the standard to which the work is to be done.
- The statement of work also indicates who is responsible and when the work needs to be delivered.

(3) **Product Breakdown Structure (PBS)**

- The products required for each activity would then be listed:
    - Long Jump
    - Sand pit
    - White board
    - Flag

- Describe the machinery and equipment required for the project.
- Compare different suppliers.

(4) **Cost Breakdown Structure (CBS)**

This will include information gathered from:

- The WBS, WP, SOW and PBS.
- Capital and revenue costs identified in the cost-benefit analysis and feasibility study documents.

It describes the categories that require costing to ensure nothing is left out of the budget process.

Numbers and costs would be allocated to each product.

This creates the detailed **financial plan (budget)** for the project.

The benefits of using breakdown structures include:

- Summarising all the activities comprising the project, including support and other tasks
- Displaying the interrelationships of the various jobs (work packages) to each other and the total project
- Establishing the authority and responsibility for each part of the project
- Estimating project cost
- Performing risk analysis
- Scheduling jobs (work in progress)
- Providing a basis for controlling the application of resources to the project.

4 Planning for quality

Project Quality Plan (PQP)

This major document details the **standards** that must be adhered to in order to ensure a successful development process. It will provide a clear indication of procedures and policies that must be followed to maintain quality within the work carried out. It generally includes:

- **Risk assessment** – of the possible internal and external risks that are likely to affect the project and the alternative actions which are required to reduce the risks.

- **Project overview** – outline of the main activities to be carried out.

- **Project requirements** – details a description of the work to be carried out, timescales and deliverables and is cross referenced to the requirements specification.

- **Project organisation** – stating management roles and responsibilities, this will help to determine the allocation of resources to each of the project activities.

- **Monitoring and reporting procedures** – cross referenced to the project standards, this section identifies how the project will be monitored and what to do if slippage occurs. It also states the frequency and content of reports as well as key control processes, such as end of stage meetings, for example, when the steering meetings will take place and procedures for evaluating the final installed system.

- **Key development stages and processes** – the activities that will need to be completed during the life cycle.

- **Key standards to be used in the project** (quality assurance) – this will help to ensure quality outputs, standards that need to be evaluated and will include hardware, software and development standards such as notation of modelling techniques.

- **Testing strategy** – this will identify the stages of development where testing is to be carried out, by whom and of what.

- **Procurement policy** – the procedures and standards for procurement will be stated and any variation from the normal procedure noted, with reasons.

- **Configuration management** – how this will be dealt with should be set out so that each version of the deliverables is identified.

5 Planning for time

Network analysis

Network analysis is a general term, referring to various techniques adopted to plan and control projects. It is used to analyse the inter-relationships between the tasks identified by the work breakdown structure and to define the dependencies of each task. Whilst laying out a network it is often possible to see that assumptions for the order of work are not logical or could be achieved more cost effectively by re-ordering them. This is particularly true whilst allocating resources; it may become self evident that two tasks cannot be completed at the same time by the same person due to lack of working hours or, conversely, that by adding an extra person to the project team, several tasks can be done in parallel thus shortening the length of the project.

Critical Path Analysis (CPA)

One of the component parts of network analysis is critical path analysis or CPA (this is often called network analysis). It is the most commonly used technique for managing projects.

The process of CPA.

(1) **Analyse the project**. The project is broken down into its constituent tasks or activities. The way in which these activities relate to each other is examined: which activities cannot be undertaken until some previous activity or activities are complete?

(2) **Draw the network**. The sequence of activities is shown in a diagrammatic form called the 'network diagram'.

(3) **Estimate the time and costs of each activity**. The amount of time that each activity will take is estimated, and where appropriate the associated costs are estimated.

(4) **Locate the critical path**. This is the chain of events that determines how long the overall project will take. Any delay to an activity on the critical path will delay the project as a whole; delays to other activities may not affect the overall timetable for completion. That is the distinction between critical and non-critical activities.

(5) **Schedule the project**. Determine the chain of events that leads to the most efficient and cost effective schedule.

(6) **Monitor and control the progress of the project**. This implies careful attention to the schedule and any other progress charts that have been drawn up, to monitor actual progress in the light of planned achievement.

(7) **Revise the plan**. The plan may need to be modified to take account of problems that occur during the progress of the project.

The network diagram:

The diagram is made up of two parts: activity lines and nodes. The diagram is drawn and read from left to right.

A complete network diagram (CPA) would look like this:

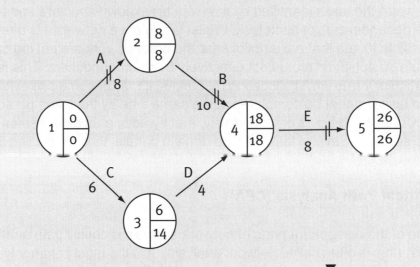

- Each activity is represented by an arrow

- The activity letter or description (or both) is written on the arrow.

- The activity duration is written below the arrow.

- The activities on the critical path are identified with //

- Activities start and finish in circles known as nodes (O).

- Nodes are numbered so that each node has a unique identifier.

- The nodes also contain information on two times:
    - The earliest event time (EET)
    - The latest event time (LET)

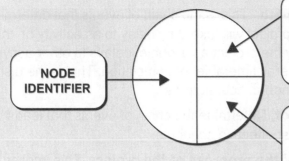

Earliest event time (EET)

(Earliest time at which activity can be reached)

NODE IDENTIFIER

Latest event time (LET)

(The latest time by which the node must be reached if the project is to be finished by its required completion date)

Drawing the diagram

- First draw a dot-to-dot diagram – this can be completed quickly and allows the logic of the diagram to be tested before you begin to draw the final version.

- Once the network has been drawn, calculate the EET and LET for each node.

- To calculate the EET, work left to right. Take the EET from the previous node and add this to the duration of the activity. **Where you have a choice of EETs, always select the highest.**

- To calculate the LET, work right to left. Take the LET from the previous node and deduct the duration of the activity. **Where you have a choice of LETs, always select the lowest**.

Reading the diagram

- The EET and LET of the final node will always be the same and this will equal the **overall duration** of the project.

- We can also identify the **critical path**, i.e. the activities where any delay will lead to a delay in the overall project. These are the activities for which EET = LET.

- Some activities could increase in duration and yet the project could still be completed by the required target date. Such activities are said to exhibit **'float'**. Float can generally be calculated as the difference between the LET and the EET.

Rules for drawing the diagram

- If two activities occur in parallel, *dummy activity lines* are inserted to allow only one activity arrow to join nodes together. Dummy activities do not consume any time or resources and are drawn in the diagram to make it clearer.

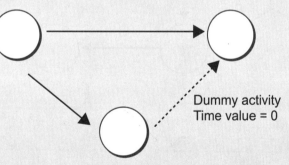

Dummy activity
Time value = 0

- Loops are not allowed because the network essentially shows a series of activities progressing through time. It focuses on the passage of time, not on the successful completion of activities. In other words, you cannot have a series of activities leading from one event that lead back to the same event. For example, this diagram is not allowed.

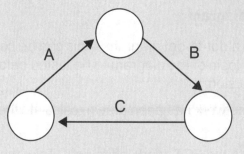

It would be redrawn including a new activity.

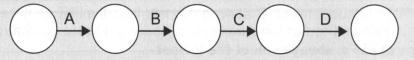

- An activity can only occur once, so there cannot be two lines with the same activity. For example, this diagram is not allowed:

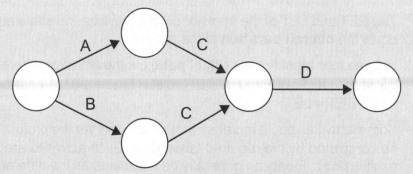

The diagram may need to be redrawn and/or a dummy activity used.

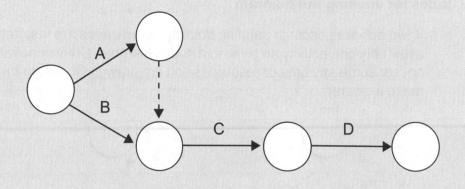

Illustration 1 – CPA worked example

Consider the follow details about a project. You are given the list of activities, their durations and the preceding activities. This last column tells you which order the activities must be drawn in.

Activity	Duration (weeks)	Preceding activity
A	8	–
B	10	A
C	6	–
D	4	C
E	8	B, D

Required:

Draw the network diagram, and identify the critical path, the estimated project duration and any float on any activity.

Solution:

Step 1: draw the basic network diagram, showing the order of the activities. Remember the rules above when you are drawing it. You are aiming to move across your page from left to right.

Each activity must start and end with a node, so the first thing to do is to identify the activities which can start straight away – these are the ones with no preceding activity. In this case A and C can start straight away.

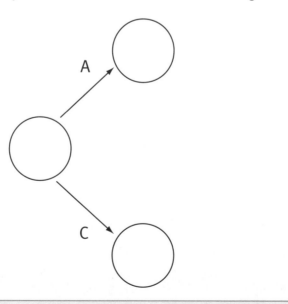

Now you can draw in the other activities. B follows A, and D follows C:

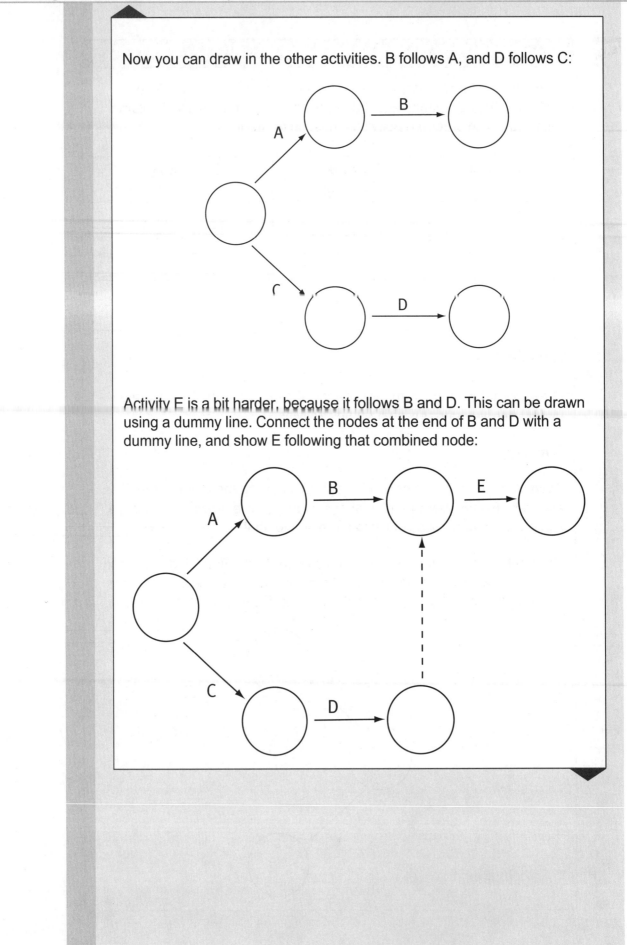

Activity E is a bit harder, because it follows B and D. This can be drawn using a dummy line. Connect the nodes at the end of B and D with a dummy line, and show E following that combined node:

You could have drawn the diagram without the dummy line, as shown below. Both of the diagrams are acceptable and both show the correct flow of activities.

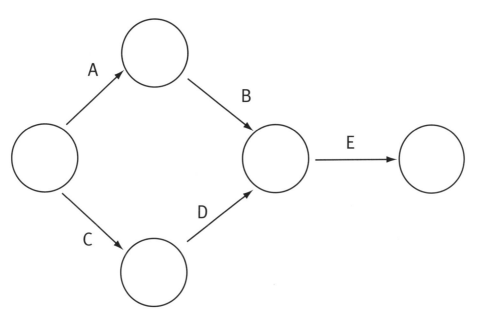

Step 2: Now the basic network diagram has been drawn, we can start to add in the details of the durations of each activity. These are shown on the activity lines. You can now draw in the node lines, ready for the calculations of EET and LET.

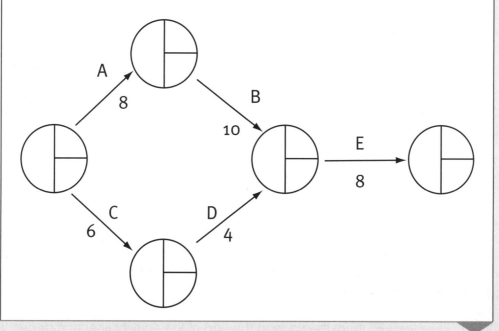

Step 3: Calculate the Earliest Event Time (EET) working left to right. Start at the first node: the EET of the first node must always be zero. You then look at each activity in turn.

Take the EET from the node at the beginning of the activity line, and add it to the duration of the activity, the answer gives you the EET for the node at the end of the activity line.

So for A, EET at the start is 0, add the duration of A, which is 8, so the EET for the node at the end of the activity line is 8. For C, we get 0 + 6 = 6.

You have to be careful when looking at B and D as they lead to the same node – this is a choice:

For B: 8 + 10 = 18, or for D: 6 + 4 = 10. Remember for the EET, when you have a choice, you select the highest, so we use 18.

E is straightforward: 18 + 8 = 26.

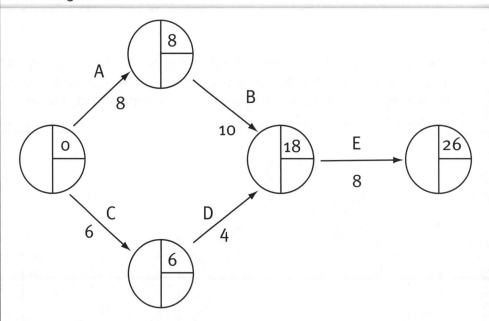

Step 4: Calculate the Latest Event Time (LET) working right to left. Start at the last node: the LET of the last node must equal the EET of the last node, so in this case the LET of the last node is 26. You then look at each activity in turn.

Take the LET from the node at the end of the activity line, and deduct the duration of the activity. The answer gives you the LET for the node at the beginning of the activity line.

So for E, the LET of the node at the end is 26, deduct the duration of E, which is 8, so the LET for the node at the beginning of E's activity line is 18. For D, we get 18 – 4 = 14, and for B we get 18 – 10 = 8.

For A and C you have a choice. Using A we get 8 – 8 = 0, or using C we get 14 – 6 = 8. When you have a choice for the LET, you always use the lowest, so we use 0.

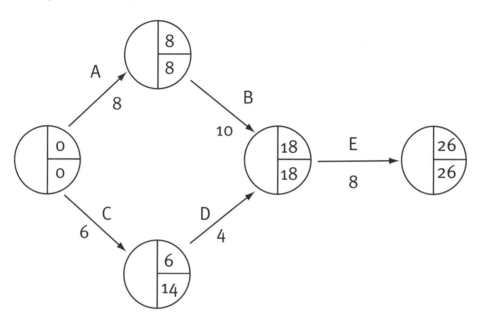

Our CPA is complete. We can now put in the reference numbers in each node (there are no rules here, just work left to right and number each node, it is just used for identification purposes).

We can now work out the critical path:

Look at your diagram. Where the nodes at the beginning and the end of an activity line have the same EET and LET, this tells you that the activity is critical. In our diagram we can see that activities A. B and E are critical. We note these on the diagram with double lines on the activity line. Always check that your critical path is a continuous path through the diagram from the first to the final node.

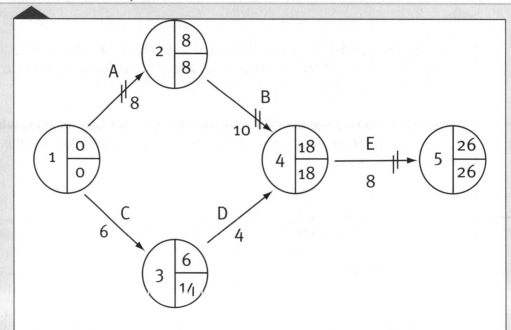

From our diagram, we can also see the overall duration of the project. This is the same as the EET and LET of the final node, so in this project, the overall duration is 26 weeks.

We can also work out of there is any slack/float on any activity. This can be seen from those activities which are not on the critical path. The amount of float can be calculated as the difference between the EET and the LET. In our diagram, activities C or D have a float of 8 weeks.

Case study style question 1

The details of activities and duration for Project YT you are managing are shown below.

Activity		Duration (weeks)	Preceding activity
A	Problem definition	2	–
B	Prepare feasibility report	3	A
C	Studying existing system	2	A
D	Logical and physical design	4	C
E	Software and hardware development	4	B
F	Systems development report	8	D, E
G	Testing	4	F
H	File conversion	3	D, E
I	Changeover	6	G, H

> ### Required:
>
> Construct a network diagram of the project's activities as detailed within the above table.
>
> Write an email to the project sponsor explaining the activities which are on the critical path, the overall project duration and any activities that have a float.
>
> ### (15 minutes)
>
> *Note, you will not be asked to produce a network diagram as part of the E2 assessment, or the management level case study but network diagrams are examinable therefore it is important to be able to draw the network so that you can understand the diagram and be able to answer questions about it.*

Limitations of CPA

- It may be time consuming to produce and monitor for large projects.

- Difficult to use for less routine projects with lots of uncertainty.

- Overly complex for some smaller short-term projects.

Benefits of CPA

- Assists in identifying all activities required for completing the project

- It will assist in identifying those activities that need to be completed before the next activity can start (dependent activities), and those that can happen at the same time (parallel activities)

- The network diagram will identify those activities that lie on the critical path. These activities cannot overrun, otherwise there would be delays in the overall project.

- The network diagram will identify those activities that are non-critical and exhibit float or buffer. This allows management to rank each activity in relation to how much flexibility is available.

- The network diagram will show the minimum completion time for the project, and will allow for sensitivity analysis to be introduced into the project.

Dealing with risk and uncertainty when planning for time

Risk and uncertainty at the initiation stage of the project was covered in the previous chapter. At the detailed planning stage, risk and uncertainty must be considered again when the project manager is planning the time aspect of the project. There are a number of techniques which can assist with this:

- Project evaluation and review technique (PERT)
- Scenario planning
- Buffering.

Project evaluation and review technique (PERT)

This can be used to overcome uncertainties over times taken for individual activities in a network diagram.

Each task is assigned a time.

- An optimistic (best) time (o)
- A probable time (m)
- A pessimistic (worst) time (p)

It then uses a formula to calculate an expected time, and by calculating variances for each activity, estimates the likelihood that a set of activities will be completed within a certain time.

The expected time for each activity is then calculated as:

$$= \frac{o + 4m + p}{6}$$

These estimates are used to determine the average completion time.

Advantages:

- It gives an expected completion time.
- It gives a probability of completion before the specified date.
- It gives a Critical Path.
- It gives slack through earliest and latest start times.
- It allows calculation of contingency to be added to the plan.

Limitations:

- The activity times are very subjective.
- Assumes probability distribution of project completion time as the critical path.

Scenario planning

Although the use of PERT is one way to cope with risk in time planning there are ways of planning in a contingency for risk that are less complex. Wherever risk is identified as taking the form of alternative outcomes, a series of contingency or scenario plans may be constructed for each alternative.

Scenario planning involves considering one or more sets of circumstances that might occur, other than the 'most likely' or 'expected' set of circumstances used to prepare the budget or plan for a project. Each set of assumptions is then tested to establish what the outcome would be if those circumstances were actually to occur.

This would allow the project manager to switch to the appropriate plan for whichever contingency arose.

Buffering

A more simplistic way to incorporate risk by adding artificial slack into risky activities. It adds padding to the original estimates and allows for the fact that it can be very difficult to ensure that all stages and activities are carried out exactly as planned. This is known as 'buffering', but should not be encouraged because it leads to a build-up of slack in the programme and may lead to complacency.

Gantt Chart

This is an alternative or complementary approach to network analysis. It also provides a graphical representation of project activities and can be used in both project planning and control.

A Gantt chart is a horizontal bar chart where the length of the bar represents the duration of the activity.

When a Gantt chart is used to help control a project it is usual to use two bars, one showing the planned duration and the second showing the actual duration.

To create a Gantt chart.

- Display a schedule of activities using bars.

- List the activities down the side of the page.

- Using a horizontal timescale, draw a bar for each activity to represent the period over which it is to be performed.

- Both budgeted and actual timescales can be shown on the same chart.

Illustration 2 – Gantt chart example

An example of a project undertaken to examine the current procedures in the accounts payable department.

The project manager's first step is to break down the project into phases:

		Estimated time to complete
Phase 1	Document current procedures	4 days
Phase 2	Produce flowcharts	3 days
Phase 3	Summarise paper flow and methods for receiving, processing and sending information	5 days
Phase 4	List problem areas and develop initial recommendations	6 days
Phase 5	Develop improved processing procedures	3 days
Phase 6	Track sample transactions for one week under existing procedures	5 days

| Phase 7 | Track sample transactions for two weeks under proposed new procedures | 10 days |
| Phase 8 | Prepare and deliver a final report to the treasurer, including recommended changes in procedures and an estimate of savings | 2 days |

This could then be expressed in a Gantt chart using the most common method, the bar chart, the start of which is shown below. The budgets for the activities are shown, together with the actual durations underneath:

Days	1	2	3	4	5	6	7	8	9	10	11
Document current procedures											
Produce flowcharts											
Summarise paper flow and methods for receiving, processing and sending information											
List problem areas and develop initial recommendations											

Benefits of Gantt charts:

The Gantt chart shares some advantages with network analysis:

- Assists in identifying all activities required for completing the project
- It will assist in identifying those activities that need to be completed before the next activity can start (dependent activities), and those that can happen at the same time (parallel activities)
- The Gantt chart will show the minimum completion time for the project, and will allow for sensitivity analysis to be introduced into the project

In addition, the Gantt chart has further advantages over network analysis:

- Easier visualisation of relationships
- Unlike CPA, activities are drawn to scale so the most significant activities can be highlighted
- It is drawn in real time
- Actual durations can be shown alongside budget
- Aids resource allocation.

Limitations of Gantt charts:

The Gantt chart is a useful tool for tracking your project and anticipating delay problems before the final deadline is compromised. However, it will be of limited use when you have to deal with a relatively large project team. The more complex the team structure the higher the likelihood of schedule delays.

Remember, charting phases and monitoring progress is only a tool, not the solution itself.

For the more complex projects the Gantt chart has the following limitations:

- It does not identify potential weak links between phases.

- The chart does not reveal team problems due to unexpected delays.

- The chart does not coordinate resources and networking requirements needed at critical phases of the schedule.

- It does not show the degrees of completion for each phase.

Case study style question 2

A new on-line order entry system is currently being developed in your organisation. As part of the implementation procedures, users of the new system will require a number of training activities.

K has just taken over as project manager from H who left the project due to ill health. K has found the following network diagram for the project but is not sure what it tells him.

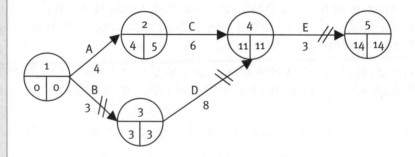

Required:

Write an email to K, explaining the information he should be able to establish from the network diagram. You should also explain how a Gantt chart might be of more use in this context.

(15 minutes)

Milestones and control gates

One of the main reasons for constructing a network diagram is to improve the control of the project duration.

In order to facilitate this, a number of milestones can be identified in the network. They are not specifically shown on the diagram (except of course for the end activities), but they are shown on a Gantt chart as a small triangle or other symbol.

A **milestone**, as the name implies, is an event that is clearly identifiable as a measure of how far the project has progressed, and how far it has to run. This involves partitioning the project into identifiable and manageable phases that are well defined key events and unambiguous targets of what needs to be done and by when, and should be established during the project planning phase.

Milestones are important in assessing the status of the project and quality of the work. Monitoring the milestones enables the project manager to keep control over the projects progress, and allows any delays to be identified immediately.

Some milestones are key points in the project life cycle which give the project sponsor or steering committee an opportunity to review project progress, and make a decision whether to proceed further or to terminate the project. These milestones are called **'control gates'** and represent the significant completion of milestones. A gate can only be 'passed' if the progress meets pre-defined performance standards. This could take the form of technical reviews or completion of documents.

'Gates' should be identified in the project plan and a review will be required to formally pass each gate. If at the gate review the criteria have not been met, the project should not continue. This may mean changes are needed to the overall project plan.

6 Planning for resources

Resource histogram

This is a graphical aid for determining the total requirement for a specific resource during the project. The histogram identifies, in block graph form, the fluctuating need for finance, staff, technology resources or vendor services at any stage in the project. This can assist in planning. Reallocation of key tasks can reduce the excessive requirement at certain periods, providing a smooth flow of resources throughout the project.

This smooth flow is easier and cheaper to plan for. The histogram may also assist in control activities.

A resource histogram shows the amount and timing of the requirement for a resource or a range of resources using a stacked bar chart.

e.g

Illustration 3 – Resource histogram example

It is very common for a project budget to be constructed as shown below. Variance analysis and financial control are much easier when a spreadsheet package is used for project budgeting.

Month	1	2	3	4	5	6	7	8	9	10	11	Total
	$	$	$	$	$	$	$	$	$	$	$	$
Salaries	420	285	662	850	122	453	411	502	850	421	409	5385
Materials	0	125	0	0	1000	250	400	325	100	125	800	3125
Overheads	180	55	320	123	249	402	111	122	451	123	201	2337
Sub-con.	0	200	200	200	200	0	0	560	560	250	0	2170
Total	600	665	1182	1173	1571	1105	922	1509	1961	919	1410	13017

Such a budget can, of course, be shown as a histogram for immediate visual impact, as shown below:

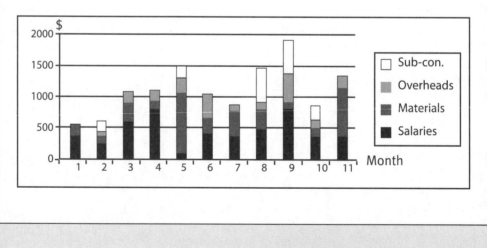

Benefits of resource histograms:

- It helps with capacity planning, resource scheduling and management
- Resource availability and allocations can be shown on a histogram, to highlight overloads and under-utilisation
- Easy visualisation of resource requirements
- It is drawn in real time

7 Project management software

While project management software can assist considerably at the planning stage, it is also useful at the other stages of the project.

The planning of the project will be assisted through the use of appropriate software. The type of output produced by the package will vary depending upon the package being used.

They may be used in a variety of ways.

Planning:

- The ability to create multiple network diagrams.
- The ability to create multiple Gantt charts.
- The ability to create Project Initiation Document (PID), Project Quality Plan (PQP) and Work Breakdown Structure (WBS).

Estimating:

- The ability to consider alternative resource allocation.
- The ability to create and allocate project budgets.
- The ability to allocate time across multiple tasks.

Monitoring:

- Network links to all project team members.
- A central store for all project results and documentation.
- Automatic comparison to the plan, and plan revision.

Reporting:

- Access to team members.
- Ability to create technical documents.
- Ability to create end of stage reports.

Advantages of using project management software

- Improved planning and control. Software includes various tools which can aid planning. All project data can be held centrally and this facilitates comparison between planned and actual data.

- Improved communication. Calendars, report generation and scheduling of activities can all aid communication during the project.

- Improved quality of systems developed.

- Accuracy. Particularly in large projects, manually drawing network diagrams can be prone to error.

- Ability to handle complexity. For large, complex projects, PM software is indispensable in managing and controlling large volumes of activities.

- What if analysis. The software allows the user to see the effect of different scenarios by altering elements of the project data. This enables the project manager to plan for contingencies and to assess consequences.

- Timesheet recording. In order to ease the project manager's burden of recording the actual effort and revised estimates to complete a task, a number of PM software packages allow this data to be captured from individual team member.

- Project management software recognises that there is a sequence in which activities need to be performed. The use of software can help to ensure that all necessary tasks are carried out as required.

When choosing project management software, or indeed any software package, it is important to:

- determine requirements of organisation including its current and future needs.

- document requirements including the essential functions/important/wish list.

- review all available packages to identify three/four products which meet the essential functions and fall within budget.

- have a demonstration of the packages on a trial basis if possible.

- select a package including 'roll out' strategy with installation, training, etc.

Despite the extensive use of project management software, projects can still go spectacularly wrong, over schedule and/or budget.

Here are some common pitfalls:

- **Emphasis on maintaining the plan rather than managing the project.** In a large project, maintaining the plan can be a full-time task. This can leave little time for dealing with important project issues. It is often better for project managers to delegate the input/maintenance responsibility to a project administrator and receive regular reports as a basis for managing the project.

- **Resources may not be managed realistically**. This especially applies when tasks are over-budget. Adding new people into a project at a late stage can make it later since the new team members will be slower at grasping what is required and actually divert the attention of other team members.

- **Estimates.** For planning purposes, the accuracy of estimates is vital to the identification of the critical path and the key milestones of the project. However, estimates are subjective and can vary wildly. Also, estimates have been made at a fixed point in time with a particular set of assumptions.

- **Skill levels.** Plans tend to talk about resources when actually they are referring to human beings with all the uncertainty that it brings. Where one individual may find a task within his/her skillset, another person may struggle. It matters which person does which task.

- **Work breakdown**. Some plans fail because the work breakdown into tasks does not match with how people work. Work breakdown assumes discrete units of work that someone will spend a fixed amount of time on a task before moving to the next task.

Case study style question 3

You are a trainee management accountant working for a firm of financial and management consultants (ZX) who have been contracted to assist in the management and control of a large international sporting event due to take place in four years' time.

A significant part of the project will be the provision of new buildings and facilities. Major new works associated with the project include the construction of a 30,000-seat indoor athletics stadium and a world press and media centre. A further consideration is the upgrade of the current transport network, with major development work required on the local rail system between the main stadium and the city centre, and an airport bus link.

Success will be measured in terms of trouble-free performance of the events, level of customer enthusiasm and satisfaction, and sustained economic activity generated in the region. Completion of the project on time is critical, even if cost or quality are adversely affected.

The main software development aspect of the project is the development of the communications software in the form of an information database. This will require development of a dedicated website to give public access to event information. The database will contain information about competitors and their events, time and location and availability of tickets.

The database will be designed to allow the general public to monitor the events, order tickets from the website for any event, and purchase merchandise. The website will also contain links to local hotels and restaurant facilities. The whole package of communications software and the telecommunications and IT hardware has been called the "Communications Infrastructure".

A work breakdown structure has been produced and the project has boon brokon down into ovor 20 activitioc, all with varying durations. Each of the activities will be carried out by individual specialist project teams, and led by a project team manager. It is critical that these events are co-ordinated and planned effectively, as timing is critical to the success of this project.

One of the key tasks to undertake immediately is the determination of the critical path.

Required:

You have been asked by your management to prepare a report which includes an explanation of the importance of undertaking critical path analysis for a project such as this and an explanation of how using project management software may assist during this project.

(20 minutes)

Project management software functions

The following is a list of functions that would commonly be found within a standard project management software package, such as Microsoft Project:

- **Budgeting and cost control.** At any time during the project, actual costs can be compared with budgeted costs for individual resources or activities, or for the whole project.

- **Calendars.** Calendars can be used for reporting purposes and to define working periods.

- **Graphics.** The ability to create and modify graphics, such as Gantt charts, is a useful feature of PM software. It will allow the tasks in Gantt charts to be linked so that preceding activities can be shown.

- **Multiple project handling.** Large projects often have to be broken down into smaller projects to make them more manageable. Alternatively, project managers may be responsible for more than one project at a time. Most PM software packages will store numerous projects quite easily.

- **Planning.** All PM software allows the user to define the activities that need to be performed. It will maintain detailed task lists and create critical path analyses. It will allow the project manager to plan several thousand activities, by allocating resources, setting start and completion dates and calculating expected time to complete.

- **Scheduling.** Most systems will build Gantt charts and network diagrams based on the task and resource list and all of their associated information. Any changes to those lists will automatically create a new schedule for the project. It is also possible to schedule recurring tasks, to set priorities for tasks, to schedule tasks to start as late as possible, and to specify 'must end by' and 'no later than' dates.

- **Resource planning.** A critical issue in project planning is resource management, that is ensuring the project has the correct level of manpower, equipment and material at the right place at the right time and in right quantities.

- **Resource histograms.** These provide the project manager with a visual display showing the usage and availability of resources over the project's life. This allows the project manager to see quickly and easily where there are either too few resources or where there are surplus resources to carry out a particular activity. The project manager then has the ability to reallocate resources or to obtain additional resources to ensure that critical activities are achieved on time and therefore the critical path is achieved. An example of a resource histogram is shown on top of next page.

- **Reporting.** The project manager has to report on the progress of the project to the stakeholders. PM software provides the facility to generate standard reports, such as progress to date, budget reports, allocation of resources reports, individual task or WBS reports and financial reports.

8 Project management methodologies

A project management methodology is a set of guidelines which defines methods and processes to be followed which should help the project be delivered successfully. It can be seen as a systematic and disciplined approach to project management. The development of standard processes is obviously helpful as these, together with standard templates for the documents used, help many project issues to be anticipated and worked around.

Since every organisation is unique, and undertakes unique projects, there is no 'one-size fits all' answer to which project management methodology to use.

A popular choice – PRINCE2 or PMBOK

PMBOK provides a knowledge base and roadmap for effective project management while PRINCE2 provides a more pragmatic 'How To' approach. Both approaches are customisable which is beneficial as it allows for better integration into the level of project management maturity the organisation is currently at and aspires to be at in the future.

Benefits and limitations of a single methodology

Benefits of a single methodology:

- Provides a structured step-by-step approach to managing projects.

- Stages in the methodology become familiar which speed up the completion of the project.

- Helps to keep the project on track and to identify any deviations at an early stage.

- Users become familiar with the tools and reports used, so can compare different projects.

- Team members and project managers become familiar with the approach used and this improves the overall management of projects.

- The methodology can be developed over time and can result in a best practice approach.

Limitations of a single methodology:

- If the methodology selected is unsuitable , it may make managing projects more difficult.

- No one methodology can be suitable for all projects.

- All projects are different, so the methodology may need modifying for each project, but this may be difficult.

- Some methodologies will be too detailed for smaller projects.

- Strictly adopting a methodology may become too bureaucratic.

- All features of the methodology may not be required for all projects.

9 PRINCE2 methodology

PRINCE2 is a project management methodology, capable of supporting complex projects. The UK Government as an open standard method for managing Information Technology projects originally launched PRINCE in 1989. Since then it has been adopted by many organisations both within government and in outside industry for projects.

PRINCE2 (PRojects IN Controlled Environments, version 2) is a process-based approach for project management providing an easily tailored and scaleable method for the management of all types of projects. Each process is defined with its key inputs and outputs in addition to the specific objectives to be achieved and activities to be undertaken.

The main purpose of PRINCE2 is to deliver a successful project, which is defined as:

- delivery of the agreed outcomes
- on time
- within budget
- conforming to the required quality standards.

To do this it contains a large number of control elements which can be applied to all sorts of projects, small and large.

The main control features are:

- It enforces a clear structure of authority and responsibility.
- It ensures the production of key products – PID, project budget, plan & progress reports.
- It gives a clear understanding of the tasks to be completed.
- It contains several quality controls, such as clearly defined procedures.

PRINCE2 structure

The major component parts of the PRINCE2 methodology address the issues of:

- **Organisation** – PRINCE2 suggests using an organisation chart for the project so that there is a clear structure of authority and responsibility. Everyone on the project should understand their role and responsibility for the delivery of objectives.

Within PRINCE2, responsibilities are defined in terms of roles, rather than individuals. The basic PRINCE2 project organisational structure is illustrated below (arrows indicate accountability):

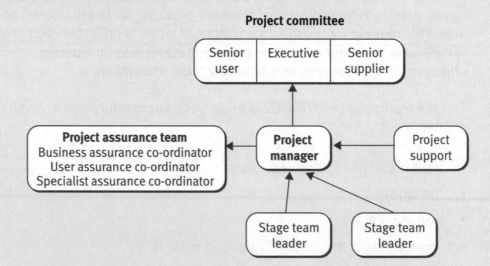

- **Plans** – successful control includes setting plans/standards for everything that needs to be delivered (time, quality, responsibility, communication).

- **Controls** – (TARA) regular and formal monitoring of actual progress against plan is essential to ensure the timeliness, cost control and quality of the project.

- **Products** – includes a number of tools associated with the control of projects (initiation document, budget, progress reports).

- **Quality** – quality should be defined and controlled on the project (zero defects). Quality plans should set the standards required (e.g. using recognised methodologies such as PRINCE2).

- **Risk management** – identifying different types of risk will allow us to plan to reduce them or avoid them.

- **Control of change management** and configuration management – any change to the project should only be after the appropriate approval has been authorised. The management of these changes means knowing which versions are the current ones.

PRINCE2 process areas

- **Starting up a project** – a pre-project process, this stage involves designing and appointing the project management team, creating the initial stage plan and ensuring that information required by the project team is available.

- **Initiation** – akin to a feasibility study, this stage establishes whether or not there is the justification to proceed with the project. The Project Board take ownership of the project at this stage.

- **Managing stage boundaries** – the primary objective at this stage is to ensure that all planned deliverables are completed as required. The Project Board is provided with information to approve completion of the current stage and authorise the start of the next. Lessons learned in the earlier stages can be applied at later stages.

- **Controlling a stage** – monitoring and control activities are carried out by the project manager at each stage of the project. This process incorporates the day-to-day management of the project.

- **Managing product delivery** – this includes effective allocation of Work Packages and ensuring that the work is carried out to the required quality standard.

- **Project closure** – bringing the project to a formal and controlled close approved by the Project Board, it establishes the extent to which the objectives have been met, the extent of formal acceptance obtained of deliverables by the Project Customer, and identifies lessons learned for the future. An End Project Report is completed and the project team disbanded.

Whilst these could all be considered to be elements of any good project management, the difference with PRINCE2 is the level of structure and documentation that is required. This helps in providing controls on the planning and execution of projects and forces the identification of potential problems.

Note: students are advised to read the article on PRINCE2 from the Cimaglobal website. It can be found using the following link:
http://www.cimaglobal.com/Documents/ImportedDocuments/
PRINCE2_P5_article.pdf

10 The Project Management Body of Knowledge (PMBOK)

While not strictly a methodology, the US-based Project Management Institute (PMI) has defined best-practice project management principles and processes. The Project Management Body of Knowledge (PMBOK) describes nine key areas in terms of inputs, outputs, tools, techniques and how they fit together.

The PMBOK describes nine Project Management Knowledge Areas:

(1) **Integration** Management – processes for ensuring that the various elements of the project are properly co-ordinated.

(2) **Scope** Management – processes for ensuring that the project includes all the work required and only the work required to complete the project successfully.

(3) **Time** Management – processes for ensuring timely completion of the project. All projects are finite, and time ranks as one of the main limits.

(4) **Cost** Management – processes for ensuring that the project is completed within the approved budget. All projects must have a budget.

(5) **Quality** Management – processes for ensuring that the project will satisfy the needs for which it was undertaken.

(6) **Human Resource** Management – processes required to make the most effective use of the people involved in the project.

(7) **Communications** Management – processes required to ensure timely and appropriate generation, collection, dissemination, storage, and ultimate distribution of project information.

(8) **Risk** Management – processes concerned with identifying, analysing and responding to project risk.

(9) **Procurement** Management – processes for acquiring goods and services from outside the performing organisation.

PMBOK is not intended as an alternative to the project life cycle, but rather as a view of the knowledge and skills required in order to carry out each of the stages of the life cycle. It can be viewed as a toolbox. So, for example, at the 'initiating' stage, the project manager would need to consider integration management activities, scope management activities, and so on.

Case study style question 4

R, a manufacturer and retailer of fashion clothes, has invested in a new technology system to improve the logistics of the movement of clothes between its warehouses and chain of 250 retail outlets. Ensuring that the outlets have the right supply of clothes is a critical success factor for the company.

However, the warehousing stock control and logistics project set up to develop and deliver the new system has experienced numerous problems. The project ended up being well over budget and was also late in delivering the system. Now, only three months after the new system has been installed, it is apparent that the project has not delivered its objective. Instead, the company is facing a crisis with many store managers complaining that they are not receiving the correct stock. Even worse, some stores are out of stock of key ranges, whereas the warehouses are full of clothing.

A meeting between the project team and project sponsor has ended up with everyone blaming each other, saying it was not their responsibility. It is clear that they did not use a project management methodology and did not have adequate control systems in place so that the problems that have now transpired could have been identified and rectified earlier in the project life cycle.

Required:

You have been asked for help by the project sponsor. Write an email to the project sponsor recommending a project management methodology/ approach, explaining how it could have helped to prevent the failures of the warehousing, stock control and logistics project.

(15 minutes)

11 Summary diagram

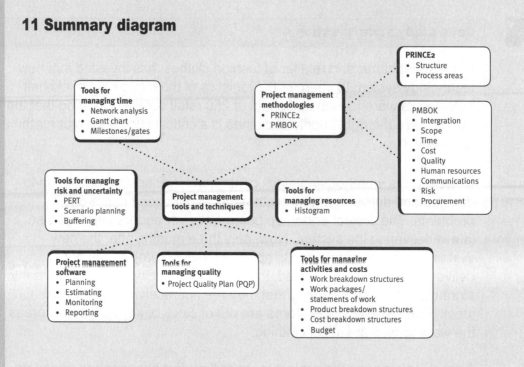

End of chapter questions

Question 1

There are a number of tools and techniques used when managing projects, including:

- Work breakdown structures
- Network analysis
- Milestones
- Resource histograms
- Product breakdown structures
- Project quality plan

Match the tool or technique to its purpose.

- To identify the product purchases required for each activity
- To graphically represent the logical order of activities
- To determine the resource requirements for the project

Question 2

Which of the following are PRINCE2 process areas? Select all that apply.

- Controlling a stage
- Identification of a need
- Managing product delivery
- Planning
- Post completion audit
- Project closure

Question 3

The following shows a network diagram for a project. The durations are shown in weeks.

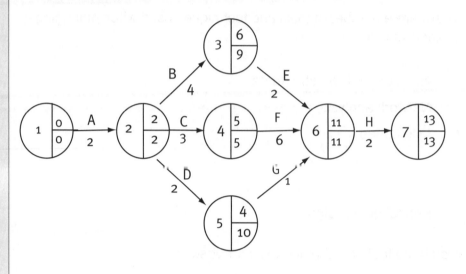

Using this diagram, which of the following statements are true? Select all that apply.

- The overall duration of the project is 13 weeks
- The critical path is ADGH
- Activities B and E have slack of 3 weeks
- Activities D and G have slack of 7 weeks
- Activity E is on the critical path
- The critical path is ACFH

Question 4

Which of the following statements regarding critical path analysis is FALSE?

A   Each activity line must begin and end with a node

B   Latest event times are calculated working left to right

C   When there is a choice in calculating the earliest event time, select the highest

D   Activities that are not on the critical path will have float

Question 5

When planning a project, there are a number of techniques that are used to take account of risk and uncertainty:

- PERT
- Scenario planning
- Buffering

Match the descriptions to the technique.

- This technique involves considering and testing one or more set of circumstances which may occur.
- In this technique artificial slack is added to risky activities.
- This technique involves using a formula to calculate an expected time for each activity.

Question 6

Which of the following are project management knowledge areas as defined by the Project Management Institute? Select all that apply.

- Communications
- Legal
- Leadership
- Procurement
- Integration
- Scope

Question 7

The following diagram shows a critical path diagram for a network. The durations are shown in weeks.

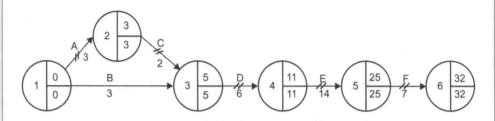

Which of the following statements regarding activity B is true?

A   There is no slack in activity B.

B   Activity B is on the critical path.

C   Activity B can overrun by 2 weeks.

D   Activity B can only start after the completion of activity A.

Question 8

Which of the following statements regarding project management software are true? Select all that apply.

- Software can only be used at the planning stage of the project
- Software improves the accuracy of drawing network diagrams
- Using project management software will ensure the success of the project
- Software can be used to undertake 'what if' analysis
- Using software can improve communication during a project

Question 9

Which of the following statements regarding milestones and gates is **incorrect**?

A   A milestone is used to measure the progress of a project

B   If a milestone is not met, the project should not continue

C   Milestones can be shown on gantt charts

D   A control gate can only be passed if progress meets pre-defined performance standards

Question 10

Which of the following statements regarding the PRINCE2 structure are correct? Select all that apply.

- In the PRINCE2 organisation chart, the project manager reports to the project committee and the project assurance team.

- The project committee is made up of senior user, senior supplier and project support.

- The PRINCE2 structure includes organisation, plans, controls, products, quality, risk management and control of change management.

- Initiation documents, budgets and progress reports are part of the PRINCE2 products.

- The project assurance team is made up of business assurance co-ordinator, customer assurance co-ordinator and supplier assurance co-ordinator.

Test your understanding answers

EMAIL

To: Project sponsor

From: Project manager

Date: today

Subject: Project YT – Network diagram

I have completed the network diagram for project YT. This is shown below:

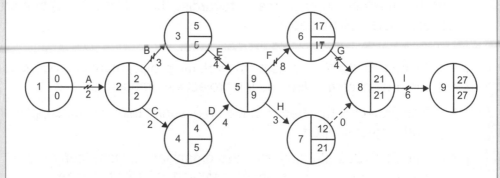

The diagram gives us a number of pieces of information which will be helpful to us in running the project.

From the diagram, the overall duration of the project is 27 weeks.

A number of the activities are deemed to be 'critical'. Critical activities are those activities which must be done on time, or the overall duration of the project will be extended to beyond 27 weeks. In project YT, the critical activities are A, B, E, F, G and I. Extra care must be taken to ensure that these activities run to plan.

The diagram also highlights those activities which have float, or slack. Activities with float or slack in this project are C and D which have one week of float, and H which has nine weeks.

I hope this information is useful to you. Please get in touch if you have any questions or want to discuss any aspects further.

Case study style question 2

EMAIL

To: K

From: Management Accountant

Date: today

Subject: Network diagram

I have reviewed the network diagram for the on-line entry system project. The diagram gives us a number of pieces of information which will be helpful to you in running the project.

From the diagram, the overall duration of the project is 14 weeks.

A number of the activities are deemed to be 'critical'. Critical activities are those activities which must be done on time, or the overall duration of the project will be extended to beyond 14 weeks. In this project, the critical activities are B, D and E. Extra care must be taken to ensure that these activities run to plan.

The diagram also highlights those activities which have float, or slack. Activities with float or slack in this project are A and C which have one week of float.

The network diagram is useful in giving the above information, but it can be difficult to understand. Another tool which could be used to show much the same information is the Gantt chart. This is a straightforward method of scheduling tasks; it is essentially a chart on which bars represent each task or activity. The length of each bar represents the relative length of the task. Its advantages lie in its simplicity, the ready acceptance of it by users, and the fact that the bars are drawn to scale.

It also has the advantage over the network diagram in that the actual activities can be added alongside the scheduled activities which is useful in monitoring progress once the project is underway.

I hope this information is useful to you. Please get in touch if you have any questions or want to discuss any aspects further.

REPORT

To: Management of ZX

From: Management Accountant

Date: today

Subject: Critical path analysis and use of project management software

Introduction

In this report the importance of undertaking critical path analysis will be explained and the useful of using project management software will also be explained.

The importance of critical path analysis

Critical path analysis is an important technique to assist with project management, when a project has to be completed within a given amount of time, or before a final target date. A CPA chart shows all the activities that must be carried out in order to complete the project, the sequence in which they must take place, the budgeted time for each activity, the minimum overall completion time for the project and the earliest times that each activity can start and must be finished to make sure that the target project completion date is achieved. The analysis therefore enables management to:

* decide whether the target date for completion is achievable

* if the target date is achievable, what is the latest time the project can begin

* identify which activities are critical to completion on time and must be started at the earliest possible time

* identify those activities that are non-critical, and how much 'slack' they have, so that they can be started late or might take longer than planned without affecting the overall project completion time

* identify which activities cannot start until another activity (or other activities) have finished, and which activities can be undertaken in parallel with each other.

Regular monitoring of actual progress against the CPA chart will provide management with valuable information to assist with efforts to ensure completion of the project on time.

Project management software

Project management software can be used throughout the project in a number of ways. It is especially useful in planning, estimating, monitoring and reporting.

Planning

Project management software can be used to enter activities, estimates, precedents and resources to automatically produce a network diagram (showing the critical path) and a Gantt chart (showing resource use). These diagrams can be difficult to produce.

Estimating

Project management software allows the entry of actual data – the hours or days actually taken to complete a particular task. Many of these tasks are the same in systems development across different projects and so a considerable amount of information can be collected about the time taken to complete common tasks.

Monitoring

Project management software allows the entry of actual data, which can be used to monitor the progress of the project and to re-plan the rest of the work.

Reporting

Most project management software packages have comprehensive reporting requirements, which allow managers to print out the progress and status of the project. This means that standard progress reports can be produced automatically.

Conclusion

This report has looked at two important project management tools, namely critical path analysis and project management software. Both of these assist in the management of the project.

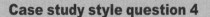

Case study style question 4

EMAIL

To: Project sponsor

From: Management Accountant

Date: today

Subject: Project management methodology

A project management methodology that could have been used by R is PRINCE2. This is an acronym for PRojects IN Controlled Environments and is a structured approach to project management, used by the UK government and private sector organisations. It includes bureaucratic controls on the planning and execution of projects, identifies some of the potential problems that may arise and early resolution. Whilst it could be argued that aspects of PRINCE2 could be considered to be just good project management, the difference is in the level of structure and documentation required.

The key processes of PRINCE2 methodology offer a number of features that would have benefited R Company including:

- A defined management structure
- A system of plans
- A set of control procedures
- A focus on product based planning.

The main purpose is to deliver a successful project, which can be defined as:

- Delivery of agreed outcomes
- On time
- Within budget
- Conforming to the required quality standards.

PRINCE2 has a set of progressive documents for a project and control is achieved through the authorisation of work packages. These include controls on quality, time and costs and identify reports and handover requirements, all of which are problems that have led to the failure of the project in R. The methodology includes a series of 'management products', for example project initiation documents, project budget, quality plan and various checkpoint and progress reports, which would have improved controls for R's project.

The key processes and documentation of PRINCE2 would have enforced the project team in R to have a clear structure of authority and responsibility between members in the project team, so that each party has clear objectives. As part of this, the control responsibilities of the various members of the project team would have been determined. This should mean that the different participants in the warehousing stock control and logistics project would have had a clearer understanding of the various tasks and the relationships between them and should have prevented the problems R is now facing.

The exception plan concept in PRINCE2 would mean that if R's project was going to exceed its tolerance, for example variances in time, cost or quality, this would have been reported to the project board. The implications on the whole project deliverables should have been discussed and plans amended to reflect any changes needed to ensure the project delivered its objectives.

I hope you have found the above useful, please get in touch if you need any more information about this.

Question 1

The correct matching is:

Product breakdown structures – To identify the product purchases required for each activity

Network analysis – To graphically represent the logical order of activities

Resource histograms – To determine the resource requirements

Work breakdown structures are used to break complex tasks into manageable pieces.

Milestones are used to assess the status of the project and how far the project has progressed.

Project quality plans are used to detail the standards required in the project.

Question 2

- Controlling a stage
- Managing product delivery
- Project closure

The other PRINCE2 process areas are:

- Starting up a project
- Initiation
- Managing stage bounderies

Question 3

The true statements are:

- The overall duration of the project is 13 weeks
- Activities B and E have slack of 3 weeks
- The critical path is ACFH

Question 4

B   Latest event times are calculated working left to right

This is false as latest event times are calculated working right to left.

Question 5

The correct matching is:

PERT – This technique involves using a formula to calculate an expected time for each activity.

Scenario planning – This technique involves considering and testing one or more set of circumstances which may occur.

Buffering – In this technique artificial slack is added to risky activities.

Question 6

- Communications
- Procurement
- Integration
- Scope

The project management institute's nine process areas are communications, procurement, intergration, scope and:

- time
- cost
- quality
- human resources
- risk

Question 7

C   Activity B can overrun by 2 weeks.

Activity B has slack of 2 weeks. It is therefore able to overrun by 2 weeks without affecting the overall duration of the project.

Given that the activity has slack, it cannot be on the critical path as activities on the critical path must start and end as scheduled.

From the diagram it can be seen that activity B can start right at the beginning of the project and has no preceeding activities.

Question 8

- Software improves the accuracy of drawing network diagrams
- Software can be used to undertake 'what if' analysis
- Using software can improve communication during a project

Project management software can be used throughout the project. Using software will contribute to the success of the project but cannot guarantee it.

Question 9

B   If a milestone is not met, the project should not continue

This is incorrect as a milestone is simply a measure of progress in the project. If a control gate is not met, the project should not continue.

Question 10

- In the PRINCE2 organisation chart, the project manager reports to the project committee and the project assurance team.

- The PRINCE2 structure includes organisation, plans, controls, products, quality, risk management and control of change management.

- Initiation documents, budgets and progress reports are part of the PRINCE2 products.

The project committee is made up of senior user, senior supplier and project support. This is incorrect. The project committee is made up of senior user, senior supplier and executive.

The project assurance team is made up of business assurance co-ordinator, customer assurance co-ordinator and supplier assurance co-ordinator. This is incorrect. The project assurance team is made up of business assurance co-ordinator, user assurance co-ordinator and specialist assurance co-ordinator.

16

People and projects

Chapter learning objectives

Discuss management and leadership issues associated with projects, including the roles of key players in projects.

1 Session content diagram

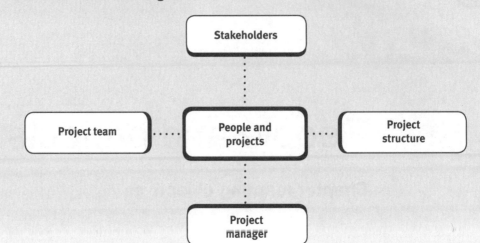

2 Who is involved in the project?

Note: A lot of the material in this chapter will be familiar from the earlier chapters on relationship management. Much of the material in the relationship management part of the syllabus will be equally applicable in the context of a project.

A key aspect in ensuring the success of a project is having the right people involved in the project. Decisions need to be made about the people involved in the project after the need for the project has been identified and the methodology has been selected.

Having the right people, with the right knowledge and skills, involved in the project will significantly enhance its chance of success.

There are various interested parties who are involved in or may be affected by the project activities. They are known as its '**stakeholders**', as they have a 'stake' or interest in the effective completion of the project. Obviously, the number of people involved will depend on the size of the project.

A project is much like an organisation in that it has a hierarchical set of relationships. This hierarchy is put in place for two main reasons:

*   to create a structure of authority so everyone knows who can make decisions, and

*   to create a series of superior-subordinate relationships so each individual or group has only one 'boss'.

Project stakeholders should all be committed to achieving a common goal – the successful completion of the project.

Stakeholder hierarchy

Based on the principles of 'one person – one boss' and a decision-making authority, the hierarchy shown below is adapted from the one shown in *Successful Project Management*, Gido J and Clements J, 1999.

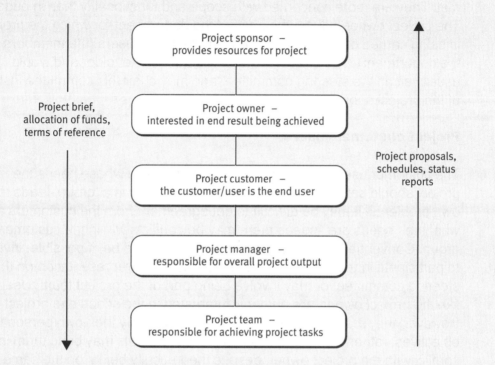

The roles of the various stakeholders:

Project sponsor:

The project sponsor makes yes/no decisions about the project.

The role of the sponsor:

- Initiates the project. They must be satisfied that a business case exists to justify the project.

- Appoints the project manager.

- Makes yes/no decision regarding the project. The sponsor is responsible for approving the project plan.

- Provides the resources for the project and are responsible for its budget.

- Monitors the progress of the project from the information provided by the project manager.

- Provides support and senior management commitment to the project.

Project owner:

The project owner is the person for whom the project is being carried out. They are interested in the end result being achieved and their needs being met. They are more concerned with scope and functionality than in budget. The project owner may be the head of the department for which the project is being carried out. The owner may represent the users (the members of the department). The project owner is a senior stakeholder and would usually sit on the steering committee, and may chair this committee instead of the project sponsor.

Project customers/users:

The customer/user is the person or group of people whose needs the project should satisfy. The fact that this stakeholder is a 'group' leads to its own problems. It may be difficult to get agreement from the customers as to what their needs are; indeed there may be conflicts within the customer group. Conventional logic dictates that users should be, if possible, invited to participate in the project. This may simply mean representation on the steering committee, or may involve being part of the project team. Users, like the project owner, are primarily interested in the scope of a project. However, they may try to 'hijack' the project to satisfy their own personal objectives, rather than those of the organisation. This may bring them into conflict with the project owner, despite theoretically being 'on the same side'. In the case of the new finance system, the users would come from the different parts of the finance function.

In small projects, the sponsor, owner and customer may be the same person.

Project manager:

The project manager is responsible for the successful delivery of project objectives to the satisfaction of the final customer. As projects are interdisciplinary and cross organisational reporting lines, the project manager has a complex task in managing, coordinating, controlling and communicating project tasks.

The role of project manager involves:

- Ensuring project objectives are achieved.
- Making decisions relating to system resources.
- Planning, monitoring and controlling the project.
- Selecting, building and motivating the project team.
- Serving as a point of contact with management hierarchy.

- Communicating with the chain of command.
- Selecting and managing subcontractors.
- Recommending termination where necessary.

In essence, the project manager takes responsibility for providing leadership to the project team who carry out the project tasks in order to achieve the project objectives. The project manager will lead and coordinate the activities of the project team to ensure that activities are performed on time, within cost and to the quality standards set by the customer. An important aspect of project management is to ensure that the team members are organised, coordinated and working together.

Project team:

The members of the project team will be given individual responsibility for parts of the project. As projects are often interdisciplinary and cross organisational reporting lines, the project team is likely to be made up of members drawn from a variety of different functions or divisions: each individual then has a dual role, as he or she maintains functional/divisional responsibilities as well as membership of the project team.

Project steering committee/project board

Overseeing the project and making all high level decision regarding the project will be a steering committee or project board. In smaller projects there will be either a steering committee or a project board, but larger scale projects will have both. Where a project has both, the project board sits above the steering committee in the hierarchy and is in charge of the overall management of the project. All high level decisions regarding the project will be made by the board.

While the steering committee may meet monthly, the board will meet less frequently, maybe only several times a year. They will require progress reports about the project, but these will be high level reports, focusing on the main aspects of the project. A strong project board can make the difference between success and failure of a large, complex project.

The steering committee/board will normally be chaired by the project sponsor and the members should represent all major areas of interest in the project, for example the project owner would sit on the committee/board. The representatives of each area should be at a sufficient level of seniority so that they have the authority to take decisions on behalf of their areas. The project manager will report all progress to the steering committee/project board.

Project Champion

Some high profile projects may have a project champion, or supporter. This is an informal role within the project, with no decision making or reporting responsibility. The role of the project champion is simply that, to campaign on behalf of the project at the highest levels of the organisation. They will show their support of the project by marketing it at every opportunity, even though they have no formal role in the project.

In addition to the above, suppliers, subcontractors and specialists are also important stakeholders. The project will often require input from other parties, such as material suppliers or possibly specialist labour, such as consultants. Each of them will have their own objectives, some of which conflict with those of the project. For example, suppliers will seek to maximise the price of the supply, and reduce its scope and quality, in order to reduce cost. This conflicts directly with the objectives of the sponsor and customers. In the case of the new finance system, suppliers may provide hardware and software, and specialists might include members of the organisation's IT, purchasing or internal audit departments.

The role of CMAs in projects

Management accounts can undertake a variety of roles within projects, including:

Project manager – many accountants undertake the role of project manager. The range of skills possessed by the management accountant, such as leadership, communication and analytical skills are the skills required by the project manager.

Project sponsor – the project sponsor, who supplies the funding for the project is often a senior member of the finance function.

Project customer/user – all areas within organisations can be affected by projects and many projects will have an effect on the financial systems and procedures, therefore the management accountants will often be involved in terms of assessing the impact the changes will have on the accounting function.

Member of project team – management accountants are often required to be part of project teams. They bring financial knowledge and are able to analyse and advise on the financial impact of the project on the organisation.

Providing financial information for the project – the finance department is often involved in supplying financial information to the project manager. At the outset of the project when the economic feasibility is being considered, the management accountant would be involved in undertaking the cost-benefit analysis. Throughout the project, the project spend should be monitored and compared to the original budget and this information is usually produced by the management accountant.

3 Managing stakeholder relationships

At the beginning of a project potential stakeholders need to be identified and their interests in the project assessed. This is a vital project management activity to enable the relationships within the groups to be managed. A plan can be drawn up to secure and maintain their support and to foresee and react to any problems. The project manager can concentrate on the critical stakeholder relationships, assess the risks associated with certain groups, indicate where attention needs to be focused and thus reduce the vulnerability of the project.

The project manager has to balance a number of values, beliefs and assumptions in attempting to navigate a project to a successful conclusion. These values, beliefs and assumptions relate to the stakeholders in the project, who may be defined as any party with a vested interest. The ability to be able to discern stakeholder values, beliefs, assumptions and expectations is a positive tool in the project manager's 'competence toolbox', not least because they often conflict and may not always be benevolent to the project.

Once stakeholders are identified they can be mapped in relation to:

- The likelihood of each stakeholder group attempting to impress their expectations on others.

- The power and means available for them to do so.

- The impact of stakeholder expectations on the project.

Mendelow's matrix, which was covered in the concept of strategy and the rational approach to strategy development chapter, could be used to aid the project manager in managing the project stakeholders.

Stakeholder conflict

Most conflict within projects arises from the interaction of individuals, and a good project manager must have the interpersonal skills to be able to manage conflict.

Within a project, there will be a number of stakeholders and they may not share the same objectives, which may cause conflict. Among the most common reasons for conflict within projects are the following:

- Unclear objectives for the project.
- Role ambiguity within the project team.
- Unclear schedules and performance targets.
- A low level of authority given to the project manager.
- Remote functional groups within the project, working almost independently.
- Interference from local or functional management.
- Personality clashes, or differing styles of working.

The project manager should establish a framework to predict the potential for disputes.

This involves:

- risk management – since an unforeseen event (a risk) has the potential to create conflict; and
- dispute management – matching dispute procedures with minimum impact on costs, progress and goodwill.

The techniques used for dispute management are:

- **Negotiation** – involving the parties discussing the problem. This may or may not resolve the problem.
- **Mediation** or 'assisted negotiation' – involves a neutral third party (the mediator) intervening to reach a mutually agreeable solution. In practice, disputes are often resolved by accepting the view of the stakeholder that has financial responsibility for the project. In such a situation, mediation and negotiation may only deliver an outcome that is a reflection of the original power imbalance.
- **Partnering** – focuses on creating communication links between project participants with the intention of directing them towards a common goal – ahead of their own self-interest.
- **Compromise** – is the most obvious approach to conflict management, although it does imply that both parties in the conflict must sacrifice something.

Case study style question 1

GPC is a project being undertaken by the Southern Regional Health Authority (SRHA) to connect all medical centres and hospitals within the region to a national information network, called the 'Healthweb'.

You are a senior management accountant working for one of the southern region hospitals, and, as part of the project team, it is your responsibility to communicate with all SRHA medical centres and hospitals on the progress of the project.

The SRHA is one of four regional government-controlled authorities, responsible to the central government Department of Health. Each regional health authority manages and controls the provision of medical care to the public within its local area. The SRHA is responsible for fifty medical centres and ten hospitals within the region, all of which are publicly funded (i.e., the SRHA is not responsible for private medical centres and hospitals).

The SRHA has been set a target by the central government to have 80% of all medical centers and 90% of all hospitals within the region connected to the Healthweb by July 2016. Prior to the project commencement, most information within the hospitals and medical centres was kept by a manual, paper-based system, and all data exchange was done by means of telephone or by post. The senior management team of the SRHA set up a project board to oversee the progress of the project and to specify the project objectives.

Required:

You have been asked by the executives of your own hospital to prepare a report to the other senior managers in the hospital which should discuss the relationship of the project manager to:

- the project sponsor (i.e., the central government)
- the project board
- the medical and administrative users (in medical centres and hospitals).

Your report should also Include a discussion of the potential conflicting project objectives of the above stakeholders.

(20 minutes)

4 Project manager

The skills required by a project manager

The skills that the project manager brings to the project are critical to its success. A project manager requires a number of varied skills:

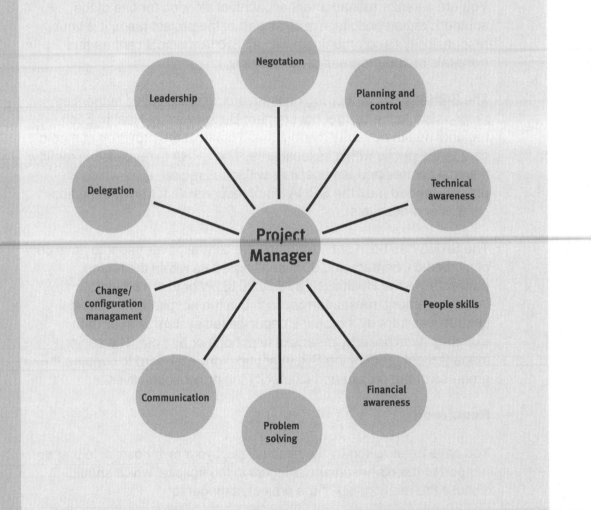

Main project management skills

Leadership

Leadership is the ability to obtain results from others through personal direction and influence. Leadership in projects involves influencing others through the personality or actions of the project manager. The project manager cannot achieve the project objectives alone; results are achieved by the whole project team. The project manager must have the ability to motivate the project team in order to create a team objective that they want to be part of.

Communication

Project managers must be effective communicators. They must communicate regularly with a variety of people, including the customer, suppliers, subcontractors, project team and senior management. Communication is vital for the progression of the project, identification of potential problems, generation of solutions and keeping up to date with the customer's requirements and the perceptions of the team.

Project managers should communicate by using a variety of methods:

- regular team meetings
- regular meetings face-to-face with the customer
- informal meetings with individual team members
- written reports to senior management and the customer
- listening to all the stakeholders involved in the project.

Negotiation

Project managers will have to negotiate on a variety of project issues, such as availability and level of resources, schedules, priorities, standards, procedures, costs, quality and people issues. The project manager may have to negotiate with someone over whom he or she has no direct authority (e.g. consultants), or who has no direct authority over him or her (e.g. the customer).

Delegation

A further key skill required for a project manager is that of delegation. A project manager will communicate and clarify the overall project objective to the team members, and will then further clarify the individual team member's role in achieving that objective by a process of delegation. Delegation is about empowering the project team and each team member to accomplish the expected tasks for his or her area of responsibility. The project manager has neither the time nor the skills to carry out all the project tasks, so he or she must delegate responsibility to those who do have the skills.

Problem solving

Project managers will inevitably face numerous problems throughout the project's life. It is important that the project manager gathers information about the problem in order to understand the issues as clearly as possible. The project manager should encourage team members to identify problems within their own tasks and try to solve them on their own, initially. However, where tasks are large or critical to the overall achievement of the project, it is important that team members communicate with the project manager as soon as possible so that they can lead the problem-solving effort.

Change-management skills

One thing is certain in projects, and that is change. Changes may be:

- requested by the customer
- requested by the project team
- caused by unexpected events during the project performance
- required by the users of the final project outcome.

Therefore, it is important that the project manager has the skills to manage and control change. The impact that change has on accomplishing the project objective must be kept to a minimum and may be affected by the time in the project's life cycle when the change is identified. Generally, the later the change is identified in the project life cycle, the greater its likely impact on achieving the overall project objective successfully. Most likely to be affected by change is the project budget and its timescale.

The project manager and negotiation

One of the required skills of a project manager is negotiation. While running a complex project, the project manager may get involved in a number of negotiations.

Project managers will have to negotiate on a variety of project issues, such as availability and level of resources, schedules, priorities, standards, procedures, costs, quality and people issues. The project manager may have to negotiate with someone over whom he or she has no direct authority (e.g. consultants), or who has no direct authority over him or her (e.g. the customer).

The following table gives examples of the types of issues for which the project manager may get involved in negotiation.

Negotiation point	Possible issues	Negotiate with
Resources	Funding	Senior management
	Staff	Line managers
	Equipment	Purchasing
	Time scale	Customer/senior management
Schedules	Order of activities	Customer/teams
	Duration of activities	Line managers/team members
	Timing of activities	Line managers/team members
	Deadlines	Customer/line managers
Priorities	Over other projects or work	Senior management
	Between cost, quality and time	Customer/team members
	Of team members' activities	Team members
Procedures	Methods	Team members
	Roles and responsibilities	Team members/customer
	Reporting	Senior management/customer
	Relationships	Team members
Quality	Assurance checks	Customer/teams
	Performance measures	Customer/teams
	Fitness for purpose	Customer/team members
Costs	Estimates	Accountants/team members
	Budgets	Customer/senior management
	Expenditure	Customer/accountants
People	Getting team to work together	Team members
	Getting required skills	Team members/line managers
	Work allocations	Team members/line managers
	Effort needed	Team members/line managers

5 Project team management

The basic project team consists of the project manager (and possible team leaders), and a group of specialists assigned or recruited for the project.

The project team should include everyone who will significantly contribute to the project, both managerial and non-managerial people, whether they are full-time or part-time.

The project team will obviously include all of the technical people responsible for the project's efforts toward research, design, development, procurement, production and testing. Team members are expected to attend all project meetings, and to participate in project decision-making. Therefore, care should be taken in making sure that the team does not have any non-performing members. The project team is likely to be made up of a range of staff with different skills and experience. Effective team working is essential for the success of a project and it is important to foster this through regular meetings to establish team cohesion, helping to develop a team which is integrated, has common objectives and positive group dynamics.

The ideal project team will achieve project completion on time, within budget and to the required specifications. They will do all this with the minimum amount of direct supervision from the project manager.

The project manager must get the individual team members to view the project from the 'big-picture' perspective, and to concentrate on overall project goals.

Lifecycle of project teams

Tuckman's model of team development was covered in the building, leading and managing teams chapter. This can be used to show the lifecycle of the project team.

To recap, the stages are:

- **Forming** – a collection of individuals are brought together, often from different areas of the organisation. The project manager has an important role at this stage to provide clear direction to the team and ensuring they understand the project objectives.

- **Storming** – As the individuals start to operate as a team, most teams go through this conflict stage. Team members may try to test the project manager's authority and may challenge the role they have been given. The project manager must demonstrate strong conflict resolution leadership skills at this stage.

- **Norming** – The individuals settle in to their roles and the team starts to perform. The project manager will begin to pass control and decision-making authority to the team members.

- **Performing** – The team is capable of operating at full potential at this stage. The project manager will concentrate on the performance of the project.

- **Adjourning** (dorming) – Once the objectives of the project have been achieved, the team can be disbanded and the individuals can go back to their previous roles, or move on to work on a new project.

These stages can be considered alongside the project lifecycle as shown below:

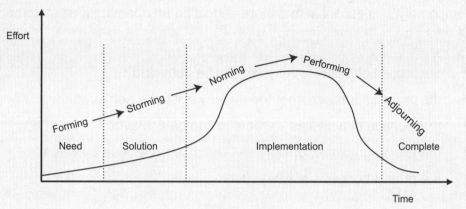

The project life cycle

Likewise the other models of team building, such as Belbin, can also be applied to project teams. These models should be reviewed at this stage and consideration given as to how they could be applied in a project scenario.

Managing project teams

In the management of project teams we must pay attention to two particular characteristics of each team:

- Each project is a complete entity, and unique in terms of experiences, problems, constraints and objectives.

- The members of the team concerned may well have not worked together as a group on any previous occasion.

The **style of management** for the team must be the relevant approach aimed at the creation of the appropriate internal team environment or, in other words, team climate. Some large organisations provide the team with initial status by providing it with all the necessary support and resources, such as office accommodation, a budget, support secretarial staff, and so on. Other organisations simply appoint a leader, authorised by the board to appoint team members and acquire resources at his or her own discretion.

The **planning and controlling of the team** activities are vital aspects of management in that a major project cost lies in the fact that team members are not undertaking their own tasks but have been taken from these temporarily. It is essential that there should be an unambiguous statement of:

- the project objective(s) – what is to be achieved?
- the project approach, methods – how is it to be achieved?
- the location of activities – where is it to be achieved?
- the allocation of responsibilities – what is to be done by whom?
- the project budget – at what cost?

Leading and motivating project teams

All aspects of leadership and motivation which were covered in the leadership and management chapter are equally applicable in the context of a project team as they are to business as usual. The models covered in the leadership and management chapter should be reviewed at this stage and consideration given as to how they could be applied in a project scenario.

The project manager does not and cannot complete a project on his or her own. It requires effective teamwork and team motivation. To foster a motivated project team environment, the project manager needs to understand his or her team members first in order to understand what motivates them. The project manager should attempt to create a project environment that is supportive and where team members feel enthusiastic and want to work towards the overall project goal.

The project manager can create such an environment by:

- Ensuring that the team is made up of the correct people. The project manager should be aware of Belbin's model and ensure that all required roles in the team are met. This will avoid conflict and foster good working relationships.
- Adequate knowledge and experience in team. The project manager must ensure that all team members are able to participate fully in their role and that they possess the required knowledge and skills
- Adopting a participative style of management.
- By encouraging participation in project decision-making.
- By delegating decisions to the team members, thus encouraging involvement and ownership.
- Holding regular project meetings whereby team members can participate and air their views and put forward their opinions.

- Holding regular one-to one meetings with individual team members, encouraging them to put forward their own ideas and suggestions for project improvement.

- Ensuring that conflict is minimised by ensuring that all team members are clear about their role and what is required of them.

The project manager needs to demonstrate that he/she values the contribution made by team members and that their contribution is important to the overall project.

Case study style question 2

AF is a large construction company that has just won a major contract for a road-widening scheme through an area of countryside that has been officially designated as an 'area of outstanding natural beauty'. The work will be carried out to some extent by direct employees of AF, but most of the work will be undertaken by sub-contractors.

The scheme has already attracted a considerable amount of publicity and the Preserve the Countryside Movement, a large national pressure group, has already announced its intention to organise demonstrations and protests against the construction work. More extreme and radical protest groups have threatened disruptive action.

The project is being financed by the transport department of the central government, and the managers of AF who are responsible for the project have already spoken to the police authorities about the preservation of public order. A security firm will be employed to provide physical protection to employees and assets.

A traffic survey conducted for the central government has suggested that, during the time that the road widening is taking place, there will be severe disruption to normal road traffic and severe delays for drivers on their journeys will be inevitable.

PC has been appointed as project manager, but this is the largest and most complex project he has managed. He knows that in this project he must give strong leadership to get the best possible performance out of the project team, but he is concerned about how he is going to manage this aspect of the project.

Required:

Write an email to PC suggesting what leadership style is most likely to be successful for a project such as this road-widening scheme. Give your reasons and make reference to any theories of leadership style with which you are familiar.

(15 minutes)

6 Project structure

Establishing an effective project management structure is crucial for its success. Every project has a need for direction, management, control and communication, using a structure that differs from line management. As a project is normally cross functional and involves partnership, its structure needs to be more flexible, and is likely to require a broad base of skills for a specific period of time. The project manager needs a clear structure, consisting of roles and responsibilities that bring together the various interests and skills involved in, and required by, the project.

In conventional (functional or divisional) structures, there is often a lack of clarity as to how authority is divided between line managers and project managers. If a project is relatively small or short term, for example an information system redevelopment, this may not be a major issue. However, if the project forms a major part of the business of the organisation, such as in a construction company, this may necessitate an organisation structure such as a matrix, where lines of authority are clearer.

Matrix and project structure

Definition: A matrix structure aims to combine the benefits of decentralisation (motivation of identifiable management teams, closeness to the market, speedy decision making) with those of co-ordination (achieving economies and synergies across all business units, territories and products).

The matrix structure seeks to add flexibility and lateral coordination. One way is to create project teams made up of members drawn from a variety of different functions or divisions. Each individual has a dual role as he/she maintains their functional/divisional responsibilities as well as membership of the project team.

Both vertical and horizontal relationships are emphasised, and employees have dual reporting to managers. The diagram below shows a mix of project and functional structures.

```
                        SENIOR MANAGEMENT
                                |
                        FUNCTIONAL STRUCTURE
```

PROJECT STRUCTURE	Production Department	Sales Department	Finance Department	R&D Department
Project Manager A				
Project Manager B				
Project Manager C				

The matrix organisation structure has been widely criticised, but is still used by many organisations in industries such as engineering, construction, consultancy, audit and even education. The characteristics of the organisation that lead to *a matrix being the most suitable organisation structure* are as follows:

- The business of the organisation consists of a series of projects, each requiring staff and resources from a number of technical functions.

- The projects have different start and end dates, so the organisation is continually reassigning resources from project to project.

- The projects are complex, so staff benefit from also being assigned to a technical function (such as finance of logistics) where they can share knowledge with colleagues.

- The projects are expensive, so having resources controlled by functional heads should lead to improved utilisation and reduced duplication across projects.

- The projects are customer-facing, so the customer requires a single point of contact (the project manager) to deal with their needs and problems.

Impact on project achievement

The matrix structure can impact on the achievement of the project as follows:

- improve decision-making by bringing a wide range of expertise to problems that cut across departmental or divisional boundaries

- replace formal control by direct contact

- assist in the development of managers by exposing them to company-wide problems and decisions

- improve lateral communication and cooperation between specialists.

There are, however, disadvantages with a matrix structure:

- a lack of clear responsibility

- clashes of priority between product and function

- functions lose control of the psychological contract

- career development can often be stymied

- difficult for one specialist to appraise performance of another discipline in multi-skilled teams

- project managers are reluctant to impose authority as they may be subordinates in a later project

- employees may be confused by reporting to two bosses

- managers will need to be able to resolve interpersonal frictions and may need training in human relations skills

- managers spend a great deal of time in meetings to prioritise tasks.

Case study style question 3

H designs and manufactures sports equipment and is currently positioned as the market leader in the industry. However, whilst operating in a growth market, there are new competitors entering the market with innovative new product offerings. The Marketing Director is aware that to retain market leader position, the company must improve its practices involved with new product development (NPD), and the time taken to get from the product idea to launch needs to be much quicker.

The company has a functional structure with the Marketing Director heading up the marketing function, and the R&D Director heading up the function responsible for research and product development; in addition, there are separate functions for Production, Human Resources, Finance, Sales and IT.

The Marketing Director feels that the functional structure is impeding the NPD process. Having recently read an article on organising for NPD, he is proposing that the best way to manage the process would be through introducing a matrix structure and the use of cross functional teams. However, at a recent meeting of the functional heads, the Research and Development Director said that, in his experience, the potential difficulties in using a matrix structure offset the benefits.

The managing director is unsure as to whether H should adopt a matrix structure and has asked for your advice.

Required:

Write a report for the managing director describing the advantages and disadvantages of H using a matrix structure in project management work for NPD.

(15 minutes)

7 Summary diagram

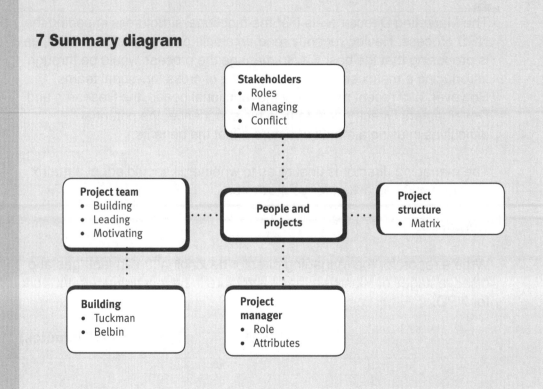

End of chapter questions

Question 1

There are a number of people involved in a project. Match the people to the correct description.

Project sponsor	Responsible for the successful delivery of the project
Project owner	The person for whom the project is being carried out
Project manager	Responsible for making all high level decisions about the project
Project board	Provides resources for the project

Question 2

The person responsible for approving the project plan is which of the following?

A   Project manager

B   Project owner

C   Project sponsor

D   Project user

Question 3

Organisations that run a number of projects often adopt the matrix structure. Which three of the following characteristics lead to the matrix structure being the most suitable? Select all that apply.

• The projects have different start and end dates.

• The projects are all of short duration.

• The organisation runs projects occasionally.

• The projects are expensive.

• The organisation has a dedicated project team which works on all projects.

• The projects are customer facing.

Question 4

H is a project manager. He has just been appointed to manage a project on behalf of X, a property development company, to build 300 low-cost family homes in R Town. X has recently acquired an area of land on the outskirts of R Town and have just received planning permission from R Town Council for the building project.

R town council see this as a way of addressing the problem of lack of affordable housing in R Town.

R Town university however are opposing the development. They say that the building will spoil the view of the university. They claim that the picturesque setting of the university is one of the main attractions for students and staff and that this development will detract from their reputation.

As project manager, H must manage the project stakeholders. Using the Mendelow matrix, match the two stakeholders to the correct management strategy

R Town Council
R Town University

Key player
Keep satisfied
Keep informed
Minimal effort

Question 5

Which three of the following statements are true regarding the matrix structure?

- Requires centralised decision making
- Employees have dual reporting to managers
- The structure seeks to add flexibility and coordination
- Reduces the time spent in meetings
- Clear lines of responsibility
- Replaces formal control with direct contact

Question 6

Which of the following would be the role of the project manager? Select all that apply.

- Selecting, building and motivating the project team
- Providing resources for the project
- Making all high level decision regarding the project
- Recommending termination of the project if necessary
- Main point of contact with the management hierarchy
- Communicating with the chain of command

Question 7

Project managers require a number of skills including:

- Delegation
- Negotiation
- Communication
- Problem solving
- Planning and control
- Leadership

Match the following activities to the required project manager skill.

- The project manager may have to deal with disputes between various stakeholders.
- The project manager must ensure that all stakeholders are kept up to date about the progress of the project.
- The project manager must clarify each team member's role and must empower them to achieve their objectives.
- The project manager must motivate the project team so that the team works hard to achieve the project objective.

Question 8

Which three of the following statements regarding the project manager are true?

- They must be effective communicators
- They must have all the technical skills required in the project
- They may have to negotiate on a variety of issues
- They must adopt the democratic style of leadership
- They are responsible for the project budget
- They must have change-management skills

Question 9

A key role of any project manager is to build and lead the project team. When putting together a project team, Belbin's model of team roles can be used.

Which of the following statements relating to Belbin's model of team roles is true? Select all that apply.

- The team worker is concerned about the relationships within the team.
- A successful team requires at least eight members.
- The plant promotes activity in others.
- All of Belbin's roles should be filled for an effective team.
- The implementer (company worker) is practical and efficient.
- The completer/finisher is thoughtful and thought provoking.

Question 10

Tuckman's model of team development can be used throughout a project. Match the project stage to the most suitable stage in Tuckman's model.

Need	Norming
Solution	Performing
Implementation	Adjourning (dorming)
Completion	Storming
	Forming

Test your understanding answers

Case study style question 1

REPORT

To: Hospital senior managers

From: Management Accountant

Date: Today

Subject: Project relationships

Introduction

This report will consider the various relationships which exist within the Healthweb project. In any project the project manager will have relationships with the project sponsor, the project board and the project users. This report will cover each of these relationships and will also consider the potential conflicting project objectives of these stakeholders.

Project manager and project sponsor

T, as the company responsible for carrying out the GPC project, is contracted directly by the central government (the project sponsor). Therefore, the project manager will need to work through the project sponsor for any contractual dealings with T.

The project sponsor is usually the party responsible for payment of projects, but in this case the amount of funding from the central government is not clear, neither in the initial funding nor the on-going running costs. Therefore, the project manager will need to work with the sponsor to resolve potential conflict over project costs. The role of the central government in this project as a fund provider may cause conflict between central government and the SRHA.

The project manager has little direct reporting/communication with the central government, as responsibility for the project progress is mainly to the project board.

However, the ultimate achievement of long-term project objectives is to the central government, who, as the project sponsor, will be evaluating strategic level objectives and who will be concerned with ensuring that the whole project is not seen to waste public resources.

Project manager and the project board

The project manager is responsible for achieving the objectives set by the project board. The project board is responsible for the overall running of the project, and their objectives are to delegate the achievement of the sponsors' targets without disrupting the achievement of their own business objectives.

Direct communication between the project manager and the project board is necessary, with on-going regular reporting of project milestone review meetings.

The project board will be concerned with the achievement of management/business level objectives, in particular that the project improves business efficiency and effectiveness.

Project manager to medical and administrative users

The project manager is responsible for the overall delivery of the final working system to the end users. The objectives of the users are to care for their patients, while minimising their workload. The first role of the project manager is to 'sell' the benefits of the new system to the users, as without their backing the project is unlikely to succeed. Good communication between the project manager and the end users is essential to the implementation of a successful project. The project manager is responsible for reviewing the needs of each group of users to ensure that systems design meets the needs of the users as far as possible within the project constraints, and ensuring that training is effective. In addition, the project manager will need to manage both medical and administrative staff expectations of the system as the project progresses.

The administrative and medical staff will be evaluating the operational day-to-day objectives of the project.

Possibility of conflicting objectives

The sponsor's objectives are the achievement of improved service to patients. This may conflict with the objectives of the staff, who will seek to minimise their workload while providing good care for their patients. Staff are likely to have concerns about the implementation workload, the on-going costs and workloads and the patient record security.

There is also likely to be conflict between the sponsor and the project board over funding. Although a technology fund has been set up by the central government, it is evident that this funding has not been easy to obtain, causing a financial burden upon the SRHA and the individual hospitals and medical centres. A number of doctors have already expressed concern over resources being spent on the new system rather than on direct patient care, but the central government has made it quite clear that this project is not discretionary. However, the central government are sending out rather mixed signals by allowing individual hospitals and medical centres to decide upon their individual method of operation.

In addition, the central government and project board may be concerned with funding and cost minimisation, whereas the end users may see this as cost-cutting, thus reducing the value of the end product.

As a public sector project, financial objectives should not be primary ones. Quality and customer perspective should be of more importance to all of the stakeholders. However, public funds must not be seen to be wasted.

Conclusion

There are many stakeholders in any project and they often have different objectives which can lead to conflict within the project. It is important to recognise potential conflict in a project to ensure that it is managed so that it does not affect the successful delivery of the project.

Case study style question 2

EMAIL

To: PC

From: Management Accountant

Date: today

Subject: Project management leadership style

The most effective leadership style within an organisation will depend on the circumstances, and might well differ for different types of employee and different types of task.

According to Adair, the most appropriate leadership style depends on the relative significance of three factors – task needs, group needs and individual needs. Task needs refer to the tasks that the leader must carry out, such as setting objectives, planning tasks, allocating responsibilities, setting performance standards and giving instructions for work to be done. Group needs refer to the management responsibilities for communication, team-building, motivation and discipline. Individual needs relate to the manager's responsibilities for coaching, counselling and motivating individual employees. The relative significance of task needs, group needs and individual needs will vary from one situation to another, and the most appropriate leadership style will depend on the relative significance of each of these three factors in the given circumstances.

In managing a road widening project, it seems likely that the task needs will be the most significant and individual needs the least. If this is the case, a task-orientated leadership style – in other words an authoritarian style of leadership – might be most appropriate.

Fiedler, another contingency theorist, argued that the most appropriate leadership style in a given situation depended on the extent to which the task is highly structured, the leader's position power and the nature of the leader's existing relationship with the work group. If the task is highly structured and the leader's position power is high, and if the relationship between the leader and the work group is already good, Fiedler suggested that the most appropriate leadership style would be a task-orientated leader. These circumstances probably apply to the management of construction projects such as a road-widening scheme.

A similar conclusion might also be made if Hersey and Blanchard's situational theory is considered. They argued that the most appropriate leadership style in a given situation depends on the maturity of the individuals who are being led. The greater the maturity of the employees, the more a leader should rely on relationship behaviour rather than task behaviour. With construction work, the maturity of many employees might be considered fairly low, however, and a task-orientated leadership style would therefore be more appropriate.

I hope you have found the above useful, please get in touch if you need any more information about this.

REPORT

To: Managing Director

From: Management Accountant

Date: today

Subject: Structure

Introduction

The structure adopted by a company when undertaking projects can have an effect on the success of the project. There are a number of possible structures which could be adopted by H. This report will consider the advantages and disadvantages of the matrix structure.

Matrix structure

As the Marketing Director in H has noted, the ability to develop new products and get them to market quickly requires the cooperation of a range of individuals from various functions. H could fundamentally reorganise to form a matrix structure. This type of structure is based on a dual chain of command and is often used as a structure in project management. In the case of H it would involve establishing a cross functional team to design and develop new sports equipment products. Each individual would have a dual role in terms of their functional responsibility as well as membership of a project team. For instance, an individual could belong both to the marketing function and to the NPD project. Employees would report both to a functional manager and a project manager.

Benefits of a matrix structure

As the Marketing Director suggests, this structure does bring a number of benefits to NPD project work. The matrix structure is particularly suited to a rapidly changing environment, such as that facing H, creating flexibility across the project, with the aim of speedy implementation. It can improve the decision-making process by bringing together a wide range of expertise to the new product development process, cutting across boundaries which can be stifled by normal hierarchical structures. Lateral communication and cooperation should be improved. From an employee's perspective it can facilitate the development of new skills and adaptation to unexpected problems, broadening a specialist's outlook.

Disadvantages of a matrix structure

Whilst there are benefits, the Research and Development Director is also correct in his view that there are downsides to the matrix structure. One of the main problems is associated with the lack of clear responsibilities and potential clashes and tensions between the different priorities of the project tasks and the specialist function. Employees may end up being confused by having to report to two bosses and deciding whose work should take precedence. There is also the question of who should do the appraisal of their performance?

The complexity of the matrix structure can often make it difficult to implement. Inevitably, conflicts will arise due to the differences in the backgrounds and interests of staff from different functional areas.

Conclusion

The matrix structure is fairly complex and can cause issues with lack of clarity in reporting lines, however it also offers a number of benefits for project work.

H will have to consider both the advantages and disadvantages carefully in deciding whether or not to implement the matrix structure.

Question 1

The correct matching is:

Project sponsor	Provides resources for the project
Project owner	The person for whom the project is being carried out
Project manager	Responsible for the successful delivery of the project
Project board	Responsible for making all high level decisions about the project

Question 2

C Project sponsor

The role of the project sponsor is to make all the yes/no decisions for the project, including approving the project plan. Note: in larger scale projects, there may be a project board. In addition the project sponsor also supplies the funds for the project.

Question 3

- The projects have different start and end dates.
- The projects are expensive.
- The projects are customer facing.

In addition, the matrix structure is most suitable when the organisation carries out a number of projects which all require teams made up of individuals from different technical backgrounds.

Question 4

The correct matching area is:

R Town Council – Key player

R Town University – Keep informed

The council have high power as they are able to give permission for the development. They also have high interest as they want the development to bring much needed housing to the area. This puts them in the category of key players.

The university have high interest as they do not want their view spoiled, but they have limited power to stop the development. This puts them in the keep informed category.

Question 5

- Employees have dual reporting to managers
- The structure seeks to add flexibility and coordination
- Replaces formal control with direct contact

A drawback of the matrix structure is that there can be an increase in time spent in meetings. In addition the lines of responsibility can be confusing as members of staff have two reporting lines. The matrix structure requires decentralised decision making.

Question 6

- Selecting, building and motivating the project team
- Recommending termination of the project if necessary
- Main point of contact with the management hierarchy
- Communicating with the chain of command

Providing resources for the project and making the high level decisions for the project will be the responsibility of the project sponsor.

Question 7

The correct matching is:

Negotiation – The project manager may have to deal with disputes between various stakeholders.

Communication – The project manager must ensure that all stakeholders are kept up to date about the progress of the project.

Delelgation – The project manager must clarify each team member's role and must empower them to achieve their objectives.

Leadership – The project manager must motivate the project team so that the team works hard to achieve the project objective.

Question 8

- They must be effective communicators
- They may have to negotiate on a variety of issues
- They must have change-management skills

Project managers do not require all the technical skills to run a project as long as someone in the project team has the required skills.

In terms of the leadership style they adopt, the democratic style has been shown to be effective. However the manager will have to make all the decisions regarding the project and they may not be able to allow team members to contribute to that decision making. They must adopt the most suitable leadership style depending on the situation.

The responsibility for the project budget rests with the project sponsor.

Question 9

- The team worker is concerned about the relationships within the team.
- All of Belbin's roles should be filled for an effective team.
- The implementer (company worker) is practical and efficient.

According to Belbin, all of the team roles should be covered, but members can hold more than one role, therefore a team does not need to have exactly eight members.

The plant is the creative, ideas person in the team. The shaper promotes activity.

The completer/finisher is the person who chases the progress of the project, ensuring all documentation is complete and deadlines are met.

Question 10

The correct matching is:

Need – Forming

Solution – Storming

Implementation – Norming/Performing

Completion – Adjourning (dorming)

Index

Index

Index

Index

Index

Index

V

W